*Oracle Press*™

Oracle Database 12c
New Features

CW00954006

Oracle Press™

Oracle Database 12c
New Features

Robert G. Freeman

New York   Chicago   San Francisco
Athens   London   Madrid   Mexico City
Milan   New Delhi   Singapore   Sydney   Toronto

Cataloging-in-Publication Data is on file with the Library of Congress

McGraw-Hill Education books are available at special quantity discounts to use as premiums and sales promotions, or for use in corporate training programs. To contact a representative, please visit the Contact Us pages at www.mhprofessional.com.

Oracle Database 12c New Features

Copyright © 2014 by McGraw-Hill Education (Publisher). All rights reserved. Printed in the United States of America. Except as permitted under the Copyright Act of 1976, no part of this publication may be reproduced or distributed in any form or by any means, or stored in a database or retrieval system, without the prior written permission of Publisher, with the exception that the program listings may be entered, stored, and executed in a computer system, but they may not be reproduced for publication.

Oracle is a registered trademark of Oracle Corporation and/or its affiliates. All other trademarks are the property of their respective owners, and McGraw-Hill Education makes no claim of ownership by the mention of products that contain these marks.

Screen displays of copyrighted Oracle software programs have been reproduced herein with the permission of Oracle Corporation and/or its affiliates.

234567890   QFR QFR   1098765

ISBN   978-0-07-179931-7
MHID   0-07-179931-1

Sponsoring Editor Paul Carlstroem	**Technical Editor** Peter Sharman	**Production Supervisor** Jean Bodeaux
Editorial Supervisor Janet Walden	**Copy Editor** Bill McManus	**Composition** Cenveo Publisher Services
Project Manager Vastavikta Sharma, Cenveo® Publisher Services	**Proofreader** Claire Splan	**Illustration** Cenveo Publisher Services
Acquisitions Coordinator Amanda Russell	**Indexer** Claire Splan	**Art Director, Cover** Jeff Weeks

Information has been obtained by Publisher from sources believed to be reliable. However, because of the possibility of human or mechanical error by our sources, Publisher, or others, Publisher does not guarantee to the accuracy, adequacy, or completeness of any information included in this work and is not responsible for any errors or omissions or the results obtained from the use of such information.

Oracle Corporation does not make any representations or warranties as to the accuracy, adequacy, or completeness of any information contained in this Work, and is not responsible for any errors or omissions.

This book is dedicated to the people who are really important in my life. First and foremost is my wife Carrie, who is the single most amazing, kind, and loving person I've ever met. Second, my six kids, Felicia, Sarah, Jacob, Jared, Elizabeth, and Amelia—you are all the brightest, kindest, and most amazing people and I'm proud to be your father. This book, and my life, are dedicated to all of you. Finally, I dedicate this book to my father and my sister. Both are very special people in my life.

About the Author

Robert G. Freeman is a Master Principle Database Expert for Oracle. He is the author of a number of books that cover a wide range of Oracle Database topics. From backup and recovery to new features to Oracle GoldenGate and more, Robert has written on the subject. Robert has been working with the Oracle Database for longer than he cares to admit (he confesses to over 20 years). Robert is the proud husband of Carrie, proud father of six children, and enjoys numerous things including swimming in his backyard pool, traveling, and flying airplanes.

About the Contributors

Scott Black currently works in the Advanced Engineering Group at Oracle, helping public sector customers leverage their investment with Oracle Database and related technologies. His main focuses are core database, RAC, Exadata, and GoldenGate. Before joining Oracle Scott worked as a database administrator in a number of industries and has been involved in IT for over 12 years. Scott has also contributed to several publications, including a newly released book on GoldenGate. When not fiddling with technology, he enjoys spending time with his wife and three children.

Tom Kyte is a Senior Technical Architect in Oracle's Server Technology Division. Before starting at Oracle, Tom worked as a systems integrator building large-scale, heterogeneous databases and applications, mostly for military and government customers. Tom spends a great deal of time working with the Oracle database and, more specifically, working with people who are working with the Oracle database. In addition, Tom is the Tom behind the AskTom column in *Oracle Magazine*, answering peoples' questions about the Oracle database and its tools (http://asktom.oracle.com/). Tom is also the author of *Expert Oracle Database Architecture* (Apress, 2005), *Expert One-on-One Oracle* (Wrox Press, 2001/Apress, 2004), *Beginning Oracle Programming* (Wrox Press, 2002/Apress 2004), and *Effective Oracle by Design* (Oracle Press, 2003). These are books about the general use of the database and how to develop successful Oracle applications.

Eric Yen, OCP, CISSP, has been working with Oracle databases since version 7.3.2. Directly recruited to Oracle out of college, Eric developed his passion to learn, understand, and implement database technology early in his career. Currently, he is a Senior Principal Consultant with Oracle's National Security Group, working with various government agencies. His previous contributions to the Oracle community includes co-authoring *Oracle 11g Streams Implementers' Guide*, a chapter in *Oracle GoldenGate 11g Handbook*, and speaking at Oracle OpenWorld.

About the Technical Editor

Peter Sharman is a Principal Product Manager with the Enterprise Manager product suite group in the Server Technologies Division at Oracle. He has worked with

Oracle for the past 18 years in a variety of roles from education to consulting to development, and has used Enterprise Manager since its 0.76 beta release. Pete is a member of the OakTable Network, and has presented at conferences around the world, from Oracle OpenWorld (both in Australia and the United States), RMOUG Training Days, the Hotsos Symposium, Miracle Open World, and the AUSOUG and NZOUG conferences. He has previously authored a book on how to pass the Oracle8i Database Administration exam for the Oracle Certified Professional program. He lives in Canberra, Australia, with his wife and three children.

Contents at a Glance

Contents

Foreword

I've been working with the Oracle software since 1987, when version 5.1.5c could be bought out of the back of a magazine for $99 USD. Oracle shipped you a box of 5¼ floppy disks with every technology they had at the time. That would have been Forms, Reports, SQL*Net, and, of course, the database.

A lot has changed in the intervening years with the addition of versions 6, 7, 7.1, 7.2, 7.3, 8.0, 8iR1, 8iR2, 8iR3, 9iR1, 9iR2, 10gR1, 10gR2, 11gR1, 11gR2, and now Oracle Database 12c Release 1. That is 16 major releases in 25 years, about one new release every one and a half years. It certainly has kept it interesting.

And with every new release comes the requisite "new features" books. This one in particular the reader will find useful as it is authored by none other than Robert Freeman, along with contributing authors Scott Black and Eric Yen. This book is a rather comprehensive guide to what you can expect with Oracle Database 12c—from installation and upgrade, to what the new Oracle Multitenant architecture in 12c means to you.

The book starts with an overview of installing and upgrading to Oracle Database 12c, a very reasonable place to begin. The step-by-step instructions for getting the software up and running are provided clearly, with graphics, making installation a snap. After that the authors delve into describing the new architecture—Oracle Multitenant. This is the first major architectural change to Oracle Database since version 6 in 1998! Version 6 was an architectural rewrite of the version 5 database, and while Oracle Database 12c is not a complete rewrite of the version 11 database, it is radically different. What Multitenant is, how it works, and what it means to you are clearly laid out.

Then the authors get into the nitty-gritty with details on the new Oracle Grid Infrastructure implementations. This is followed by Robert Freeman's core area—backup and recovery. He has literally written the book on backup and recovery with RMAN. Next is a series of chapters on new features—new features in SQL and PL/SQL, in partitioning, and in Business Intelligence and Data Warehousing.

The next two areas covered are of extreme interest to me—what's new in Oracle Database security and what's new in manageability and performance. This is the section of the book I was most looking forward to, and I wasn't disappointed; like everyone else who is reading this book, I have an abiding interest in both securing my database and making it run faster.

Lastly, the authors close out the book with some odds and ends, cool new features that need to be introduced but don't fit nicely into any of the above categories. All in all, it's a nice way to end the book.

While Robert has authored several Oracle Database New Features books in the past, that doesn't mean this is just a simple update of the previous one—this is all new work, done from scratch, looking at only the newest, never-before-seen features of the latest generation of Oracle Database technology—version 12*c* Release 1. Have fun with it.

Tom Kyte
http://asktom.oracle.com

Acknowledgments

As I write this acknowledgment, I am in Albuquerque, New Mexico. At this moment I'm mindful of the many people who have helped with the production of this book, as well as all of the other books, training manuals, and magazine articles I've written. Further, I'm mindful of all the people who have been a part of my professional life beyond writing and, of course, and most important, those who have been and are a part of my personal and family life. What I'm saying is that there are a lot of people who deserve to be acknowledged here. The sad truth is that I don't have enough space, or a good enough memory, to recall them all. So, to the unnamed masses who have made a difference in my life and deserve thanks, thank you.

Now, there are some people who I must thank and acknowledge. Not because I'd get in trouble or have to sleep on the couch, but because they had a significant part in the writing of *this* book. First, and topping the list of all of those who deserve my profound thanks, is my wife, Carrie. Never have I met a person who has such power to make a difference in the life of a human being as she does. We married as this book was maturing from a proposal to an actual writing project. This is a woman who has the power to take a broken heart and spirit and mend it. We have been married over a year now, and she has walked with me through heaven and hell without batting an eyelash or even having to fix her hair. I can't imagine my life without her. She is the reason this book got written, and that is a simple fact. It is a way overused notion, but Carrie is, truly, my muse and my inspiration. Her smile soothes my soul, her words comfort my heart, and, hey, she's darned easy on the eyes, too.

Then, there is Amelia, my sixth child. She was born while the writing and editing of this book was going hot and heavy. She too has been such a positive light in my life. She has shown me that even at 47, I still have a lot of life to live. You should see her, 3 months old at the time I wrote this. She would melt even the hardest of hearts. I know, everyone says that about their baby, but in my case, it's true. Oracle Press should put a copy of her picture on the front of this book. It would result in at least an additional 5,000 copies sold!

As always, my five other children ... not so much children anymore ... are the source of profound pride for me. Felicia, Sarah, Jacob, Jared, and Elizabeth are the best adult children a parent could ever hope for. I am watching every one of them grow up to be a responsible adult. I almost feel like I can't call them children anymore. However, they will always be my children in my heart, even when they are 40 years old and I'm a grumpy old man who can't even write children's books. They have always been, and continue to be, a source of eternal inspiration.

I must mention Bennett, our little goldendoodle, or I'd get barked at. He's a cute fuzz ball of fun who loves playing the "I'm not licking you" game with Amelia. Also I must mention Clifford, the very old cat, though he's living at my son's nowadays. I must mention him because I always do, and he'd scratch my eyes out if I didn't. Of course, he has cat sundowner's, so he might not even remember me now.

I also want to thank my friends Paul and Kris, who have been helping me with a special project of late. I can tell you that you can't go wrong when these two are behind you. Thanks for everything!

Huge thanks also go to the contributors of this book. First, my friend Scott Black, who I have known for years, helped out with the RAC chapter and also provides technical advice to me at various times, just when I need it. I've always tried to surround myself with people smarter than I, and Scott certainly falls into this category. Thanks to Scott's family for loaning his skills to this book; you all should take a vacation now!

Then, there is Eric Yen. While I have not known Eric that long, I have found him to be quite the stand-up guy. Eric came into this writing project, I dare say, not quite knowing what he was signing up for. He wrote the chapters on security, partitioning, and data warehousing. Eric quickly discovered just how hard writing a book can be, and he ended up sacrificing what I'm sure was much more time to this project than he anticipated. I told Eric that he would feel a ton of pride when he got his printed copy of this book. He should, as he has done a great job with his chapters.

Then, there is Tom Kyte. I almost should write a separate acknowledgment for Tom, as he's actually had quite the pivotal role in my life, far beyond his contribution in this book. I really don't need to tell you much about Tom, unless you have been hiding under a rock somewhere. Tom has added some great thoughts and an awesome Foreword to this book, and I am very grateful to him for his participation. Thanks to Tom for everything. Someday I will figure out a way to pay you back.

Special thanks goes to Penny Avril, Vice President, Database Product Management at Oracle, who was always great about getting me answers about the things coming up in Oracle Database 12c and in general just being a help whenever I needed it. Also, Timothy Chien, who is the Principle Product Manager at Oracle in charge of RMAN, was especially helpful, so thank you Timothy! Thanks to the many other folks on the product management and development side who helped me. There are too many names to mention, some of which I am sure I have forgotten.

The people I work for at Oracle deserve much thanks, and have my utmost respect. These people include Larry Ellison (who I've never met—can you believe that!?)—to whom I owe my career. Further thanks go to Peter Doolan (who left Oracle just as I was writing this—we will miss you, Peter), Ken Currie, Paul Tatum, Adilson Jardim, Aaron Cornfeld, and Venkataraman Girish. All deserve a big thanks! This management team is awesome. Oh, the stories I could tell (but then someone would have to kill me)! Thanks also to Lauren Farese, who was my first manager at Oracle and helped me to get up to speed.

Then there are my co-workers at Oracle. I can't list them all individually, as that would consume a whole book in and of itself. So please forgive me for not doing so. Again, that would just create a long, immense list of names. There are a few, though, who I must mention. Special thanks to Tyler Muth, Tom Roach, Dave Partrage, Craig Dickman, Derrick Lawson, Frank Wickham, Michelle Hoyt, Chris Hildrum, Venkatesh Kalipi, Mikel Manitius, and Matt Miller. Thanks also to Peter Bostrom, Franck Goron, Christine Ryan, Ralf Dossmann, Su Sheth, and Robert Lindsley.

Of course, I have to thank the folks at Oracle Press. There is Paul Carlstroem, Amanda Russell, Janet Walden, and Jean Bodeaux, as well as Vastavikta Sharma of Cenveo Publisher Services and freelancers Bill McManus and Claire Splan. All of them made this book possible. Poor Paul ... we kept falling behind schedule, and I'm sure I've cost him a head of hair—or two.

Finally, there are some people from my past that just deserve thanks for their part in where I am now. These include Gary Chancellor, Rich Niemiec, Joe Trezzo, Paul Winterstein, Glen Webster, Charles Pack, Mark Blomberg, Mike Ault, Jonathan Lewis, Cary Millsap, and a host of others I've probably forgotten. Then there is my dad, who was my greatest mentor when I was growing up.

There are so many more to thank. If I missed your name, I apologize. My life is full.

Introduction

Welcome to *Oracle Database 12c New Features*! This is the fourth book in the Oracle Database New Features series that I've written for Oracle Press. I am excited about this book, and I'm very excited about Oracle Database 12c. If you have picked up this book, then I have little doubt that you are also excited about Oracle Database 12c and all of its new features.

Oracle Database 12c is perhaps one of the biggest releases of Oracle Database ever. With features such as Oracle Multitenant, online datafile movement, cross-platform movement, and many more, Oracle Database 12c provides an even stronger feature set, providing power and flexibility for both administrators and users.

With all the new features included in Oracle Database 12c, you might be concerned about the stability of the first release of the product. While I can't promise that it (or anything else) is bug-free, I can say that my testing on the actual released code has proven it to be quite stable. No doubt, there will be some things to iron out as time goes on, but with this release Oracle has proved, again, that it can release a very large product with a huge code base that works pretty well. Among the reasons you buy the Oracle database are its stability, availability, performance, and recoverability.

There's something else worthy of mention here in the introduction. While my contributors and I wrote the initial chapters of this book using pre-release versions of Oracle Database 12c, the final version of this book was tested on the real deal. The results you see in the code here are from the production database release. I've always done the books in this series that way, because I understand that it's important. In the past, I've seen many things change between pre-release versions and the production release, and I've read other books that were clearly written with pre-release code that didn't work in the production release. You won't find any of that here. As a result of this approach, our book takes a bit longer to get to press, but I think it's worth the extra time, and I hope you do too.

A couple of notes about this book. First of all, this book was not designed with the Oracle Certified Professional Upgrade Exam in mind. Therefore you may find that some of the objectives in that exam are not aligned with the content of this book. Second, you will find in some cases that what is touted as a new feature in this book may have been available in Oracle Database 11g Release 2. My benchmark on what to include in this book as a "new feature" is if that feature is touted as a new feature in the Oracle Database 12c documentation. If it is, I considered it a new feature. In some cases the new feature has been backported to Oracle Database 11g Release 2. Data Redaction is one such feature as it has been backported to Oracle Database 11.2.0.4.

I also hope that you enjoy this book and find that it helps you to easily transition to Oracle Database 12c. Please also check out my blog, at http://robertfreemanonoracle.blogspot.com, where I talk about all things Oracle, including 12c new features, Exadata, tuning, and a whole lot more. Also, I will post errata for this book there.

If you find that you like this book, please go to your favorite online place to buy books and leave a kind comment. Five stars are always welcome! If you find something missing, please go to my blog. There you will find an email link that you click to send an email to me with your thoughts and comments. I always look to improve my books, and if you find an error, I want to correct it.

Finally, remember that if you like this book, my name is Robert G. Freeman. If you don't like this book, then my name is Tom Kyte (I say with a big smile). Now! It's time to move into the world of Oracle Database 12c. Engines full ahead—full attack!

CHAPTER
1

Getting Started with
Oracle Database 12c

I t's here! Oracle Database 12*c*! Better yet, you are here, reading this book on Oracle Database 12*c*. This hopefully means that you have a keen interest in learning about all of the new features contained within Oracle Database 12*c*. In this book, we will cover a lot of these features, and get you excited about what's in this latest version of the Oracle Database.

This first chapter is the beginning of the Oracle Database 12*c* journey. In this chapter, we are going to cover getting started with Oracle Database 12*c*. You will find discussions on:

- Downloading and staging Oracle Database 12*c*

- Preparing to install Oracle Database 12*c*

- Installing Oracle Database 12*c*

- Introducing Oracle Enterprise Manager Database Express 12*c*

Downloading and Staging Oracle Database 12*c*

Oracle Database 12*c* is available through the Oracle Software Delivery Cloud (https://edelivery.oracle.com) or through the Oracle Database 12*c* home page (a web search for Oracle Database 12*c* Download should help you find it). You should create a directory on your database server and download the installation files (Zip files, usually) into that directory. Once you have downloaded the compressed images onto your computer, unzip them into the same directory using the **unzip** command.

Tom Says

Another great source of information on new features is the New Features Guide itself available on www.otn.oracle.com under the documentation for Oracle Database 12*c*. In addition, all of the documentation for the database can be found there as well. To top it all off, be sure to check out the first chapter of the documentation relevant to you to find out what's changed in Oracle Database 12*c*; for example, the first chapter of the Administrators Guide is "What's Changed in 12*c* for Administrators." There are too many new features to fit in any single book; this book you are reading covers many of the most important new capabilities.

Tom Says

Also, please note that raw partitions are desupported in Oracle Database 12c; you cannot use them at all in this release. Raw partitions must be migrated to ASM or a regular filesystem. See support note "Announcement of De-Support of using RAW devices in Oracle Database Version 12.1 [ID 578455.1]" for further details.

NOTE
Make sure you unzip the two Zip files into the same directory (as the installation instructions indicate) or the install will fail. It's possible that Oracle will change the install process at some point in the future and no longer require you to unzip the files into the same directory, so review the latest read-me files to double-check.

The install image for the database itself comes in the form of two compressed (Zip) files. Additional files will be available for the Oracle Grid Infrastructure, gateways, client, web tier and other related products. This chapter addresses the installation of Oracle Database 12c only, and not the installation of the Oracle Grid Infrastructure. See Chapter 4 for information on new features associated with the Oracle Database 12c Grid Infrastructure components.

Preparing to Install Oracle Database 12c

There are a number of steps that you need to complete before you start your Oracle Database 12c software install. Many of these steps will seem very familiar to you if you have been working with the Oracle Database for a long time. Even if that's the case, however, you should carefully consider all the following preparatory steps before you begin to install the new Oracle software:

- Review the install guides and read-me files

- Make sure your OS platform has all required updates installed

- Make sure your platform meets the minimum hardware and software requirements

- Create the required OS groups and users

- Configure the required kernel parameters

- Check whether any patches are required prior to the install

- Finish the pre-install steps

Let's look at each of these items in some additional detail next.

Review the Install Guides and Read-Me Files

It's always a good practice to review the installation guide a few times before you install the Oracle Database, especially if you're dealing with a new version. The install guide provides you with a concise list of steps that you should perform as you prepare to install Oracle Database 12c. Additionally, the install media often contains read-me text files that you should review for any last-minute instructions that Oracle provides related to the install. These instructions might include prerequisites to install additional software (for example, Oracle may recommend that you download a new version of the Oracle Universal Installer (OUI) before installing the database software).

Make Sure Your OS Platform Has All Required Updates Installed

Review the install guide for your specific Operating System (OS) platform to ensure that you are running on a version of that OS that supports Oracle Database 12c. Additionally, check that guide along with the associated read-me files and the My Oracle Support (MOS) portal to make sure that you have installed all the OS patches and fixes that are required before installing Oracle Database 12c. MOS offers a Certification page that can assist you in determining the combinations of software and hardware that are supported by Oracle Database 12c.

Tom Says
This is a key point! If you are upgrading an earlier release of an Oracle install, make sure to read the Upgrade Guide (available on www.otn.oracle.com) before doing so in addition to reading the installation guide. It will be time well spent—trust me. The number one cause of failed upgrades is the failure to read the upgrade guide.

Make Sure Your Platform Meets the Minimum Requirements

Before you begin your install, make sure the platform on which you will be installing Oracle Database 12*c* meets the minimum hardware and software requirements. Of course, minimum requirements are just that—*minimum* requirements—and don't ensure peak performance of your databases. Factors such as adding additional databases in the future, the nature of the processing that occurs in the databases, and so on will impact the total requirements of the platform with respect to disk space, memory, and CPU usage.

The general minimum server requirements vary by platform. To give you an example, some of the stated requirements for a Linux x86-64 (64 bit) install are described in the following sections.

Oracle Database 12*c* Software Storage Requirements

A Linux x86-64 install has the following Oracle Database 12*c* software storage requirements:

- Oracle Database 12*c* Enterprise Edition: 6.4GB

- Oracle Database 12*c* Standard Edition: 6.1GB

- Oracle Database 12*c* Standard Edition One: 6.1GB

Additional space would be required if you plan to use the fast recovery area (FRA). Diving into the factors that feed into configuring the FRA is well beyond the scope of this book. Please take a look at *Oracle Database 11*g *RMAN Backup and Recovery* by Robert Freeman (yours truly) and Matt Hart for more information on sizing the FRA. We cover backup and recovery in quite a detailed manner in that book.

The /tmp directory requires a minimum of 1GB of space. If you do not have enough space in /tmp, you need to either increase the amount of space in that file system or set the TMP or TMPDIR environment variables in the Oracle environment.

Oracle Database 12*c* Memory Requirements

The Oracle memory requirements for a Linux x86-64 install are as follows:

- Minimum of 1GB (recommend 2GB of RAM or more).

- If you have between 1GB and 2GB of memory on your system, then you should allocate 1.5 times the amount of RAM for swap space.

- If you have more than 2GB of memory on your system, then you should allocate an amount of swap space equal to the amount of memory available on the system, up to 16GB.

NOTE
To reiterate, these are minimum, bare-bones requirements for database memory. Typically, you will want a great deal more memory on your system. The amount of memory that you will need is very dependent on the nature and number of the databases that you intend to run on the system. Frankly, running an Oracle Database that you expect to perform on any hardware with less than 8GB of memory is probably bordering on the insane.

Operating System Requirements

As of this writing, Oracle Database 12*c* supports the following Linux distributions:

- Oracle Linux 6 with the Unbreakable Enterprise kernel: 2.6.39-200.24.1.el6uek.x86_64 or later.

- Oracle Linux 6 with the Red Hat Compatible kernel: 2.6.32-71.el6.x86_64 or later.

- Oracle Linux 5 Update 6 with the Unbreakable Enterprise kernel: 2.6.32-100.0.19 or later

- Oracle Linux 5 Update 6 with the Red Hat compatible kernel: 2.6.18-238.0.0.0.1.el5 or later

- Red Hat Enterprise Linux 5 Update 6: 2.6.18-238.0.0.0.1.el5 or later

- Red Hat Enterprise Linux 5 Update 6 with the Unbreakable Enterprise Kernel: 2.6.32-100.0.19 or later

- SUSE Linux Enterprise Server 11 SP2: 3.0.13-0.27 or later

Also note that there are a number of packages that you will need to ensure are installed on your system before you can install the Oracle Database. Each version of the Operating System has a different list of packages, so we won't list them all here.

Probably the easiest way to ensure that you have installed all the packages is to use the Oracle Database preinstall RPM that is available from ULN (linux.oracle.com). The RPM is named differently for the different operating systems in use. For example, the name is oracle-rdbms-server-12cR1-preinstall-1.0-3.el6.x86_64.rpm for Oracle Database 12*c*. The instructions on downloading and using this RPM are somewhat lengthy. You can find them in the Oracle Database 12*c* Installation Guide for Linux. There are often OS specific instructions related to the Oracle Database install, so it's always a really good idea to go through the install guide for your specific hardware, even if you are an Oracle old timer (like me).

After checking your install requirements, you can use a command such as **cat /etc/oracle-release**, **cat /etc/redhat-release**, or **lsb_release -id** to determine the distribution and version of Linux that is installed, making sure that everything lines up and is good to go. Here is an example of running the **/etc/oracle-release** command and the expected output:

```
[root@server12c ~]# cat /etc/oracle-release
Oracle Linux Server release 6.3
```

You will also want to determine whether the required kernel errata is installed by using the **uname -r** command, as shown here:

```
[root@server12c ~]# uname -r
2.6.39-300.26.1.el6uek.x86_64
```

In the case of my release the current install guide at the time of this writing says that I need to have release 2.6.32-100.0.19 or later, so I've got the correct server release installed. The current install guide (or updated read-me file) will contain the latest minimum release level that is required.

For Linux distributions, a number of packages must be installed. Check the current install guide for a list of these required packages. Use the **rpm** command to query the system to determine if the correct packages are installed. For example, I might want to check that the correct release for binutils (binutils-2.17.50.0.6 or later as of this writing) is installed. I can use the following command to check this information:

```
[root@server12c ~]# rpm -q binutils
binutils-2.20.51.0.2-5.34.el6.x86_64
```

Create the Required OS Groups and Users

If this is the first install on the system you are using, then you need to create the Oracle environment. The process to do this has not changed in Oracle Database 12c. You still create the Oracle inventory group (e.g., oinstall), the OSDBA group (e.g., dba), the Oracle software owner (e.g., the oracle OS account), and the OSOPER group (e.g., oper). As with earlier versions of the Oracle Database (and mentioned earlier in this chapter), there is an RPM package that you can download and install that will create the oracle OS account and groups for you. This is known as the Oracle RDBMS Pre-Install RPM. Along with creating the oracle user and required install groups, the RPM will install all required kernel packages for both the Oracle Grid Infrastructure and the Oracle Database. It will also configure the kernel parameters and resource limits to the values recommended by Oracle.

Configure the Kernel Parameters

On a new system, you need to set the OS kernel parameters (if you have not used the YUM Oracle RDBMS Pre-Install RPM). Refer to the Oracle Database 12c install guide for your specific operating system for recommended minimum values. The Oracle install guide for your operating system also provides methods to determine the current settings and reset those settings if required.

NOTE
I often find that the minimum values for the parameters recommended by Oracle quickly become insufficient for larger database installations. If you are not familiar with the operating system you are working with, you should discuss the recommended settings with an experienced OS administrator and determine if higher values are advisable.

I often find that one of the places that I run into problems is with the resource limits defined for the Oracle database owning account. Make sure that the limits for the Oracle account are set to the minimum values listed in the install guide.

Check Whether Any Patches Are Required Prior to the Install

Often, the initial release of the Oracle Database product is available on the public download sites but the updated releases are only available through Oracle's support platform (MOS). Whether you are installing the first release of Oracle Database 12c or any release for that matter, you should check MOS and download the most current version of that version of the Oracle Database.

Finish the Pre-Install Steps

You are almost ready to install Oracle Database 12c. Before you can begin the install, you need to complete the following steps:

- Determine the location of the ORACLE_BASE directory. If you already have a previous version of Oracle Database installed on the system, then you should use the same ORACLE_BASE directory that is already defined. This is not required but highly recommended.

- Ensure that you can start an X terminal session (if installing on Linux) so that you can run the Oracle Universal Installer (OUI).

- Unset parameters such as ORACLE_HOME, TNS_ADMIN, and the like.

- Make sure that the PATH environment variable does not include $ORACLE_HOME/bin.

NOTE
In earlier Oracle Database versions, it was common to set ORACLE_HOME to the location of the new ORACLE_HOME before starting a new software install. It is now recommended that you set the ORACLE_BASE parameter instead. When ORACLE_BASE is set, the OUI creates an ORACLE_HOME path that is compliant with Oracle's Optimal Flexible Architecture (OFA). It is recommended that you accept the ORACLE_HOME path that the OUI recommends.

Installing and Deinstalling Oracle Database 12*c*

Now that you have made sure your system is ready to install Oracle Database 12*c*, you are ready to install the database product. For purposes of demonstration, in this section we are installing Oracle Database 12*c* Enterprise Edition on Oracle Linux x86-64. We assume you have downloaded the database software and unzipped it into a directory called /u01/download/database. In this section you will

- Prepare to start the OUI

- Install Oracle Database 12*c* using the OUI

- Deinstall Oracle Database 12*c* using the OUI

NOTE
Oracle Database 12c cannot be installed over an existing ORACLE_HOME location, so you will be installing it into a new ORACLE_HOME.

Prepare to Start the OUI

Before you can start the install, you first need to set up the environment so that you can run an X Windows session, and then you need to log in as the oracle user. There are many ways to run an X Windows session. In our case, we are logged directly into the server. You could use other methods, like VNC or SSH tunneling with some X Emulator. As with many things, there are a number of ways to get the job done.

In Figure 1-1, we've enabled X Windows (using **xhost +**), switched over to the Oracle user directory, and then changed to the /u01/oracle/download/database/database directory, which is where we unzipped the Oracle Database 12c install software and therefore, where we will be performing our install from.

Before performing the install, we set the ORACLE_BASE directory to /u01/app/oracle:

```
export ORACLE_BASE=/u01/app/oracle
```

Now we are ready to start the Oracle Universal Installer and begin the database install.

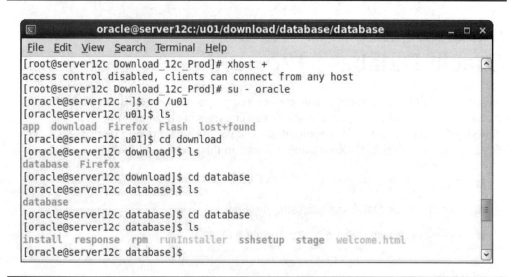

FIGURE 1-1. *Setting up Unix environment for install*

Install Oracle Database 12c Using the OUI

To begin the install process, we start the old familiar runInstaller program:

```
[oracle@server12c database]$ ./runInstaller
```

This launches the Oracle Universal Installer. Oracle will go through some OUI pre-install checks, and then the OUI will appear.

During the install, the OUI presents you with several screens to enter your install information into. The Oracle Database 12c OUI interface has not changed a great deal since Oracle Database 11g Release 2 (though the install screens themselves have changed a lot), so if you have installed Oracle Database 11g Release 2 (or, frankly, even older versions) then this process should feel familiar to you.

Figure 1-2 shows the opening screen of the OUI, where you can enter your email address and your My Oracle Support password to get automated security updates. You can also choose to skip this step and move on if you prefer.

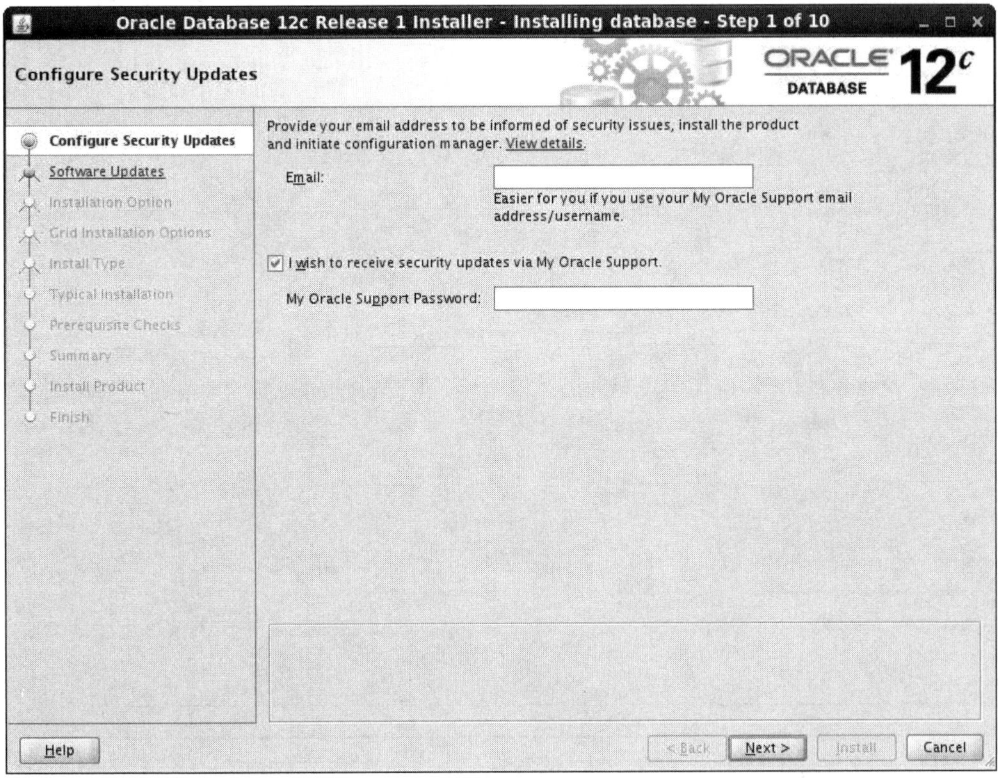

FIGURE 1-2. *Oracle Universal Installer Configure Security Updates screen*

If you click Next, and you did not enter an email address at the installer prompt, you will be asked to confirm that you wish to remain uninformed of critical security features. This is a rather onerous sounding message. You may, or may not, wish to enable security updates for a great many reasons. At the end of the day, you are the DBA and you understand your architecture. Since this is not a new feature, we won't dive into best practices of this feature, and we assume you already know what to do here.

Completing the first screen, you will click Next to move to the Download Software Updates screen (see Figure 1-3), where you can enter your My Oracle Support credentials so that you can easily download and install patches and other updates from Oracle. You can enter the information requested and click Next to continue, or you can click the Skip Software Updates button and click Next to

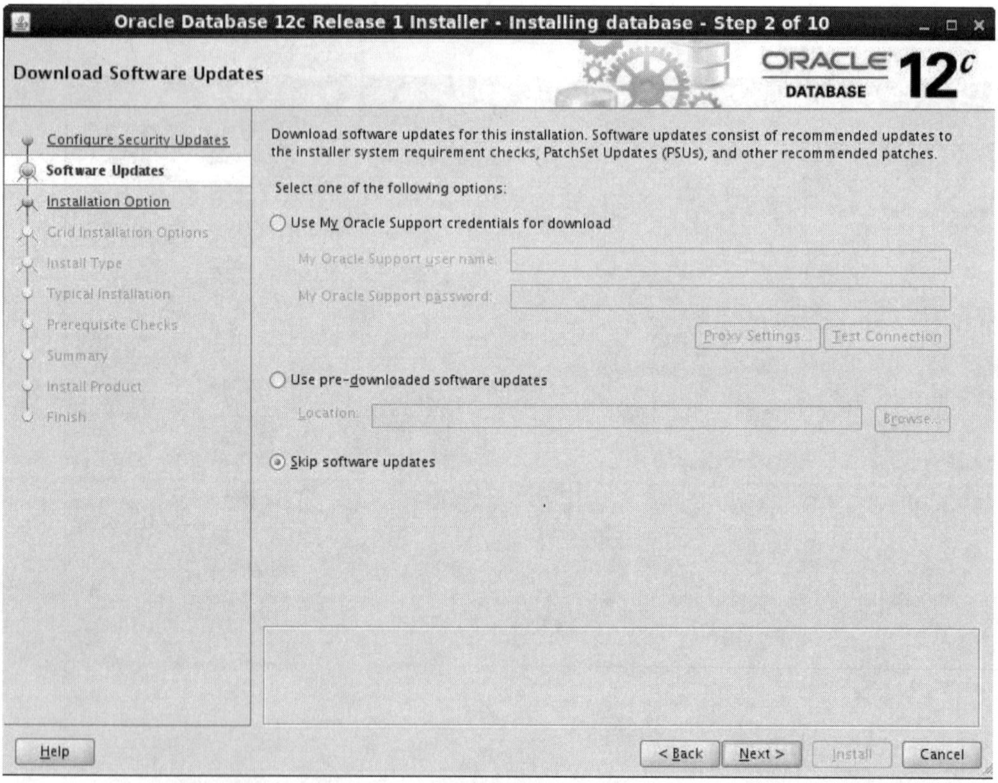

FIGURE 1-3. *OUI Download Software Updates screen*

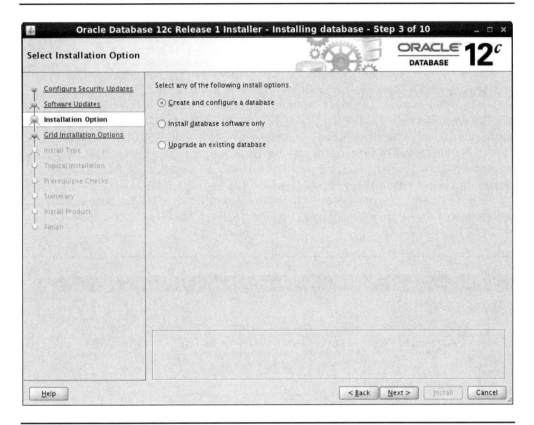

FIGURE 1-4.   *OUI Select Installation Option screen*

continue. If you opt to skip software updates at this time, you can always choose to configure them at a later date. For now, we have opted to skip updates and continue. As this is not new in Oracle Database 12*c*, we will move on in the install process.

The Select Installation Option screen (see Figure 1-4) that appears next gives you the following three choices:

■ **Create and configure a database**   Installs the Oracle Database 12*c* software and also creates a small Oracle database and configures the networking associated with that database.

■ **Install database software only**   Installs the Oracle 12*c* software only. You would need to manually create a database afterward using the Oracle Database Creation Assistant.

- **Upgrade an existing database** Starts the Oracle Database Upgrade Assistant, which will give you an option to upgrade an existing database to Oracle Database 12c.

Generally, I recommend choosing the first option because it not only installs the Oracle software for you but also stands up an Oracle database at the same time. The reason I like this option is so that I can quickly test the new Oracle environment that I've created. Once the install is done, you can check that the database came up successfully and that the networking components work. So, in this case, we will select the first option. I also like to manually start the Database Upgrade Assistant (DBUA) if that is the tool I'm going to use to upgrade a database with (which it often isn't). We discuss upgrading a database to Oracle Database 12c in Chapter 2 of this book.

Next, as shown in Figure 1-5, the OUI asks you which "class" of database you wish to install. The options are Desktop Class and Server Class. The main difference

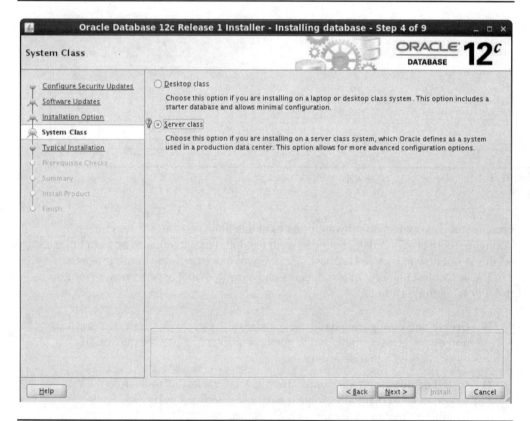

FIGURE 1-5. *OUI System Class selection screen*

is that if you choose Server Class, you get more install options. If you are new to Oracle Database, you might want to start with the Desktop Class option. Most Oracle DBAs use the Server Class option, and that is what we will select in this demonstration. Click Next to continue.

Next, the Grid Installation Options screen (see Figure 1-6) asks if you want to install a single instance database, an Oracle Real Application Clusters (RAC) database, or an Oracle RAC One Node database. In our case, we want to install a single instance database (we will cover Oracle RAC new features in Chapter 3), so we choose the first option and click Next.

Figure 1-7 shows the next screen, Select Install Type, which gives you the option of performing either a typical install or a more advanced install. If this is your first time installing Oracle Database, then you may want to choose the Typical Install

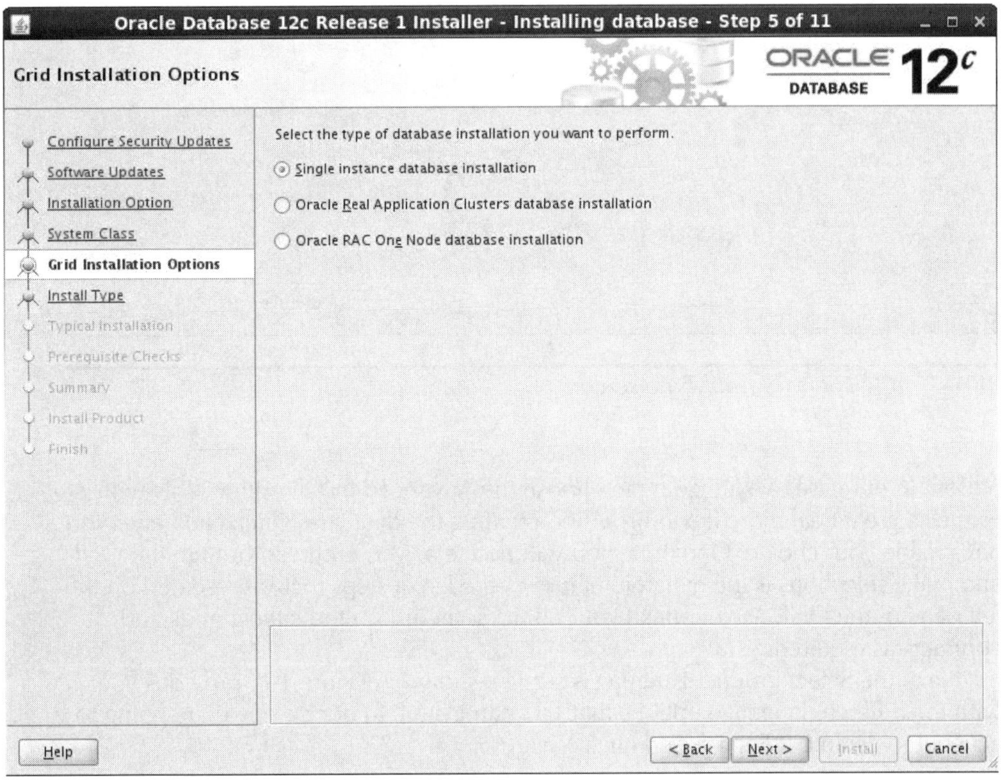

FIGURE 1-6.   *OUI Grid Installation Options screen*

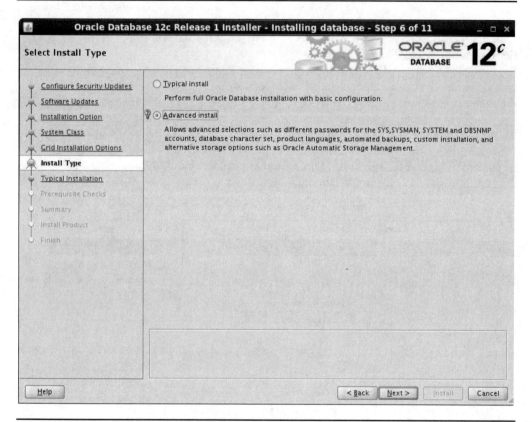

FIGURE 1-7. *OUI Select Install Type screen*

option. In our case, we are going to choose the Advanced Install option. This will give us a great deal more flexibility when creating the database. Click Next after you have made your choice. One thing you will notice as you progress through the OUI and make selections is the dynamic nature of the list of steps that is presented on the left pane of the OUI. As you make your choices, the list on the left expands and contracts as required.

Next, the Select Product Languages screen, shown in Figure 1-8, provides you with the different language options that you can install. In our case, we are going to accept the default of English and click Next.

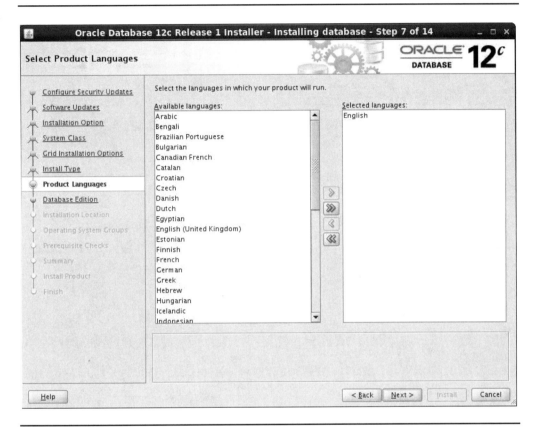

FIGURE 1-8. *OUI Select Product Languages screen*

The Select Database Edition screen (see Figure 1-9) gives you options to choose which database edition you want to install. You are currently given three options (Oracle could always choose to add or remove or rename database editions at any time):

- Oracle Database 12c Enterprise Edition

- Oracle Database 12c Standard Edition

- Oracle Database 12c Standard Edition One

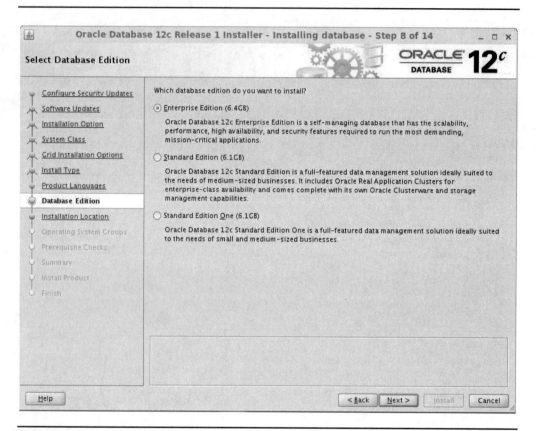

FIGURE 1-9. *OUI Select Database Edition screen*

Select the Oracle Database 12c edition that you are licensed to install. Each version has varying levels of features and capabilities. In our case, we are going to choose to install the Enterprise Edition of Oracle Database 12c and then click Next.

Next you are presented with the Specify Installation Location screen, shown in Figure 1-10, where you define the location of the ORACLE_BASE directory. We specified the location of the ORACLE_BASE directory earlier in this chapter, in the section "Finish the Pre-Install Steps." When you fill in the ORACLE_BASE location (that is, the Oracle Base field in the OUI), the OUI automatically completes the Software Location field below it. This directory will become the ORACLE_HOME

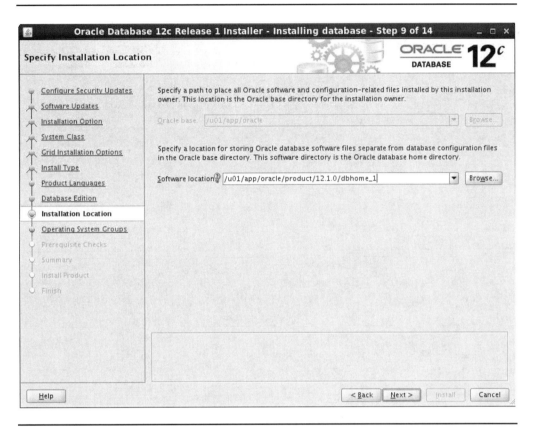

FIGURE 1-10. *OUI Specify Installation Location screen*

directory for the software. In our case, we have accepted the default ORACLE_BASE
directory (/u01/app/oracle), which we planned on using anyway. Note that the
Software Location information is also prefilled using the directory $ORACLE_BASE/
product/12.1.0/dbhome_1. Typically, we accept these defaults. Click Next to continue.

If you are installing the Oracle Database software into this ORACLE_BASE
location on this machine for the first time, then the Create Inventory screen is
displayed next, as shown in Figure 1-11. The Oracle Inventory (contained in the
inventory directory) is its own small metadata repository that keeps track of which
Oracle software is installed on your system, and other metadata such as where the
different ORACLE_HOME directories are, any patches that have been applied, and

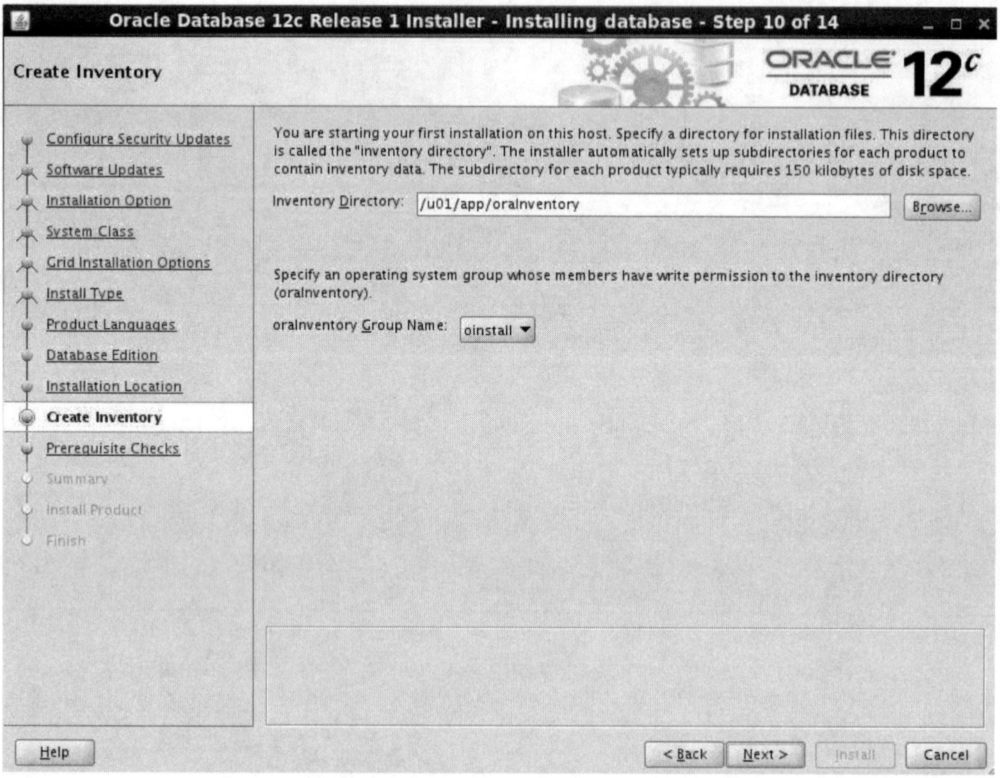

FIGURE 1-11. *OUI Create Inventory screen*

so forth. In our case, let's just leave the defaults and click Next. If you have already installed Oracle into this ORACLE_BASE location then the inventory has already been created.

The Select Configuration Type screen (see Figure 1-12) gives you a couple of options with respect to the type of starter database that Oracle Database will create after it has installed the Oracle Database Software. Two options are available, General Purpose/Transaction Processing and Data Warehousing. Based on the option you choose, Oracle Database will use an existing Oracle Database Configuration Assistant (DBCA) template to create the database configuration you have chosen.

Because we are just creating a starter/test database, we are going to choose the General Purpose/Transaction Processing option. If you are an experienced DBA, you know that you'll invest a great deal of time and thought in how you will create and

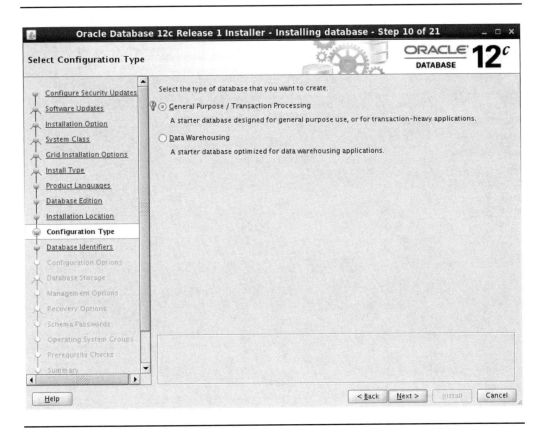

FIGURE 1-12. *OUI Select Configuration Type screen*

configure the database that you will actually use. For now, we just want a database that we can use for test purposes. Click the Next button to continue.

The next OUI screen is the Specify Database Identifiers screen, shown in Figure 1-13. First, this screen enables you to define the global database name and the Oracle Service Identifier (SID). Both of these default to a value of orcl, which is fine in most cases. However, if you are installing Oracle Database 12*c* on a system that already has a database called orcl (running on Oracle Database Version 11.2, perhaps), then you need to select a different global database name and a different SID for the database.

In our case, this is not a new install, and an orcl database already exists. Therefore we will make the name of this Oracle Database 12*c* database orcl12c as seen in Figure 1-13.

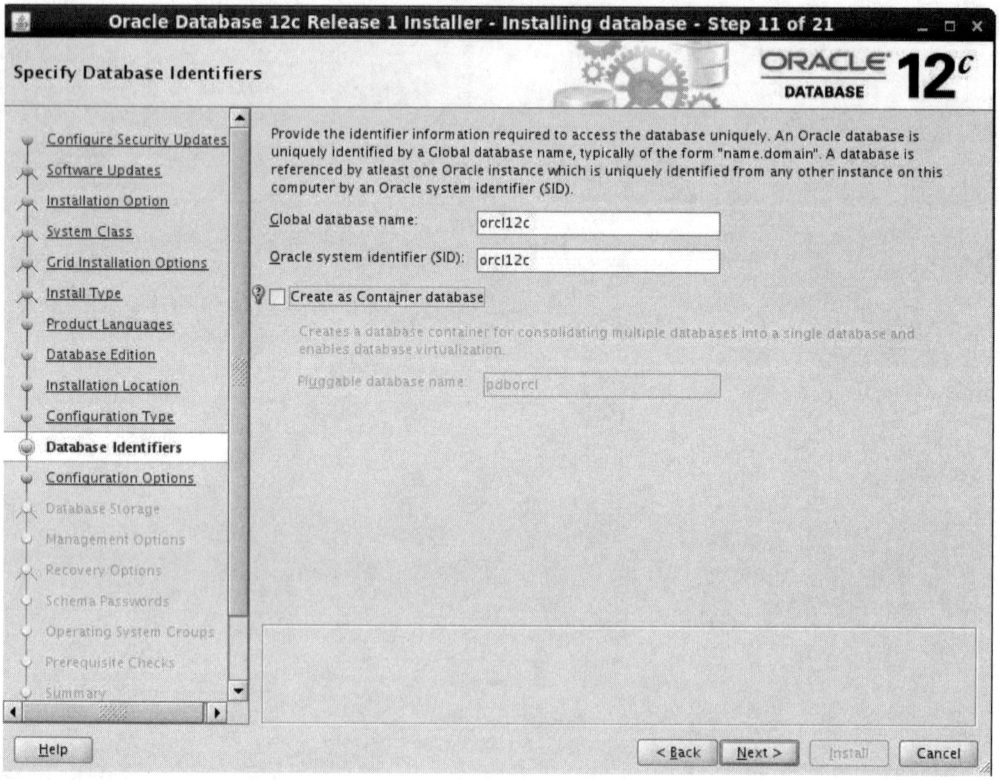

Oracle Database 12c Release 1 Installer - Installing database - Step 11 of 21

Specify Database Identifiers

ORACLE **12**c
DATABASE

- Configure Security Updates
- Software Updates
- Installation Option
- System Class
- Grid Installation Options
- Install Type
- Product Languages
- Database Edition
- Installation Location
- Configuration Type
- **Database Identifiers**
- Configuration Options
- Database Storage
- Management Options
- Recovery Options
- Schema Passwords
- Operating System Groups
- Prerequisite Checks
- Summary

Provide the identifier information required to access the database uniquely. An Oracle database is uniquely identified by a Global database name, typically of the form "name.domain". A database is referenced by atleast one Oracle instance which is uniquely identified from any other instance on this computer by an Oracle system identifier (SID).

Global database name: orcl12c

Oracle system identifier (SID):   orcl12c

☐ **Create as Container database**

Creates a database container for consolidating multiple databases into a single database and enables database virtualization.

Pluggable database name: pdborcl

[Help]   [< Back] [Next >] [Install] [Cancel]

FIGURE 1-13. *OUI Specify Database Identifiers screen*

NOTE
In this book, we use all lowercase letters for Oracle database names (which can be up to eight characters). Case sensitivity with Oracle database names is a platform-specific feature. What's important is that you develop and follow a set of conventions with respect to how you name your databases and the like, so that the names are consistent throughout your database. Also, make sure your naming conventions meet your platform-specific requirements.

The next option on the Specify Database Identifiers screen is related to a new feature in Oracle Database called Oracle Multitenant. Notice the Create as Container Database check box. This provides the ability for you to create this new database as a Multitenant Container Database. I discuss Multitenant Container Databases in much more detail in Chapter 3.

The Create as Container Database check box is checked by default. For now, just to keep things simple and make sure everything installs correctly before we start exercising all of the new features in Oracle Database 12c, clear this check box and then click the Next button to continue.

On the Specify Configuration Options screen, you can configure the memory allocation, change the character sets, and specify whether you want to install the sample schemas in the database. On the Memory tab, by default, the OUI allocates 40 percent of the available physical memory to the database to be installed. Frankly, because this is a test database, that's likely more than enough memory to allocate to the database that you will create. In our case, the OUI wanted to allocate 2.5GB (2594MB) to the database. That seems excessive, so I reduced the amount of memory allocated to the database to 1GB (1024MB, which is still probably more than enough), as shown in Figure 1-14. Notice that I decided not to enable Automatic Memory

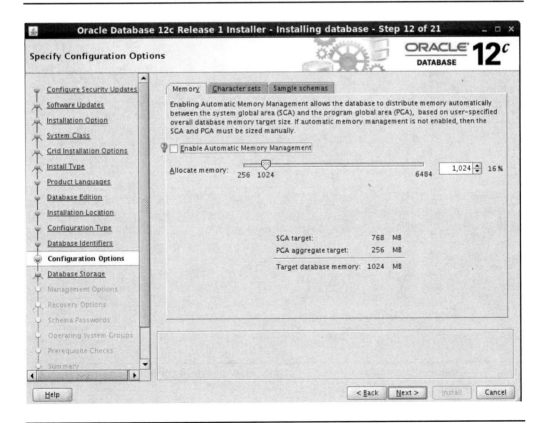

FIGURE 1-14. *Memory tab of the OUI Specify Configuration Options screen*

Management (AMM). Again, because this is a test database, I don't see any need to enable AMM at this point.

The Character Sets tab of the Specify Configuration Options screen seen in Figure 1-15 enables you to change the character set. Again, because this is just a test database, there is really no need to change the default character set (which can vary based on platform—the default on our Oracle Linux system is WE8MSWIN1252).

Next, click the Sample Schemas tab, shown in Figure 1-16. Many of the examples later in this book use the sample schemas, so when you create this database (or whatever database you create to experiment with Oracle Database 12c new features), you will want to have the sample schemas installed. Therefore, check the Create Database with Sample Schemas check box. Click Next to continue.

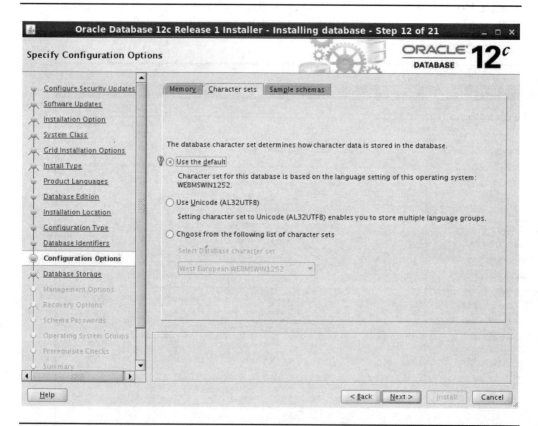

FIGURE 1-15. *Character Sets tab of the OUI Specify Configuration Options screen*

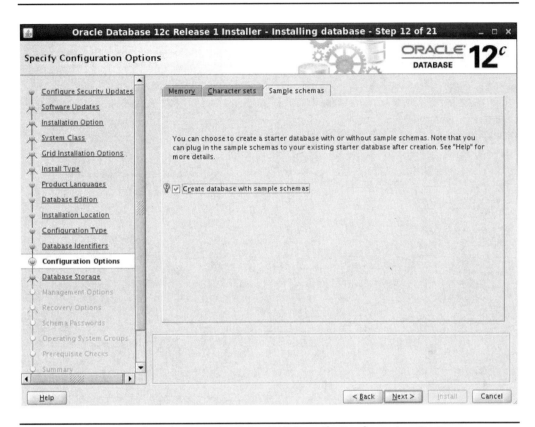

FIGURE 1-16.   *Sample Schemas tab of the OUI Specify Configuration Options screen*

Next, the OUI presents the Specify Database Storage Options screen, where you specify the location in which to store the database files that will be created for your database. The other option, Oracle Automatic Storage Management (ASM) is used if you have Oracle ASM configured. Typically, ASM would be configured if you are installing the Database on an Oracle Database RAC cluster (though RAC is not required). I discuss Grid- and RAC-related new features in Chapter 4.

In this case, as shown in Figure 1-17, we are going to leave the File System radio button selected and accept the default location listed for the database files in the Specify Database File Location text box.

Next, you will find yourself on the Specify Management Options screen. If you have some experience with installing previous versions of the Oracle Database then you will notice that the next screen is slightly different than you will have seen previously. First, you will not find an option to set up Oracle Enterprise Manager

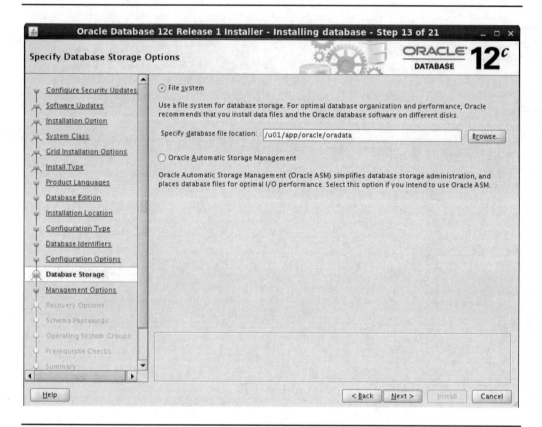

FIGURE 1-17.   *OUI Specify Database Storage Options screen*

Database Control for the database. Oracle has discontinued Database Control and replaced it with a new product called Oracle Enterprise Manager Database Express. We will discuss the removal of Database Control and the addition of EM Database Express later in this chapter.

   The Specify Management Options screen also provides you with an opportunity to connect your database with the Oracle Management Server infrastructure (that is, Oracle Enterprise Manager Cloud Control 12c). For now we will leave the screen as is and click Next to continue. Since you're not really doing anything on this screen, I decided to save paper and not give you a screen shot.

   The Recovery Options screen, shown in Figure 1-18, is where you define the location of the fast recovery area (called *Recovery Area location* on the screen— don't ask me, I don't know). Check the Enable Recovery check box, leave the File

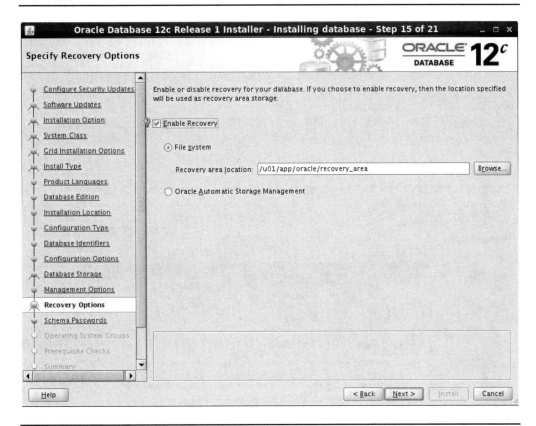

FIGURE 1-18. *OUI Specify Recovery Options screen*

System radio button selected, and accept the default file system as the FRA. Also note that when you enable recovery, this will enable redo log archiving.

NOTE
This book is not about backup and recovery of Oracle databases, so we won't go into the specifics of the FRA, how to manage it, RMAN backups, or anything like that in this chapter, though we will do a quick backup of our new database toward the end of this chapter. (For detailed information about backup and recovery, check out Oracle Press's book Oracle RMAN 11g Backup and Recovery, *by Robert Freeman and Matthew Hart.)*

This is a good spot to mention the help options that the OUI offers as you proceed through the install process. If you want additional information about the screen you are viewing, click the Help button (in the lower-left corner). A window with helpful information specific to the install step you are currently on will appear. Figure 1-19 provides an example showing the Help Topic Window that appears when you click the Help button (which I highlighted for you just for fun!) on the Specify Recovery Options screen of the OUI.

Having selected the FRA, click Next to proceed to the Specify Schema Passwords screen, shown in Figure 1-20, which enables you to set the passwords for the SYS,

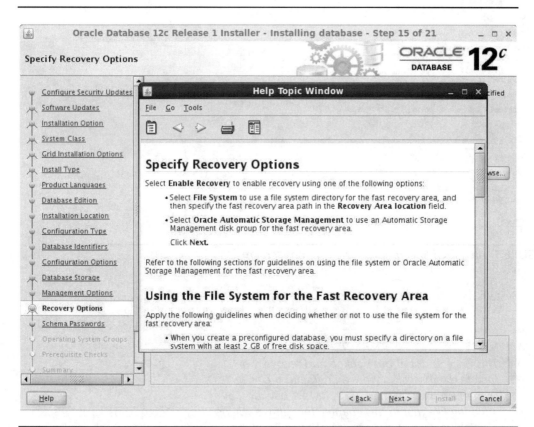

FIGURE 1-19. *Getting help from the Oracle Universal Installer*

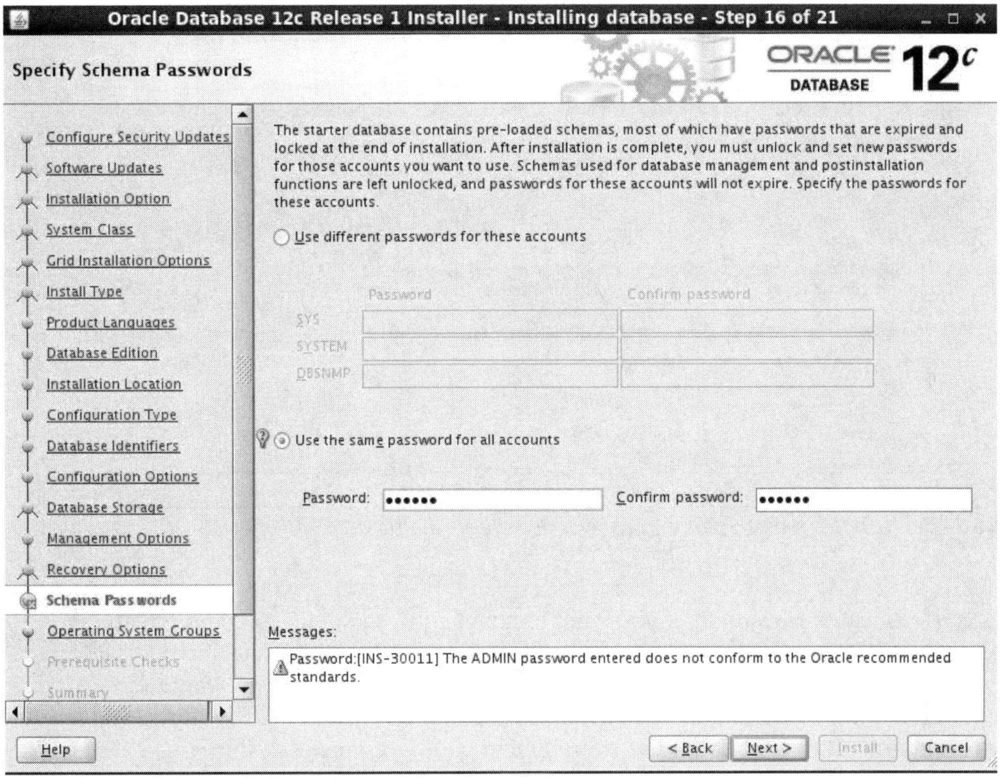

FIGURE 1-20. *OUI Specify Schema Passwords screen*

SYSTEM, and DBSNMP schemas. You can choose to use separate passwords for each schema (considered the best practice), or you can use a common password for all the schemas. Since this is a simple test database, we will opt to use the same password for all accounts.

Note in the Messages box (at the bottom of Figure 1-20) that the OUI lets you know if your password does not meet certain complexity requirements. (To view the minimum password requirements click the help button). If you click Next, the OUI warns you that the password does not meet Oracle's recommended standards and

FIGURE 1-21. *OUI Specify Schema Passwords screen dialog box with details*

asks if you want to continue. If you want to change the password to comply with the Oracle standards, click the No button and then re-enter the password. If you wish to continue with a nonconforming password, click the Yes button. If you want more information, then you can click the Details button and the dialog box will provide you with more information on the warning that you have received. This is demonstrated in Figure 1-21.

On the next screen, Privileged Operating System Groups, you can define the various operating system groups that are associated with different privileges (such as the OSDBA group). In our case, we will accept the default values (shown in Figure 1-22) and click the Next button.

After you click the Next button, the OUI proceeds to run the install prerequisite checks on the system. These checks ensure that all the required system settings are correct prior to the install. The system checks whether the proper packages have been installed, whether the proper kernel parameters are set, and so on.

As shown in Figure 1-23, the prerequisite checks have detected a problem with the free space in the /tmp file system and issued a warning (as seen in the status column). We can see at the bottom of the figure that there needs to be at least 1GB of free space and we only have some 835MB space available.

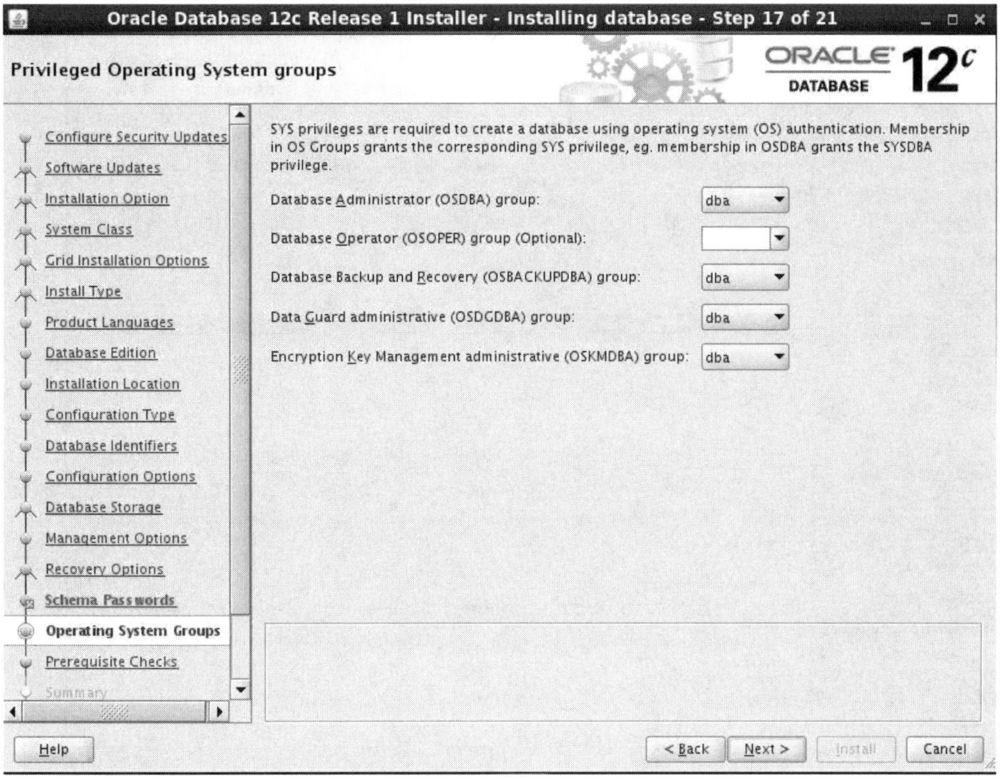

FIGURE 1-22. *OUI Privileged Operating System Groups screen*

Figure 1-23 shows that a warning was issued (as shown in the Status column). The Fixable column is marked No. If the Fixable column were marked Yes then we could prompt the OUI to generate a fix script for us to correct the problem. Many problems detected in the Perform Prerequisite Checks screen are automatically fixable. The reason this one is not is that the OUI does not know if the /tmp file system is just too small, or if we just have some big files that need to be removed. Also, it would not know which files it could safely remove to correct the condition. So we have to intervene manually to correct the problem. In this case, we could just go in, remove some big files, and click the Check Again button. The OUI would re-check the configuration and find that we had cleared enough space. At this point no error or warning message would appear.

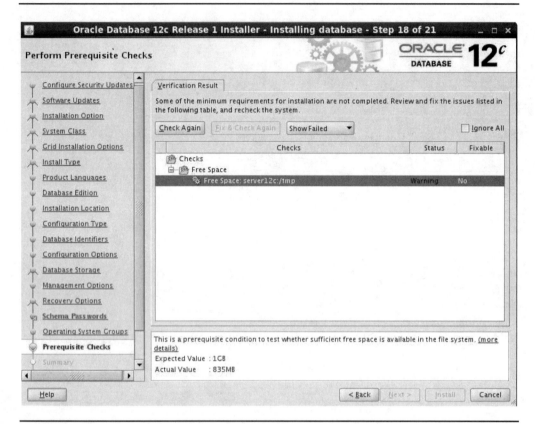

FIGURE 1-23.   *OUI Perform Prerequisite Checks screen with warning*

Now, let's look at another case. In Figure 1-24, we see that the prerequisite checks have found a problem with the setting of the system memory parameter semmsi. It should be set to 250 and it appears to be set to 200.

Notice that this time, the Fixable column says Yes. This means that we can have Oracle Database help us correct the problem. If you are sure the problem is not significant, click the Ignore All check box. This prompts the OUI to ignore all the errors and warnings detected and proceed with the install as if there were no issues. However, I want to correct the problem, so I'll click the Fix & Check Again button near the top of the screen. In response, Oracle creates a script and opens a dialog box, labeled Execute Fixup Scripts (see Figure 1-25), that lists the name of the script and gives us instructions on how to proceed. In our case, we will open another

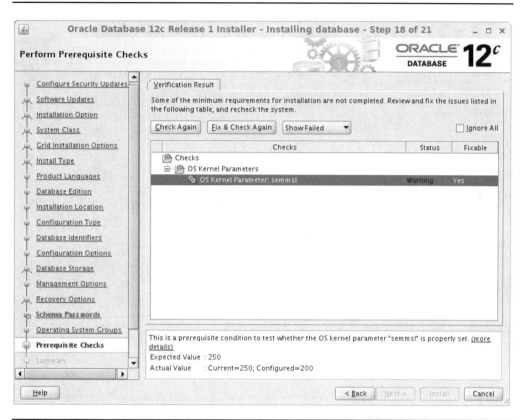

FIGURE 1-24. *A warning in the OUI about the semmsi parameter*

terminal window, make sure we are the root user and execute the script called
runfixup.sh.

Here is the result of actually running the fixup script created by the OUI:

```
[root@server12c Desktop]# /tmp/CVU_12.1.0.1.0_oracle/runfixup.sh
All Fix-up operations were completed successfully.
```

After running the fixup script, click OK in the Execute Fixup Scripts dialog box. The
OUI will rerun the checks. If all of the errors and warnings are not cleared, the OUI
displays the screen shown in Figure 1-23 again, with any remaining errors or
warnings listed. In that case, proceed to correct any additional errors or warnings as
previously described.

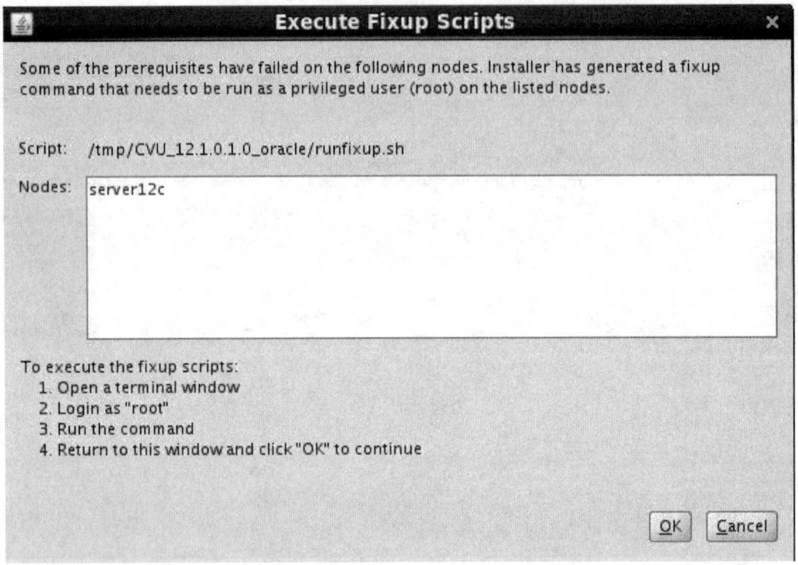

Execute Fixup Scripts   ✕

Some of the prerequisites have failed on the following nodes. Installer has generated a fixup command that needs to be run as a privileged user (root) on the listed nodes.

Script: /tmp/CVU_12.1.0.1.0_oracle/runfixup.sh

Nodes: server12c

To execute the fixup scripts:
1. Open a terminal window
2. Login as "root"
3. Run the command
4. Return to this window and click "OK" to continue

OK   Cancel

FIGURE 1-25.   *OUI Execute Fixup Scripts dialog box*

If the problems were corrected, then you will see the OUI Summary screen, as shown in Figure 1-26. You can review the various settings and configurations that will be applied to the install. If the settings all look correct, then you are ready to install the Oracle Database software. Simply click the Install button.

If you want to reset a setting, click the Edit link next to that setting. You are taken back to the OUI screen where that setting is configured. Optionally, you can click the Back button to reverse through the configuration pages one at a time, or you can click the Cancel button to cancel the install.

NOTE
Clicking the Save Response File button allows you to save your selections as a response file that you can use later in "silent" installs.

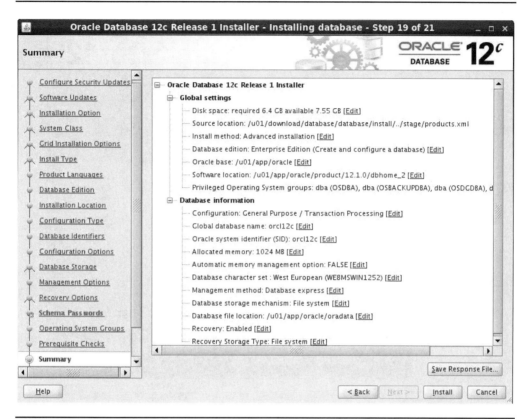

FIGURE 1-26. *OUI Summary screen*

In our case, we are ready to install Oracle Database 12*c*, so we click Install and, voilà, the OUI begins to install our database for us! Figure 1-25 shows an example of the OUI installing the Oracle software. You can click the Details button to see additional details of the install process. How long the OUI takes to complete the install process depends on a number of factors, including memory, disk speeds, CPU speed, system load, and so forth. Note the details box that is available to click. This will present even more detailed information on the install process if you desire.

After the OUI has installed the database software itself, but before it can create the first database, we need to perform a few manual steps as root to complete the database software install. This step is shown by the Execute Root Scripts step in the status box of the section of the OUI Install Product screen that you can see in Figure 1-27.

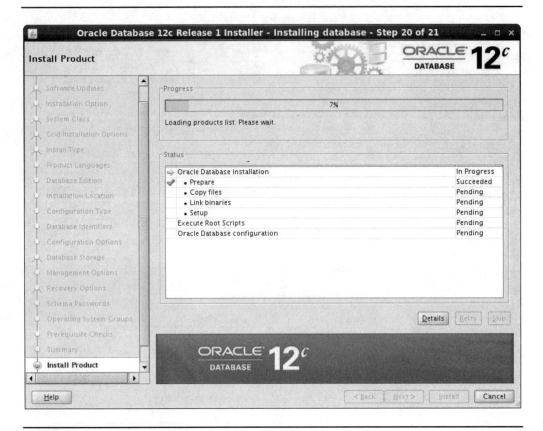

FIGURE 1-27.   *OUI Install Product screen*

During this step the OUI presents you with a list of scripts that you need to run as the root owner. An example of the dialog box that indicates the script or scripts you need to run to complete the software install is shown in Figure 1-28.

As directed in the Execute Configuration Scripts dialog box (shown in Figure 1-28), we will run the /u01/app/oracle/product/12.1.0/dbhome_2/root.sh script as the root user. During your install you may be prompted to run more than one script as root.

To run these scripts, open a separate terminal session as root and then run each of the scripts in the order shown in the Execute Configuration scripts dialog box seen in Figure 1-28. Here is an example:

```
[root@server12c Desktop]# /u01/app/oracle/product/12.1.0/dbhome_2/root.sh
Performing root user operation for Oracle 12c
The following environment variables are set as:
    ORACLE_OWNER= oracle
```

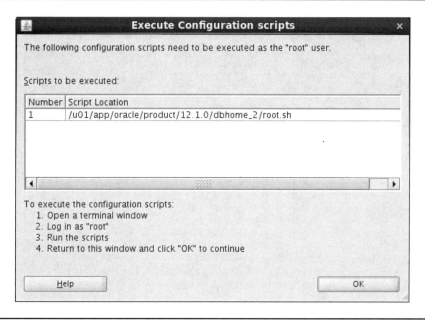

FIGURE 1-28.   *OUI Execute Configuration Scripts dialog box*

```
    ORACLE_HOME=  /u01/app/oracle/product/12.1.0/dbhome_2
Enter the full pathname of the local bin directory: [/usr/local/bin]:
The contents of "dbhome" have not changed. No need to overwrite.
The contents of "oraenv" have not changed. No need to overwrite.
The contents of "coraenv" have not changed. No need to overwrite.
Entries will be added to the /etc/oratab file as needed by
Database Configuration Assistant when a database is created
Finished running generic part of root script.
Now product-specific root actions will be performed.
[root@server12c Desktop]#
```

Once the scripts have successfully executed, click the OK button in the Execute Configuration Scripts dialog box. At this point, the OUI will indicate that the install of the Oracle Database was successful, as shown in Figure 1-26. To complete the installation, click the Close button to close the OUI.

Once the OUI has installed the Oracle Database 12c software, it will then start to create the Oracle Database and configure Oracle Database networking for you. During this install, you will notice some other new features when the Oracle Database Configuration Assistant (DBCA) starts to create that database. One nice feature of the DBCA in Oracle Database 12c is that there is a button that will open

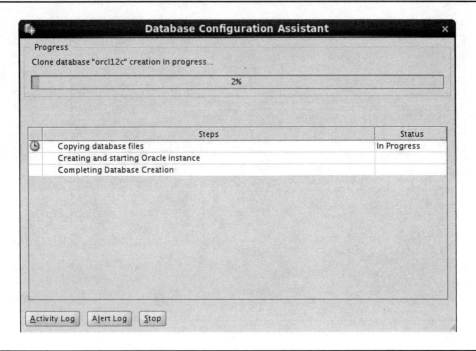

FIGURE 1-29. *The OUI/DBCA creating a database*

the alert log of the database for you, so that you can monitor the log as the database is being created. You can see the DBCA doing its thing in Figure 1-29.

Figure 1-30 provides a look at the new Alert log output screen, and the Activity Log dialog box output during the install process.

Once the OUI and the DBCA are complete, the DBCA returns information about the database that has just been created, as shown in Figure 1-31. At this point, the database should be up and running.

Let's check that the database is actually running by logging in as follows:

```
[oracle@server12c ~]$ . oraenv
ORACLE_SID = [orcl12c] ?
The Oracle base remains unchanged with value /u01/app/oracle
[oracle@server12c ~]$ sqlplus / as sysdba
SQL*Plus: Release 12.1.0.1.0 Production on Sun Jul 21 00:28:08 2013
Copyright (c) 1982, 2013, Oracle.  All rights reserved.
Connected to:
Oracle Database 12c Enterprise Edition Release 12.1.0.1.0 - 64bit
Production
```

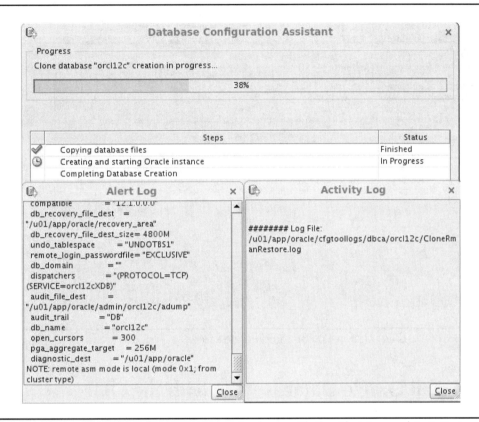

FIGURE 1-30. *The OUI/DBCA creating a database with the Alert Log and Activity Log boxes active*

```
With the Partitioning, OLAP, Advanced Analytics and Real Application
Testing
options
SQL> select open_mode from v$database;
OPEN_MODE
--------------------
READ WRITE
```

Before you click the OK button on the DBCA, make sure you write down the URL for EM Database Express URL. You will want that. Then, to complete the install, simply click the OK button on the DBCA screen. This will return you to the OUI Finish screen. You can then click the Close button on the OUI Finish screen to complete the install.

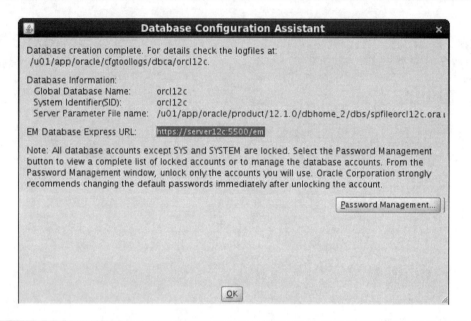

FIGURE 1-31. *The OUI database creation complete screen*

Deinstall Oracle Database 12c with the OUI

A quick word about deinstalling Oracle Database 12c is in order. The way you deinstall the database software has changed in Oracle Database 12c. The deinstall tool that you used to use is now deprecated and you now deinstall the database using the OUI interface. To do this, you first will start the installer from an Oracle Database 12c ORACLE_HOME. Figure 1-32 shows you the Welcome screen of the OUI. Notice that it looks different than the OUI Welcome screen that you started from the Oracle Database install media.

To remove an Oracle Database ORACLE_HOME, you select the Deinstall Product button that you see on the right side of the OUI Welcome screen. When you select this button, the OUI Inventory screen will appear as seen in Figure 1-33. Select the ORACLE_HOME that you wish to deinstall, and click the Remove button as seen in Figure 1-33.

The OUI will present you with a confirmation screen, making sure you really want to remove the ORACLE_HOME. If you do, just click the Yes button and the OUI will remove the Oracle software in the selected ORACLE_HOME. When the deinstall is complete, the OUI will return to the OUI Inventory screen, allowing you to remove another ORACLE_HOME if you wish.

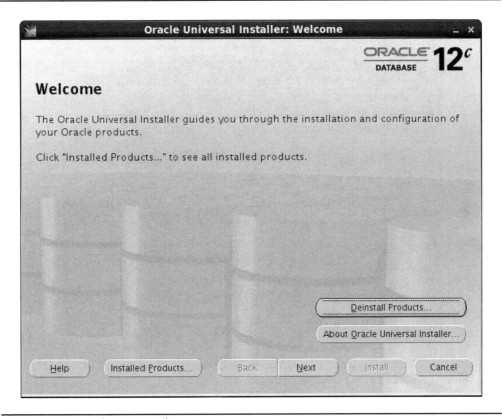

FIGURE 1-32.   *The OUI Welcome screen*

NOTE
If an ORACLE_HOME has a dependent HOME location (as indicated by the + sign by the ORACLE_HOME name), then you need to remove that dependent object first, and then you can remove the remaining ORACLE_HOME.

Note that, as of this writing, the OUI does not clean up the databases that are running under that ORACLE_HOME. In fact, the remaining instances are terminated, pretty abruptly, since the software that was running them will have disappeared all of a sudden. So, in the best of worlds, you should either remove the databases under the ORACLE_HOME directory you are removing first, or you should move them to run under a different ORACLE_HOME before you execute the delete operation.

FIGURE 1-33. *The OUI Inventory screen*

The Death of Database Control and Birth of Database Express

If you looked closely at the output from the DBCA shown in Figure 1-31, you might have noticed something different if you are a veteran Oracle Database installer. Instead of receiving a URL for Database Control, as in the past, you are given a URL for EM Database Express. This refers to Oracle Enterprise Manager Database Express, a lightweight replacement to Database Control. You might have missed it, but Oracle announced in My Oracle Support document 1484775.1 that Database Control will no longer be supported after Oracle Database 11*g* Release 2.

Database Express is still web based, but it has a much smaller footprint and is easier to manage than Database Control. That's the good news. The bad news is that Database Express does not have nearly the same functionality that Database Control had. And, *no*, there isn't a copy of Database Control left over for you to use—it's gone, history, just plain not there. If you aren't convinced, just look for the old **emca** or **emctl** commands that were used to manage Database Control.

Database Express Prerequisites

Before you can start Database Express, the following must be true:

- The database that you want to manage with Database Express is up and running (you can't start or stop the database with Database Express).

- The listener is running and is servicing the database you want to manage with Database Express.

- You know the name of the server that the database is on.

- You know the port number that Database Express is listening on. By default, the port number on the first Database Express database created on a database server is 5500. You can determine the correct port number for a specific database by making a call to the **dbms_xdb_config.gethttpport()** package in the database, as shown in this example:

```
SQL> select dbms_xdb_config.gethttpport() from dual;
DBMS_XDB_CONFIG.GETHTTPPORT()
-----------------------------
                         5500
```

You can also change the port for a given database using the procedure **dbms_xdb_config.sethttpport**, as seen here:

```
sql>  exec dbms_xdb_config.sethttpsport(5500);
```

You will find additional instructions related to Database Express in *Oracle Database 2 Day DBA 12c Release 1 (12.1)*, available at Oracle's documentation website at http://tahiti.oracle.com.

Accessing Database Express

Now it's time to open your web browser and type in the EM Database Express URL (which you received in the Database Configuration Assistant screen shown earlier in Figure 1-26). If you forgot it, the format of the URL is as follows: https://server_name:port number/em. In the case of the server we're using, the URL is https://server12c:5501/em. After you type the URL and press ENTER, you should see the Database Home screen, described next.

Navigating Database Express

Figure 1-34 provides an example of the Database Home screen for Oracle EM Database Express 12c.

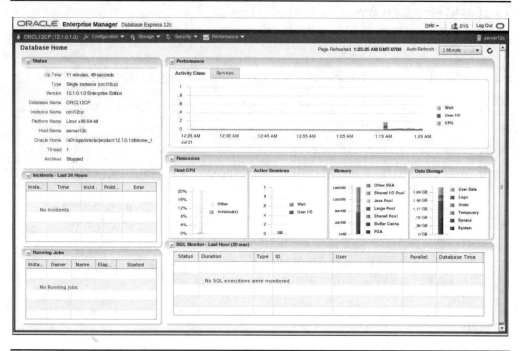

FIGURE 1-34. *Oracle EM Database Express Database Home screen*

NOTE
The loss of Database Control and the impacts to your database operations should be seriously considered when doing your Oracle database upgrade planning. It is possible that you have configured notifications, jobs, and other types of administrative and monitoring functions in Database Control that will no longer be available when you upgrade to Oracle Database 12c.

As you can see, the look and feel of Database Express is much different from that of Database Control and is a bit more like Enterprise Manager Cloud Control 12c. The Database Home screen provides a single place from which you can review and monitor the database. It provides the following database-related information:

- Basic database status information

- Summary performance information

- Resource information, including host CPU, active sessions, memory utilization, and storage

- Database incidents that occurred in the last 24 hours

- SQL monitoring information

- Information on running jobs

As you move your cursor over the various graphs, bubbles will appear with additional information. You can click some of the buttons in the regions and drill down for additional information. For example, in the SQL Monitor region you will see SQL statements that Oracle is actively monitoring. You can click the status button of a given SQL statement to see more details about that SQL statement, including its execution plan, time and wait statistics, and IO statistics.

Although Database Express has rather limited functionality compared to Database Control, it still has a great deal of functionality to assist both junior and senior DBAs. Some of the major functionality is accessible from the following drop-down menus at the top of the Database Home screen:

- Configuration

- Storage

- Security

- Performance

Each of these drop-down menus has several options. Let's finish up this chapter by looking at some of that functionality in additional detail.

NOTE
Database Express represents a single management interface for an individual database (or individual instance if you are running a RAC install). Database Express is much more limited than Database Control. If you are managing a few or a bunch of databases, we strongly recommend that you implement Oracle Database 12c Cloud Control in your enterprise, if you haven't already done so. It really is the way to manage Oracle databases in the enterprise.

Configuration

Configuration, the leftmost drop-down menu in Database Express, enables you to manage the following:

- **Database Installation Parameters**   This page allows you to view and manage the various parameter settings of the database.

- **Database Memory Settings**   This page provides information about the various memory areas used by your Oracle database. For example, the page displays the current memory settings, the SGA and PGA advisor, top sessions by PGA, and other memory-related items. The page also provides an option to configure memory allocations. By clicking this option, you can modify the database memory settings (dynamic or static) as required.

- **Database Feature Usage**   Often, DBAs will ask, "Which features in the database are we actually using?" When licensing time comes around, sometimes it's hard to tell which products you are using and which you are not. The Database Feature Usage screen provides the information you need to determine which features are currently in use, the number of times that each feature has been detected as having been used, and other information with respect to the usage of the features in the database.

- **Current Database Properties**   This page displays the current Oracle Database properties, which impact the entire database. While initialization parameters are specific to a database instance (which is significant in RAC installations), properties describe behaviors and settings of the database as a whole. Examples include the global database name, various NLS database settings, and other global database settings.

Storage

The Storage drop-down menu enables you to look at a number of storage-related database items. These include the following:

- **Tablespaces**   This page provides a list of each tablespace assigned to the database (including those with temporary datafiles, such as temporary tablespaces). It includes information regarding how much space is allocated to the tablespace, how much free space is in the tablespace, and how much of the tablespace is currently in use.

   On the Tablespaces page, you can also create or remove tablespaces, add datafiles to existing tablespaces, and drill down in a given tablespace and look at its individual datafiles.

■ **Undo Management**   This page provides an overview of undo-related database statistics. Information presented includes the Undo Advisor, undo space usage, undo generation rate, and general information related to database undo.

■ **Redo Log Groups**   This page provides information about the online redo logs in the database (instance). It displays all the available online redo logs, and shows you which one is the current online redo log, the log sequence number, and the location of the current online redo log file.

The Redo Log Groups page also lets you create and drop new online redo log groups and files, force a checkpoint, and switch logfiles.

■ **Archive Logs**   This page provides information about each online redo log that has been archived.

■ **Control Files**   This page provides information about the database control files, including number, location, and name.

Security

The Security drop-down menu enables you to manage the following basic database security functions:

■ **Users**   This page provides a list of all the users in the database and a variety of other information, including whether the account is locked, when it was created, the default user and temporary tablespaces, and when the account expires. Clicking the name of an individual user opens a page called User View, which provides a lot of details about the individual user, including their roles, system, and object grants.

The Users page also enables you to create or drop users; create a user like another user (for example, if you have a user named Robert, you can create a user named Carrie that is just like the Robert user account); manage privileges and roles; and manage grants to database objects.

■ **Roles**   This page enables you to manage database roles. You can see all the roles that currently exist in the database, create new roles, and delete existing roles. You can also look at specific roles and see the privileges assigned to those roles.

■ **Profiles**   This page enables you to see all profiles defined in the database. It also lets you create or remove profiles in the database.

Performance

The Performance drop-down menu is perhaps the handiest of the four menus in Database Express. From the Performance menu, you can access

- The Performance Hub
- The SQL Tuning Advisor

Performance Hub The Performance Hub provides a real-time look at database performance. It also enables you to go back in time, somewhat, and see what past performance looked like. Figure 1-35 provides an example of what the Performance Hub looks like.

Figure 1-35 shows quite a bit of information about our database. The top graph indicates that a peak in user activity occurred shortly after 1:30 A.M. (which is when we ran a backup). Below the graph, the Summary tab is selected, which provides a general overview of the performance of the system. The Host: Runnable Processes pane shows that we are not using very much CPU. The Memory: Host pane shows how much memory was allocated to the database and how much is allocated to

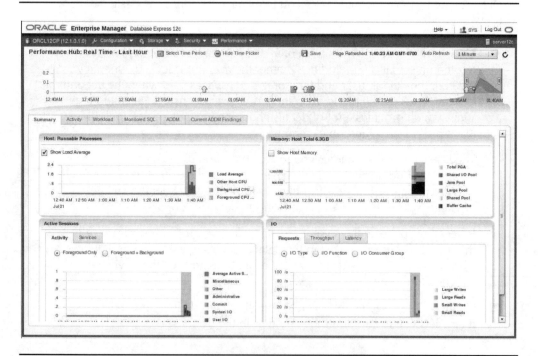

FIGURE 1-35. *Oracle EM Database Express Performance Hub with Summary tab selected*

specific areas (such as the SGA and PGA). You can also check the Show Host Memory check box to see how much memory the database has allocated relative to the total amount of memory allocated to the database server itself. The other two panes include information about active sessions and IO-related information.

Unfortunately, the Performance Hub Summary tab offers no real drill-down capabilities. So, for example, if you see a spike in performance, you usually can't click that spike and drill down into additional information. Other views, such as the Activity view, do provide drill-down capabilities.

So, if you click the Activity view, a graph located in the middle of the page provides wait-related information by default. The drop-down box above the graph provides a number of alternative views that you can select. You can choose to look at such information as top sessions, resource consumption, and other metrics that can help you to not only tune your database but also respond to database performance issues.

The bottom of the Activity tab shows the SQL that is executing on the system and shows the different user sessions that are running in the database. The SQL and user sessions are sorted based on what is being displayed in the upper graph. For example, as shown in Figure 1-36, if you choose to have the upper graph show SQL statements by top-level SQL ID, you can then view below the graph the individual SQL statements and user sessions sorted by the top-level SQL ID you have selected.

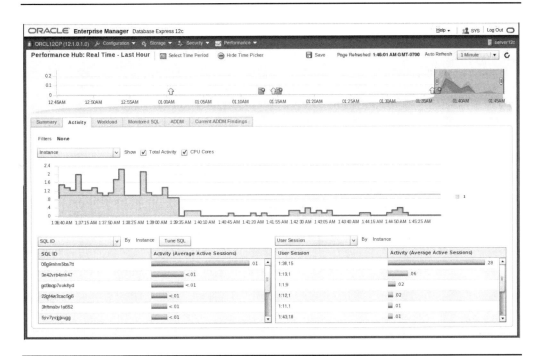

FIGURE 1-36.   *Oracle EM Database Express Performance Hub with Activity tab selected*

SQL Tuning Advisor   The SQL Tuning Advisor provides a window into Oracle's SQL Tuning Advisor (STA). The STA runs automatically during the maintenance window. Also, if you wish, you can run the STA manually from the Performance Hub (with the Activity tab selected) if you find a SQL statement that is performing poorly. Simply pick the SQL statement(s) you want to have analyzed and then click the button to schedule the STA in Figure 1-36 we mentioned earlier. You can then view the results by clicking the SQL Tuning Advisor tab. Automated runs will be displayed on the Automatic tab, and your manual runs will be displayed when you click the Manual tab.

Database Express has a lot of functionality, and we have just scratched the surface in this chapter. Frankly, covering all of its functionality could probably take up its own book. While it is now missing some of the functionality that you might have gotten used to with Database Control, it's much lighter weight and the performance for what it does do is exceptional. We have given you a good introduction to the tool, but the best way to really understand Database Express is to actually use it.

End of Line

We have started our journey to exploring Oracle Database 12c new features by installing the product and creating a starter database. Quite the first step! In each chapter, we will wrap up the chapter with a section I call "End of Line." If you read *Oracle Database 11g New Features*, you will know that "end of line" is a quote from the first *Tron* movie, indicating that the MPC has completed its communication. In true geek style, I am borrowing the line as it sounds so much more fun than using "summary" or "chapter conclusion."

There is nothing boring about Oracle Database 12c. This version of the Oracle Database has perhaps some of the biggest changes and new features of any of the Oracle major releases in some time, if ever. You might have glimpsed some of that in this chapter as you installed Oracle Database. In the next chapter, you will see even more as we cover migrating and upgrading to Oracle Database 12c from previous versions of the Oracle database.

Then in the chapters that follow Chapter 2, we will really get things into high gear talking about new features like there is no tomorrow. By the time you are done reading this book, you will feel beyond excited to start playing with all the things that the Oracle developers have given you in Oracle Database 12c. So, head on to Chapter 2 and let's continue our quest for Oracle Database 12c knowledge!

CHAPTER
2

Upgrading and Migrating
to Oracle Database 12c

This chapter covers the basics involved in upgrading or migrating your existing Oracle database to Oracle Database 12*c*, including:

- Introductory comments

- New features related to upgrading to Oracle Database 12*c*

- Preparing for an upgrade to Oracle Database 12*c*

- Upgrading to Oracle Database 12*c* with the Database Upgrade Assistant

- Upgrading to Oracle Database 12*c* manually

- Upgrading to Oracle Database 12*c* with Oracle Data Pump

- Activities to complete after upgrading to Oracle Database 12*c*

- Rolling back the upgrade

- Miscellaneous changes to be aware of after upgrading

Before we get started here I'd like to address a couple of topics.

Introductory Comments

I'd like to open this chapter by making a few comments on things related to upgrading Oracle databases. These conversations have come up from time to time that I feel require addressing. So, I'd like to discuss the following:

- The difference between upgrading and migrating a database

- Upgrading is complex—tread carefully

- Why upgrade? What's the big deal?

The Difference Between Upgrading and Migrating a Database

First, what is the difference between upgrading a database and migrating a database? The terms seem to be treated like synonyms, and in reality—they are not. Upgrading a database is the process of upgrading the data dictionary of a given database to a later version. During an upgrade, the data in the database is not changed, moved, or touched in any way. I use the word *data* very carefully, because the datafiles themselves might be changed during an upgrade (as has happened in the past).

A migration then is the movement of the database to new hardware, operating system platform, or character set. For example, moving a database from AIX to

Solaris is a migration. You might be moving from Oracle Database 11*g* on AIX to Oracle Database 12*c* on Solaris, but it's still a migration.

We also use the terms *in-place* and *out-of-place* software upgrades. An in-place software upgrade is one where the new software is installed into an existing software location. An out-of-place software upgrade occurs when the software is installed in a new software location.

Upgrading Is Complex—Tread Carefully

Second, the upgrade process can be a very complex process that involves a number of different permutations based on the hardware your database is running on, the Oracle Database version you are moving from, the database features you are using, security you have implemented, and many other considerations. Because of these complexities, it's not possible for this chapter to be anything close to the be-all and end-all to upgrading to Oracle Database 12*c*. Instead, it serves as a quick summary of the basic methods and tasks involved in upgrading to Oracle Database 12*c*.

That being said, this chapter does provide some insights into the upgrade process and I interject some of the experience I've garnered in over two decades that I've been managing Oracle databases, including countless upgrade projects. So it's a good place to start. If your source database is a basic installation of Oracle Database and a version that supports direct upgrade, then a quick read of this chapter and a quick glance at the *Oracle Database Upgrade Guide 12*c and all associated readme files should be more than enough to steer you through a successful upgrade (of course, test the thing first!).

If your upgrade path is more complex, then you will need to read this chapter and the *Oracle Database Upgrade Guide 12*c more closely. Depending on which features you are using, you might also need to refer to other material, such as Oracle GoldenGate documentation, the *Oracle Database Security Guide 12*c, and so forth.

NOTE
Although this book discusses a myriad of new features that you will find in your newly upgraded Oracle Database 12c database, it does not cover every new feature for every product associated with the database. So, you may need to do further reading in your product-specific documentation. Make sure you check out the "What's New in Oracle Database 12c" section (provided in each book in the Oracle Database 12c documentation set) for information about the new features for the specific database product(s) that you are using.

With those caveats in mind, let's take a look at how you can upgrade to Oracle Database 12*c*.

Tom Says

I am often asked how I know so much about the large set of features in the database, or even how I know about the existence of many of these features. The answer to that is the New Features Guide and the "Changes in This Release" section in most of the manuals. I start out by reading the New Features Guide and then drill down into the Administrators Guide, the Application Developers Guide, the SQL Reference, the Reference Guide and so on, reading the "Changes in This Release" in each document. This gives a very comprehensive overview of the new features and changes to the database.

Why Upgrade? What's the Big Deal?

Because upgrading Oracle Databases can be a complex and involved process, I've been in more than one enterprise where they tended to put off upgrades. Many reasons are offered for this approach—the complexity of application testing, the time, manpower requirements and cost of upgrading a large number of Oracle databases—and there is always the fear of the new and unknown. However, I would argue that there are some very compelling reasons to upgrade.

The first reason has to do with support. At the time this book was written Oracle has four levels of support: Premier, Waived Extended, Extended, and Sustaining Support. Each of these different support models have a cost and timeline associated with them. The bottom line is that the longer you wait to upgrade your database, the higher your support costs go up. Additionally, after about eight years you will find you can no longer get new bug fixes. So, if you run into a problem once your version has moved out of support, you will find yourself in bad shape. Oracle Premier support ends in Jun 2018 for Oracle Database 12*c*. Extended Support ends in January 2021. Both of these give you an extra three years of support life as opposed to Oracle Database 11*g* Release 2, which will go out of Premier support in January of 2015. For more information on support policies, please go to the MyOracle Support Portal (support.oracle.com). You can also find information on Oracle's support policy at www.oracle.com/us/support/lifetime-support/index.html.

NOTE
You might also want to look at note 742060.1 for more information on current database release schedules and for information on platform desupport and patching end dates.

Another compelling reason to keep up to date with your database versions is security. Unless you have lived under a rock in the last many years, you will no doubt be aware of the numerous database security breaches that have occurred.

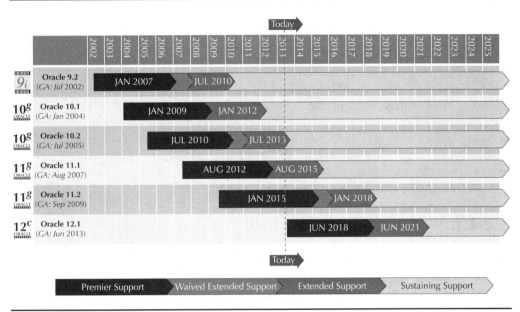

FIGURE 2-1.   *Current lifetime support dates for the Oracle Database*

Oracle releases security patches on a regular basis. Not applying those patches can then put your databases at significant risk. Upgrading your database is another way of ensuring that you have the most current in database patches and security-related features. See Chapter 9 for a list of all the new security features available in Oracle Database 12*c*.

Finally, take a look at Figure 2-1. This provides a graphical look at the current support status for various versions of the Oracle Database. I'm sure you don't want to be caught with your database out of support, do you?

New Features Related to Upgrading to Oracle Database 12*c*

Before you actually start upgrading your existing Oracle databases to Oracle Database 12*c*, you will want to be aware of the following new features that Oracle has added to assist you in the upgrade process:

- The Pre-Upgrade Information Tool
- Parallel processing for database upgrades

- Restartable Database Upgrade Assistant (DBUA)

- Pre- and post-upgrade summary report enhancements

- Installation of Oracle XML Database during the upgrade

The following sections briefly discuss these new features. Later in this chapter I will cover some of these features in much more detail.

NOTE
See Chapter 4 for more information related to upgrading Oracle RAC databases and the Oracle Grid Infrastructure components.

Pre-Upgrade Information Tool

A new tool has been added to your upgrade toolkit. Oracle Database 12c introduces the Pre-Upgrade Information Tool. This tool is a script that you can run before you perform a manual upgrade to Oracle Database 12c. If you choose to use the DBUA, it runs the same checks as this script before it executes the database upgrade. The Pre-Upgrade Information Tool looks for any issues that might occur during an upgrade. If it finds known issues, it creates a fixup script to correct the problems. The tool is also used to perform post-upgrade checks. Again, if the script finds specific problems, it will generate fixup scripts to correct the problems. Later in this chapter you will see the Pre-Upgrade Information Tool in use.

Parallel Processing for Database Upgrades

Previous database upgrades involved the use of the catupgrd.sql script to perform the upgrade. Oracle Database 12c replaces the catupgrd.sql script (deprecated in Oracle Database 12c) with a new Pearl script called catctl.pl. Because catctl.pl is a Perl script, it will *not* run from SQL*Plus. The script takes full advantage of parallelism during the upgrade process. You can opt to upgrade the database in parallel or in serial (but you can select only one of these options). The DBUA and the manual upgrade process can take advantage of parallelism. The default for both is to run in parallel mode.

NOTE
The catupgrd.sql script is deprecated in Oracle Database 12c.

Restartable DBUA

In the past, a DBUA upgrade failure or error often meant that you had to restore the database to a point before you started the upgrade and then start over. In Oracle

Database 12*c*, the DBUA toolkit adds achievement logging, which keeps track of the upgrade process. Achievement logging, combined with the creation of guaranteed restore points during the upgrade process, provides the capability to recover from DBUA errors during pre-upgrade and post-upgrade activities.

Pre- and Post-Upgrade Summary Report Enhancements

The DBUA provides HTML-based pre- and post-upgrade reports on the status of the upgrade of the database. The reports provide a look at various components of the database so that you can confirm that they are configured correctly. The reports provide a means to detect issues associated with the upgrade that may need to be dealt with, such as invalid objects.

Installation of Oracle XML Database During the Upgrade

In previous versions of Oracle Database, Oracle XML Database (Oracle XML DB) was an optionally installed component. With Oracle Database 12*c*, installation of Oracle XML DB is now required. Therefore, Oracle XML DB will be installed when you upgrade your database to Oracle Database 12*c*. Oracle XML DB is now required because Oracle Enterprise Manager Database Express (EM Express), which replaces Database Control, is built using Oracle XML DB.

Preparing for an Upgrade to Oracle Database 12*c*

To quote Alexander Graham Bell, "Before anything else, preparation is the key to success." That certainly applies when upgrading your Oracle database from a previous version of Oracle Database to Oracle Database 12*c*. This section covers the various tasks that you need to perform when preparing for a successful Oracle Database upgrade:

- Read, and then read some more
- Testing
- Check for compatibility issues
- Consider removing Database Control before you upgrade
- Back up the source database

- Choose an upgrade or migration method

- More about the Pre-Upgrade Information Tool

- Getting ready to upgrade or migrate

Read, and Then Read Some More

Oracle Database 12*c* comes with a plethora of documentation. As previously mentioned, you should not consider this chapter to be the essential guide to upgrading to Oracle Database 12*c*. Rather, this chapter is just a basic guide. A variety of factors can impact the upgrade process, and the best way to start your preparation for an upgrade is to read the actual Oracle-provided documentation. In particular, you should read the *Oracle Database Upgrade Guide 12*c and the installation documentation that pertains to your specific hardware.

This book will provide you with good insight into a number of new features in Oracle Database 12*c*. With over 500 new features in Oracle Database 12*c*, it's possible we will not cover a new feature associated with a database component you are using. A quick read of the new features section of the documentation related to the components you are using will round out your reading list and help you to put together a plan to upgrade your Oracle databases.

Testing

The pre-upgrade testing process is a critical part of any successful upgrade plan. In fact, I think that inadequate or improper testing is one of the major failures in the upgrade projects that I've seen. I don't have any quantifiable facts behind this number, but I'd wager that of all the failed upgrade projects that I've seen, the root cause of some 75 percent of them has been something that was not done right in the testing phase.

With that reminder of the importance of pre-upgrade testing, let's look at a few key components of the pre-upgrade testing process:

- Testing and test plans

- Testing infrastructures

Testing and Test Plans

It is generally considered a best practice to put together test plans before you start your upgrade process. These plans should mandate testing of the database, the application itself, database and application performance, and data integrity issues. The plans should also specify to test backup and recovery, monitoring and alerting, and other infrastructure-related items to make sure they are compatible with Oracle Database 12*c*.

Testing connectivity is another item your plans should include. I've had more than one migration that encountered last-minute problems because one part of the middle tier was not compatible with the new version of Oracle. The middle tier can be so vast that it's often difficult to find all the components and ensure they are compatible. But, finding those components and ensuring compatibility before you have completed the migration is much better than waiting until after the production migration has completed. I've seen cases where test migrations went successfully, but the production middle tier included components that were not present in the test environment.

The bottom line is that you need to prepare for these contingencies in your planning and try to address as many of them as you can. Also, document the problems you run into so that you, and everyone else, will have a record of these problems and the solution, in case the problem arises again. I don't know about you but I go through a lot in a month's time. I don't tend to remember everything, and even when I remember the big stuff, I often forget the details. The point is, keep records, and keep them somewhere that's accessible to your co-workers so that they can benefit from your experiences.

Testing Infrastructures

Once in a while, when I write a book, I come across a subject that I feel passionate about and almost want to turn into a rant. Testing is one of these subjects. I've worked in a number of different environments. I suspect that number is somewhere in the mid one-hundreds to be honest, maybe higher. The one common theme I find in these environments is that there is a lack of an adequate test environment. As I talk to the folks in the trenches, I hear war stories and horror stories on numberless things that have gone wrong in the past with the release of new applications, from the upgrading of new databases to the addition of new hardware and changes in infrastructure. The stories continue about unplanned changes, undocumented changes, changes that were documented but the actual change was something other than what was documented, and of course, there are the emergency changes that happen at two o'clock in the morning that nobody really hears the details about.

Then, you hear the ultimate results of these events. They come in sentences like "Well, we don't apply the quarterly patches because we had a failure applying one a year ago." Or something like "We don't like to upgrade the database because the last time we did we had a week-long outage because of significant performance problems." And the reasons and excuses continue.

More often than not, at the end of these conversations I finally drill down to the root cause of the problem. What is that root cause? Lack of an adequate test environment.

On the one hand, there is invariably a strong discussion with management and the top technical folks with a clear message about how important production is,

Tom Says

Many times I find it is lack of a test environment period. A test environment is the first step in any high-availability solution. The test environment should mirror the production environment as much as possible—and the testing taken seriously. It takes time, it takes money, it can delay a production rollout, but it can also ensure that the production rollout will happen "silently." The production rollout will be a boring event. How many of you can say your upgrades are boring? There is where you want to be—bored.

how the upgrade has to go smoothly and how the users can't be affected by the upgrade in any way (i.e., performance or outage).

On the other hand, you start to dive into the test infrastructure and its associated processes and the things you find there don't match the expectations expressed by management or the top technical folks you just had your meeting with. There is a disconnect, a terrible, dangerous disconnect.

What surprises me even more are the stories I hear from the guys in the trenches. The history of failed this and failed that, all of which clearly evidence a test infrastructure and set of processes that do not truly reflect the message that I've just heard that production is important, that the users are important, and that we can't take risks.

I find it confusing sometimes that management often does not realize the impedance to the goal of successful upgrades (database and otherwise) is wholly predicated on well-designed test environments that help ensure those successes. I often hear the lament of cost and time and availability of resources and a host of other reasons. At the end of the day, I'm often left wondering what is really important.

Let me be clear. If your test system cannot replicate your production system in every respect, then you are taking a risk. It might be a measured risk, it might be a risk that you and your management are willing to accept, but it's a risk nevertheless. I've often found that this risk isn't properly managed or understood by anyone, from the guys in the trench up to management. So it's important to understand the risks. In understanding the risks, we might find some solutions to manage them.

To establish a successful test environment in which you can craft a process that repeatedly produces results that reflect the results that would appear in production, you need to address the following considerations:

- Make sure the hardware components are the same in the test and production environments.

- Make sure that the operating system and its associated patch levels are the same between the production and test environments, unless there is a good reason (such as testing) for a difference.

- Make sure the networking configuration is the same between the test and production environments. This would include hardware, settings, switches, cabling and all other aspects of the network.

- Make sure the Oracle configuration (including items such as Clusterware, the number of RAC nodes, the database version, and parameter settings) is the same across the test and production platforms unless a divergence is expected for testing.

- Review any parameters derived by system configuration information (for example, the number of CPUs or amount of memory) subject to change based on hardware differences. Make sure you understand those differences and how they might impact your test results.

- Ensure that data volumes are the same across the test and production platforms.

- Make sure the disk characteristics are the same between the test and production platforms, if at all possible. This would include the number of disks that the data is spread across, and the physical connections. For example, do both systems have the same number of host bus adapters (which can make a huge difference with respect to throughput)?

- Do you accurately reproduce expected transaction types that the application will execute?

- Do you simulate the mix of transaction types and, just as important, simulate concurrency?

- Do you simulate based on the current database footprint (data, transaction rate, and concurrency) or do you determine the future usage footprint and simulate based on that?

- Do you stress-test the system?

- Is your change management process sufficient to manage the overall enterprise configuration and in particular the production and test environments. It is important to make sure that any change to either configuration is tracked to ensure that test results are meaningful.

I've seen each of the issues above cause problems at one time or another. The most common issues seem to be a test environment that does not even come close to replicating the production environment in any way. I also often see that the testing methodology really does not represent the activity that will be occurring in production. Most frequently there is no volume/concurrency testing. That is to say, often the goal of the testing is to make sure that the right answers are being produced, in a reasonable amount of time, from a single process. Many times I've seen these "tested" processes fail when moved into production because tens if not hundreds of users start running them all at the same time.

Whole books have been written about how to do appropriate testing, a topic that's beyond the scope of this book. Oracle provides a number of tools to help you with your testing. In particular, we recommend that you use Oracle Real Application Testing as you plan your Oracle Database 12c upgrade. It will make your upgrade process much easier and provide a higher likelihood that your upgrade will be successful.

Check for Compatibility Issues

Compatibility issues frequently cause problems in upgrade projects. Often, some component is not compatible with the new version of Oracle Database. You want to make sure that new prerequisites for OS, hardware, and other component versions, settings, or certification issues are reviewed and if need be, any discrepancies are addressed. This section addresses the following compatibility issues:

- Infrastructure and application compatibility

- OS and hardware compatibility

- The database COMPATIBLE parameter

Infrastructure and Application Compatibility

When an upgrade project is delayed by a problem, the problem usually is not with the database upgrade process itself, but rather is a result of a compatibility issue with another component in the system. Therefore, before you upgrade your database to Oracle Database 12c, make sure Oracle Database 12c is compatible with the other parts of your infrastructure. For example, check for the following:

- Application support and/or certification for Oracle Database 12c

- Driver (such as ODBC or JDBC) support for Oracle Database 12c

- Infrastructure support for Oracle Database 12c, such as hardware-related version support (e.g., firmware), network compatibility, storage compatibility, and so on

OS and Hardware Compatibility

You need to check that your current operating system and hardware components are compatible with Oracle Database 12c. Oracle Database 12c contains install guides for each OS platform that it supports. Make sure that you check this install guide to ensure that the OS is compatible with Oracle Database 12*c*. Also check to ensure your system includes all patches and OS components (such as specific RPMs) that Oracle recommends be installed. You very likely will need to upgrade and patch your OS to install Oracle Database 12*c*. It's also possible that you will need to install new or updated libraries to install Oracle Database 12*c*. All of these prerequisites are listed in the Oracle-specific documentation that is associated with your specific database platform.

The Database COMPATIBLE Parameter

The COMPATIBLE parameter has two main purposes. The first is to control which features you can use in the Oracle database. The second, somewhat related to the first, has to do with your ability to back out of a migration done by DBUA or done manually, as we will discuss later in this chapter.

Generally, when you are migrating your database, we recommend that you keep COMPATIBLE set to the version of the source database until you are comfortable that the migration has been successful with respect to things like connectivity and application performance.

Rolling back the database upgrade (discussed later in the chapter) should be a last-gasp affair. It is often indicative of a failure in the planning and testing previous to the production upgrade. Generally, if you find that you have a significant problem after upgrading, call Oracle Support and work with them to correct your problem. Don't panic and roll back the upgrade, as this makes finding a solution much more difficult.

Once you have migrated the database and tested it, go ahead and let it run in production mode with the COMPATIBLE parameter set to a value of 11.0.0.0 (the minimum required for an Oracle Database 12*c* database) until you are convinced that everything is working well. Then, after several weeks of successful operation, start using your normal change-control process (meaning, test it with gusto!) to modify the COMPATIBLE parameter from 11.0.0.0 to 12.0.0.0.

Consider Removing Database Control Before You Upgrade

As indicated earlier in the chapter, Database Control has been replaced in Oracle Database 12*c* by Oracle Enterprise Manager Database Express. Each of the upgrade processes will remove Database Control. This can make the upgrade process take longer than it otherwise would. To eliminate this issue, you can manually remove Database Control prior to the upgrade by using the **emremove.sql** script contained in the Oracle Database 12*c* ORACLE_HOME/rdbms/admin directory. In addition, in some cases you may need to remove the following files associated with Database

Control. These files may or may not exist in your environment, depending on whether your database was previously upgraded.

- $ORACLE_HOME/HOSTNAME_SID.upgrade

- $ORACLE_HOME/oc4j/j2ee/OC4J_DBConsole_HOSTNAME_SID

If you are running Windows, you will want to remove the DB Console service associated with the database you are upgrading. This service is normally called OracleDBConsole<SID>. Oracle does provide a method of preserving and referencing historical DB Console information. See the *Oracle Database Upgrade Guide 12*c for more information on this capability.

Back Up the Source Database

One of the most critical actions a DBA can take before upgrading to Oracle Database 12*c* is to make sure the source database is backed up. This should be a physical backup, and we strongly recommend that you use RMAN for this backup. To ensure you have a complete backup, you should back up the entire database (an online backup will do), back up all the needed archived redo logs, and back up the current control file.

CAUTION
Physical backup means do not use Oracle Data Pump for your pre-upgrade backup! Oracle Data Pump is not a physical backup of a database. If you want to do an Oracle Data Pump export of the database, that might not be a bad idea, but it should not be your primary means to ensure you can recover your database after an upgrade failure.

Tom Says
I second this sentiment 100 percent. Oracle Data Pump, and the legacy export and import tools—they are *not* backup tools, they do *not* provide a physical backup. There is much confusion on this. The only thing that is a backup is—a backup. Exports are logical copies of data that you might be able to use to reconstruct your database, maybe. *Do not* rely on them as a backup *ever*.

Choose an Upgrade or Migration Method

You can upgrade (or migrate if needed) your database to Oracle Database 12c. You have several options depending on the version of the database you are upgrading from, if you are moving to a different platform during the upgrade, and even your personal preferences.

In this section we will discuss the following:

- Direct and indirect upgrades

- Upgrading using the Oracle Database Upgrade Assistant (DBUA)

- Upgrading using the manual upgrade method

- Other upgrade/migration methods

Additionally, you can use these methods along with Oracle GoldenGate or Oracle Standby Database to facilitate the switch over to the new Oracle Database 12c database with a minimum of downtime. Refer to the *Oracle Database Upgrade Guide 12c* and the product-specific guides for information on using these Oracle products/tools during an upgrade.

Direct and Indirect Upgrades

All methods used to upgrade the Oracle Database are categorized into two different types. The first is the direct upgrade and the second is the indirect upgrade.

The direct upgrade provides the means to upgrade your database on the same platform either with the Database Upgrade Assistant (DBUA) or through a manual process. Oracle Database 12c allows for direct migration from one of these Oracle Database versions:

- Oracle Database 10g Release 2 version 10.2.0.5 or later

- Oracle Database 11g Release 1 version 11.1.0.7 and later

- Oracle Database 11g Release 2 version 11.2.02 and later

If you are not running one of these versions of the Oracle database then you cannot directly upgrade to Oracle Database 12c. Instead you must either:

- Upgrade the source database to a version of the Oracle Database that does support direct upgrade.

- Upgrade the database via an indirect upgrade method.

Database migrations to Oracle Database 12*c* are supported through these means:

- Use of Oracle Database Data Pump Export and Import utilities (or imp/exp utilities if Data Pump is not available on your database version) to migrate the Oracle database to another Oracle instance.

- Use of Oracle Transportable Tablespaces technology to

    - Migrate specific tablespaces to an upgraded Oracle Database 12*c* database instance. This feature has been available for some time, so we won't be covering it in much detail in this book.

    - Move an entire database to an upgraded Oracle Database 12*c* database instance. This is a new feature in Oracle Database 12*c* that we cover in more detail in Chapter 5.

- Oracle GoldenGate Technologies

    - You can find out a lot about Oracle GoldenGate in my book *Oracle GoldenGate 11g Handbook* from Oracle Press. So, we won't be mentioning it much in this chapter.

- Use of the Oracle **create table as select** command over Oracle Net.

Figure 2-2 provides a graphic example of the upgrade/migration path you will need to follow based on the version of the Oracle Database you wish to upgrade/migrate from. The most common ways of upgrading or migrating to Oracle Database 12*c* include

- Upgrading using the DBUA

- Upgrading using the manual upgrade method

- Migrating using the Oracle Data Pump utility

- Migrating using transportable tablespaces

- Migrating using the Oracle SQL **create table as select** command

We will briefly review each of these options in more detail next.

Upgrading Using the DBUA

Oracle introduced the DBUA many versions ago, and over time it's gotten better and better. This tool makes the process of upgrading your existing Oracle database

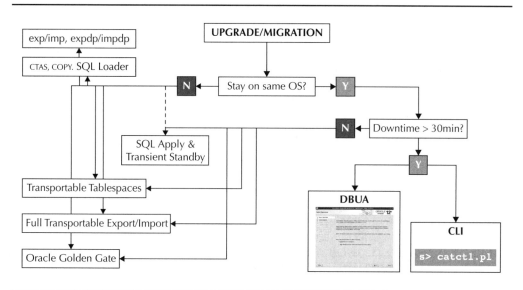

FIGURE 2-2. *Paths to upgrade to Oracle Database 12c*

very easy. You can use the DBUA tool when you are upgrading from the following versions of Oracle Database:

■ Release 10.2.0.5

■ Release 11.1.0.7

■ Release 11.2.0.2 or later

If you are using any other release, you will need to either:

■ Upgrade from that release to one of the releases noted above, and then perform a direct database upgrade

■ Use one of the alternative database migration methods listed later in this chapter

You can determine which version your database is currently at by issuing the following query:

```
SQL> select * from v$version;
BANNER
-----------------------------------------------------------------------
Oracle Database 11g Enterprise Edition Release 11.2.0.3.0 - 64bit Production
```

```
PL/SQL Release 11.2.0.3.0 - Production
CORE  11.2.0.3.0  Production
TNS for Linux: Version 11.2.0.3.0 - Production
NLSRTL Version 11.2.0.3.0 - Production
```

In this case we are running Oracle Database 11g Version 11.2.0.3. This version is supported by DBUA, so we can use the DBUA tool to perform the upgrade. If you are upgrading from a version of Oracle Database earlier than Oracle Database 11g, you will need to set the COMPATIBLE parameter to a value of at least 11.0.0.0 after the upgrade is complete. Note that you cannot downgrade your database to a version earlier than 11.1.0.7.

Upgrading Using the Manual Upgrade Method

As the name suggests, the manual upgrade method is used to manually upgrade from an earlier version of Oracle Database to Oracle Database 12c. The Oracle Database versions that support the manual upgrade method are the same versions that support upgrades via the DBUA, as listed in the previous section (10.2.0.5, 11.1.0.7, and 11.2.0.2 or later). The manual upgrade method required the execution of a number of scripts, and is not fronted by any kind of GUI. The manual upgrade process can be a bit more error-prone since you have to manually execute the steps in the right order, which the DBUA does for you.

Migrating Using the Oracle Data Pump Utility

The first option available to you if you cannot do a direct migration of your database to Oracle Database 12c is to use the Oracle Data Pump utility. If you are migrating from a particularly old version of the database, then you would use Oracle's older Import and Export utilities to migrate to Oracle Database 12c.

When you use Oracle Data Pump, you create the Oracle Database 12c database first, and then you load the database metadata and data using Oracle Data Pump. The main drawback to using Oracle Data Pump over the previously described upgrade methods (DBUA and manual database upgrade) is that Oracle Data Pump is slower. You can use Oracle Data Pump features such as compression, direct network connection, and parallelism to improve performance of the export/import operations.

Migrating Using Transportable Tablespaces

Transportable tablespaces can be an easy method of migrating to Oracle Database 12c from another database. This is especially true if the target database is on another platform, or if you just want to upgrade specific objects or schemas to Oracle Database 12c. Oracle Database 12c now supports transport of entire databases across platforms through the use of a combination of transportable tablespaces and Oracle Data Pump, including those platforms with byte-ordering differences (e.g., Endian byte format).

Migrating Using the create table as select Command

The Oracle **create table as select** (CTAS) command is another supported method of migrating to Oracle Database 12*c*. Using this method, you create an Oracle Database link, and then move the data over that database link from the old database to the new Oracle Database 12*c* database.

This method has a few drawbacks that are readily apparent. First, you are dependent on your network bandwidth for movement of the data. Second, you have to create a CTAS statement for each table. Third, you have to re-create the various constraints and indexes and other supporting structures in the new database. As a result, this method is rarely used, as it can be quite time-consuming to write the scripts to re-create a given database in its entirety. Oracle Data Pump is preferable to the use of this method. Because this method has been around for some time, and is rarely used, we will not be covering it in any great detail within this book.

More About the Pre-Upgrade Information Tool

As mentioned earlier in the chapter, the Pre-Upgrade Information Tool (also called the Pre-Upgrade Utility) is designed to perform checks on the database before it is upgraded, and then report on the results of those checks. The tool will also generate scripts, and suggest manual actions on the part of the DBA, that need to be run to address issues in the database both before and after the upgrade has occurred. Additionally, the tool creates a log file that provides the results of the execution of the Pre-Upgrade Information Tool.

Using the Pre-Upgrade Information Tool with the Database Upgrade Assistant

If you are upgrading the database via the Database Upgrade Assistant (DBUA) then that tool will run the Pre-Upgrade Information Tool for you. After the tool has run, the DBUA will display the results as seen in Figure 2-3. The DBUA will categorize the errors as warnings or failures. You should always make sure that the failure items are corrected before you upgrade. In most cases the warning items can be corrected after the upgrade but it's still a good idea to correct them before the upgrade.

In some cases, the DBUA can correct the problem for you as is the case with the DBMS_LDAP dependencies exist warning that appears. In the case of the EM repository the tool can't fix the problem, but provides information on how to correct the problem.

Running the Pre-Upgrade Information Tool Manually

To run the Pre-Upgrade Information Tool manually, you need to set your environment to the pre-Oracle Database 12*c* database environment. As shown in this example, we are setting our environment for an Oracle Database 11.2.0.3 database called orcl:

```
[oracle@server12c ~]$ . oraenv
ORACLE_SID = [oracle] ? orcl
```

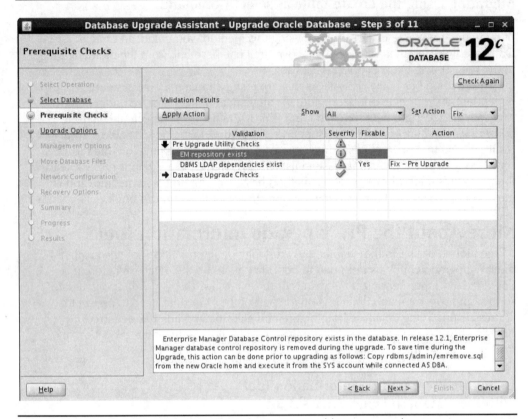

FIGURE 2-3. *The DBUA after the Pre-Information Tool has executed*

```
The Oracle base has been set to /u01/app/oracle
[oracle@server12c ~]$ env|grep ORACLE
ORACLE_SID=orcl
ORACLE_BASE=/u01/app/oracle
ORACLE_HOME=/u01/app/oracle/product/11.2.0.3/dbhome_1
```

After you have the environment set correctly, run the Pre-Upgrade Information Tool. The tool is in the Oracle 12c Database ORACLE_HOME/rdbms/admin directory in the form of a script called preupgrd.sql, as shown here:

```
[oracle@server12c admin]$ pwd
/u01/app/oracle/product/12.1.0.1/dbhome_1/rdbms/admin
[oracle@server12c admin]$ ls -al pre*
-rw-r--r-- 1 oracle oinstall 5231 Apr  2 00:16 preupgrd.sql
```

Next, you need to log into the database you will be upgrading using the SYS user with the SYSDBA privilege and run the Pre-Upgrade Information Tool. Here is an example of the execution of this tool:

```
[oracle@server12c admin]$ pwd
/u01/app/oracle/product/12.1.0.1/dbhome_1/rdbms/admin
[oracle@server12c admin]$ . oraenv
ORACLE_SID = [orcl12cp] ? orcl
The Oracle base remains unchanged with value /u01/app/oracle
[oracle@server12c admin]$ sqlplus sys as sysdba
SQL*Plus: Release 11.2.0.3.0 Production on Thu Jul 25 15:29:11 2013
Copyright (c) 1982, 2011, Oracle.  All rights reserved.
Enter password:
Connected to:
Oracle Database 11g Enterprise Edition Release 11.2.0.3.0 - 64bit Production
With the Partitioning, OLAP, Data Mining and Real Application Testing options
SQL> @preupgrd.sql
Loading Pre-Upgrade Package...
Executing Pre-Upgrade Checks...
Pre-Upgrade Checks Complete.
        ************************************************************
Results of the checks are located at:
/u01/app/oracle/cfgtoollogs/orcl/preupgrade/preupgrade.log
Pre-Upgrade Fixup Script (run in source database environment):
/u01/app/oracle/cfgtoollogs/orcl/preupgrade/preupgrade_fixups.sql
Post-Upgrade Fixup Script (run shortly after upgrade):
/u01/app/oracle/cfgtoollogs/orcl/preupgrade/postupgrade_fixups.sql
        ************************************************************
    Fixup scripts must be reviewed prior to being executed.
        ************************************************************
        ************************************************************
            ====>> USER ACTION REQUIRED  <<====
        ************************************************************
The following are *** ERROR LEVEL CONDITIONS *** that must be addressed
            prior to attempting your upgrade.
    Failure to do so will result in a failed upgrade.
    You MUST resolve the above errors prior to upgrade
        ************************************************************
```

Note that the resulting log and scripts are created in a directory called ORACLE_ BASE/cfgtoollogs/orcl/preupgrade, the contents of which are shown here:

```
[oracle@server12c admin]$ cd $ORACLE_BASE/cfgtoollogs/orcl/preupgrade
[oracle@server12c preupgrade]$ ls -al
total 24
drwxr-xr-x 2 oracle oinstall 4096 Mar 13 10:18 .
drwxr-xr-x 3 oracle oinstall 4096 Mar 13 10:00 ..
-rw-r--r-- 1 oracle oinstall 1987 Jul 25 15:29 postupgrade_fixups.sql
-rw-r--r-- 1 oracle oinstall 3243 Jul 25 15:29 preupgrade_fixups.sql
-rw-r--r-- 1 oracle oinstall 6880 Jul 25 15:29 preupgrade.log
```

The preupgrade.log file contains the output from the Pre-Upgrade Information Tool execution. Suffice it to say that the tool checks a number of components in the database, such as the Oracle catalog views, the Oracle packages and types installed in the database, the database JVM, and all the other components installed in the database. The tool also ensures there is sufficient tablespace space and that database settings (such as the setting for processes), time zone–related configurations, and other configuration settings are correctly configured. The tool also may recommend that you perform certain actions, such as running the **dbms_stats.gather_dictionary_ stats** PL/SQL package, statistics on fixed objects, and other database-related items.

While the output log is a bit lengthy to produce in its entirety, here are some snippets from a run that I did. First, we can see that my database process count might be too low:

```
WARNING: --> Process Count may be too low
Database has a maximum process count of 150 which is lower than the
default value of 300 for this release.
You should update your processes value prior to the upgrade
to a value of at least 300.
For example:
    ALTER SYSTEM SET PROCESSES=300 SCOPE=SPFILE
or update your init.ora file.
```

This alert indicates that a directory for Database Control has been found and suggests some actions based on that finding:

```
WARNING: --> Enterprise Manager Database Control repository found in
the database
In Oracle Database 12c, Database Control is removed during
    the upgrade. To save time during the Upgrade, this action
    can be done prior to upgrading using the following steps after
    copying rdbms/admin/emremove.sql from the new Oracle home
  - Stop EM Database Control:
   $> emctl stop dbconsole
  - Connect to the Database using the SYS account AS SYSDBA:
SET ECHO ON;
SET SERVEROUTPUT ON;
@emremove.sql
   Without the set echo and serveroutput commands you will not
   be able to follow the progress of the script.
```

You might well get several different kinds of warnings and errors produced in the log file, so you should carefully go over each of these warnings and clean up the database to be upgraded in advance.

The Pre-Upgrade Information Tool creates two SQL scripts. The first is the **preupgrade_fixups.sql** script. You should execute this script before you begin the upgrade of the database using either the DBUA or the manual upgrade process.

These scripts contain platform-specific updates that should be executed both before and after the upgrade. The updates are designed to fix issues in the database both before and after the upgrade of the database. In the following example, we are running the **preupgrade_fixups.sql** script in the orcl database—I've printed part of the results (which are quite long again):

```
[oracle@server12c preupgrade]$ sqlplus / as sysdba @preupgrade_fixups.sql
SQL*Plus: Release 11.2.0.3.0 Production on Thu Jul 25 15:44:46 2013
Copyright (c) 1982, 2011, Oracle.  All rights reserved.
Connected to:
Oracle Database 11g Enterprise Edition Release 11.2.0.3.0 - 64bit Production
With the Partitioning, OLAP, Data Mining and Real Application Testing options
Pre-Upgrade Fixup Script Generated on 2012-07-25 15:29:38  Version: 12.1.0.1
Build: 006
Beginning Pre-Upgrade Fixups...
PL/SQL procedure successfully completed.
PL/SQL procedure successfully completed.
*********************************************************************
Check Tag:     DEFAULT_PROCESS_COUNT
Check Summary: Verify min process count is not too low
Fix Summary:   Review and increase if needed, your PROCESSES value.
*********************************************************************
Fixup Returned Information:
WARNING: --> Process Count may be too low
    Database has a maximum process count of 150 which is lower than the
    default value of 300 for this release.
    You should update your processes value prior to the upgrade
    to a value of at least 300.
    For example:
        ALTER SYSTEM SET PROCESSES=300 SCOPE=SPFILE
    or update your init.ora file.
*********************************************************************
PL/SQL procedure successfully completed.
*********************************************************************
Check Tag:     EM_PRESENT
Check Summary: Check if Enterprise Manager is present
Fix Summary:   Execute emremove.sql prior to upgrade.
*********************************************************************
Fixup Returned Information:
WARNING: --> Enterprise Manager Database Control repository found in the database
    In Oracle Database 12c, Database Control is removed during
    the upgrade. To save time during the Upgrade, this action
    can be done prior to upgrading using the following steps after
    copying rdbms/admin/emremove.sql from the new Oracle home
  - Stop EM Database Control:
   $> emctl stop dbconsole
  - Connect to the Database using the SYS account AS SYSDBA:
  SET ECHO ON;
  SET SERVEROUTPUT ON;|
  @emremove.sql
  Without the set echo and serveroutput commands you will not
    be able to follow the progress of the script.
          ***************************************************
              ************ Fixup Summary ************
 4 fixup routines generated INFORMATIONAL messages that should be reviewed.
```

```
PL/SQL procedure successfully completed.
**************** Pre-Upgrade Fixup Script Complete *********************
PL/SQL procedure successfully completed.
```

Note that the steps listed in the log file also appear in the output of the **preupgrade_fixups.sql** script. Don't be confused, the **preupgrade_fixups.sql** script does not fix the manual things that you are instructed to fix. So, for example, you still need to go in and drop the OEM repository as instructed by the script.

The *Oracle Database Upgrade Guide 12c* provides a reference for diagnosing and solving the various errors that you might see reported in the Pre-Upgrade Information Tool.

After the **preupgrade_fixups.sql** script is complete, and you have run the manual fixes that it's indicated need to be completed, you can proceed with the database upgrade. Once the upgrade is complete, you will want to run the post-upgrade fixup that the pre-upgrade information tool also created. That script is called **postupgrade_ fixups.sql**.

Getting Ready to Upgrade or Migrate

While the pre-upgrade information tool is very helpful in finding things that need to be taken care of within the source database before it's upgraded, you will probably want to do your own checking first. Also, you might like to clean up some things that would get flagged by the pre-upgrade information tool otherwise. There are some things to address on both the source database environment and the destination environment. Let's look at these issues quickly.

Preparing the Source Database Environment

Here are a few things to do on the source database before you start the upgrade or migration:

1. Check the recycle bin for each schema. These will need to be cleared before either the DBUA or a manual upgrade can occur.

2. Check for any objects in the DBA_OBJECTS view that have a status of INVALID and that are owned by SYS or SYSTEM. If you cannot figure out why the objects are invalid then open a support ticket with Oracle and correct the problem. You can use the $ORACLE_HOME/rdbms/admin/utlrp.sql script to recompile database objects before the upgrade.

3. There are some cases where you might have duplicate objects in SYS or SYSTEM. If this is the case, reference MOS note 1030426.6 on how to clean up these objects or open an SR with Oracle support.

4. Review and remove outdated parameters on the source database before the upgrade. I often find databases with old outdated parameters set, and

these settings can cause problems in later versions of Oracle. Also, having parameters set that are not needed can increase the time it takes to upgrade your database, significantly in some cases (by a factor of 7 or more). Make sure that you follow the instructions of your application vendor with respect to setting parameters, of course.

5. Make sure all components in the DBA_REGISTRY view have a status of VALID. If they don't, open an SR with Oracle and correct the problem.

6. Standardize the components you install in the database. Remove any components that you don't use. This will speed up the upgrade process, sometimes significantly. The total time to upgrade a database is directly related to the number of components in the database.

7. Preserve the performance statistics.

    ■ Start collecting AWR statistics for at least a month before the upgrade. You can use the **dbms_stats.alter_stats_history_retention** PL/SQL procedure to modify the retention. The **dbms_stats.get_stats_history_retention** function can be used to display the current retention setting for the AWR. Finally you can display the space consumption of AWR by using the SYSAUX_OCCUPANTS view by using a query such as this one:

    ```
    select space_usage_kbytes/1024 space_mb
    from v$sysaux_occupants where occupant_name='SM/OPTSTAT';
    ```

    ■ Make your AWR snapshot intervals 30 minutes with a retention of > 31 days.

    ■ Before the upgrade or migration, extract the AWR information from the source database using the $ORACLE_HOME/rdbms/admin/awrextr.sql script. You can use the script $ORACLE_HOME/rdbms/admin/awrload.sql to then load the data into your target database.

    Having imported the previous AWR data, you can execute a performance snapshot comparison report between current AWR data and the imported AWR data from the source database using the PL/SQL stored procedure **dbms_workload_repository.awr_diff_report_html**. Note that this requires a Diagnostic Pack license. Review MOS note 785730.1 for more information on using awrextr.sql and awrload.sql to move AWR data between different databases/schemas.

    ■ You might also want to review MOS note 1477599.1 for more information on collecting data for performance issues.

8. Check the network and ensure that it has the stability and bandwidth to support your upgrade or migration plan. Make sure that it's stable and that you won't get disconnected from the database server in the middle of the upgrade. Also, ensure that it's fast enough to support the DBUA or the migration of the database through whatever method you select. Be aware that real world speed might well be less than the theoretical speed that is offered by the interface for a number of different reasons.

9. You may want to consider running integrity checks against the source database such as using the RMAN **backup check logical validate database** command to validate the blocks in your database are not corrupt. You might also want to review MOS notes 101466.1 and 136697.1 and the information about the h* helper script contained in those notes.

10. Review MOS note 1565082.1 (12.1.0.1 Base Release - Availability and Known Issues) for up-to-date information on known issues with Oracle Database 12.1.

11. Determine what client versions will be connecting to your new Oracle Database 12c Database. If the clients are less than version 11.0 then you will need to set the new parameter **allowed_logon_version_server** to the correct version of the network authentication protocol that needs to be serviced.

NOTE
Consider that your project to upgrade to Oracle Database 12c might well be a golden opportunity to get your environment under control. It's a great opportunity to implement standards, source, and version control; right size your memory usage; update your security models; and many other enterprise-oriented best practices. While these practices are well beyond the scope of this book, now is an excellent opportunity.

Preparing the Target Database Environment

The target database environment may be on the same physical environment or in a completely different database environment. Before you start your upgrade you will want to do the following on the target database environment:

1. Carefully check all of the certification requirements including the following:

   - Hardware

   - Operating system version and patch level

- Firmware revision levels

- Compatibility with enterprise components

2. Check that all installation requirements have been met with respect to the target database environment. Ensure that you have sufficient memory, CPU, disk and other resources available.

3. Check for any patches to software or firmware that might need to be applied.

4. Check for any Oracle patches that might need to be applied to the database software before you start the upgrade or migration process.

5. Install the following Oracle software and patches:

   - Install either the current base release of Oracle Database 12*c* or the newest patch set released for Oracle Database 12*c* into a new ORACLE_ HOME. You can have a single ORACLE_HOME for each database, or one for many databases.

   - Apply the latest patch set updates (PSU) or any recommended bundled patches (BP).

   - Research and apply any interim patches for known database issues that might impact your database operations.

Upgrading to Oracle Database 12*c* with the Database Upgrade Assistant

The Oracle Database Upgrade Assistant (DBUA) is a graphical tool that guides you through the steps of successfully performing a database upgrade. It makes the upgrade process simple and easy to complete. This section shows you how to use the DBUA to upgrade your database to Oracle Database 12*c*.

This discussion assumes that you have already installed Oracle Database 12*c*, completed all of the database upgrade prerequisite tasks outlined earlier in this chapter (with the exception of running the pre-upgrade tool, which the DBUA will do for you), and also completed any related tasks not covered in this book that might be specific to the hardware, OS platform, or database features that you have installed.

Starting the DBUA

Before you start the DBUA, you need to ensure that you have your environment set so that the DBUA Java application can start. Typically, on a Unix-based system such as Linux, this involves using the **xhost** command to enable your X Windows System and then testing using **xclock** or some X utility.

NOTE
Even the simplest of things can cause an upgrade to stall or fail. Make sure, for example, that you have enough space in your fast recovery area (FRA) to accommodate the additional archived redo logs that will be generated during the upgrade.

Next, set your Oracle environment for the Oracle Database 12*c* ORACLE_HOME. To make changing Oracle environments easy, you can set up a dummy entry in the /etc/oratab file that has the ORACLE_HOME for Oracle Database 12*c* set in it so that you can use **oraenv** to set the environment. Once you have the environment set correctly, you can start the DBUA from the OS command-line prompt with the command **dbua**. The following example configures the /etc/oratab file with a dummy database entry, sets the environment with **oraenv**, and then starts the DBUA utility:

```
[oracle@server12c preupgrade]$ cat /etc/oratab
dummy:/u01/app/oracle/product/12.1.0.1/dbhome_1:N
elevendb:/u01/app/oracle/product/11.2.0.3/dbhome_1:N
orcl:/u01/app/oracle/product/11.2.0.3/dbhome_1:N

[oracle@server12c preupgrade]$ . oraenv
ORACLE_SID = [orcl] ? dummy
The Oracle base remains unchanged with value /u01/app/oracle
[oracle@server12c preupgrade]$ dbua
```

Upgrading with DBUA

After you launch the DBUA application, the DBUA main page (Select Operation) opens, as shown in Figure 2-4.

This page gives you two options: upgrade Oracle Database, or move a database to a different Oracle Database 12*c* ORACLE_HOME, thereby upgrading to a different edition of Oracle (say, from Oracle Express Edition to Oracle Enterprise Edition). Choose the first option, Upgrade Oracle Database, and then click Next.

On the Select Database page, you choose the database that you want to upgrade. Note that there is a Source Oracle Home drop-down menu. From that menu, choose the ORACLE_HOME directory for the database you want to upgrade to Oracle Database 12*c*. As shown in Figure 2-5, for purposes of this upgrade example, we are upgrading an Oracle Database 11*g* database running Version 11.2.0.3 to Oracle Database 12*c*, so that is what we selected in the drop-down menu.

NOTE
During the DBUA upgrade process, the Recycle Bin is emptied. If you have objects in the Recycle Bin that you want to preserve, make sure you back them up before the upgrade process.

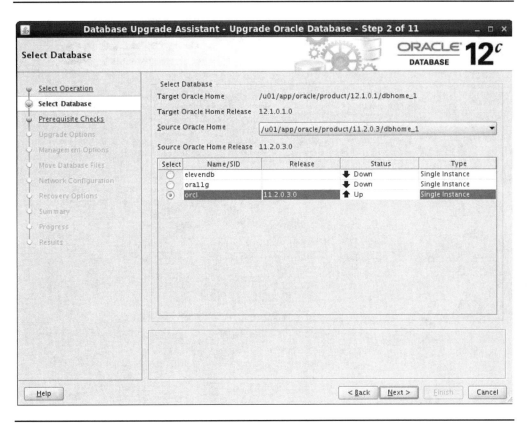

FIGURE 2-4. *DBUA main page*

After you choose the correct ORACLE_HOME, the databases assigned to that ORACLE_HOME are displayed. Click the radio button for the database that you want to upgrade. As shown in Figure 2-5, in our case, we chose the orcl database. Click Next.

After you click Next, the DBUA collects information about the database that you have chosen to upgrade. This can take a little while, so be patient. Once it has collected the information that it needs, the DBUA will perform two sets of database checks. First it will execute the Pre-Upgrade Utility, described earlier in this chapter. Then another set of checks called the Database Upgrade checks are performed. These checks include things such as:

■ A check of the current database to ensure that it is eligible for upgrade

■ A check of the oratab file to find the ORACLE_HOME for the database being upgraded

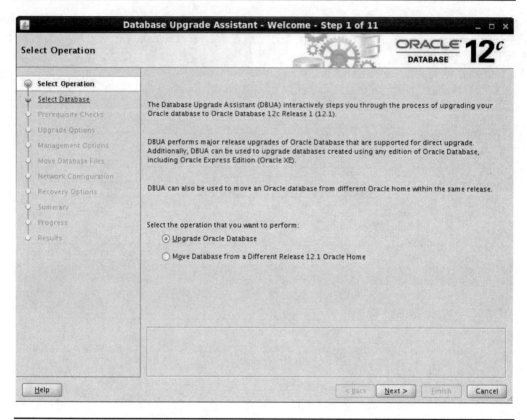

FIGURE 2-5. *DBUA Select Database page*

- A check of the ORACLE_HOME OS user ownership
- A check of Oracle Automatic Storage Management (ASM) to ensure that the new Oracle Database 12c database that will result from the upgrade will still be compatible with ASM

As shown in Figure 2-6, the Pre-Upgrade Utility check flagged several issues in our database. On the page, each individual item will be displayed as a line item if the pre-upgrade information utility detects a warning or fatal condition during the execution of the pre-upgrade utility. You can click on one of the individual items that appear on the page and review more details about the issue at the bottom of the page.

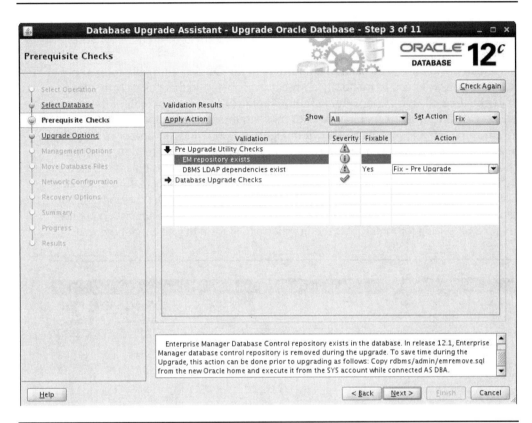

FIGURE 2-6.   *DBUA Prerequisite Checks page*

NOTE
The DBUA Prerequisite Checks page groups the checks in the validation results window. Make sure you click on the arrows next to the Validation column to see all the results.

In some cases the DBUA will give you an option to apply fixes needed to correct the issue reported. If the DBUA can correct the issue, you will see, in the Action column, an option to fix the item. Clicking on the action column, you will see in a drop-down box that you have three options:

- Fix the item.

- Ignore the error or warning.

- Revalidate (in case you manually fixed the problem).

You can also select these actions globally at the top right of the DBUA screen. If you wish to correct the items, make sure that the items say Fix-Pre Upgrade and click on the Next button to continue. The DBUA will correct the actions for you during the upgrade.

If there is nothing in the Action column, then the DBUA is not able to fix the item and you will need to manually correct the problem. In this case, correct the item and then click the Check Again button on the DBUA screen. If all of the checks are now coming out as OK, click Next to move to the Upgrade Options page.

The Upgrade Options page, shown in Figure 2-7, provides a number of upgrade-related options that you can select from. In the Upgrade Options section, you can choose to recompile invalid objects during the post-upgrade process (this is selected by default). Recompilation parallelism is also supported. This is a new feature on Oracle Database 12c that can significantly speed up recompiling objects after the upgrade. You can choose the degree of parallelism (DOP) to be used when the schema is recompiled. The default setting for the DOP is the number of CPUs on the host machine.

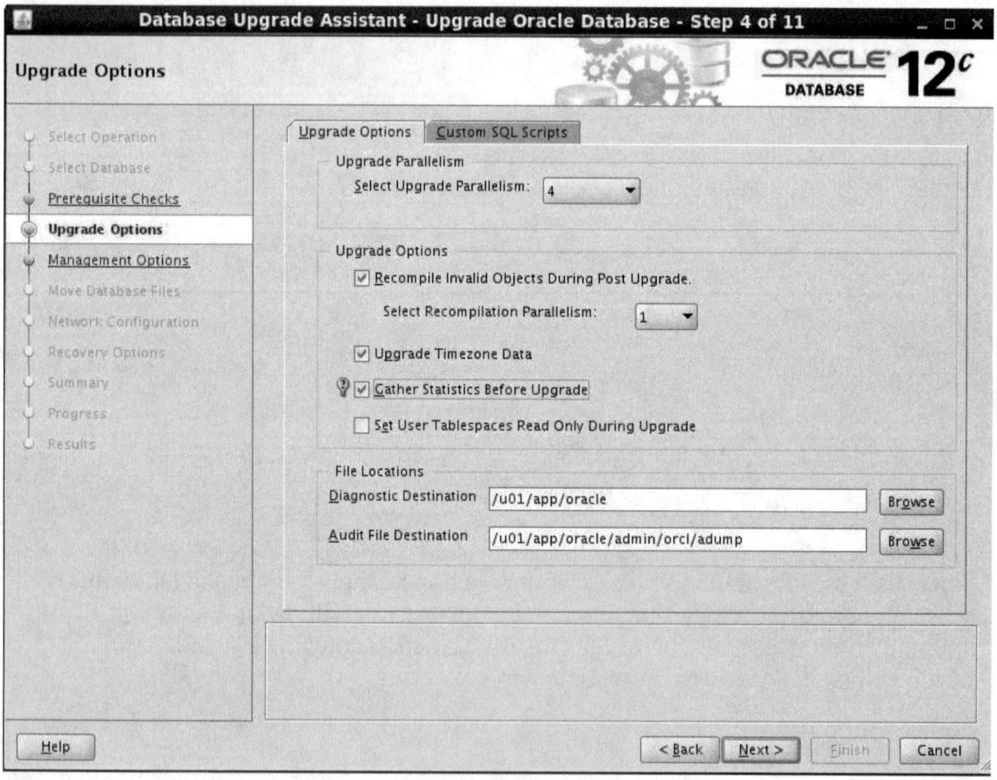

FIGURE 2-7. *DBUA Upgrade Options page*

From the DBUA Upgrade Options page you can also choose to upgrade the time zone data, collect statistics before the upgrade, and set the user tablespaces to read-only mode. You might have noticed that some of these are items that show up in the pre-upgrade utility (like the statistics and time zone data). So this is a nice place to get those items taken care of.

The two fields in the File Locations section of the upgrade Options page allow you to define the diagnostic destination directory and the audit file destination directory. These fields are populated for you by default and generally the defaults are the right way to go.

Finally, the Custom Scripts tab of the Upgrade Options page enables you to run custom scripts both before and after the upgrade. This can be handy, for example, if you want the DBUA to run an RMAN backup both before and after the upgrade.

After you have selected the options that you want to use, click Next to proceed to the Management Options page as seen in Figure 2-8. This page gives you the ability to configure Enterprise Manager Database Express (which replaces Database Control) or register the new database with Oracle Enterprise Manager Cloud

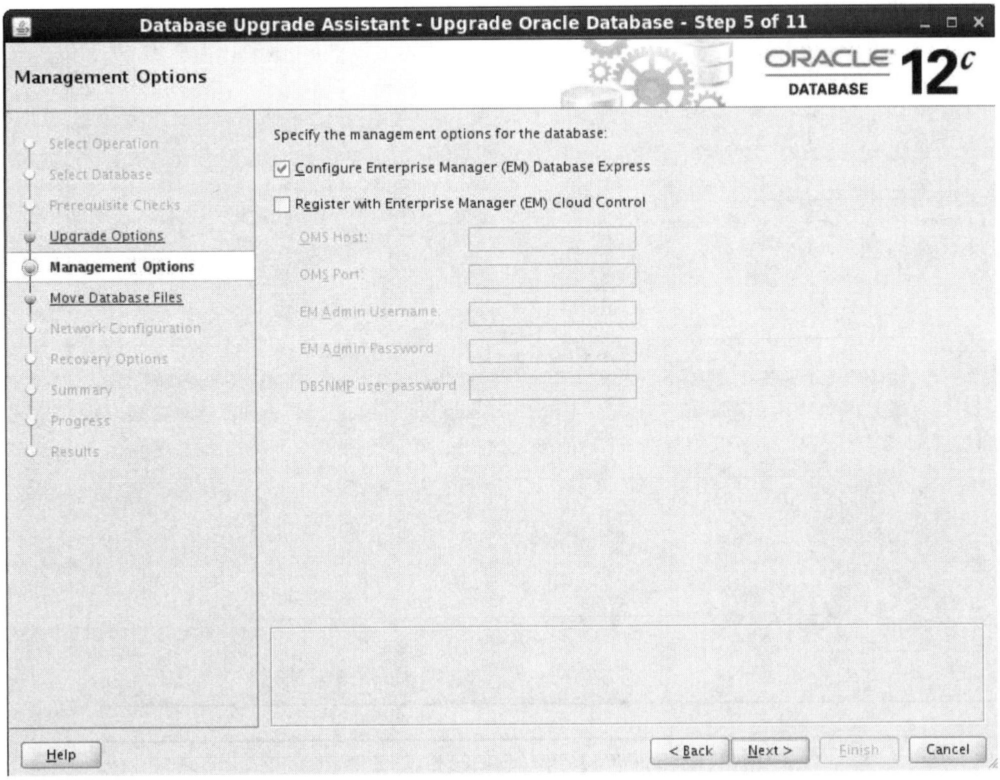

FIGURE 2-8. *DBUA Management Options*

Control. We discuss Enterprise Manager Database Express later in this chapter. If you are running Cloud Control, then you should select that option and fill in the fields to point the database to the correct Enterprise Manager components. Otherwise, select Configure Enterprise Manager (EM) Database Express and click Next to go to the Move Database Files page.

The Move Database Files page, shown in Figure 2-9, is where you can choose to move the database files and the FRA as part of the upgrade process. You should use these options if you want to move your database to or from ASM during the migration process. In our case, we are not moving files at all so we will just click Next to move to the Network Configuration page.

On the Network Configuration page, seen in Figure 2-10, you can choose the listener that you want to support the database you are migrating. Choose the listener that you want to service the database. This should be an Oracle Database 12c or

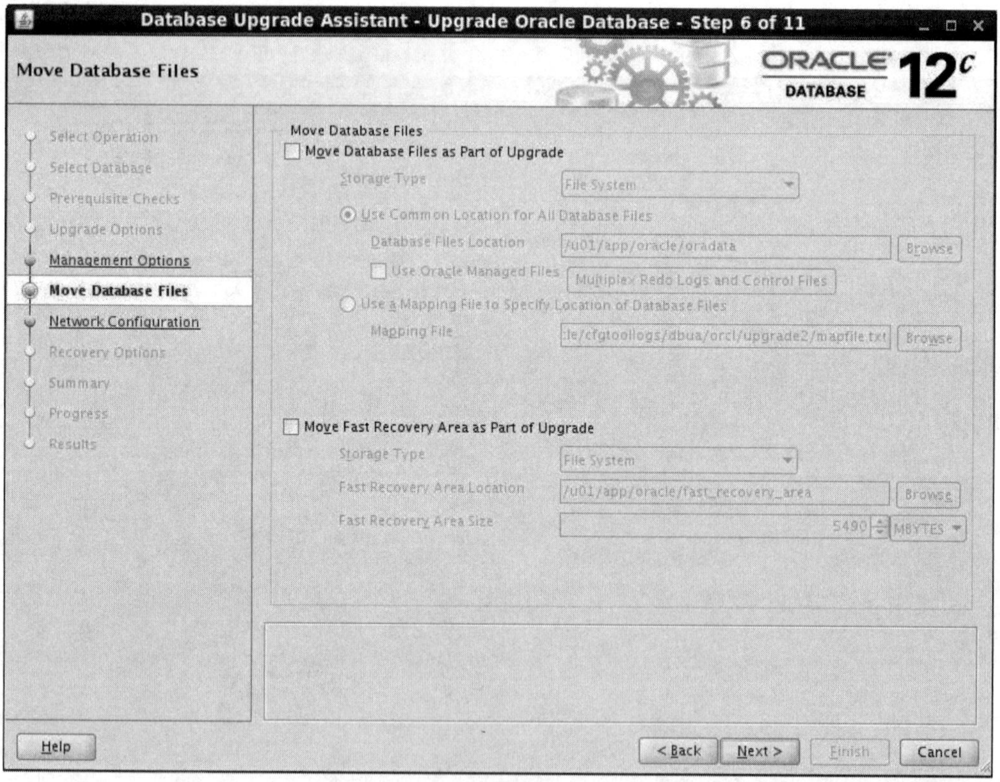

FIGURE 2-9. *DBUA Move Database Files page*

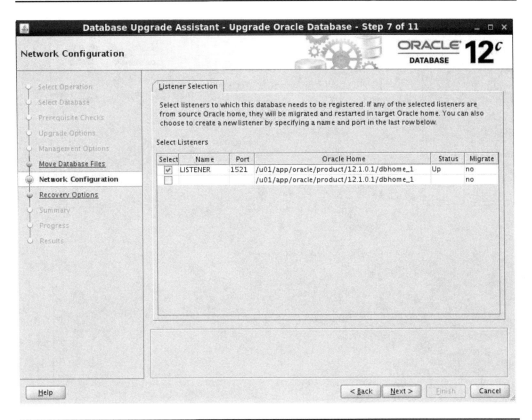

FIGURE 2-10. *DBUA Network Configuration page*

later listener. If you have not yet created an Oracle Database 12c listener, you can create one from this page. When you have made your selection, click Next to move to the DBUA Recovery Options page.

On the DBUA Recovery Options page, seen in Figure 2-11, you can choose to have the DBUA process perform an RMAN backup, or you can indicate that you have your own backup and recovery strategy and that the DBUA should not perform a backup.

The Recovery Options page also provides what I think is one of the most important new features in the DBUA. That is the ability to use Flashback Database while running an upgrade. In Oracle Database 12c the DBUA will create guaranteed restore points during the upgrade that can be used to flash back to specific points in the upgrade process. This provides the ability to recover from upgrade failures and restart the process at the point of the restore point. This is a significant improvement in

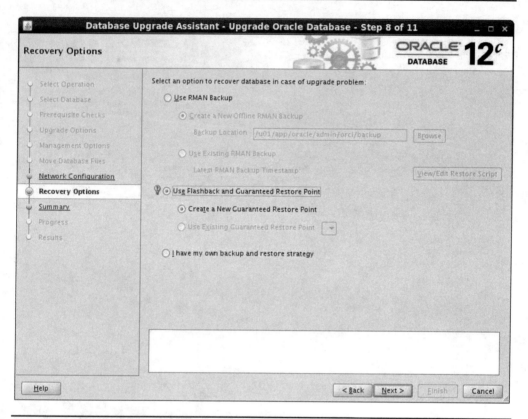

FIGURE 2-11. *DBUA Recovery Options page*

the DBUA. So significant, in fact, that we think it makes using this tool preferable to performing a manual upgrade in many cases.

NOTE
Enabling Flashback Database and ARCHIVELOG mode will have some performance impact on your database and require some additional disk space in your FRA. The cost of this disk space is far outweighed by the flexibility you get should the DBUA encounter an error during the upgrade. The time required to restore a large database may well outweigh the additional cost of storage, and slightly slower performance, in the event of a failure.

In our case, we are going to have the DBUA create a restore point for us. I would strongly recommend a RMAN backup be taken before you start the upgrade. After you choose the option that is correct for you, click Next to move to the DBUA Summary page, shown in Figure 2-12.

NOTE
The DBUA will check to ensure that you have enough disk space available in the FRA and in $ORACLE_HOME. Make sure you review the space availability notice at the bottom of the DBUA Recovery Options page to ensure you have enough space.

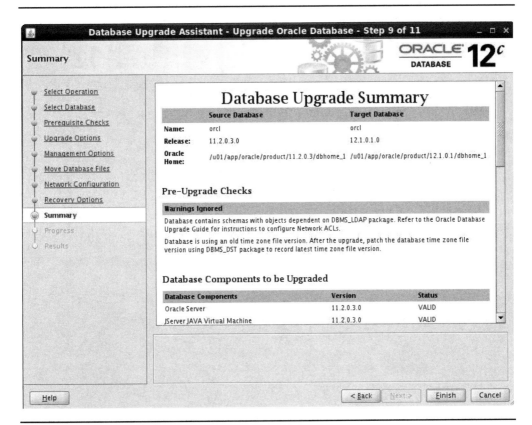

FIGURE 2-12.   *DBUA Summary page*

The DBUA Summary page provides an overview of the upgrade process that is about to occur. Review the Summary page carefully to ensure that it correctly identifies the upgrade you intend to perform. If it is correct, click the Finish button and the upgrade will begin. If it's incorrect, you can click the Back button to move back through the DBUA steps and make the necessary changes.

After you click Finish, the DBUA Progress page appears, as shown in Figure 2-13. It displays the progress as the different upgrade steps occur. Note that the steps shown are high-level detail steps. There are arrows to the left that you can click on that will give you more details on the progress. You can also see that the entire upgrade process has a completion bar that indicates the total completion percentage to that point in time. As each step completes, the time it took to execute that step shows up in the time column. An example of the timings and the additional step details seen by clicking on the arrows in the progress box are seen in Figure 2-14.

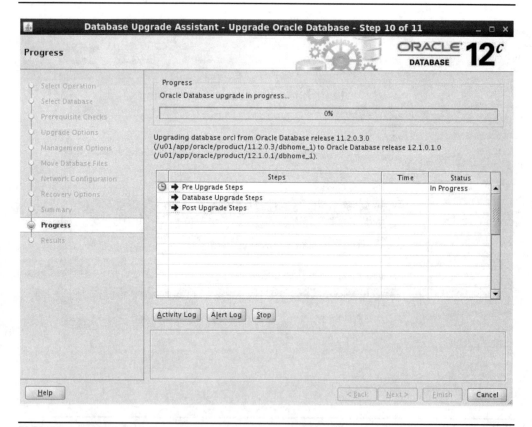

FIGURE 2-13.   *DBUA Progress page*

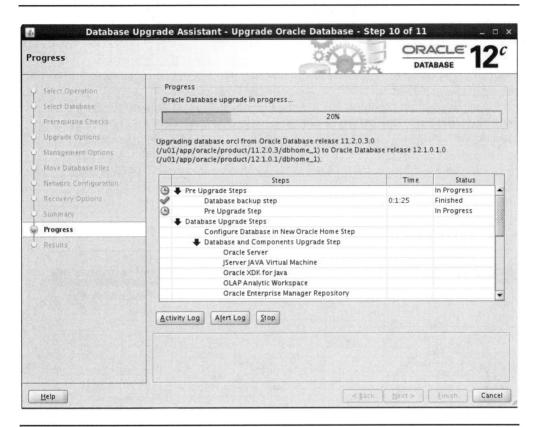

FIGURE 2-14. *DBUA Progress page with timing and step details*

The DBUA has also added buttons at the bottom that will display the activity log that is updated during the upgrade. Another button allows you to look at the database alert log. Both of these can be quite helpful to monitor the upgrade process. You can also click the Stop button to stop the upgrade process completely. Oracle recommends that if you stop the upgrade, that you restore the database that was being upgraded from a backup or to flashback the database to the guaranteed restore point if you indicated one should be created at the beginning of the upgrade.

As shown in Figure 2-13 earlier, the upgrade process has three main stages:

- Pre-upgrade steps

- The actual database upgrade

- Post-upgrade steps

The pre- and post-upgrade steps generally don't take very long to perform. How long the upgrade process itself takes depends on a number of factors, such as memory, number and speed of CPUs, and IO throughput. The upgrade also changes parameters in the database as required, such as ensuring that the database is assigned to the correct listener, that the /etc/oratab file is correctly updated, and that any services (i.e., Windows services) are correctly updated.

Once the upgrade is complete, click the Upgrade Results button on the Progress page. The DBUA will display the Results page, which contains the results of the upgrade, including any errors or warnings and details related to the upgrade operation that has just completed. Review the details displayed on the Results page and then click the Close button. Figure 2-15 shows an example of the main DBUA page after a completed upgrade. Note that it's kind of subtle when the upgrade

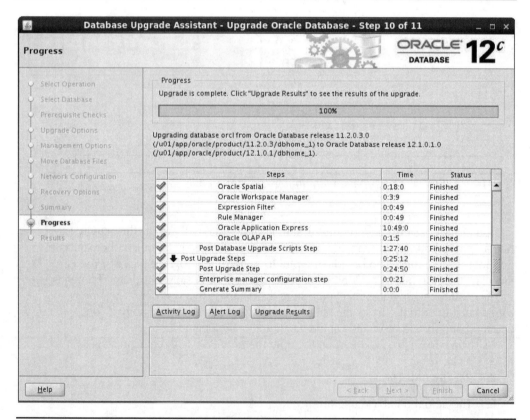

FIGURE 2-15. *DBUA Upgrade Completed page*

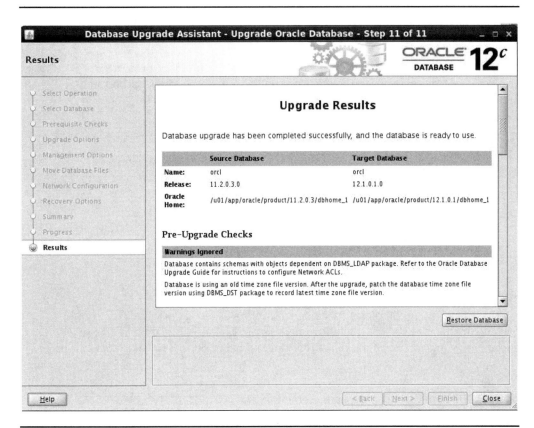

FIGURE 2-16. *DBUA Upgrade Results page*

completes, so you will need to kind of pay attention to the progress message when it says the upgrade is complete.

Figure 2-16 provides a look at the Upgrade Results page that appears after clicking on the Upgrade Results button. Note that the results page provides general information about the upgrade including:

- Results of the pre-upgrade checks

- Details about the upgrade process itself

- Specific information on the individual steps of the upgrade including:

    - How the database was backed up, and how it can be restored if required

    - Information on the new SPFILE

- Information on how EM Database Express was set up

- Information on any changed initialization parameters

Notice on the Upgrade Results page that there is a button that provides the ability to restore the database. Pressing this button will cause DBUA to restore the database, or flashback the database, to a point-in-time prior to the start of the upgrade process.

NOTE
During the upgrade process, errors may pop up as separate dialog boxes. It's also possible that the upgrade process will just seem to stall, which may indicate that the archivelog destination directory (or the FRA) has filled up. The Oracle Database Upgrade Guide 12c contains a list of error codes and potential resolution steps for many of the errors that surface in the DBUA utility.

Once the DBUA completes successfully, your database is upgraded. You should back up the database before you allow any users to access it. Once the database is backed up, you can connect applications to it and begin normal database operations.

NOTE
The DBUA also provides a silent method for the upgrade process. Refer to the Oracle Database Upgrade Guide 12c *for more information on using the silent mode install.*

Upgrading to Oracle Database 12c Manually

If your database is at a version of Oracle that supports the use of DBUA (10.2.0.5, 11.1.0.7, or 11.2.0.2 or later), then you can choose do a manual upgrade. If the database is not at a version that supports the DBUA, then it will not support a manual upgrade. This section discusses the following topics related to performing a manual upgrade from Oracle Database version 11.2.0.3 to Oracle Database 12c. (This discussion assumes that you have already installed the database, as described in Chapter 1.)

- Manual upgrade pre-upgrade steps

- Performing the manual upgrade

- ■ Manual upgrade post-upgrade steps
- ■ Other post-upgrade steps to continue

NOTE
*In the past, I've preferred manual upgrades over use of the DBUA. This was mainly because the DBUA tended to be a bit touchy, and if it failed, that often required restarting the upgrade from scratch. As described in the previous section, the DBUA now has a number of features that can make recovering from errors easier and reduce the chances of having to start over from scratch. Given this new feature set and the stability of the DBUA in my testing of Oracle Database 12*c*, I highly recommend the use of DBUA over manual upgrades.*

Manual Upgrade Pre-Upgrade Steps

To begin the manual upgrade process, complete the following pre-upgrade steps:

1. Back up the database to be upgraded.

2. Run the Pre-Upgrade Information Tool, as described earlier in the chapter.

3. Copy the existing database parameter file to the new ORACLE_HOME. You may not need to do this if you are using ASM to store the database parameter file.

Performing the Manual Upgrade

You are now ready to start the manual upgrade. The following steps assume you are using a Linux system, but we also point out specific Windows system tasks where relevant.

1. Set the Oracle environment (for example, using the **oraenv** utility) for the database that you want to migrate. Your environment will then be set to the old ORACLE_HOME.

2. From SQL*Plus, log into the database using an account that has privileges to shut down the database.

3. Shut down the database with the **shutdown immediate** command.

NOTE
*Do not use the **shutdown abort** command, as you need to perform a clean shutdown of the database.*

4. If you are using Microsoft Windows, you need to

   a. Stop the Oracle service associated with the database.

   b. Delete the Oracle service associated with the Oracle Database 11*g* database using the **oradim** utility.

   c. Create the new Oracle service associated with the database that is being upgraded to Oracle Database 12*g* with the **oradim** utility.

5. Modify your /etc/oratab file by changing the ORACLE_HOME path for the database you are upgrading. Change the path from the previous ORACLE_HOME to the new ORACLE_HOME that the database is being upgraded to. (Windows systems do not have an /etc/oratab file.)

6. Set the Oracle environment to the new ORACLE_HOME for the Oracle database you are upgrading to. This includes setting the following environment variables:

   ■ ORACLE_HOME

   ■ ORACLE_BASE

   ■ ORACLE_SID

   ■ PATH

NOTE
If you are using any scripts that manually set the Oracle environment variables, you will need to change those scripts.

7. Copy the database PFILE or SPFILE from the old ORACLE_HOME/dbs directory to the new ORACLE_HOME/dbs directory. (If you are storing the SPFILE for the database in ASM, you can skip this step.)

8. From the command line, change to the $ORACLE_HOME/rdbms/admin directory. This is the Oracle Database 12*c* directory.

9. Start SQL*Plus and connect to the database as the SYS user.

10. Start up the database instance by using the **startup upgrade** command from SQL*Plus. You might need to use the **pfile** option of the **startup** command, depending on the location of your database's parameter file.

11. Note any parameters that are listed as desupported. You will want to remove these parameters later, after the upgrade is complete.

12. Run the **catctl.pl** script from the $ORACLE_HOME/rdbms/admin directory, as shown in this example:

```
cd $ORACLE_HOME/rdbms/admin
$ORACLE_HOME/perl/bin/perl catctl.pl catupgrd.sql
```

NOTE
*The **catclt.pl** script is a Perl script that takes a parameter, **catupgrd.sql**, which is the actual SQL script that performs the upgrade. As mentioned earlier in the chapter, the **catupgrd.sql** script is deprecated and Oracle has announced that it will be removed in future versions of Oracle.*

By default, the script runs the upgrade in parallel. The DOP is determined based on the number of cores/CPUs allocated to the database by the hardware or virtual environment. You can disable parallelism using the **parallel=no** parameter. To do so, start SQL*Plus and, after starting the database with the **startup upgrade** command, run the **catupgrd.sql** script manually from that interface rather than from the Perl script, as shown here:

```
SQL>@catupgrd.sql parallel=no
```

During the upgrade, the script reports what phase of the upgrade it is in. The number of phases may vary depending on your database and the components contained within it. Some phases run quickly, while others can take some time to execute. Also, the output of the script will show you if it's using parallelism, as shown in this snippet of the execution of the script (Phases 48 and 49 are serial threads, whereas Phase 50 is a parallel thread that is using four processes):

```
[Phase 48] type is 1 with 1 Files
ora_restart.sql
[Phase 49] type is 1 with 1 Files
cmpupend.sql
[Phase 50] type is 1 with 1 Files
catupend.sql
Using 4 processes.
Serial   Phase #: 0 Files: 1
```

13. After the **catupgrd.sql** script completes the upgrade, it shuts down the database. If there are no errors, then proceed to step 14. If errors appear, then research the cause of the errors in the *Oracle Database Upgrade Guide 12c* and perform the corrective actions recommended.

TIP
As the database upgrade proceeds, you can monitor the alert log (for example, tail -f alert*.log) to see if any errors are generated in it during the upgrade.

14. Restart the database instance from SQL*Plus with the **startup** command.

15. Run the post-upgrade tool utlu121s.sql to display a summary of the results of the upgrade. If the post-upgrade tool reports errors, refer to the *Oracle Database Upgrade Guide 12c* for more information on troubleshooting those errors.

16. Review the log output from the utlu121s.sql script. Make sure that the SQL script **catuppst.sql** was successfully executed. If it was not (typically because of an error in the upgrade process), then you need to run the script to complete the upgrade process. The script is contained in the Oracle Database 12*c* $ORACLE_HOME /rdbms/admin directory.

This completes the upgrade process. You are now ready to perform the manual upgrade post-upgrade steps.

Manual Upgrade Post-Upgrade Steps

Now that you have upgraded your database to Oracle Database 12*c*, you can complete the upgrade process by following these steps:

1. Run the **utlrp.sql** script to recompile any invalid objects. You can monitor the progress of **utlrp.sql** by issuing the following query:

```
-- List of objects that need recompiled
select count(*) from obj$ where status in (4, 5, 6);
-- list of objects already compiled
select count(*) from utl_recomp_compiled;
-- list of jobs created by utl_recomp
select job_name from dba_scheduler_jobs
where job_name like 'utl_recomp_slave_%';
-- List of jobs running
SELECT job_name FROM dba_scheduler_running_jobs
WHERE job_name like 'UTL_RECOMP_SLAVE_%';
```

2. Run the **utluiobj.sql** script to validate that all expected packages and classes are valid.

3. Gather fixed object statistics with the PL/SQL procedure **dbms_stats.gather_fixed_object_stats** (optional step recommended by Oracle).

4. Run the **ut1u121s.sql** script again (optional step recommended by Oracle).

5. If you are going to be using the new 32k extended data types, you will need to do the following:

   - Modify the parameter **max_string_size** to a value of EXTENDED. It's not dynamic, so you will need to use **scope=spfile** when modifying the parameter.

   - Shut down the database in a consistent matter, and then start up the database using the **startup upgrade** command.

   - Execute the script **$ORACLE_HOME/rdbms/admin/utl32k.sql**. This will modify the data dictionary tables so that they can support the new extended string sizes.

   - Issue a **shutdown immediate** to shut down the database consistently again and then start the database with the **startup** command.

   The database can now support the new extended string sizes. This new feature is discussed in more detail in Chapter 6 of this book.

6. Back up the database after the upgrade.

This completes the manual upgrade of your database to Oracle Database 12*c*.

NOTE
If you are upgrading an Oracle RAC database, make sure to refer to the Oracle Database Upgrade Guide 12c *as well as the other Oracle RAC manuals for additional steps to upgrade your database.*

Other Post-Upgrade Steps to Consider

There are a few other post-upgrade things you will probably want to do at some point in time. You may not want to do them immediately after the upgrade because you will want to test the upgrade first to make sure it's successful. When you make some of these changes it will be more difficult to downgrade the database. Keeping this in mind, the post-upgrade steps are the following:

1. After you have finished your initial testing, reset the database parameter COMPATIBLE to a value of 12.0.0.0. Oracle Database 12*c* allows for compatible to be set to a value of 10.0.0 or higher. As long as COMPATIBLE is set to the previous version of your Oracle database, you will not be able to use any new features of Oracle Database 12*c*.

   The COMPATIBLE setting impacts your ability to roll back your upgrade. We discuss rolling back database upgrades later in this chapter.

   Resetting COMPATIBLE to a value of 12.0.0.0 will enable the new features of Oracle Database 12*c*. Once you change the COMPATIBLE parameter to a value of 12.0.0.0 or higher you cannot roll back the upgrade of your database without using a tool like Oracle Data Pump.

2. Enable the new extended data type capability by setting the MAX_STRING_SIZE database parameter to a value of EXTENDED. This new feature provides the ability to define VARCHAR2, NVARCHAR2, and RAW data types to 32KB.

3. Check the value for the PARALLEL_MIN_SERVERS parameter, as the default setting has changed from 0 to a derived value based on the hardware platform you are running on. Ensure the new default setting is sufficient.

4. If you are using an RMAN recovery catalog, upgrade it if it is not compatible with the Oracle Database 12*c* version of RMAN.

5. If the Pre-Upgrade Information Tool instructed you to upgrade the time zone file version after completing the upgrade, do that now. Oracle provides the **dbms_dst** PL/SQL procedure to assist you in updating the time zone file.

6. Depending on the products and features you are using (such as APEX, Oracle Database Vault, externally authenticated SSL users, and others), you may need to perform specific actions for particular products or features. Please refer to the *Oracle Database Upgrade Guide 12*c and the product-specific documentation for more information on post-upgrade activities for a particular product or feature.

Migrating to Oracle Database 12*c* with Oracle Data Pump

For any of a number of reasons, you might not be able, or even want, to use the DBUA tool or the manual upgrade method to upgrade your database. In these cases, Oracle Data Pump is the preferred alternative. This section explores the following topics:

- The benefits of using Oracle Data Pump when migrating to Oracle Database 12*c*

- Using Oracle Data Pump to migrate your database to Oracle Database 12*c*

The Benefits of Using Oracle Data Pump When Migrating to Oracle Database 12*c*

Following are a number of reasons that might lead you to choose to use Oracle Data Pump instead of the DBUA or the manual upgrade method to migrate a database to Oracle Database 12*c*:

- You are upgrading across platforms with different endian byte formats.

- You are migrating from a version of Oracle Database that does not support direct migration via the DBUA or a manual database migration.

- You want to upgrade with a minimum of downtime. You have decided to use Oracle Data Pump (and you have a license for this tool) in combination with other tools, such as Oracle GoldenGate or Oracle Streams, to facilitate near-zero-downtime migrations to Oracle Database 12*c*. In this case, you use Oracle Data Pump to instantiate the GoldenGate target database. The other nice thing about this method is that, if you have configured GoldenGate properly, rolling back to your previous version of Oracle Database is a breeze. For mission-critical, low-downtime, low data loss/corruption mission databases, this method of migrating to Oracle Database 12*c* is strongly recommended.

NOTE
In some cases, you can also use RMAN to instantiate the GoldenGate database, which is an even better solution because RMAN will be faster and may pose less hassle than Oracle Data Pump.
Oracle GoldenGate is beyond the scope of this book, so check out my Oracle GoldenGate 11g Handbook *(Oracle Press, 2013) to find out how to set up this tool in such a way that you can do a near-zero-downtime upgrade of your database. In fact, there is even a chapter in that book on near-zero-downtime database migrations using Oracle GoldenGate!*

One nice thing about using the Oracle Data Pump method is that you can stand up your Oracle Database 12c database and make sure that it's running properly and stable before you actually move the data over. You can perform test migrations over to the new database and time how long the actual migration is likely going to take so that you can appropriately set outage windows and set user expectations with respect to outages and the like.

Oracle GoldenGate provides the ability to do replication across Oracle databases, including many versions that do not support direct upgrade to Oracle Database 12c. Oracle GoldenGate offers the choice of one-way replication or multimaster replication, which is particularly handy.

NOTE
If you are not already familiar with the features of Oracle Data Pump, refer to Oracle Database Utilities 12c in the Oracle documentation set.

Using Oracle Data Pump to Migrate Your Database to Oracle Database 12c

The process of migrating using Oracle Data Pump is pretty straightforward. For purposes of this discussion, we assume that you know how to use Oracle Data Pump, but we also provide a few examples to get you going. We also assume that your environment is unique in some way that will require you to customize this process to your needs. As such, these instructions are not intended to be the ultimate guide to migration using Oracle Data Pump. Rather, these steps are intended to serve a guideline for building your own migration process.

NOTE
*When you are migrating via Oracle Data Pump, consider properly configuring the **resumable timeout** setting for the process. That way, if you run into space issues, instead of failing, the import process will sit and wait, giving you time to correct the space problem.*

These are the general steps for migrating to Oracle Database 12c using Oracle Data Pump:

1. Create a new Oracle Database 12c database using the Oracle Database Configuration Assistant (DBCA).

2. Validate all connectivity to the database before you start your migration process. This includes connectivity from/to the source database (going both directions) and connectivity to the mid-tier components such as the application servers and Enterprise Manager Cloud Control 12*c*.

NOTE
*In these steps, the pre–Oracle Database 12*c
database is called the source database and the
*new Oracle Database 12*c *database that you are*
migrating to is called the target database.

3. Ensure that the target database is "productionized." This would include setting up and enabling any monitoring, ensuring backups are scheduled and tested and that other production-like activities have been implemented.

4. Create a complete migration plan, which should include procedures for the actual migration, testing, and all backout contingencies.

5. Test the migration process in a test environment before you attempt it in production. Test it several times until you are comfortable with the process. Oracle Data Pump **impdp** and **expdp** in particular can have odd idiosyncrasies when importing object and or data (such as problem inserting data into tables with enabled constraints), so make sure that you test with a set of schemas that exactly replicates the production database you are going to migrate.

6. On the target system, we recommend that you create the tablespaces that you will need in the target database before you start any imports. If you have a large number of database datafiles in your source system, consider consolidating them into one physical datafile associated with individual bigfile tablespaces when migrating. For example, if you have an HR tablespace with 20 datafiles of 2GB each, create a single bigfile HR tablespace in the new Oracle Database 12*c* database with one 40GB database datafile. Here is an example of the creation of a bigfile tablespace called HR:

```
create bigfile tablespace
datafile '/u02/oradata/hr01.dbf' size 40g;
```

7. From the source database, use the **create directory** command to create a directory for the dump file your Oracle Data Pump will create. Then, use Oracle Data Pump to create an export dump file that is a metadata-only export. This will contain just the information needed to re-create the various schemas, schema objects, and so on. Here is an example of what the **create**

directory and Oracle Data Pump **expdp** command might look like (note: this example doesn't create a log file—you may wish to create a log file when you run your export):

```
[oracle@server12c admin]$ . oraenv
ORACLE_SID = [new12c] ? mydb
create directory metadata_exp_dir as '/ora/mydb/export';
```

8. In the source database, create a privileged user with the ability to do Data Pump exports. Note that you will need to grant access to any user-defined tablespaces as we have in the SQL code here:

```
[oracle@server12c admin]$ . oraenv
ORACLE_SID = [new12c] ? mydb
sqlplus / as sysdba
create user robert_admin identified by robert
quota unlimited on users;
grant create session to robert_admin;
grant datapump_exp_full_database to robert_admin;
grant read, write on directory metadata_exp_dir to robert_admin;
```

NOTE
Yes, in step 8 we could have opted to grant DBA privileges and reduced the grants we needed to issue. However, in keeping with the principle of granting accounts the minimum privileges needed, we have opted to issue only the grants required to complete the task at hand. You will find that we have done the same thing in step 10.

9. Now, let's export the metadata from the Oracle Database 11*g* source database. We will import this metadata into the 12*c* Oracle database in a later step:

```
[oracle@server12c admin]$ . oraenv
ORACLE_SID = [new12c] ? mydb
expdp robert_admin/robert full=y content=metadata_only
dumpfile=metadata_exp_dir:mydb_metadata.dmp  nologfile=yes
reuse_dumpfiles=yes
```

or you could just export specific schemas if you prefer, as in this example:

```
expdp robert_admin/robert schemas=scott content=metadata_only
dumpfile=metadata_exp_dir:mydb_scott_metadata.dmp  nologfile=yes
reuse_dumpfiles=yes
```

10. Now, we need to create the user on the target Oracle 12*c* database that
    we will use to import the Data Pump Dump file. Note, we only grant the
    minimum privileges that are required to perform the import. You might need
    to grant additional privileges (for example, quotas on tablespaces) to the
    import account that you will create. Here is an example:

```
oracle@server12c admin]$ . oraenv
ORACLE_SID = [new12c] ? new12c
The Oracle base remains unchanged with value /u01/app/oracle
sqlplus sys/robert as sysdba
select name from v$database;
create directory metadata_import as '/ora/new12c/import';
create user robert_admin identified by robert quota unlimited on users;
grant create session to robert_admin;
grant datapump_imp_full_database to robert_admin;
exit
```

NOTE
*In steps 8 and 10 we create the robert_admin user
in both the source and target databases to facilitate
our network Data Pump processing. Note that
the roles we grant the robert_admin account in
both databases are powerful roles (especially the
DATAPUMP_FULL_[IMP|EXP]_DATABASE roles!).
Make sure the robert_admin account is well secured
on both machines when not in use. (I'd remove
it when you are done with it or at least lock the
account out when not in use.)*

11. (Optional) Consider using Oracle Flashback Database technologies to
    provide the ability to rollback your database should the import not work as
    you expected. Make sure your target database is in ARCHIVELOG mode,
    and then create a guaranteed restore point. In our case we did the following
    and suggest you consider doing the same:

```
[oracle@server12c admin]$ . oraenv
ORACLE_SID = [new12c] ? new12c
create guaranteed restore point rsp_one guarantee flashback
database;
```

12. Using the dump file that you created in step 9, create the schemas and
    schema objects in the target database. Note that this will create the indexes
    associated with the database, which can make the import take longer.
    Optionally, you can use the **exclude** parameter of the **impdp** command to

exclude the creation of indexes during this import, and then create them after you have loaded the database data. Here is what the **impdp** command might look like to import the schema objects:

NOTE
You might well see errors while running this and the later Data Pump import. This is not uncommon—for example, objects or tablespaces might be flagged as already existing. Review the log file after the import and determine whether or not the errors are significant.

```
[oracle@server12c admin]$ . oraenv
ORACLE_SID = [new12c] ? new12c
The Oracle base remains unchanged with value /u01/app/oracle
impdp robert_admin/robert full=y content=metadata_only
dumpfile=metadata_import:mydb_metadata.dmp  logfile=metadata_
import:metadata_import.log exclude=tablespace table_exists_
action=skip
```

If you opted to just export data for specific schemas then you would use the following Data Pump **impdp** command:

```
oracle@server12c admin]$ . oraenv
ORACLE_SID = [new12c] ? new12c
impdp robert_admin/robert schemas=scott content=metadata_only
dumpfile=metadata_import:mydb_metadata.dmp  logfile=metadata_
import:metadata_import.log exclude=tablespace table_exists_
action=skip
```

NOTE
During the import you might get errors about objects that exist. Generally, you can ignore such errors.

13. In the target database, connect as a privileged user and create a database link to a privileged account on the source database. Here is an example:

```
[oracle@server12c admin]$ . oraenv
ORACLE_SID = [new12c] ? new12c
sqlplus robert_admin/robert
create database link MYLINK
connect to robert_admin
identified by robert
using 'mydb';
-- test the dblink
select count(*) from dba_objects@mylink;
```

14.   Make sure your environment is set for the target database.

15.   Use the Oracle Data Pump **impdp** command to import the source database
into the target database using the database link created in step 10. You will
use the **network_link** parameter to facilitate the movement of the data over
the network. This reduces the need to create a dump file, move it to another
location, and then import it, which reduces the time required to perform the
import operation.

Here is an example of the **impdp** command that you might use. Note
that you will get a number of errors. Most of these errors will be fine (for
example, there will be errors on APEX objects, and constraint violations).
Review the logfile after the import to make sure that no unexpected errors
occurred. You can also perform select count(*) operations on the
tables to ensure that the tables were loaded with data.

```
oracle@server12c admin]$ . oraenv
ORACLE_SID = [new12c] ? new12c
impdp robert_admin/robert full=y network_link=MYLINK
logfile=metadata_import:explog.all content=data_only
```

Instead of importing the entirety of the database, you might want to just
import specific schemas. Note that in this case, you will have probably
imported foreign key constraints. You will need to disable any foreign key
constraints before running this specific import, as in this example:

```
select 'alter table scott.'||table_name||' disable constraint
'||constraint_name||';'
from user_constraints
where constraint_type='R';

alter table scott.EMP disable constraint FK_DEPTNO;
alter table scott.PATTERN_DETAIL disable constraint FK_PATTERN_
DETAIL_HEADER;
```

Having disabled any foreign keys, then you can import the data into the
schema(s):

```
oracle@server12c admin]$ . oraenv
ORACLE_SID = [new12c] ? new12c
impdp robert_admin/robert schemas=scott network_link=MYLINK
logfile=metadata_import:explog.all content=data_only
```

Once the import is complete, re-enable foreign keys by taking the code you
used earlier to disable them, and simply change the **disable** keyword to **enable**:

```
alter table scott.EMP enable constraint FK_DEPTNO;
alter table scott.PATTERN_DETAIL enable constraint FK_PATTERN_
DETAIL_HEADER;
```

NOTE
*We are demonstrating the most elementary use of **impdp**. Other options you might consider are parallelizing the **impdp** streams (while not saturating your network) using the **parallel** command. You might run multiple **impdp** commands, having one command load all but five of the largest tables, and have separate **impdp** commands loading the five largest tables in parallel.*

16. If you chose not to import the indexes earlier, you can now import the indexes. To do this, you might use the following command:

```
oracle@server12c admin]$ . oraenv
ORACLE_SID = [new12c] ? new12c
impdp robert_admin/robert schemas=scott include=INDEX network_
link=MYLINK nologfile=y
```

17. Having imported the data into the target database, run the **utlrp.sql** script to revalidate all objects in the database.

18. Back up the database with RMAN.

19. Validate that all data in the database is correct and then begin to switch users over to the new database.

Rolling Upgrades

Rolling upgrades provide a method of upgrading the database while incurring a minimum of downtime. There are various tools for performing rolling upgrades including:

- Oracle Clusterware and Oracle RAC
- Oracle Data Guard Physical and logical standby databases
- Oracle GoldenGate

If you have a need to perform a rolling upgrade, please reference the Oracle documentation for more information about how these tools can be used to support a rolling upgrade strategy. Also note that Oracle Cloud Control 12c provides support when performing a database rolling upgrade.

Rolling Back the Upgrade

Oracle Database 12*c* provides the ability to roll back an upgrade, but that ability is somewhat limited. If you choose to roll back an upgrade, you will need to plan on rolling back to the base release that the upgrade started from. As such, you can roll back from one of the following versions of Oracle Database:

- Oracle Database 11*g* Release 2 versions 11.2.0.2 and 11.2.0.3

- Oracle Database 11*g* Release 1 version 11.1.0.7

Note that the versions you can roll back to are not as comprehensive as the versions you can upgrade from. Thus, if you do a direct upgrade from 10.2.0.5, you cannot downgrade back to 10.2.0.5. You would, instead, be required to downgrade to 11.2.0.2, 11.2.0.3, or 11.2.0.7. Additionally, patchset downgrades are supported for Oracle Database 11.2 patchsets, except for Oracle Database release 11.2.0.1.

Note that the use of the COMPATIBLE parameter is key to being able to roll back your database upgrade. If COMPATIBLE is set to 10.0.0.0 or 11.0.0.0 or 11.1.0.0 then you can still roll back the upgrade (to version 11gR1 or 11gR2 as mentioned above). To roll back a database with COMPATIBLE set to 10.0.0.0, you will need to change COMPATIBLE to 11.0.0.0, and then roll back to one of the versions mentioned earlier in this section. If you have changed the COMPATIBLE parameter to 12.0.0.0 or higher, then no rollback is available and you will need to use Oracle Data Pump or your restore point to perform a rollback. Note that using Flashback Database will cause data loss and rollback with Oracle Data Pump will require an outage.

Also, note that changing COMPATIBLE will provide the ability for users to use Oracle Database 12*c* features. This can complicate any rollback efforts, so make sure your system is performing well before you change COMPATIBLE to 12.0.0.0. However, this is not a license not to ever change COMPATIBLE either. At the end of the day, the best practice is to make sure the new Oracle Database 12*c* environment is stable and then change the COMPATIBLE parameter.

Another method of rolling back (more complex but with limited outage time and no data loss) would be to use Oracle GoldenGate to replicate back and forth between the Oracle Database 12*c* database and the older Oracle version database you wish to rollback to.

If you have upgraded a database from Oracle Database Express Edition, you will not be able to downgrade that database. Additionally, you cannot downgrade to a version previous to Oracle Database version 11.1.0.7.

This was just a few highlights on downgrading your database. There are a number of other considerations for downgrading your database that you should review in the *Oracle Database Upgrade Guide 12*c as a part of your upgrade planning. Make sure you are comfortable with your backout plan. I strongly recommend that if you have upgraded and are having problems that you stay the course, fix the problems, and just move forward.

Miscellaneous Changes to Be Aware of After Upgrading

Earlier versions of Oracle Database included a stand-alone deinstallation utility that was required to deinstall the software in a given ORACLE_HOME. While this utility is still available in Oracle Database 12c, it is also now available through the OUI. Also the SEC_CASE_SENSITIVE_LOGON parameter is deprecated in Oracle Database 12c. This is because standards-based verifiers (SHA-1 and SHA-512) do not support case-sensitive password matching. All Oracle passwords, by default, are now case sensitive.

The audit trail has changed quite a bit in Oracle Database 12c. A new feature, Unified Auditing, has been introduced. You will want to review Chapter 9 to find out about Unified Auditing. The reason I mention it here is that to use Unified Auditing you will have to re-compile the Oracle executable to enable Unified Auditing. You may want to consider this before you start upgrading or migrating your databases.

End of Line

Upgrading and migrating to Oracle Database 12c is quite a job. This is a long chapter and we have only scratched the surface. To further your education, please read the *Oracle Database Upgrade Guide 12c Release 1*. Additionally, there are some good Metalink Oracle Support (MOS) notes including these documents:

- 1516557.1—Complete Checklist for Upgrading to Oracle Database 12c Release 1 using DBUA

- 1503653.1—Complete Checklist for Manual Upgrades to Oracle Database 12c Release 1 (12.1)

- 1520299.1—Master Note For Oracle Database 12c Release 1 (12.1) Database/Client Installation/Upgrade/Migration Standalone Environment (Non-RAC)

- 1515747.1—Oracle Database 12c Release 1 (12.1) Upgrade New Features

The documentation for Oracle Database 12c is available by surfing over to www.oracle.com/pls/db121/homepage. Now that we have upgraded or migrated our database, it's time to learn about all the new features in Oracle Database 12c! In the next chapter we will start by exploring one of the biggest changes to Oracle Database in a long time—Oracle Multitenant.

CHAPTER
3

Oracle Multitenant

Oracle Database 12c introduces *Oracle Multitenant,* perhaps one of the biggest architectural changes to the Oracle database. The pluggable database (PDB) feature is designed to address a number of problems, including:

- Provisioning

- Patching

- Consolidation

- Efficient resource utilization

Using the Oracle Multitenant architecture is optional (and involves license considerations). As such, the Oracle PDB feature does not replace the existing Oracle database architecture. Thus, if you prefer, you can run your Oracle database in Oracle Database 12c without ever having to know a thing about Oracle Multitenant and PDBs.

That being said, we recommend that you at least read this chapter and consider incorporating PDBs because they have a number of benefits and features that make them a very attractive option in the enterprise. So, this chapter introduces you to Oracle Multitenant, container databases, and pluggable databases and, along the way, points out the benefits of Oracle Multitenant DBs. This chapter covers the following:

- An introduction to the PDB feature

- Multitenant Container Databases (CDBs) and PDBs and the data dictionary

- Creating and deleting PDBs

- Using PDBs as a consolidation tool

- PDBs and resource management

- Administration of CDBs and PDBs

- Backup and recovery of CDBs and PDBs

So, let's get on with it and talk about Oracle Multitenant DBs and what they are!

Tom Says

That said, ultimately there will be a single architecture for the Oracle database—that of the Oracle Multitenant. There are no license considerations for running the Multitenant architecture with a single pluggable database. The initial Oracle Database 12c releases will support the legacy architecture as well as Multitenant, but ultimately the legacy architecture will be de-supported. Therefore, it will be beneficial for all DBAs to become familiar with this architecture.

Introducing Oracle Multitenant

Oracle Multitenant introduces some interesting changes to the traditional architecture of the Oracle Database from both the physical and logical points of view. Until now, it has always been a given that a particular Oracle Database instance (or set of instances, in the case of an Oracle RAC database) is always associated with only one database. With the introduction of Oracle Multitenant, that basic assumption is no longer always true.

A Multitenant database provides the capability for the Oracle database to function as a *container database*. A container database provides the ability for the Oracle database to include from zero, one, or many unique and isolated database environments called PDBs or containers. Each environment can have its own set of schemas, schema objects, users, and so on. To the application, once connected to a given PDB, the PDB looks just like a non-CDB. Figures 3-1 and 3-2 provide a graphic that demonstrates an example of the relationship between the Multitenant database, the PDB, and the CDB.

While you might need a moment to conceptualize the changes involved with the introduction of Oracle Multitenant, you will find in many ways that it still feels a lot like the Oracle Database we all know and love. So it won't be that hard to introduce this new feature into your enterprise and managing it wouldn't be too difficult. In fact, after completing this chapter, you might very well determine that your organization would benefit by taking advantage of this new feature. (We will describe the potential advantages in detail later in this chapter.)

FIGURE 3-1. *A CDB and a single PDB*

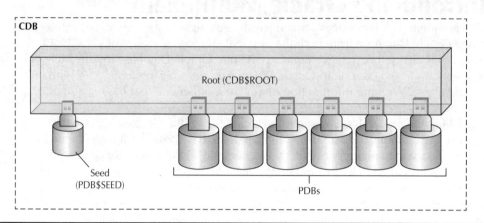

FIGURE 3-2. *A CDB and many PDBs*

NOTE
Oracle Multitenant is a separately licensed product that you need to purchase if you are going to take advantage of its features. At the time of this writing the normal Oracle license will allow you to create a container database with one pluggable database in it. If you wish to have more than one pluggable database in your container database, then you will need to purchase Oracle Multitenant.

When you first create an Oracle Database 12c database (either through DBCA or manually), you have the option to create that database as a Multitenant Container Database. Thereafter, you can create pluggable databases (PDBs) from scratch in an existing CDB, or you can remove a PDB from one CDB and attach that PDB to another CDB that you have created either on the same platform, or on another platform. I will discuss all this in more detail as we move through this chapter.

The use cases for Multitenant databases are several. Consolidation of a large number of disparate databases often rises to the top of the list. Oracle Multitenant is a great tool for database consolidation. Beyond the typical use cases for consolidation (reduction in power and cooling costs, reducing space requirements and so on) using Oracle Multitenant Database can be a much more efficient platform to run multiple databases on from a performance and resource utilization point of view. It is simply more efficient to run more databases as PDBs in an Oracle Multitenant database than to run them individually on the same machine. We will discuss more reasons to use Oracle Multitenant Database throughout this chapter.

Tom Says
It is interesting to note that the Multitenant architecture will affect DBAs only. From a developer's perspective and from an applications perspective—*nothing will have changed*. You will still connect to a database, perform transactions in the same exact fashion you always have. The goal of the Multitenant architecture is to provide an environment that is more resource friendly—without impacting existing applications and the way they work at all.

NOTE
Many of the Oracle data dictionary views use the term container to reference individual PDBs. For example, the column CONT_ID represents the container_id of the container.

The Multitenant Container Database

The *Multitenant Container Database (CDB)* is the parent, or *root*, structure within the Multitenant architecture. This section discusses the following CDB topics:

- Creating the Multitenant Container Database

- The architecture of a CDB

- How to name a CDB

- The benefits of a CDB

- Version requirements for creating a CDB

- The CDB root container

- CDB common users

Creating the Multitenant Container Database

An Oracle Database 12c database is not created as a CDB by default. So, if you are manually creating a database with the **create database** command, and you wish to create the database as a Multitenant Container Database, you need to include the **enable pluggable database** clause. If you use the Oracle Database Configuration Assistant (DBCA), it gives you an option to create the database as a CDB when you configure the database to be created. An additional option is provided to create the first PDB in that CDB. We will discuss the creation of a PDB from within a CDB later in this chapter in more detail.

Note that once you decide to create an Oracle Database 12*c* database as either a CDB or a non-CDB (the default), you cannot change that database back to the other state. For example, you can't later convert an existing Oracle Database 12*c* non-CDB to a CDB if you decide you want to take advantage of the features of the CDB. Likewise, you can't convert a CDB to a non-CDB. However, you can create a CDB and then attach an Oracle Database 12*c* non-CDB (or databases) to the CDB as a PDB database. We will talk more about moving non-PDB databases into a CDB later in this chapter.

NOTE
Of course, you can also use Oracle Data Pump import and export and Transportable Tablespaces to move data in and out of a database using Oracle's Multitenant architecture.

You can also run Oracle CDBs and non-CDBs on the same database server. They can share the same ORACLE_HOME or live in different ones, whichever you prefer. You can also run Oracle Database 12*c* on the same server where other versions of Oracle Database are running, just as you have probably done in the past.

Now that you understand the distinction between an Oracle database that has Multitenant configured and one that does not, you might be concerned that managing a CDB will require that you learn a whole new set of skills. Don't be concerned, because regardless of whether the database is a CDB or non-CDB, it is still an Oracle database. You will find that many of the management and administrative tasks are the same or very similar. Yes, a few things have changed and some new functionality has been added, but a CDB is still an Oracle database.

Architecture of the CDB

As mentioned, the CDB is very much like an Oracle database. One might say it's an "Oracle database on steroids." As we discuss the architecture of the CDB in this section, you will find that it is very familiar. As we progress through the different components of the CDB, use Figure 3-3 as a reference to help put all the pieces together. The components of the CDB are as follows:

- **The Instance** As with normal Oracle databases the CDB is associated with an Oracle instance. Obviously, if the CDB is an Oracle RAC database, then it will have one or more instances associated with it. The CDB and all of the PDBs associated with that CDB share the same instance. Therefore they share all of the same SGA memory structures, and there is just one set of parameters that is used to configure memory.

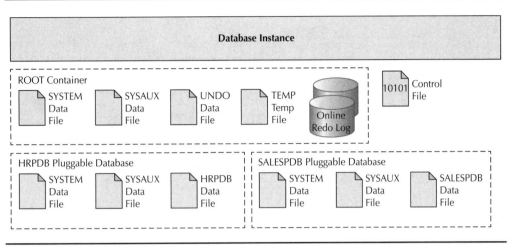

FIGURE 3-3.   *CDB architecture*

- **The CDB**   The CDB represents the database as a whole. The CDB contains multiple containers that store metadata and database data.

- **Containers**   The container is the principle storage location for system metadata and system schema information (see the root container) or a unique and isolated storage location for specific database metadata and schema data.

- **Root container**   Each CDB has exactly one root container. This container provides a location for schemas, schema objects, and non-schema objects that belong to the CDB as a whole. System metadata required for the database to manage the individual PDBs are stored in the root container. The root container is named CDB$ROOT. Figure 3-4 provides a graphic look at the root container and its contents.

- **Seed PDB**   Each CDB has an Oracle supplied PDB called the *seed*. This PDB is called PDB$SEED and it's used to create new PDBs within the CDB. You cannot add or modify objects in PDB$SEED.

- **PDB**   A user-created entity that contains user schemas, data, code and other database related objects. A PDB is designed to provide what is essentially a unique and isolated database environment within a CDB. A given CDB can have many PDBs.

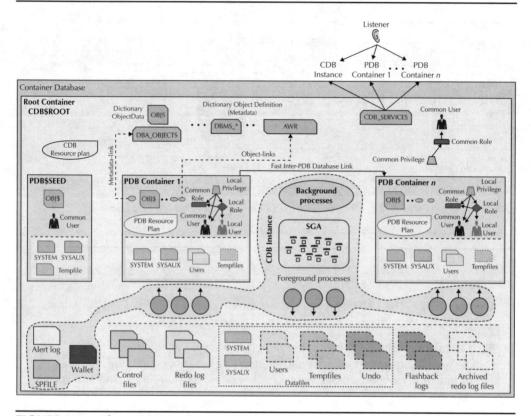

FIGURE 3-4. *The root CDB*

- **Oracle Database instance**   This includes the normal instance-related items such as the instance parameter files, system global area (SGA), and background processes.

- **At least one control file**   As with a non-CDB, you would typically multiplex the control file. This control file supports the CDB and all PDBs that are plugged into that CDB.

- **Online redo logs**   As with a non-CDB, you would typically create several groups and multiplex them. These redo logs support the entire CDB, along with all the PDBs that are plugged into it. Because the online redo logs serve the entire CDB and all associated PDBs, they need to be large enough and sufficiently numerous to avoid performance problems. If you add PDBs to a CDB, you may need to analyze the online redo log requirements for the CDB and determine if you need to enlarge the size of or increase the number of online redo logs. The online redo logs are considered to be stored as a part of the root container. If the CDB instance/database is in ARCHIVELOG mode, then archived redo logs will also be created. The configuration of ARCHIVELOG mode itself is done at the level of the CDB. You cannot opt to disable ARCHIVELOG mode for individual PDBs.

■ **One or more sets of temporary files**   A CDB has a minimum of a single temporary tablespace, called TEMP by default. This tablespace is contained in the root container and supports the temporary tablespace needs of the root CDB and all the attached PDBs. You can create and define a different default temporary tablespace for the CDB, if you choose. You can also give individual PDBs their own individual temporary tablespaces.

■ **An UNDO tablespace and related tempfiles**   A single UNDO tablespace and its tempfiles reside in the root container of the CDB in a non-RAC configuration. In a RAC configuration, you will have an UNDO tablespace for each thread. The UNDO tablespace supports the entire CDB and all PDBs.

■ **SYSTEM and SYSAUX**   These CDB system-related tablespace datafiles contain the data dictionary for the root container. These tablespaces also contain pointers to data dictionary information associated with attached PDBs (more on this later). The CDB has no user tablespaces or related datafiles. No data should ever be stored in the CDB. Though it's possible to create objects in the SYSTEM and SYSAUX tablespaces, as always those tablespaces are reserved for Oracle only.

Naming the CDB

Just as a given database server can host many non-CDB Oracle databases, it can also host many CDBs. Like a regular Oracle database, each CDB has its own ORACLE_SID that identifies that CDB uniquely from every other database (CDB or not) on that database server. For example, on my Oracle Database 12*c* server I currently have two

Tom Says
This cannot be stressed enough, regardless of the chosen database instance architecture—you should never create any objects in SYSTEM or SYSAUX, just as you should never create any objects in the SYS or SYSTEM schemas. In fact, you should never log in as SYS or SYSTEM either—consider these private, internal accounts.

database SIDs. One is a non-CDB (called orcl) and one is a CDB (called contdb). The following example shows the two LGWR processes running:

```
[oracle@server12c ~]$ ps -ef|grep lgwr
oracle    4135    1  0 18:52 ?    00:00:00 ora_lgwr_CONTDB
oracle    5127    1  0 19:30 ?    00:00:00 ora_lgwr_orcl
```

In fact, there are no additional processes running when you have a CDB or a non-CDB running on your database. You won't see additional processes start when you plug in or unplug PDBs—except for the user processes that connect to those PDBs.

Because not all Oracle databases are CDBs, you will want to be able to determine whether you are dealing with a CDB or not. For example, you might need to know this information if you want to be able to create or plug in a PDB, since the related database must have been created as a CDB. To see if your database has been created as a CDB, you can query the V$DATABASE view column named CDB as shown here:

```
select name, cdb from v$database;
NAME        CDB
---------   ---
CONTDB      YES
```

The preceding output shows that a database called CONTDB has been created as a Multitenant Container Database. Also note that the same instance and database naming restrictions on non-CDBs applies to CDBs.

CDB Benefits

We have mentioned a few of the benefits of using a CDB, but here's a more complete list:

- **Reduced costs** With more efficient use of enterprise resources, costs are reduced through consolidation of hardware, software, storage, and labor.

- **Easier and quicker movement of data** Using a CDB and PDBs allows for quick movement of databases (PDBs) and data across CDBs (by unplugging a PDB and plugging it into another CDB). This includes moving databases across servers.

- **Easier management of databases** With a single CDB to manage (with multiple PDBs), management is more centralized and simplified. Instead of managing several dozen different databases, you manage one CDB and the individual PDBs within it. If you are thinking, "But these PDBs might interfere with each other and cause problems," Oracle has already thought of that and thus added...

- **Support for Oracle Database Resource Manager**   Oracle Database 12*c* has improved the Oracle Database Resource Manager so that it can manage the resource utilization of the different PDBs within the CDB.

- **Isolation of PDBs**   Each PDB is isolated from the other PDBs. This provides an additional degree of granularity and separation for applications, while still providing the ability to share resources in an efficient, controlled manner.

- **Provision for more granular separation of duties**   You can have separate administrators for each individual PDB, and for the CDB as a whole. Additionally, common users within PDBs are isolated from the CDB and the other PDBs in the database. Local users in PDBs do not have privileges in other PDBs.

- **Easier performance tuning**   You only need to tune the memory for the CDB so that it efficiently provides services for all the PDBs attached to the database. You can easily monitor the CDB and its attached PDBs for SQL performance issues, and with the Oracle Database Resource Manager, you can easily control the PDBs so that they don't interfere with each other.

- **Easier patching and upgrades**   Rather than having to upgrade dozens of databases, you can upgrade a CDB and its PDBs all at one time.

Version Requirements for Creating a CDB

Oracle supports running a CDB only on Oracle Database version 12*c* and later. The COMPATIBLE parameter must be set to 12.0.0.0 or greater to be able to create a CDB. The version of the CDB and the PDBs that you will plug into the CDB must be the same. Thus, you cannot have an Oracle Database 11*g* PDB plugged into an

Tom Says
While you can upgrade a CDB, and thus all of its associated PDBs, all at one time, another option exists for those that cannot upgrade/patch all databases at the same exact time. When you go to apply a patch or upgrade to the next release, you can opt to create and configure a new Multitenant Container Database instance instead of upgrading the existing one. Then to upgrade or patch a PDB, you will simply unplug it from the old CDB and plug it into the new CDB—an operation that takes seconds or minutes to perform. In that fashion, you can upgrade/patch your PDBs over the course of a few days or weeks as you test each application against the new release.

Oracle 12*c* CDB. We will discuss the migration and upgrade concerns of CDBs and PDBs in more detail in Chapter 3 when we discuss upgrading Oracle databases to version 12*c*.

The CDB's Root Container

When you create the CDB (as described later in the chapter), it contains the root container (introduced a bit earlier in the section "Architecture of the CDB"). Each CDB has only one root container. It is used to store system information about the CDB itself and to store all the metadata required for PDBs that will later become part of the CDB Oracle Multitenant. The root container is also used for global database administration activities. The root container is a single PDB called CDB$ROOT.

The information contained in the root container of the CDB is stored in the SYSTEM and SYSAUX tablespaces that are created when the CDB is created. You will find that the data dictionary views that you are familiar with in non-CDBs are still available in CDBs, such as DBA_TABLES, DBA_USERS, and so on. There are also new data dictionary views in CDBs that support the administration of PDBs. We will discuss those new data dictionary views shortly.

CDB Common Users

Common users are a new type of user associated with CDBs and PDBs. The common user exists throughout the CDB and can also be assigned to one or more PDBs, or to all PDBs.

When the CDB is created, common users are created that allow the DBA to administer not only the CDB but also all PDBs that are a part of the CDB. Although these users are called "common," they actually are very powerful users. They have access not only to the CDB itself but also to every PDB. The most powerful common user is the SYS user.

Common users can log into the CDB directly by setting the ORACLE_SID and simply logging into the database, as shown in the following example, where we are logging into the CDB CONTDB as the user c##robert using the **sysdba** privilege:

```
[oracle@server12c contdb]$ sqlplus c##robert/robert as sysdba
SQL*Plus: Release 12.1.0.1.0 Production on Mon Jul 29 19:34:30 2013
Copyright (c) 1982, 2013, Oracle.  All rights reserved.
Connected to:
Oracle Database 12c Enterprise Edition Release 12.1.0.1.0 - 64bit Production
With the Partitioning, OLAP, Advanced Analytics and Real Application Testing options
```

That looks pretty normal—well, except for the c## business....

Common users have the same identity in the root container and in every PDB attached (or that will be attached) to the database. A common user can log into any container, but the privileges of a common user can be administered separately within each PDB. For example, a common user might have the privilege to create a table in one PDB but not in another.

You can also create your own common users. Each common user account must be prefixed by the naming convention c## followed by the common user name (for example, c##robert). Of course, Oracle-supplied user accounts such as SYS and SYSTEM are exempt from this rule. The namespace for a given common user exists across all the containers of the CDB. Thus, if you create a c##robert user, that user exists in all containers in that database. This means that you cannot have a local user c##robert in any individual PDB.

Also, although the common users have the capability to create objects in the root container, they should never do so. This restriction is much like that of never creating objects in the SYS schema of a non-CDB Oracle database. You might be tempted to do so, but you shouldn't do it.

Creating a Common User   Creating a common user is very similar to creating a normal user. You use the **create user** command to create the user. The following rules apply:

- You must be logged in with a user account that has the following privileges: **create user** and **set container**.

- Your current container must be the root container (CDB$ROOT). This can be determined by using the **show con_name** SQL*Plus command, as follows:

```
show con_name
CON_NAME
-----------------------------
CDB$ROOT
```

If you are logged in as a privileged user and need to change to the CDB$ROOT container, you can use the SQL command **alter session set container**. In this example, we log into the PLUG_TEST PDB, and then switch to CDB$ROOT. Note that we use the TNS name for the:

```
 [oracle@server12c contdb]$ sqlplus c##robert/robert@plug_test
show con_name
CON_NAME
-----------------------------
PLUG_TEST

alter session set container=CDB$ROOT;
Session altered.

show con_name
CON_NAME
-----------------------------
CDB$ROOT
```

- Use the **create user** command to create the common user using the **container=all** option. Remember that the common user must start with c## or C## and end with the user name.

- When creating a common user, if you define default tablespaces, temporary tablespaces, quotas, and profiles when issuing the **create user** command, those objects must exist in all containers attached to the CDB. Otherwise, the **create user** command will fail.

NOTE
If you create a schema-level object as a common user, that object can be shared across the CDB.

Here is an example of creating a common user called c##robert:

```
show con_name
CON_NAME
------------------------------
CDB$ROOT

create user c##robert identified by robert container=all;
```

Of course, we still live by the Oracle security rules, so when we try to log into the database using this newly created user, the following happens:

```
connect c##robert/ robert
ERROR:
ORA-01017: invalid username/password; logon denied
Warning: You are no longer connected to ORACLE.
```

We need to grant the **create session** privilege to the common user first, and then we can log in:

```
grant create session to c##robert;
connect c##robert/robert
```

In the previous example, we connected to the root container but not to a PDB. The procedure for connecting to a PDB is a bit different, as discussed later in this chapter.

Removing a Common User   Deleting a common user is quite simple: you connect to the root container as a user with privileges to drop other users, and use the **drop user** command as you always have. The following example drops the c##robert common user. The use of the **cascade** option causes a recursive removal of all objects that c##robert owns.

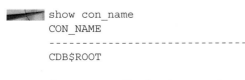

```
show con_name
CON_NAME
------------------------------
CDB$ROOT

drop user c##robert cascade;
```

NOTE
*Did you notice that I use the show con_name
SQL*Plus command a lot? With multiple PDBs it's
even easier to find yourself in the wrong place within
an Oracle database. So, before you run a command,
make sure you are in the right PDB.*

The Pluggable Database

A PDB is a logical collection of schema objects (tables, indexes, users, and so on).
From the perspective of the application and local users, a PDB appears to be an
independent database. This section discusses the following PDB topics:

- What is a pluggable database?

- PDB performance

- Naming PDBs

- PDB local users

- Accessing PDBs

What Is a Pluggable Database?

A PDB represents what is, essentially, a distinct database with its associated
metadata (such as users, tables, and statistics) and actual physical data for that
database. A PDB is also called a *container*, which is a fitting name because a PDB
contains the basic elements that comprise a single and unique database entity.

NOTE
*For all practical purposes, a PDB is a database,
so sometimes this book uses the terms database
and PDB interchangeably when referencing
a specific PDB.*

Like a normal database or the parent CDB, a PDB contains physical datafiles that store the data contained within that PDB. The datafiles also contain a local copy of the data dictionary, which contains the metadata associated with that PDB. The data in the PDB is isolated to the PDB itself, and is not shared across other PDBs.

All PDBs that are plugged into a given CDB must be the same version as the CDB (and the version must be Oracle Database 12c or later). Thus, you cannot have PDBs within a given CDB that are at different versions. This also means that if a CDB is upgraded, all the PDBs within the CDB will be upgraded at the same time, and to the same version of the database.

All PDBs are owned by the parent CDB SYS user. A given CDB can have up to 252 PDBs plugged into it at any one time.

A PDB is attached to a CDB by an account with DBA privileges. Each PDB is an independent and isolated unit from any other PDB. Likewise, PDBs can be detached from a given CDB by the administrator. The PDB can be moved among various CDBs, and can even be replicated within a given CDB.

PDBs serve several purposes:

- Each PDB is able to store data specific to a given application. In other words, each PDB is an independent and isolated data store.

- Administration of a PDB by local users (which are discussed a bit later) is isolated to that unique PDB. Administration by common users (discussed earlier) is constrained by system privileges and object grants.

- PDBs allow you to easily move data between different CDBs.

- Oracle provides a way to quickly copy and provision PDBs, which can speed up the provisioning process of new data stores.

Each PDB has, at a minimum, its own SYSTEM, SYSAUX, and USERS tablespaces. You can create additional tablespaces in a PDB just as in any other database.

Just as you can plug a PDB database into a CDB, you can unplug a PDB database from a CDB. When you unplug a PDB from a CDB, that PDB is disassociated from the CDB. You can also take a copy of a PDB from a CDB and move it to another CDB—the result being two copies of a PDB in two separate CDBs.

PDB Performance

Using a CDB and consolidating existing databases into PDBs within the CDB offers a number of features, a major one being the sharing of system resources such as CPU and memory. You might think that adding additional PDBs will incur a linear cost with respect to resources, but this is not the case. As shown in Figure 3-5, as additional PDBs are added, the total memory requirements of the CDB do not increase rapidly. In fact, in many cases, using a CDB can make much more efficient

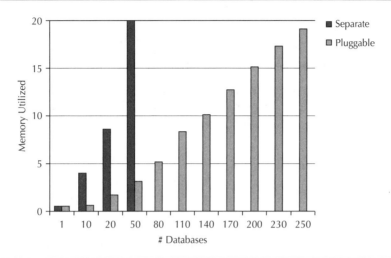

FIGURE 3-5. *Memory utilization as you add PDBs*

use of system resources than does using individual databases all with their own
database instances.

Naming PDBs

Just as a CDB has a name (contdb in our earlier example), each PDB has a unique
name within the context of a CDB. The rules for naming PDBs are the same as the
rules for naming service names, which is important because local users can connect
to an individual PDB only through a service name.

Tom Says

This cannot be stressed enough—one of the main benefits of the Multitenant
architecture is the savings in resources needed to run multiple databases on a
single host. If you consider that an Oracle instance takes approximately 25
separate background processes at a minimum, then running 10 databases on a
single host would necessitate 250 background processes using the legacy
architecture of an instance per database. Using the Multitenant architecture, we
can run the same 10 databases using just 25 processes, with 25 PGA's. The
resource savings in the reduced number of processes the operating system has
to manage as well as the reduced instance memory footprint can be quite large.

Rules for naming a PDB are as follows:

- The first character must be an alphabetical character.

- Subsequent characters can be alphanumeric or an underscore character.

- PDB names are case insensitive. So you cannot create a PDB called MYPDB and a PDB called mypdb—Oracle will not allow this.

PDB Local Users

As mentioned earlier, common users are created at the root level of the CDB and have the potential to roam across all attached PDBs. Within the confines of a PDB there are local users (which are also associated with schemas). The scope for a local user and its associated schema and schema objects is limited to the PDB that the user name is assigned to.

The same local user name, the schema name, and any object names can be created in multiple PDBs within the same CDB. Each is created in its own separate and distinct user namespace. Here is an example of the creation of a local user in the PLUG_TEST PDB:

```
-- connect as a privileged user to the root container.
connect / as sysdba
 -- Change to the container we want to create the local user in.
alter session set container=plug_test;
 -- Create the local user in the container.
create user plug_test_local identified by robert;
-- allow the local user to connect to the PDB
 grant create session to plug_test_local;
Grant succeeded.
```

As you can see next, this local user is truly a *local* user because it cannot be used to log into the root container:

```
[oracle@server12c ~]$ sqlplus plug_test_local/robert
SQL*Plus: Release 12.1.0.1.0 Production on Mon Jul 29 19:59:48 2013
Copyright (c) 1982, 2013, Oracle.  All rights reserved.
ERROR: ORA-01017: invalid username/password; logon denied
```

Note that we got an error. This is because the method we are using to login only allows us access to the root CDB. Each of the individual PDBs are isolated from the CDB and the local users are specifically allocated to the PDB in which they are created. As a result of this isolation, connecting to a PDB directly is a bit different, you have to connect to it using the service that exists for that PDB. Let's look a little bit more at how to connect directly to a PDB then.

Accessing PDBs

To access the root container, you simply need to set the ORACLE_SID and then connect to the database using SQL*Plus, like this:

```
ORACLE_SID = [orcl] ? contdb
The Oracle base remains unchanged with value /u01/app/oracle
```

This is one method you have used to access Oracle databases for a very long time. Notice that this connection is done with a privileged user. You can also log into the database root container with any Oracle-supplied account or with any common user account that you have created and granted the appropriate privileges.

If you want to access PDBs via administrative accounts or through common user accounts, you can still connect directly to the root container via SQL*Plus and then user the **alter session** command to change the container, as previously demonstrated in several examples.

If you want to access a PDB directly with a local user account, you must use a service name. Each PDB has an associated service name assigned to it (and possibly more than one, of course). In this chapter we approach services from the perspective of a non-RAC environment. If you are running in a RAC environment, you use the **srvctl** command to create the services for the PDBs. In a non-RAC CDB environment, the service is created and managed from within the database.

First, let's look at an example of connecting to a PDB via a service. In this case, we use the EZConnect naming method and SQL*Plus to connect to the PDB called PLUG_TEST, and we connect through the local user PLUG_TEST_LOCAL:

```
[oracle@server12c ~]$ sqlplus plug_test_local/robert@server12c:1521\/plug_test
SQL*Plus: Release 12.1.0.1.0 Production on Tue Jul 30 07:29:48 2013
Copyright (c) 1982, 2013, Oracle.  All rights reserved.
Connected to:
Oracle Database 12c Enterprise Edition Release 12.1.0.1.0 - 64bit Production
With the Partitioning, OLAP, Advanced Analytics and Real Application Testing
options
```

Looking at the connect string we can see that we are connecting to a service called PLUG_TEST. PLUG_TEST is a service for a PDB named PLUG_TEST. The PLUG_TEST PDB is attached to a CDB called CONTDB. PLUG_TEST lives on the database server called server12c, and the listener port that the service is listening on is 1521.

To successfully connect to a PDB using a service, the following must be true:

- The main CDB is up and running.

- The PDB is running. We discuss managing PDBs later in this chapter. For now, you can tell if a PDB is open by using the V$PDBS view, as shown here:

  ```
  select con_id, name, open_mode, restricted from v$pdbs order by 1;
       CON_ID NAME                                OPEN_MODE  RES
  ```

```
---------- ------------------------------ ---------- ---
        2 PDB$SEED                         READ ONLY  NO
        3 PLUG_TEST                        READ WRITE NO
```

If the PDB is open, you can connect to it using the service assigned to that PDB. The service typically has the same name as the PDB. So, in our example, the service is called PLUG_TEST. Through SQL*Plus, you can connect to the PDB through the PLUG_TEST service as we did earlier using the EZConnect string.

You can see a list of available services for a PDB, from within the PDB, by using the DBA_SERVICES view:

```
show con_name
CON_NAME
------------------------------
PLUG_TEST

select service_id, name, network_name,global_service, pdb, enabled
from dba_services;
SERVICE_ID NAME                      NETWORK_NAME         GLO PDB        ENA
---------- -------------------       -------------------- --- ---------- ---
         6 plug_test                 plug_test            NO  PLUG_TEST  NO
```

Note that if you issue this query from the root container, the results look different:

```
select service_id, name, network_name,global_service, pdb, enabled
from dba_services;
SERVICE_ID NAME                      NETWORK_NAME  GLO PDB        ENA
---------- -------------------       ------------- --- ---------- ---
         1 SYS$BACKGROUND                          NO  CDB$ROOT   NO
         2 SYS$USERS                               NO  CDB$ROOT   NO
         5 CONTDBXDB                 CONTDBXDB      NO  CDB$ROOT   NO
         6 CONTDB                    CONTDB         NO  CDB$ROOT   NO
```

NOTE
If you look at DBA_SERVICES or CDB_SERVICES from the root container, the service for the PDB will not appear.

However, you can see all of the services from the ROOT CDB using the V$SERVICES view as seen here:

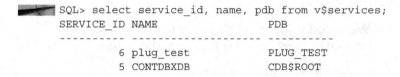

```
SQL> select service_id, name, pdb from v$services;
SERVICE_ID NAME                      PDB
---------- -------------------       ----------
         6 plug_test                 PLUG_TEST
         5 CONTDBXDB                 CDB$ROOT
```

```
6 CONTDB                 CDB$ROOT
1 SYS$BACKGROUND         CDB$ROOT
2 SYS$USERS              CDB$ROOT
```

If you would rather not use the EZConnect string (which may well be the case) then you can put the service information within a tnsnames.ora file and use that entry instead. Our tnsnames.ora entry for PLUG_TEST looks like this:

```
PLUG_TEST =
  (DESCRIPTION =
    (ADDRESS = (PROTOCOL = TCP)(HOST = server12c)(PORT = 1521))
    (CONNECT_DATA =
      (SERVER = DEDICATED)
      (SERVICE_NAME = PLUG_TEST)
    )
  )
```

The service for the PDB should have been created when the PDB was created. If the service was not created, you will need to create the service manually, but this should be a rare occasion. If you need to create a service for a PDB manually, this is documented in the *Oracle Database Administrator's Guide 12*c in the section "Creating, Modifying, or Removing a Service for a PDB."

CDBs and PDBs and the Data Dictionary

As a DBA you have no doubt used the data dictionary views to manage your database. The introduction of Oracle Multitenant has added quite a few new data dictionary views as you might expect. These data dictionary views generally come with the prefix of CDB_ or PDB_. Let's look at the data dictionary views in a bit more detail next.

This section covers the following topics:

- The CDB data dictionary

- The PDB data dictionary

- CDB/PDB administrative queries

- CDB/PDB object administration data dictionary queries

The CDB Data Dictionary and V$ Views

Both the CDB and each PDB contain data dictionary views. This includes both the standard DBA, USER, and ALL data dictionary views. Additionally, there is now a set of views called the CDB views. Finally, there are new and changed V$ views that are available. Let's look at the data dictionary views and then the V$ views in more detail next.

CDB Data Dictionary Views

At the CDB level, multiple views are available to you. First, the Oracle CDB has the standard set of data dictionary views (i.e., DBA, ALL, and USER views) that Oracle Database has included for years. These views provide a view this is based only on the container you are in. So, for example, if you are logged into the root container, the DBA_TABLES view shows you only what's in the root container, and if you are logged into a container called HR, the DBA_TABLES view represents only what is in the HR container.

PDBs introduce a new layer of objects for DBAs to worry about. You need to be able to see all the objects in the CDB and its associated PDBs. Therefore, Oracle has added an additional layer of views called container data objects that provide this overall view of all CDB and PDB objects. Using these views from the root container enables you to see everything in all containers of the CDB.

The Contained Data Object views are similar to the regular administrative views but are prefixed with CDB_ instead of DBA_. Thus, the root of the CDB includes a CDB_TABLES view that gives you a view of all the tables in all the PDB containers of the CDB (including the root container).

Now, that being said, you might think that the CDB_ views and the DBA_ views are one in the same, and they are not. For example, look at this result:

```
SQL> select count(*) from dba_objects;
  COUNT(*)
----------
     90756

SQL> select count(*) from cdb_objects;
  COUNT(*)
----------
    272228
```

That settles that, the views are somewhat different. What is different here is that the DBA views provide data dictionary information for the current container (in this case the ROOT container) and that's it. When you are in the root container, the CDB views contain all of the information in the DBA views but also contain information that is linked in from the attached PDBs.

There are actually three kinds of data stored in the CDB views. First is the data stored in the root container. The second type is called an object link. This is a pointer to a data dictionary object definition within a PDB. Also there are metadata links that are pointers to data dictionary object data within each PDB. We can see these different object types in the CDB_OBJECTS view column SHARING as seen here:

```
SQL> select distinct sharing from dba_objects;
SHARING
-------------
```

```
METADATA LINK
NONE
OBJECT LINK
```

CDB V$ Views

Additionally, many existing V$ (and the associated GV$) views have been adjusted to reflect the presence of PDBs in the database, and additional V$ views, such as V$CONTAINERS, have been added to provide container-specific information. Finally, several AWR-related views are now adjusted to reflect the presence of PDBs. Most of these new and modified views include a new column called CON_ID that identifies the container that the object resides in. For example, the V$CONTAINERS view contains the following columns:

NOTE
It is interesting that the new V$CONTAINERS and V$PDBs view names are plural, whereas most of the other V$ view names (i.e., V$DATAFILE) are singular. You can thank my brilliant technical editor Pete Sharman for pointing this out to me!

```
desc v$containers
 Name                                     Null?    Type
 ---------------------------------------- -------- -----------------
 CON_ID                                            NUMBER
 DBID                                              NUMBER
 CON_UID                                           NUMBER
 GUID                                              RAW(16)
 NAME                                              VARCHAR2(30)
 OPEN_MODE                                         VARCHAR2(10)
 RESTRICTED                                        VARCHAR2(3)
 OPEN_TIME                                         TIMESTAMP(3)
 CREATE_SCN                                        NUMBER
 TOTAL_SIZE                                        NUMBER
```

For now, the main columns to focus on in the V$CONTAINERS view are CON_ID and NAME. Each PDB container has a container identifier (CON_ID) and a name (NAME) associated with it. You will find that the CON_ID column is present in the CDB_ views and in the altered V$ views.

Figure 3-6 provides an example of how the various views all fit together between PDBs and the CDB. You will see many examples of the use of these views as you read this chapter.

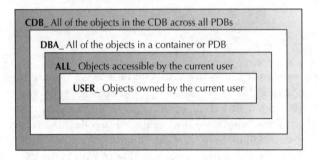

FIGURE 3-6. *Data dictionary view relationships*

The PDB Data Dictionary

The data dictionary within an individual PDB is visible only to that PDB. So, for example, the DBA_TABLES view in a container called MYCONT contains only the tables that are contained in the PDB called MYCONT.

Physically, the PDB data dictionary data is stored locally within the SYSTEM tablespace of each individual PDB. Of course, the CDB_ views in the root container need to have access to all the data dictionary information in the PDBs. To save space and time and improve performance, the PDB data is not copied and stored in the CDB. Rather, a set of pointers between the PDB data dictionary and the CDB data dictionary is created when the PDB is created or plugged in. A data dictionary is maintained within the root container as well.

On the other hand, all Oracle-supplied code and system-level information (such as data dictionary table definitions) are stored in the root container. Thus, copies of Oracle-supplied packages like **dbms_output** are stored in a single place, the root container. This not only makes storage for commonly used Oracle-supplied packages more efficient but also makes database upgrades easier.

Some PDB data is stored only in the root container, such as Automatic Workload Repository (AWR) data. Oracle creates links in the PDBs to the data that is stored in

Tom Says

It is interesting to note that the CDB_ views exist in the various plugged-in databases, but they only display information for that one plugged-in database. In short, in a PDB, the CDB_ views are equivalent to the DBA_ views. It is only in a CDB that the CDB_ views will contain information across all PDBs.

the root container. This PDB-specific data that is stored in the root container may contain either summarized records or detailed records for PDBs.

CDB/PDB Administration

The new CDB/PDB architecture adds some additional administration duties and also adds additional layers of information related to the data dictionary, as previously depicted in Figure 3-6. This section explains first how to start up and shut down the PDB, and then we look at some of the new data dictionary views associated with the administration of Oracle Multitenant Databases.

Starting and Stopping the PDB

It's always nice to know how to start something up, and then how to shut it down again. In this section, we will cover those topics from the perspective of the PDB. First we will talk about starting up the PDB, and then we will talk about shutting down the PDB.

Starting the PDB   As a DBA, the first thing that you might want to look at is a list of the containers in the database and their current status. The V$PDBS view is probably the best place to go for that information. Here is an example of a query against V$PDBS that lists the current PDBs in the database:

```
select con_id, name, open_mode, restricted from v$pdbs order by 1;
     CON_ID NAME                          OPEN_MODE  RES
---------- ----------------------------- ---------- ---
         2 PDB$SEED                      READ ONLY  NO
         3 PLUG_TEST                     MOUNTED
```

This query reports that the database currently has two PDBs: the PDB$SEED container and the PLUG_TEST container. The PLUG_TEST PDB is mounted and not open. Opening a PDB is pretty easy: you simply need to connect to the database, switch over to the container you want to start, and then open the container.

Let's look at an example. First we log into the root container using the SYS account, including the SYSDBA privilege. We then use the **show con_name** SQL*PLUS command to double check that we are currently logged into the CDB$ROOT container. Recall that in a CDB, CDB$ROOT container is the main container:

```
[oracle@server12c ~]$ sqlplus / as sysdba

show con_name
CON_NAME
------------------------------
CDB$ROOT
```

We need to change the container that we want to start, which is the PLUG_TEST container. We query the V$PDBS view to determine the status of our PDBs, and we find that PLUG_TEST is indeed mounted as seen here:

```
select con_id, name, open_mode, restricted from v$pdbs order by 1;
    CON_ID NAME                             OPEN_MODE  RES
---------- -------------------------------- ---------- ---
         2 PDB$SEED                         READ ONLY  NO
         3 PLUG_TEST                        MOUNTED
```

Now, as SYS (or another privileged user) we need to change into the PLUG_TEST container to open it. Only then can we connect to that container as a regular user. We can change the currently working container from CDB$ROOT to PLUG_TEST by using the **alter session** command as seen here:

```
alter session set container=PLUG_TEST;

show con_name
CON_NAME
------------------------------
PLUG_TEST
```

We then simply use the **startup** command to start the PDB.

```
SQL>startup
Pluggable Database opened.
connect / as sysdba
```

Consider here that the CDB of the Multitenant database was already up and running, but that the PLUG_TEST PDB was not running. This is important to note - just starting the CDB does not automatically cause the PDBs associated with the CDB to open. You need to make sure you open those PDBs too.

In this case, we switched to the PLUG_TEST PDB, and we started it up with the **startup** command, much like we would a normal database. Notice that the output is much less verbose, which makes sense. The memory is already allocated by the CDB, so there is no SGA to report on. The control files are already open, so there really is nothing to mount, as it were. Really, all that remains to be done is to open the data files associated with the PDB, ensure they are consistent, and then open the PDB.

Once the PLUG_TEST database is up and running, we recheck the status of the databases using the V$PDBS view, ensuring that the PLUG_TEST PDB is indeed in READ WRITE mode.

```
select con_id, name, open_mode, restricted from v$pdbs order by 1;
    CON_ID NAME                             OPEN_MODE  RES
---------- -------------------------------- ---------- ---
         2 PDB$SEED                         READ ONLY  NO
         3 PLUG_TEST                        READ WRITE NO
```

Note that when using the **startup** command on a PDB you have a number of different options including:

- **startup force**   Forces an inconsistent shutdown of the PDB and then re-opens it in READ WRITE mode.

- **startup restrict**   Starts the database and only allows users with **restricted session** system privileges to access the PDB.

- **startup open** [**read write** | **read only**]   Indicates that the PDB should be open in READ WRITE or READ ONLY mode. The default on a normal database is READ WRITE. If the database is a Data Guard database, then the default is READ ONLY.

For a user to open a PDB that user must have one of the following privileges granted. The user can either be a common user and have the grant apply to that common user, or a local user in the PDB with the privilege granted to that local user. The privileges are

- SYSDBA

- SYSOPER

- SYSBACKUP

- SYSDG

Of course, it would be nice to be able to open all of the pluggable databases at once. This can be accomplished using the command **alter pluggable database all open**. For this command to work the CDB itself needs to be open. You can also use the alter pluggable database command to open specific PDBs as in this example:

```
alter pluggable database pdb_one open;
```

Shutting Down the PDB   Shutting down the PDB is not much different than starting it up. You simply issue an **alter session** command to change to the correct PDB first as seen here:

```
alter session set container=PLUG_TEST;

SQL> show con_name
CON_NAME
------------------------------
PLUG_TEST
```

Then you issue the **shutdown** command to shut down the PDB. You can indicate that the PDB should be shutdown in an immediate mode with the **shutdown immediate** command. If either the **shutdown** or **shutdown immediate** commands complete, then that PDB will have been shut down in a consistent manner and the dirty blocks associated with that PDB will have been flushed to the database datafiles. Note that this does not ensure that any other part of the database is consistent in any way.

For a user to shut down a PDB that user must have one of the following privileges granted. The user can either be a common user and have the grant apply to that common user, or a local user in the PDB with the privilege granted to that local user. The privileges are

- SYSDBA

- SYSOPER

- SYSBACKUP

- SYSDG

You can also use the alter pluggable database command to close pluggable databases as in this example:

```
alter pluggable database pdb_one close;
```

PDB Administrative Views

So, let's look at some other data dictionary views that are relevant to CDBs and PDBs. As previously indicated, the first thing you might want to look at is information about every container in the database. You already saw the V$PDBS view, but you might have noticed that the root container was missing from the output of that view. If you want information on all containers, use the V$CONTAINERS view, as shown in this example:

```
show con_name
CON_NAME
------------------------------
CDB$ROOT

select con_id, name, open_mode, restricted, open_time from v$containers;
   CON_ID NAME       OPEN_MODE  RES OPEN_TIME
---------- ---------------- ---------- --- ------------------------------
        1 CDB$ROOT        READ WRITE NO  01-AUG-13 08.56.07.352 PM
        2 PDB$SEED        READ ONLY  NO  01-AUG-13 08.56.07.556 PM
        3 PLUG_TEST       READ WRITE NO  01-AUG-13 09.05.27.077 PM
```

The preceding output is what we get when connected to the root container. If we were connected the PLUG_TEST container, the output would look like this:

```
alter session set container=PLUG_TEST;

show con_name
CON_NAME
------------------------------
PLUG_TEST

select con_id, name, open_mode, restricted, open_time from v$containers;
   CON_ID NAME     OPEN_MODE   RES OPEN_TIME
---------- --------------- ---------- --- ------------------------------
        3 PLUG_TEST       READ WRITE NO  01-AUG-13 09.05.27.077 PM
```

In this case we can see that when we are connected to the PLUG_TEST container all we can see is information related to PLUG_TEST from the V$CONTAINERS view. The ROOT and SEED containers disappear when we are within a given PDB. This demonstrates how important it is to make sure that you are connected to the correct container when performing any operation.

CDB/PDB Object Administration Data Dictionary Queries

Just as with a non-CDB, you use data dictionary views to look at objects within the CDB as a whole and to look at objects within a given PDB. This section gives you a feel for how to use the additional views that Oracle provides to manage the CDB and any given PDB within that CDB.

When you are connected to a given PDB, you use the same DBA, ALL, and USER views as you use in regular Oracle databases. For example, suppose you are connected to the PLUG_TEST PDB and you want to see what's in the ROBERT schema in that PDB. You would issue this familiar-looking query:

```
show con_name
CON_NAME
------------------------------
PLUG_TEST

select owner, table_name from dba_tables where owner='ROBERT';
OWNER               TABLE_NAME
------------------- ------------------------------
ROBERT              MY_TABLE
```

As mentioned earlier in the chapter, Oracle provides a set of new views (whose names start with CDB_) that give you a global view of the data dictionary for the entire CDB and all of the plugged-in PDBs. When logged into the ROOT of the CDB then the CDB_ views have a visibility of all of the CDBs. When logged into a given PDB then the CDB_ views only have a visibility within that PDB as demonstrated here:

```
show con_name
CON_NAME
------------------------------
CDB$ROOT

select distinct con_id from cdb_tables;

    CON_ID
----------
     1
     2
     3

alter session set container=PLUG_TEST;

show con_name
CON_NAME
------------------------------
PLUG_TEST

select distinct con_id from cdb_tables;
    CON_ID
----------
     3
```

As you can see, when connected to the ROOT container, then we can see CON_IDs 1, 2 and 3 (each CON_ID represents a given container including ROOT). When connected to PLUG_TEST, which is CON_ID 3, we can only see the contents of that container.

   If we were logged into the root container and wanted to see the table called ROBERT.TEST in the PDB called PLUG_TEST, we would query the CDB_TABLES view instead of the DBA_TABLES view, adding an additional predicate indicating the name of the PDB we want to see the information from. Here is an example:

```
show con_name
CON_NAME
------------------------------
CDB$ROOT

-- First, get the container_id
select con_id, name from v$containers;
---------- ------------------------------
         1 CDB$ROOT
         2 PDB$SEED
         3 PLUG_TEST
         4 NEWPDB
```

```
select b.owner, b.table_name
from cdb_tables b
where b.con_id=3
and b.owner='ROBERT';

OWNER                           TABLE_NAME
------------------------------  ------------------------------
ROBERT                          MY_TABLE
```

NOTE
*Yes, I could have easily done this query as a join, but
I wanted to break it down into a more elementary
query to clearly demonstrate the relationship
between a container name (represented by
the NAME column in V$CONTAINERS) and the
CON_ID column. Oh, and I also ran into a bug
when I tried to join the two together that caused
my join query to fail.*

Let's look at one final example. As you know, the CDB has its own datafiles,
as does each of its PDBs. When logged into the root container, you can see all the
datafiles of the CDB and all of its children PDBs, as shown in this example:

```
show con_name
CON_NAME
------------------------------
CDB$ROOT

select a.name, b.tablespace_name
from v$containers a, cdb_data_files b
where a.con_id=b.con_id;

NAME                           TABLESPACE_NAME
------------------------------ ------------------------------
PLUG_TEST                      SYSTEM
PLUG_TEST                      SYSAUX
PLUG_TEST                      USERS
PDB$SEED                       SYSTEM
PDB$SEED                       SYSAUX
CDB$ROOT                       USERS
CDB$ROOT                       UNDOTBS1
CDB$ROOT                       SYSAUX
CDB$ROOT                       SYSTEM
9 rows selected.
```

Note that if you were attached to the root container and you queried the DBA_DATA_FILES view, you would see only the tablespaces that belong to the root container. If you were attached to any PDB container and you wanted to see the datafiles from that PDB, you would still use the DBA_DATA_FILES view, as shown here:

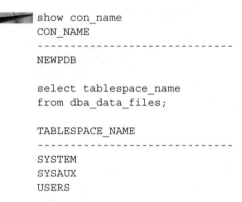

```
show con_name
CON_NAME
------------------------------
NEWPDB

select tablespace_name
from dba_data_files;

TABLESPACE_NAME
------------------------------
SYSTEM
SYSAUX
USERS
```

Creating, Deleting, and Modifying PDBs

As mentioned earlier in the chapter, there are a number of different ways to create PDBs. The two primary methods are the copy method and the plug-in method.

The copy methods that are available include

- Copying an "empty" PDB from a static source PDB, or *seed database*, that is contained within each CDB

- Cloning new PDBs from existing PDBs that already exist in the CDB

- Cloning a new PDB from a remote PDB

The plug-in methods that are available include

- Plugging in an unplugged PDB (for example, a PDB that has been unplugged from another CDB)

- Plugging in a non-CDB as a PDB

You can also delete and modify the name of a PDB. Let's look at each of these methods in more detail next.

Creating a PDB from the Seed Database

Perhaps the easiest way to create a PDB is to create it from the seed database. This section first looks at the prerequisites for creating a PDB and then explains the process of creating a PDB from the seed PDB.

Preparing to Create the PDB

The following prerequisites must be met when you are preparing to create a PDB from the seed database:

- The CDB exists.

- The CDB is open and is not in read-only, upgrade, or downgrade mode.

- You are logged in as an administrative or common user and are logged into the root container. This user must have the **create pluggable database** system privilege.

- You have determined the name of the new PDB. The name must be unique to the CDB. It also must be unique across any other CDB that shares the same listener, because the PDB name is also the service name for the PDB.

With these prerequisites in place, you are ready to create the PDB.

Creating the PDB from the Seed Database

You use the **create pluggable database** command to create a new PDB using the seed PDB. This command copies the files from the PDB and uses them to create the new PDB. For example, to create a new PDB called NEWPDB in a CDB called CONTDB, you would follow these steps:

1. Using SQL*Plus, connect to the root container using a common user that has the privileges to create the PDB. In this case, we are using the common user c##robert, which has been granted SYSDBA privileges at some point in time in the past:

   ```
   [oracle@server12c ~]$ . oraenv
   ORACLE_SID = [CONTDB] ?
   The Oracle base remains unchanged with value /u01/app/oracle
   [oracle@server12c ~]$ sqlplus c##robert/password as sysdba
   ```

2. Use the **create pluggable database** command to create a new PDB called NEWPDB from the seed database. This command has many options and variations that you might use based on your requirements. In this case,

we will keep it as basic as possible. Here is an example of the successful creation of the PDB newpdb:

```
create pluggable database newpdb admin user newpdbadm identified
by robert;
Pluggable database created.
```

The result of this command is the creation of the new PDB called newpdb. When the new PDB is created, new datafiles will be created

We can see the new PDB in the V$CONTAINERS view now, as shown here. Notice that the PDB is mounted at the moment.

```
select con_id, name, open_mode, restricted from v$pdbs order by 1;
    CON_ID NAME                              OPEN_MODE RES
---------- ------------------------------ ---------- ---
         2 PDB$SEED                          READ ONLY  NO
         3 PLUG_TEST                         READ WRITE NO
         4 NEWPDB                            MOUNTED
```

3. Connect to the PDB and open it:

```
show con_name
CON_NAME
------------------------------
CDB$ROOT

alter session set container=newpdb;

startup
```

You should now be able to connect to the database directly from the SQL*Plus prompt using the service name for the PDB:

```
[oracle@server12c admin]$ sqlplus newpdbadm/robert@server12c:1521\/newpdb
```

Cloning a PDB from an Existing PDB

Cloning a PDB from an existing PDB is similar to creating a PDB from the seed database. First, you need to start in READ ONLY mode the PDB you intend to clone by using the **startup open read only** command in the PDB to be copied from. With the source PDB in READ ONLY mode, you use the same command as in the previous section, **create pluggable database**, and add a **from** clause that specifies the database that is to be the source database. In the following example, we create a new PDB called CLNDB by cloning it from the PDB NEWPDB created earlier:

NOTE
*In some of the SQL examples you will find that I've removed the SQL prompt and most of the output from the commands. I do this to save space and also when I feel like the output from the command is not really that important. For example, you expect that when the **alter session** command is executed that it will say Session altered. It seems redundant to keep displaying that response. I also often remove the SQL> prompt to make copy/paste easier if you are using electronic media.*

```
sqlplus / as sysdba
show con_name
alter session set container=newpdb;
show con_name
shutdown
startup open read only
connect / as sysdba
create pluggable database clndb from newpdb;
```

You will notice that in this case I didn't need to define an administrative user; the target PDB will use the same administrator account as the source PDB. As before, when creating a PDB from the seed PDB, you need to start the new PDB before it can be accessed by local users:

```
alter session set container=clndb;
startup
```

We also want to shut down and reopen the source PDB (newpdb) in READ WRITE mode:

```
alter session set container=newpdb;
shutdown
startup
```

Once this procedure is complete, we are able to connect to the new PDB through SQL*Plus:

```
sqlplus newpdbadm/robert@server12c:1521\/clndb
```

Cloning a PDB from a PDB in a Remote CDB

ALERT!
At the time this book was written, Oracle Database 12c Release 12.1.0.1 had been made available. This functionality did not make it into this release and it is scheduled to be fixed in Oracle Database 12c Release 12.1.0.2. This prevents you from successfully cloning a PDB from a PDB in a remote CDB, which is the subject of this section. The other PDB clone functionality, as demonstrated in this book, does work. For now, we present the examples as they should work.

Cloning a PDB from an existing PDB is a great way to quickly stand-up a new database environment. For example, you can take an existing PDB database (say a test database) and create a development or QA database from the source PDB. As you have seen in earlier sections, this is easy to accomplish if the PDB is already in the CDB. However, you can also clone a PDB from a PDB that is in a remote CDB.

NOTE
There is a difference between cloning and plugging in a PDB. Cloning means that the source PDB remains in place and that a new target PDB is created. Plugging in means that you actually physically remove the PDB from the source CDB and plug it into the target CDB. Thus, the PDB no longer exists in the source CDB and exists in the target CDB.

As an example of cloning a PDB from a PDB in a remote CDB, assume that we have two CDBs: cdbone and cdbtwo. From the cdbone CDB we will copy a PDB called CLNDB to a PDB called TSTDB within the cdbtwo CDB. So, in the end we will have two PDBs: CLNDB in the cdbone CDB and TSTDB in the cdbtwo CDB.

Before we can make the PDB clone, we need to do some setup first.

Preparing to Clone the Remote PDB

The following prerequisites must be met when preparing to clone the remote PDB:

- The CDB exists that you are cloning the remote PDB into.

- Both the target and source CDBs are open and are not in read-only, upgrade, or downgrade mode.

■ You are logged into the CDB that is the target of the cloning process as an administrative or common user, and you are logged into the root container of the target CDB. The user that will clone the new PDB must have the **create pluggable database** system privilege.

■ You have determined the name of the new PDB. The name of the PDB must be unique to the CDB. It also must be unique across any other CDB that shares the same listener, because the PDB name is also the service name for the PDB.

■ If the PDB clone is occurring across platforms, the platforms have the same endianness (sorry, no AIX to Linux PDB clones).

■ The source and target database CDB platforms have the same database options installed.

■ The character sets of both CDBs are compatible.

Having met these prerequisites, you are ready to clone the remote PDB.

Cloning the Remote PDB

In this example, we will clone a PDB from one CDB to another CDB. The source CDB is called cdbone. The destination CDB is called cdbtwo. The source PDB is called clndb, and we will create a new PDB called tstdb in this example:

1. Connect to the CDB that contains the source PDB as an administrative user or common user with privileges to put the source PDB in READ ONLY mode. In our case we will connect to the cdbone CDB.

   ```
   [oracle@server12c ~]$ . oraenv
   ORACLE_SID = [cdbone] ? cdbone
   The Oracle base remains unchanged with value /u01/app/oracle
   [oracle@server12c ~]$ sqlplus / as sysdba
   ```

2. Use the **alter session set container** command to connect to the source PDB. In our example, we connect to the CLNDB container as shown here:

   ```
   alter session set container=clndb;
   ```

3. Create the user on the CLNDB PDB that you will use to connect to when performing the PDB clone. In our case, we will call the user **robert** and grant that user two privileges, **create session** and **create pluggable database**:

   ```
   create user robert identified by robert;
   grant create session, create pluggable database to robert;
   ```

4. Shut down the CLNDB PDB and then reopen it in READ ONLY mode:

   ```
   shutdown
   startup open read only
   ```

5. Switch over to the target CDB (cdbtwo). This is the CDB that you want to clone your PDB to. From there, create a database link to either the source CDB or the source PDB. We also recommend that you test the database link. Here is an example:

```
[oracle@server12c ~]$ . oraenv
ORACLE_SID = [CONTDB] ? cdbtwo
sqlplus / as sysdba

create database link move_pdb_link
connect to robert identified by robert
using 'server12c:1521/clndb';

-- test the db link.
select count(*) from user_objects@move_pdb_link;
```

6. Double-check that you are logged into the target CDB (cdbtwo) before you perform the cloning operation:

```
select name from v$database;
NAME
---------
CDBTWO

show con_name
CON_NAME
------------------------------
CDB$ROOT
```

7. Clone the database. Use the **create pluggable database** statement. We will use the **from** clause to specify the source PDB (CLNDB), which is on the source CDB cdbone. The result will be that the target CDB (cdbtwo) will receive a new PDB (TSTDB).

```
create pluggable database tstdb from clndb@move_pdb_link;
```

8. The cloned PDB will be in READ ONLY mode. Shut down the clone PDB and restart in READ WRITE mode.

```
alter session set container=tstdb;
shutdown
startup open read write;
```

Unplugging a PDB and Plugging a PDB into a CDB

This section looks at the next method of adding a new PDB to your CDB: taking an unplugged PDB and plugging it into an existing CDB. This section discusses

- Unplugging a PDB

- Plugging an unplugged PDB into a CDB

NOTE
Oracle SQL Developer and Oracle Enterprise Manager 12c also provide functionality to manage container databases including plugging and unplugging PDBs. In this chapter, we are limiting ourselves to using the command line interface.

Unplugging a PDB

Unplugging a PDB from a CDB does not completely remove the PDB from that CDB. Unplugging a PDB creates an XML file that packages the PDB so that it can be plugged into another CDB. So, the PDB will still show up as a container in V$CONTAINERS, but it will show a status of MOUNTED in the OPEN_MODE column. Also note that the service associated with that PDB is not dropped either.

Because the PDB is still part of the database, it will be backed up as part of any RMAN operation, which is handy. However, this can make your RMAN backups take longer if you no longer need the PDB.

So, let's look at an example of how to unplug a PDB. Our source CDB is called cdbone and includes a PDB called UNPLUGDB. The process for unplugging the unplugdb PDB from the sourcedb CDB is really pretty simple, as shown here:

1. Create an OS-level directory to store the XML metadata that will be created when the PDB is unplugged. Make sure that Oracle has access to this directory. In our case, we have created a directory called /u01/app/oracle/unplug/unplugdb.

NOTE
Yes, I know that placing the directory in /u01/app/oracle/unplug/unplugdb (which is in the ORACLE_BASE path) is a bad idea. You should never do such a thing in a production environment.

2. Set the correct ORACLE_SID and access the root container from SQL*Plus:

```
[oracle@server12c ~]$ . oraenv
ORACLE_SID = [new12c] ? cdbone
The Oracle base remains unchanged with value /u01/app/oracle
[oracle@server12c ~]$ sqlplus / as sysdba

select name from v$database;
NAME
---------
CDBONE
```

```
show con_name
CON_NAME
------------------------------
CDB$ROOT
```

3. What PDBs are in our Multitenant database?

```
select name from v$pdbs;
NAME
------------------------------
PDB$SEED
UNPLUGDB
```

4. Let's unplug the UNPLUGDB PDB.

```
alter session set container=unplugdb;
shutdown immediate
```

5. Reconnect with SYSDBA privileges.

```
connect sys/password as sysdba
```

6. Query the V$PDBS view to ensure that the UNPLUGDB PDB is in MOUNTED mode. Note that you can also see the total size of the PDBs in the database:

```
select name, open_mode, total_size from v$pdbs;
NAME                             OPEN_MODE   TOTAL_SIZE
------------------------------   ----------  ----------
PDB$SEED                         READ ONLY   283115520
UNPLUGDB                         READ WRITE  288358400
```

7. Use the **alter pluggable database** command to unplug the PDB. In the following example, we use the option **unplug into** to indicate where we want to create the metadata file associated with the PDB:

```
alter pluggable database unplugdb unplug into '/u01/app/oracle/
unplug/unplugdb/unplugdb.xml';
```

8. Query the V$CONTAINERS view on the SOURCEDB CDB. This shows that the unplugdb PDB is still listed in the view and it's still in MOUNTED mode:

```
select name, open_mode, total_size from v$pdbs;
NAME                             OPEN_MODE   TOTAL_SIZE
------------------------------   ----------  ----------
PDB$SEED                         READ ONLY   283115520
UNPLUGDB                         MOUNTED             0
```

9. We can see that the PDB is actually unplugged by querying the DBA_PDBS view as seen here:

```
select pdb_name, status from dba_pdbs;
PDB_NAME          STATUS
```

```
--------------- -------------
PDB$SEED          NORMAL
UNPLUGDB          UNPLUGGED
```

10. Try to open the PDB. You will find that you can no longer do so:

```
alter session set container=unplugdb;
shutdown
ORA-65086: cannot open/close the pluggable database
startup
ORA-65086: cannot open/close the pluggable database
```

Thus, the CDB maintains its knowledge of the PDB (and, in fact, the datafiles are still present in the same location), but because it's unplugged, the PDB can't be opened (though RMAN will back it up). If you wanted to reuse the PDB, you will need to drop the PDB with the **drop pluggable database** command as seen here:

```
drop pluggable database unplugdb;
```

and then plug it back in to your CDB, as discussed in the next section.

Plugging in an Unplugged PDB

Continuing with our example, now that we have unplugged the PDB, we are going to turn around and plug it into a different CDB. Our goal is to take the unplugged PDB that was named unplugdb and plug it into a different CDB that is called pdbtwo. In this case, both CDBs run on the same server, but we could easily move the PDB to another server if we wanted to.

Right now, the files for the unplugdb PDB that we unplugged are still in their original location. In this example, we are going to keep the PDB files there and create a copy of them in another location. This way, the files of the newly plugged-in PDB will align with the other PDB database files that are in the CDB that we are moving to. This lets us keep the original files of the source PDB, should we wish to move it somewhere else or even plug it back into the original CDB for some reason. In this case we will be moving the files associated with the PDB from the file system /u01/app/oracle/oradata/contdb/datafile/ to the file system /u01/app/oracle/oradata/cdbtwo/datafile/.

We will also be renaming the PDB. In the source system, the PDB that we unplugged was called unplugpdb. When we plug this PDB into the target server, we will rename it to mypdb.

Figure 3-7 provides a graphical overview of what we are going to do in this section.

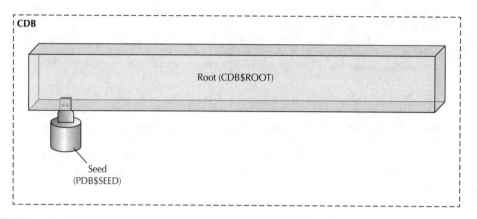

FIGURE 3-7. *Plugging in a PDB*

Preparing to Plug in the PDB   Before we plug in the PDB, the following prerequisites must be met:

■ The XML file associated with the unplugged PDB is accessible to the CDB that is going to plug in the CDB. If the XML file is not available, you can use the Oracle-provided package called DBMS_PDB.RECOVER to create a replacement XML file for you.

■ The datafiles associated with the PDB are accessible to the CDB that the PDB will be plugged into.

There are other restrictions for more exotic CDB moves (for example, if you are moving to another server, or your PDB has temporary files in it). For such scenarios, review the Oracle documentation for specific information related to the kind of PDB move that you are going to make. The Oracle-supplied package called DBMS_PDB .CHECK_PLUG_COMPATIBILITY can determine if all the requirements have been met to plug a specific PDB into a CDB.

Plugging in the PDB   To plug in the PDB, we will use the **create pluggable database** command. We want to copy the datafiles to a new location, so we will use the **copy** option to plug in the database. Note that the act of copying the files will make this activity take a little longer than if we just left the files in place.

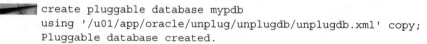

```
create pluggable database mypdb
using '/u01/app/oracle/unplug/unplugdb/unplugdb.xml' copy;
Pluggable database created.
```

When the PDB is plugged in, it's in READ ONLY mode, so we want to log into the PDB and open it. Then we want to test to make sure the service works. Here are examples of these operations:

```
alter session set container=mypdb;
startup
Pluggable Database opened.

[oracle@server12c datafile]$ sqlplus system/robert@server12c:1521\/mypdb
```

One thing to notice is that the Oracle Net service associated with the mypdb PDB was created when the PDB was plugged in. There are a number of different options you can use when plugging in a PDB that has been unplugged. For example, you can move the PDB database files, copy them, or use them in their existing location. The Oracle Database SQL Reference provides a complete list of all the options that you have to choose from.

CAUTION
Make sure that you back up the PDB after you have plugged it in. Backup and recovery of PDBs is covered later in this chapter.

Plugging in a Non-CDB as a PDB

Another option to plugging in a PDB is to take an existing non-CDB Oracle Database 12c database and plug it into a CDB. This section first describes the steps you need to follow to prepare the database to be plugged in, and then explains how to actually plug the database into an existing CDB. The next section, "Using Oracle Multitenant as a Consolidation Tool," discusses the various reasons why you might want to take an existing database and plug it into a CDB.

Oracle actually suggests three different methods of moving a non-CDB into a PDB within a CDB:

- Create a PDB in a CDB and use Oracle Data Pump to export the data from the non-CDB to the PDB you created in the CDB.

- Create a PDB in a CDB and use Oracle GoldenGate to move the data into the PDB and keep it synchronized with the non-CDB until you are ready to switch over to the new PDB.

- Plug the non-CDB into a CDB, making it a PDB within that CDB.

This section looks at the third option in some detail. The first two options really do not involve the use of new features except for the creation of a PDB, which we

> **Tom Says**
> Another dimension of the Multitenant architecture that might prompt you to
> consider options 1 or 2 above is the fact that all PDBs associated with a given
> CDB must share the same character set. If you are planning on consolidating
> multiple legacy architecture databases into a single CDB, you will have to
> convert character sets if they are different—that will take you down the path of
> a data pump export/import or GoldenGate.

have already discussed. Which method you should choose depends on various
considerations, such as the size of the non-CDB, the complexity of the movement
method, whether you are crossing endian boundaries, the length of outage you can
take during the conversion, and other considerations.

In the example presented in this section, we will plug the non-CDB called ORCL
into a CDB called targetdb and rename the new PDB neworcl.

Preparing to Plug in the Non-CDB as a PDB

Before you can plug in the non-CDB, you need to perform some preliminary activities:

1. If the CDB does not exist, then create it.

2. Perform a backup of the non-CDB.

3. Make sure that this really is a non-CDB by querying the CDB column of the
    V$DATABASE view:

    ```
    [oracle@server12c admin]$ . oraenv
    ORACLE_SID = [new12c] ? orcl
    The Oracle base remains unchanged with value /u01/app/oracle
    [oracle@server12c admin]$ sqlplus / as sysdba

    select name, cdb from v$database;
    NAME       CDB
    ---------- ---
    ORCL       NO
    ```

4. Shut down the non-CDB in a transitionally consistent state (using either
    shutdown immediate or shutdown transactional). Do not use **shutdown
    abort** to shut down the database, as this can leave the datafiles in an
    inconsistent state.

    ```
    shutdown immediate
    ```

5. Put the non-CDB into READ ONLY mode:

```
startup open read only;
```

6. Prepare the non-CDB to be plugged into the CDB. Remember earlier when we unplugged a PDB how we created an XML file. Well, we need an XML file to be created from this non-CDB database so we can plug it into a CDB. To do this, we use the **dbms_pdb.describe** command as shown here:

```
BEGIN
DBMS_PDB.DESCRIBE(pdb_descr_file => '/tmp/orcl.xml');
END;
/
```

Make sure that you check that the XML file was created.

7. Shut down the non-CDB.

The non-CDB is now ready to be plugged into a CDB.

Plugging in the Non-CDB as a PDB

Now that we have shut down the non-CDB, we are ready to plug it into a CDB as a PDB. To do so, we will use the **create pluggable database** command. Here are the steps:

1. Set your Oracle environment for the CDB that you are going to plug the non-CDB into. In this example, we import the non-CDB into the CDB targetdb:

```
  [oracle@server12c admin]$ . oraenv
ORACLE_SID = [orcl] ? cdbtwo
The Oracle base remains unchanged with value /u01/app/oracle
```

2. Having logged into the root of the CDB, you are ready to create the PDB. In the following example, just as we did earlier when we plugged in an unplugged PDB, we indicate the location of the XML file for the non-CDB that was created in the previous section. We also use the **copy** command to copy the datafiles to an OMF-compliant location related to the CDB. Finally, we rename the PDB neworcl.

```
create pluggable database neworcl
using '/tmp/orcl.xml' copy;
```

3. Now that we have plugged in the non-CDB, we need to run a script before we can open it. First we need to log into the root of the CDB that the new PDB was created in. We then use the **alter session set container** command to switch into the new PDB that we created, as shown next. Then we run a script that will convert our non-CDB to a PDB database.

The name of the script is $ORACLE_HOME/rdbms/admin/noncdb_to_pdb.sql. The output of the script is quite long, so we won't include it here. The end result is that our PDB is now completely plugged in, ready to open.

```
alter session set container=neworcl;
startup
```

Make sure you back up the CDB after you have plugged in the PDB.

Removing a PDB

Removing a PDB is a fairly easy process: close that PDB, and then drop the PDB from the root container. Here are the commands that you would use to drop a PDB called PLUG_TEST:

```
sqlplus / as sysdba
alter pluggable database PLUG_TEST close;
drop pluggable database PLUG_TEST;
```

In this case, the datafiles associated with the PLUG_TEST PDB would not be removed as this is the default behavior. If you wish the datafiles to be removed when you drop the PDB, then you would add the **including datafiles** clause to the **drop pluggable database** command as seen here:

```
drop pluggable database PLUG_TEST including datafiles;
```

Renaming a PDB

To rename a PDB, you need to switch into the PDB and then shut it down. You then open it in restricted mode and issue the **alter pluggable database rename global_ name** command. Here is an example where we have renamed the PDB unplugdb to unplugdb1.

```
alter session set container=unplugdb;
shutdown
startup open restrict
alter pluggable database unplugdb rename global_name to unplugdb1;
exit

[oracle@server12c oradata]$ sqlplus sys/robert@server12c:1521\/unplugdb1 as
sysdba
show con_name
CON_NAME
------------------------------
UNPLUGDB1
```

Using Oracle Multitenant as a Consolidation Tool

One of the problems that currently challenges enterprises is the almost unconstrained growth of systems within the enterprise. Different organizations within the enterprise often design their own applications and choose their own hardware and databases. Over time, this de-centralization can lead to a proliferation of varying hardware and software that can be incompatible, networking, and costs. Physical space becomes more difficult to procure, and resources such as power and cooling become more expensive and data center space itself becomes harder to find. Overall costs mount as well, including facility, labor, and other costs. Management of this sprawl of servers is also increasingly difficult.

Over the past few years, the concept of "consolidation" has sprung up as a solution to sprawling infrastructure. Many times, an analysis of existing system components such as CPU, memory, network, and storage will demonstrate that they are underutilized, sometimes grossly so.

The Oracle Pluggable Database is one solution that can help you take full advantage of the hardware and resources you have in place, and even possibly reduce some of your hardware needs. In consolidating non-CDBs into a single CDB, you can more efficiently use memory and other system resources.

Oracle Multitenant and Resource Management

Some resist consolidation because they are concerned about possible performance impacts that might be caused by other database tenants within a given shared system. The Oracle Database Resource Manager can control various resources within a specific PDB, including:

- CPU
- Sessions
- Parallel server processes
- Disk I/O resources among the PDBs and the CDBs on the system (if you are running on Oracle Exadata)

With PDBs, you can divide the CPU into shares, with each share defining how much CPU a given resource is assured. This can be helpful in a consolidated environment where you want to be able to assure your customer that they will always have access to a minimum amount of CPU availability. Also, you can price your services based on a minimum guaranteed CPU allowance.

The guarantee of CPU is based on the distribution of shares across the CDB. The total number of shares divided by the individual shares that a PDB is assigned indicates the amount of guaranteed CPU that the PDB will have access to.

For example, assume you have the following three PDBs within a CDB and your resource plan defines that the PDBs have the indicated number of shares of CPU:

- MYPDB; two shares

- ORCL; one share

- YOURPDB; one share

In this case, a total of four shares are allocated within all the resource plans. As a result, MYPDB, with two shares, is assured access to 50 percent of the CPU. ORCL and YOURPDB are each assured access to 25 percent of the CPU since they have one share each.

The Oracle Database Resource Manager also enables you to define a CPU utilization limit for a given PDB. For example, if you define a utilization limit of 50 percent for the ORCL PDB, it still has a guaranteed 25 percent of the CPU (based on its one share) but it will never be able to use more than 50 percent of the CPU at any time.

The Oracle Database Resource Manager also enables you to define a default directive for shares and utilization that will apply to PDBs by default. In that case, you can simply plug in the PDB and the default directives of the resource plan will take effect.

Administration of CDBs and PDBs

With a few exceptions, the typical administrative activities that DBAs will perform in a Multitenant database do not differ much from the administrative activities from a database that is not a Multitenant database. In this section, we will discuss some of these exceptions for CDBs and PDBs that you will want to know about.

Administration of CDBs

As mentioned, most administration duties associated with CDBs are not much different from those associated with non-CDBs. If you are not familiar with the basic administration commands, refer to the *Oracle Database Administrator's Guide 12c*.

Some of the new administrative-related topics for CDBs that you will want to be familiar with include the following:

- Starting the CDB instance:

  - You must be logged into the CDB's root container with a user account that has privileges to start the CDB.

- PDBs will be mounted when the CDB is opened.

- A new option to the **startup** command, **startup open recover**, will cause the database to automatically start recovery mode and then open the database.

- Creation and administration of common users:

    - You assign system and object grants to common users just as you would to other users, but you cannot create a non-common user name in a CDB. So, a command such as this one would fail:

```
create user testuser identified by testuser;
create user testuser identified by testuser
                  *
ERROR at line 1:
ORA-65096: invalid common user or role name
```

- Most other operations that you perform on non-CDBs you can perform on a CDB, including adding tablespaces, creating objects in those tablespaces (owned by common users), and so on.

- Online redo logs and the control files are managed from the CDB.

- Each CDB has its own UNDO tablespace, which is used by the CDB and all PDBs.

- The alert log belongs to the CDB but also contains information related to PDBs.

- Dropping a CDB drops all the associated PDBs as well.

Refer to the *Oracle Database Administrator's Guide 12c* for further details on managing CDBs.

Administration of PDBs

With the addition of PDBs, you need to perform additional administrative activities. In this section we discuss:

- New views associated with PDBs

- Determining which PDB you are in

- Opening, closing, and altering the open mode of PDBs

- Setting the default and temporary tablespaces for a PDB

- Setting storage limits for a PDB

- Removing a PDB

- Using the **alter system** command from within a PDB

New Views Associated with PDBs

Oracle provides the following new views that provide information about PDBs:

- The CDB_PDBS or DBA_PDBS views provide information on the PDBs in the database, such as their names and their status.

- The V$CONTAINERS view provides information on the PDBs, such as the open mode of the containers and other information.

- The V$PDBS view provides information about the individual PDBs, such as when they were opened, their current open mode, and if they are open in restricted session mode.

- CDB_PDB_HISTORY provides information about the history of a PDB.

Determining Which PDB You Are In

If you need to know which PDB you are in, you can use the **show con_name** SQL*Plus command, as you've seen frequently in this chapter. You can display the container ID by using the **show con_id** SQL*Plus command.

Oracle also provides functions that return the container ID of the container based on passing specific information to the function, including the container name, the container dbid, the container uid, and the container guid. For example, if you know the container name, you can get the container ID by using the **con_name_to_id** function as shown here:

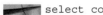
```
select con_name_to_id('MYPDB') from dual;
```

There are four functions in total:

- **CON_NAME_TO_ID**   Returns the container ID based on the container name

- **CON_DBID_TO_ID**   Returns the container ID based on the container DBID

- **CONTAINER_UID_TO_ID**   Returns the container ID based on the CONTAINER_UID

- **CONTAINER_GUID_TO_ID**   Returns the container ID based on the CONTAINER_GUID

You can find the DBID, UID, and GUID for a container in the V$CONTAINERS view.

Opening, Closing, and Altering the Open Mode of PDBs

Opening, closing, and altering the open mode of PDBs is similar to doing the same for CDBs. You can manage the state of the PDB either from the root of the CDB or from within the PDB itself.

Opening and Closing PDBs from the CDB   To open or close a PDB from the root of a CDB, you use the **alter pluggable database** command. Here is an example of using that command to open a PDB called MYPDB:

```
alter pluggable database mypdb open;
```

You will notice a message in the alert log that indicates that the database has been opened.

Another option is to open the PDB in READ ONLY mode:

```
alter pluggable database mypdb open read only;
```

You can also close a PDB from the root container. Again, use the **alter pluggable database** command:

```
alter pluggable database mypdb close;
```

The following is another option for closing the PDB:

```
alter pluggable database mypdb close immediate;
```

Opening and Closing PDBs from the PDB   You can also open and close a PDB from within the PDB itself. After signing into the root container as a privileged or common user, use the **alter session** command to switch to the container, as shown here:

```
alter session set container=mypdb;
```

Once you have entered the PDB, you can use the following **startup** and **shutdown** commands:

- **startup force**   Shuts down and then restarts the PDB.

- **startup restrict**   Starts the PDB in restricted session mode. Only users with **restricted session** privilege can connect to the database when it's in this mode.

- **startup, startup open**   Starts the database. Can be in READ WRITE mode (the default) or READ ONLY mode (**startup open read only**).

- **shutdown**   Shuts the PDB down in a consistent manner after all sessions have disconnected.

- **shutdown immediate**   Shuts the PDB down in a consistent manner, killing sessions that are active or in flight.

■ **shutdown abort**   Shuts the PDB down in an inconsistent state.

■ **shutdown transactional**   Shuts the PDB down, waiting for all in-flight transactions to complete.

While CDBs have the **shutdown abort** and **shutdown transactional** commands, PDBs do not.

Setting the Default and Temporary Tablespaces for a PDB

You can set the default and temporary tablespaces for a PDB by using the **alter pluggable database** command from the PDB, as shown in these examples:

```
alter pluggable database default tablespace pdb_tbs
alter pluggable database default temporary tablespace pdb_temp_tbs
```

Setting Storage Limits for a PDB

You can set storage limits for a given PDB by using the **alter pluggable database** command from within the PDB when logged in as SYS or a common user with the appropriate privileges. In the following example, we set the default storage for the PDB to 2G:

```
alter pluggable database storage(maxsize 2g);
```

You can also reset the storage limits to unlimited, as shown here:

```
alter pluggable database storage(maxsize unlimited);
```

Using the alter system Command from Within a PDB

You can use the **alter system** command from within a PDB to perform many tasks. The following **alter system** commands are available from within a PDB:

alter system flush shared_pool	alter system flush buffer_cache
alter system enable restricted session	alter system disable restricted session
alter system set use_stored_outlines	alter system suspend
alter system resume	alter system checkpoint
alter system check datafiles	alter system register
alter system kill session	alter system disconnect session
alter system set *initialization_parameter*	

Backup and Recovery of CDBs and PDBs

Most DBAs agree that performing backup and recovery is one of the most important parts of their job. Chapter 5 covers a majority of the Oracle Database 12c backup and recovery new features, but we felt that a quick discussion of backup and recovery within the context of CDBs and PDBs would be more useful to you here.

NOTE
This section only touches upon the basics of backup and recovery of CDBs and PDBs. As with traditional backup and recovery, many different combinations of things can influence how you actually restore your CDBs or PDBs.

Backup Features Available at the CDB Level

In large part, at the CDB level, backup and recovery has not changed much from traditional backup and recovery. In this section, we first look at which backup features have not changed (to ease your concerns), and then we look at using RMAN to back up the root container. After this section, we will talk about RMAN backups of a PDB.

Backup Features That Have Not Changed

If you use RMAN to back up your non-CDBs, you can also use it to back up a whole CDB in the same way using the RMAN **backup database** command, along with other options (such as **plus archivelog delete input**). Tablespace, datafile, control file, and SPFILE backups at the CDB level also work the same as they always have. The only difference is that you perform these backups while connected to the root container. Even the way you log into RMAN is no different in this case, as shown here:

```
rman target=/
backup database plus archivelog delete input;
```

Of course, you can perform incremental backups and section size backups, add tags, and do all the other typical things that you do in a normal backup. For incremental backups, the block change tracking file is still fully supported. In short, everything for a CDB backup is pretty much the same (beyond the new features mentioned in Chapter 5).

With CDBs, it is generally recommended to use an incremental backup strategy and back up the whole CDB all at once. This is because restoring an entire CDB is much faster than restoring the CDB first followed by restoring the individual PDBs within that CDB. So, in many ways, you shouldn't need to change how you back up your CDB from a production point of view.

Backing Up the Root Container

If you have made major changes in the root container of the CDB, you may want to do a quick backup of the root container. This is supported in Oracle Database 12c with the addition of the **backup database root** RMAN command, as shown in this example:

```
[oracle@server12c admin]$ rman target=/
connected to target database: CDBTWO (DBID=1371718279, not open)
backup database root;
```

This will just back up the root container datafiles. If control file auto backups are enabled, then SPFILE and control file autobackups will occur. If the database were in ARCHIVELOG mode, then you would also back up the archived redo logs as shown in this example:

```
backup database root plus archivelog delete input;
```

Backup Features Available for PDBs

As you might expect, there are new features associated with the backup and recovery of PDBs. This section discusses the main features that you will want to be aware of with respect to PDBs, but make sure you read Chapter 5 for even more information. In this section we look at

- Backing up PDBs with RMAN from the root container
- Backing up the PDB from within the PDB with RMAN

Backing Up PDBs with RMAN from the Root Container

RMAN also supports the backup of individual PDBs. You can back up a PDB while connected to the root container with an Oracle administrative user (such as SYS) or a common user that has the SYSBACKUP or SYSDBA privilege. If you choose this option, you use the **backup pluggable database** RMAN command to back up whichever PDB you wish to back up. Here are some examples:

```
[oracle@server12c admin]$ rman target=/
connected to target database: CDBTWO (DBID=1371718279, not open)
backup pluggable database neworcl;
```

Again, if the database were in ARCHIVELOG mode then you could backup the archivelogs at the same time as seen here:

```
backup pluggable database neworcl plus archivelog;
```

You can back up multiple PDBs at the same time. The command would look similar to this:

```
backup pluggable database mypdb, neworcl plus archivelog;
```

In this case, two PDBs are backed up, mypdb and neworcl. Also, the archived redo logs get backed up during the backup.

> **NOTE**
> *The backup pluggable database only works from the root container, not from within a pluggable database. Use the **backup database** command if you are within a pluggable database and want to backup that database. Understand though, you can't back up archived redo logs from within a PDB at this time. So if you back up a PDB, you should either shut it down first, or make sure you back up the archived redo logs from the root container.*

Backing Up PDBs with RMAN from the PDB

You can also back up a PDB by directly connecting to a PDB with a user created in that PDB. The user that you connect to must be either a common user or a user created within the PDB. Either of these users must have SYSDBA privileges. Here is an example of backing up the PDB while RMAN is connected to the PDB CDBTWO:

1. Create the common user that you will use for the backup. In this case, we will create a common user called c##robert:

   ```
   . oraenv
   ORACLE_SID = [cdbtwo] ? cdbtwo
   sqlplus / as sysdba
   create user c##robert identified by robert container=all;
   grant resource, create session, sysdba to c##robert
   container=all;
   ```

2. Use RMAN to connect to the PDB using the common user:

   ```
   rman target=c##robert/robert@server12c:1521\/neworcl
   ```

3. Since connections directly to a PDB do not support backups of archived redo logs, you will want to shut down the PDB from the RMAN prompt before starting your backup. This will ensure the datafiles that are backed up are consistent. Since you are logged in to a specific PDB, the **shutdown** command at the RMAN prompt will only shut down that PDB.

   ```
   shutdown
   ```

4. Issue the **backup database** command (as opposed to the **backup pluggable database** command):

```
backup database;
```

NOTE
Because archived redo logs cannot be backed up when attached directly to a PDB, you will need to back up the archived redo logs from the root container after you perform an online backup from within a PDB.

The **backup tablespace** command will only back up the tablespaces that are in the PDB that you are currently connected too. This is because a given tablespace name can exist in more than one PDB. For example, assume that you have four PDBs. First there is the ROOT PDB and then there are MYPDB, NEWPDB and NEWORCL in your database (and technically the SEED PDB too). We know each PDB has its own SYSAUX tablespace. So, what happens when we login to the root container and try to back up SYSAUX? The answer is that only the SYSAUX tablespace that is owned by the root container will be backed up. The same is true for any PDB that you connect to, including the ROOT PDB.

The **backup datafile** command is a bit different. If you execute the **backup datafile** command from the root container, then it can be used to back up any datafile in any of the PDBs. This is because datafile numbers are unique across a given CDB. If you issue the **backup datafile** command from any other PDB, then that datafile must exist in that PDB or an error will occur indicating that RMAN cannot find the datafile you wish to back up.

NOTE
My preferred way to back up a pluggable database would be to use the backup pluggable database from the root contained and back up the archived redo logs at the same time.

RMAN Restrictions When Connected to a PDB

At present there are a number of restrictions that apply to RMAN when connected directly to a PDB. The functionality restrictions of the different backup commands have already been described. Other commands that are not supported from a PDB include

- Archivelog backups, deletions, and nonmedia-recovery related restores.

- Point-in-time recovery

- Tablespace point-in-time recovery

- Connecting to recovery catalog

- Report/Delete obsolete

- Any RMAN configuration changes via the **configure** command

- **reset database**

- **import catalog**

- **register database**

- Data Recovery Advisor

- Flashback operations from RMAN

- **duplicate database**

- Table recovery

RMAN Restore and Recovery Features for CDBs and PDBs

As with any database, if you decide to use CDBs and PDBs, you need to know how to restore and recover them if something goes awry. This section concentrates on recovery using Oracle's RMAN backup and recovery tool. We discuss recovery related to CDBs first, and then discuss recovery related to PDBs.

Recovering the Entire CDB

The procedure to restore and recover an entire CDB with RMAN is no different from the procedure to restore and recover a non-CDB database with RMAN. Normal recovery, point-in-time recovery, and even flashback database operations are pretty much the same at this level. So, restoring and recovering a CDB, at the most elemental level, is the same as always:

```
restore database;
recover database;
alter database open;
```

The previous commands work as they always have, restoring and then recovering the entire database, including all PDBs. We then open the database with the **alter database open** command. This is just like a regular database recovery that you have no doubt done before. The PDBs will only be mounted, and you will need to re-open them.

As you might expect you can also issue **restore tablespace** and **restore datafile** commands from the root, as well as any of the other normal RMAN functionality that you have used in the past and that are new in Oracle Database 12c!

Recovering the Root Container of a CDB

RMAN provides the ability to restore just the root container, with the **restore database root** and **recover database root** RMAN commands. After the recovery, you will need to open the CDB and all of the associated PDBs.

If you find yourself in a position where you need to restore the root CDB, Oracle strongly recommends that you also recover all the PDBs, including the seed PDB, as discussed next.

Recovering the PDBs

You can choose either of two methods to perform the recovery of a PDB: recover from the root container, or recover from within the PDB. The biggest difference is that you can recover one or multiple PDBs from the root container, whereas you can only recover the PDB you are connected to if you are recovering from within the PDB. Therefore, most PDB recoveries will probably be from the root container.

Restoring and Recovering from the Root of the CDB   To start the recovery, connect RMAN to the root container and then use the **restore pluggable database** command followed by the **recover pluggable database** RMAN command. Then, simply open the PDBs that you have restored with the **alter pluggable database open** command. Here is an example:

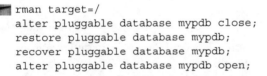

```
rman target=/
alter pluggable database mypdb close;
restore pluggable database mypdb;
recover pluggable database mypdb;
alter pluggable database mypdb open;
```

Restoring and Recovering from Within the PDB   To perform a restore from within the PDB, do the following:

1. Use RMAN to connect to the PDB as you normally would (using the PDB service):

   ```
   rman target=c##robert/robert@server12c:1521\/neworcl
   ```

2. From within the PDB, use the normal RMAN **restore** and **recover** commands. You can restore and recover the entire PDB, specific tablespaces, or specific datafiles, just as with a regular non-CDB. Here is an example of the commands used to perform a complete PDB restore and recovery:

```
alter pluggable database close;
restore database;
recover database;
alter pluggable database open;
```

NOTE
*Oracle supports point-in-time recovery for both the CDB and for individual PDBs. However, because of the complexities of point-in-time recovery of PDBs, this feature is supported only if you are using RMAN. These operations must occur from within the PDB itself, and you use the **restore database until time** and **recover database until time** commands as you normally would. You can still do manual point-in-time recoveries of the entire CDB, however.*

Other Backup and Recovery Features for CDBs and PDBs

You might use other Oracle features and tools for backup and recovery operations on CDBs and PDBs. These tools include Oracle Data Pump and Oracle Database Flashback features. Oracle Data Pump fully supports CDBs and PDBs. Oracle Flashback Database functionality generally supports CDBs and PDBs, but you might encounter some interesting issues. For example, if you have recovered a PDB using RMAN to a point in time different from that of the rest of the PDBs in the CDB (or the root container), then there can be some issues with flashback database. Please see the *Oracle Database Backup and Recovery User's Guide 12c* for more information on these "outlier" issues with flashback functionality.

Oracle Data Pump does not support CDB-wide operations. To use Oracle Data Pump, you need to connect to the individual PDB that you want to export or import into, rather than connecting to the CDB. Oracle Data Pump works pretty much the same way with a PDB as it does with a non-CDB.

You can use Oracle Data Pump to move a PDB from one CDB to another CDB. One thing to be aware of is that any common users (c##) that are present in the source DB, those users will not get created in the destination CDB during the import. While the common user is actually exported, Oracle Data Pump will raise an error during the import to the new PDB. This is the expected behavior. If you want to keep that common user, then you need to create it in the target CDB after creating the target PDB (or after importing the data into the PDB).

If the common user owns objects in the PDB, then you need to either create the common user in the target PDB before the import or use the Oracle Data Pump **remap_schema** parameter of the **impdp** command.

End of Line

In this chapter we have introduced you to Oracle Multitenant. As you might have guessed from the content in this chapter, we could well have spent a whole book on this and associated topics (like managing multitenancy and the like). We have flooded you with information. Once you get the basics down, continue to learn about this powerful new feature in Oracle Database 12c. What you see in Oracle Multitenant, I think, is the future of Oracle Database.

Now, we move on to Chapter 4 where we will talk about Oracle Grid Infrastructure new features. There you will find some really interesting information related to Oracle Cluster Ware, ASM, and Oracle Real Application Clusters.

CHAPTER
4

Oracle Grid Infrastructure

Oracle has a long tradition of investing in cluster technologies as a deeply integrated core component, and not as add-on or afterthought. The capability to have a single copy of a database available on more than one server is still an unrivaled technology more than a decade after the initial release of RAC.

The basic technologies behind Real Application Clusters are

- Storage that is shared between two or more servers, allowing each server concurrent access to the same data blocks. Storage devices traditionally used in RAC include storage-area networks (SANs) and Network Files System (NFS) devices.

- A cluster file system to store the data and to ensure data integrity between the servers in the cluster. Popular file systems include Oracle Automatic Storage Management (ASM), Veritas Cluster File System (VxCFS), and NFS.

- A communications network for the servers participating in the cluster to utilize for cluster management and to pass data. The Internet Protocol (IP) using either Ethernet or, more recently, InfiniBand is the predominant medium used.

Each release of RAC has introduced major advances in functionality and ease of management, so much so that it is easy to forget how far RAC and its predecessor, Oracle Parallel Server (OPS), have come. The *Getting to Know Oracle8*i *Release 8.1.5* documentation (1999) described the following as new features for Parallel Server:

A new "diskless" ping architecture, called cache fusion, that provides copies of blocks directly from the holding instance's memory cache to the requesting instance's memory cache. This functionality greatly improves inter-instance communication. Cache fusion is particularly useful for databases where updates and queries on the same data tend to occur simultaneously and where, for whatever reason, the data and users have not been isolated to specific nodes so that all activity can take place on a single instance. With cache fusion, there is less need to concentrate on data or user partitioning by instance.

And at Oracle OpenWorld, a demo featuring a four-node RAC cluster running was highlighted as a major advancement. In the following years block pinging was completely eliminated, clustering software and a clustered file system were bundled with RAC, and many additional features were added.

Tom Says

It is interesting to note that Oracle Parallel Server—the precursor to RAC—was introduced in version 5 of Oracle, way back in the 1980s. This technology has been around for a long time.

With the release of 12c Grid Infrastructure, Oracle's rich tradition of adding industry-leading features continues. In this chapter we will cover the main new features in the release of 12c Grid Infrastructure.

Before diving into 12c, let's review the basic architecture for 11g as a guide for comparing the changes in 12c. Figure 4-1 depicts a basic two-node cluster. In this cluster, an ASM instance, an RDBMS instance, and two listeners (a local listener and a SCAN listener) are running. Running optional services such as Grid Naming Service (GNS) does not significantly alter the diagram.

Flex Clusters

In Figure 4-1, each node in the 11g cluster is the same as far as membership and abilities are concerned. Each node runs the same cluster software, runs an ASM instance and listeners and any cluster resource can run on any node and every node

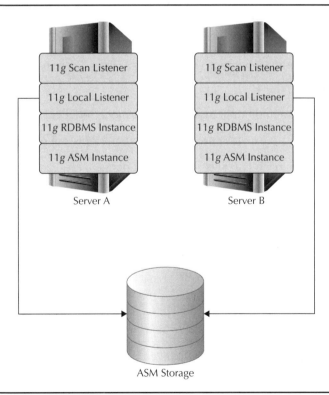

FIGURE 4-1.   *11g cluster overview*

has direct access to the storage. Beginning with 12*c* Grid Infrastructure, there is a new type of cluster called Flex Cluster that has two types of nodes—hub and leaf.

■ **Hub** A node that contains the full cluster software stack, has direct access to storage, and represents traditional RAC nodes; 64 hub nodes may exist in a given cluster.

■ **Leaf** A node that runs a lightweight RAC software stack and does not necessarily have direct access to the shared storage.

Leaf nodes are optional in a Flex Cluster, while hub nodes are required. Leaf nodes are members of the cluster, but at least one hub node must be included in the cluster to support leaf nodes. Since leaf nodes may not have direct access to the storage, they can rely on hub nodes to provide the requested data. Virtual IP addresses (VIPs) are required for hub nodes but are optional for leaf nodes.

An example of a situation that would be a good fit for leaf nodes is one in which workloads require a large amount of CPU but do not require a large amount of data. Certain spatial operations can consume a large amount of CPU resources on relatively small data sets. The process could be started on leaf nodes, thus lessening the impact on the hub nodes.

When you are deciding whether to build a Flex Cluster, keep in mind the following considerations:

■ Changing from a traditional mode to a Flex mode requires a cluster outage.

■ Changing from a Flex Cluster to a traditional cluster is not supported.

■ Grid Naming Service (GNS) is required to operate a Flex Cluster.

In the following example, we check the current mode of the node and then change the node from a hub node to a leaf node. After the change is complete, we restart the cluster software and verify the change.

```
[root@node11 ~]$ crsctl get node role config
Node 'node11' configured role is 'hub'

[root@node11 ~]# crsctl set node role leaf
CRS-4408: Node 'node11' configured role successfully changed; restart
Oracle High Availability Services for new role to take effect.

[root@node11 ~]# crsctl stop crs
CRS-2791: Starting shutdown of Oracle High Availability Services-
managed resources on 'node11'

....
....
```

```
[root@node11 ~]# crsctl start crs -wait
CRS-4123: Starting Oracle High Availability Services-managed resources

...

...

[root@node11 ~]# crsctl get node role config
Node 'node11' configured role is 'leaf'

[root@node11 ~]# crsctl check cluster
CRS-4537: Cluster Ready Services is online
CRS-4529: Cluster Synchronization Services is online
CRS-4533: Event Manager is online

[root@node11 ~]# ps -ef | grep pmon
root     10865  6285  0 15:14 pts/0    00:00:00 grep pmon
```

Notice that after starting as a leaf node, the cluster software is running but no ASM instance is up.

After changing from a hub to a leaf node is it possible to change from a leaf node back to a hub node. If you are changing a leaf node to a hub node and the leaf node previously has never been a hub node, you will need to assign VIPs to the leaf node and set up access to the shared storage on the leaf node.

Flex ASM

In previous releases of RAC, the role of ASM in the cluster is primarily to handle metadata about the data being stored on the ASM disks and to manage the allocation units that make up a diskgroup. The actual process of reading and writing of data to datafiles stored on ASM disks is done directly by the RDBMS instance processes. The ASM instance does not sit between the database and datafiles while a database is performing regular I/O. In 11*g*, in the event that ASM is not available on a particular server, all RDBMS instances on that server will crash, to prevent data corruption. For our purposes, we will call this classical ASM.

12*c* introduces an optional *Flex ASM*, where the ASM instance and the RDBMS instance do not have to reside on the same server. In prior versions of RAC, having each node in the cluster running ASM does not provide any more protection from outages, as each RDBMS instance can communicate only with the local ASM instance. In addition, running an ASM instance on each server requires memory, CPU, and cluster resources. In a small, two- or three-node cluster, the impact of running two or three ASM instances is small, but as larger six-node, eight-node, or even larger clusters have become more common and the total resources to run an ASM instance on every node is larger compared to a smaller cluster. In addition the extra ASM instances running on every node in the cluster provided no additional benefits in regards to high availability of the services provided by ASM. Two major benefits of Flex ASM are that it reduces the number of ASM instances for larger clusters and removes the dependency of having an ASM instance functioning on a node for RDBMS instances to run.

By default, clusters running a Flex ASM configuration will run an ASM instance on every node for clusters with three or fewer nodes. This is to provide high availability of the services provided by ASM. The cluster will be able to withstand two ASM instances failing. For clusters with four or more nodes, only three nodes will have an ASM instance.

The following example shows that a database in a two-node cluster is still fully functional after one ASM instance is shut down. First, we search for PMON processes that show an ASM instance and an RDBMS instance running. Next, we stop the ASM instance with the **–f** (force) option. Since diskgroups are cluster resources that depend on ASM, we could either dismount all the diskgroups and then stop ASM or use the force option. Next, we search for PMON processes again, but this time only the RDBMS PMON process is found. Had this been a non-Flex ASM cluster or an 11g R2 or earlier cluster, the instance would have stopped when the local ASM instance was no longer available. Last, we query the RDBMS instance to verify that it is still functional.

```
$ ps -ef | grep pmon
oracle    9983     1   0 Apr29 ?          00:00:09 ora_pmon_a056_1
grid      24419    1   0 00:04 ?          00:00:00 asm_pmon_+ASM1
grid      24765 24361  0 00:09 pts/0      00:00:00 grep pmon

$ srvctl stop asm -n node10 -f

$ ps -ef | grep pmon
oracle    9983     1   0 Apr29 ?          00:00:09 ora_pmon_a056_1
grid      24847 24361  0 00:09 pts/0      00:00:00 grep pmon

$ sqlplus / as sysdba

SQL> select open_mode from v$database;

OPEN_MODE
--------------------
READ WRITE
```

Flex ASM Architecture

As previously stated, when using a Flex ASM configuration, the database and ASM instances do not have to be on the same server. Figure 4-2 helps to illustrate this. The RDBMS instance still requires a connection to an ASM instance, and it also

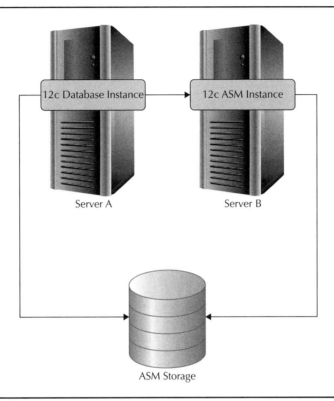

FIGURE 4-2. *12c Flex Cluster overview*

requires direct access to the actual ASM storage, as I/O operations go directly from the server hosting the RDBMS instance to the ASM storage. Figure 4-2 shows a cluster with an RDBMS instance running a server that doesn't have an ASM instance running. The ASM instance is running a separate node. The RDBMS communicates with the remote ASM instance, and both the RDBMS and ASM instances need access to the shared storage.

Installing and Configuring Flex ASM

During the installation of Flex ASM, the Oracle Universal Installer (OUI) will present a screen similar to the one shown in Figure 4-3. If you choose the option to configure a Flex Cluster, Flex ASM is automatically enabled, as a Flex Cluster requires Flex ASM. Also, if you intend to run pre-Oracle Database 12c databases on the cluster, you will have to either use classical ASM or change the Flex ASM configuration to run an ASM instance on every node in the cluster, because pre-Oracle Database 12c databases are not able to communicate with remote ASM instances.

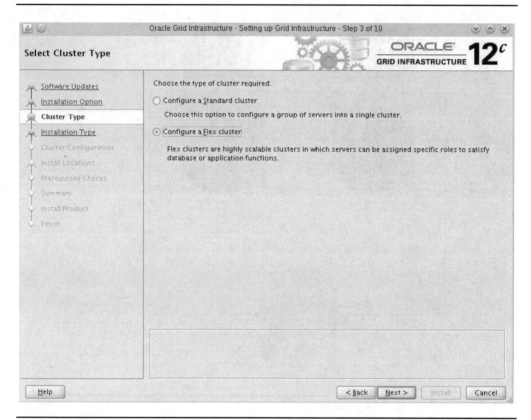

FIGURE 4-3. *Choosing the cluster type*

As part of the installation process, the OUI will ask you which network the ASM clients should use to communicate with remote ASM instances. The network used for ASM connections can be shared with the private network used for normal RAC traffic or it can be a separate dedicated network that is also a private network to the cluster. To facilitate remote ASM connections, a listener is required to run on the ASM network. The following is an excerpt of a cluster resource listing showing the new ASM listener:

```
$ $ crsctl stat res ora.ASMNET1LSNR_ASM.lsnr -n node10
NAME=ora.ASMNET1LSNR_ASM.lsnr
TYPE=ora.asm_listener.type
TARGET=ONLINE
STATE=ONLINE
```

If you choose to run Flex ASM, you will have SCAN listeners, local listeners, and ASM listeners!

If you plan on running pre-Oracle Database 12c databases on your cluster or if you wish to run non default number of three ASM instances, you can use the **srvctl** command to specify how many ASM instances the cluster should run (remember, a server can run only a single ASM instance). In the following example, we use the **asmcmd** tool to check to see if Flex ASM is configured, and then we use **srvctl** to find which servers are running an ASM instance and to get the number of ASM instances configured to run. Recall that modifying the ASM instance count returns no output.

```
$ asmcmd showclustermode
ASM cluster : Flex mode enabled

$ srvctl status asm -detail
ASM is running on node10,node11
ASM is enabled.

$ srvctl modify asm -count ALL

$ srvctl config asm
ASM home: /u01/app/12.1.0/grid
Password file: +OCR/orapwASM
ASM listener: LISTENER
ASM instance count: ALL
Cluster ASM listener: ASMNET1LSNR_ASM
```

Next, we use **srvctl** again to specify that each node should run an ASM instance (note that no output is given after modifying the ASM count). Next, we verify the configuration. Finally, we set the configured ASM instance count to 3 and verify the configuration.

```
$ srvctl modify asm -count 3
$ srvctl config asm
ASM home: /u01/app/12.1.0/grid
Password file: +OCR/orapwASM
ASM listener: LISTENER
ASM instance count: 3
Cluster ASM listener: ASMNET1LSNR_ASM
```

ASM Enhancements

Flex ASM may be the major ASM feature in Oracle Database 12c, but there are other enhancements that continue to make ASM one of the best file systems for running Oracle databases. This section covers those enhancements.

Password Files

ASM does not have a data dictionary, so user authentication is provided either by
the OS or by a password file. The default location for the password file is $ORACLE_
HOME/dbs. Since this is not a shared location, each node maintains its own version
of the password file. That creates the possibility the password file will be out of sync
and cause authentication issues. With 12c, the required enhancements have been
made to the grid infrastructure to store the password file in an ASM diskgroup,
allowing all nodes in a cluster to share a single ASM password file. By running the
srvctl command, we can list the diskgroup and path of the ASM password file:

```
$ srvctl config asm
ASM home: /u01/app/12.1.0/grid
Password file: +OCR/orapwASM
ASM listener: LISTENER
ASM instance count: 3
Cluster ASM listener: ASMNET1LSNR_ASM
```

ASM Rebalance and Resync

In Oracle Database 11g, diskgroup rebalances were limited to operating on a single
group at a time. In Oracle Database 12c, multiple diskgroups can be rebalanced
simultaneously within an instance.

ACFS Enhancements

Oracle Automatic Storage Manager Cluster File System (ACFS; also known as
CloudFS) is an interesting piece of technology. Regular file systems such as ext3,
NTFS, and JFS are well known and easy to use but can be complex to configure for
peak database performance. ASM is a fast, easy-to-use cluster file system, but you
cannot use standard file system tools to manage or even access data stored in ASM.
This is where ACFS provides the ability to bridge the gap between fast, database
optimized file systems and at the same time allowing administrators to manage
ACFS like any other file system. Figure 4-4 shows how ACFS fits in with ASM
Dynamic Volume Manager (ADVM) and ASM to be able to provide a traditional
cluster file system. ADVM is a volume device that uses ASM diskgroups for storage.

ADVM takes I/O requests from clients and maps the requests to the corresponding
ASM diskgroup. ADVM also extends ASM by providing a disk driver interface into
ASM storage that has been configured for ADVM volumes. ACFS provides the final
link between ASM and a regular file system. With ACFS, administrators and DBAs
can interact with ACFS file systems just like regular file systems with tools such as
cp and **df**.

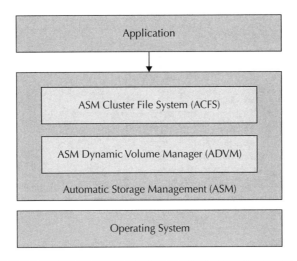

FIGURE 4-4. *ADVM overview*

File Support

Until the release of Oracle Database 11.2.0.4, no datafiles or derived files such as DataPump exports, archive logs, or RMAN backups were supported on ACFS. ACFS was tightly integrated with the cluster software but had little use to DBAs. With Oracle Database 12*c*, all database files are supported on ACFS (except for the Windows platform). When running a 12*c* cluster, this support is also extended to 11.2.0.4 databases.

In the following example, we are going to use an existing ASM diskgroup and create a 12*c* ACFS file system. Since ACFS is a kernel module, first check to ensure that the O/S and kernel version are supported. Use the following command to see if the current version of 12*c* ACFS is supported:

```
$ acfsdriverstate supported
ACFS-9200: Supported
```

If the result is unsupported, you may want to check the latest Oracle documentation to see if a newer version of 12*c* supports your platform. Next, we check to see if all the kernel modules are installed and if they have been loaded:

```
$ acfsdriverstate installed
ACFS-9203: true

$ acfsdriverstate loaded
ACFS-9204: false
```

The preceding output indicates that the modules are present but are not loaded. Loading the modules requires running the following command as root:

```
$ acfsload start
ACFS-9391: Checking for existing ADVM/ACFS installation.
ACFS-9392: Validating ADVM/ACFS installation files for operating
system.
ACFS-9393: Verifying ASM Administrator setup.
ACFS-9308: Loading installed ADVM/ACFS drivers.
ACFS-9154: Loading 'oracleoks.ko' driver.
ACFS-9154: Loading 'oracleadvm.ko' driver.
ACFS-9154: Loading 'oracleacfs.ko' driver.
ACFS-9327: Verifying ADVM/ACFS devices.
ACFS-9156: Detecting control device '/dev/asm/.asm_ctl_spec'.
ACFS-9156: Detecting control device '/dev/ofsctl'.
ACFS-9322: completed

$ acfsdriverstate loaded
ACFS-9203: true
```

Next, we create a directory where we want the ACFS file system to be mounted:

```
$ mkdir /acfs
```

With the required drivers loaded, we are ready to create an ADVM volume and ACFS file system. There is a graphical user interface (GUI) called asmca, but will use the command-line tool. Using the ASMCMD command-line tool, we create a volume with the **volcreate** command and then get the volume device path using the **volinfo** command:

```
ASMCMD> volcreate -G data -s 3G vol1
ASMCMD> volinfo -G data vol1
Diskgroup Name: DATA

        Volume Name: VOL1
        Volume Device: /dev/asm/vol1-249
        State: ENABLED
        Size (MB): 3072
        Resize Unit (MB): 32
        Redundancy: UNPROT
        Stripe Columns: 4
        Stripe Width (K): 128
        Usage:
        Mountpath:
```

Now we are ready to create an ACFS file system and register it with the cluster. The first command, **mkfs**, formats an ACFS since **–t acfs** specified an ACFS format. The parameter is the device path found by running the **volinfo** command within

ASMCMD. Lastly, the **acfsutil** command registers the ACFS system with the cluster. Note that registering an ACFS file system is not supported in an Oracle Restart configuration, but you can still use ACFS file systems; you will need to manually mount them.

```
$ mkfs -t acfs /dev/asm/vol1-249
mkfs.acfs: version              = 12.1.0.1.0
mkfs.acfs: on-disk version      = 39.0
mkfs.acfs: volume              = /dev/asm/vol1-249
mkfs.acfs: volume size         = 3221225472
mkfs.acfs: Format complete.

$ acfsutil registry -a /dev/asm/vol1-249 /acfs/
```

The ACFS volume is ready for use and will be automatically mounted by the cluster on startup. If we were using Oracle Restart or wanted to manually mount the file system, the procedure would be the same as mounting ext3 or a similar file system:

```
$ mount -t acfs /dev/asm/vol1-249 /acfs/
```

Highly Available NFS

Network File System (NFS) was developed by Sun in 1984 as a method to access files on a remote system. Since then, NFS has become the clear standard in sharing files in a Unix environment, with many major storage vendors offering native NFS in their products. Using ACFS and 12c Clusterware, it is now possible to export an ACFS file system and use the Clusterware to ensure the NFS resource is highly available.

Note the following about using NFS to export an ACFS file system:

■ ACFS relies on an existing NFS server already configured on the host.

■ Deployment is not supported on Oracle Restart systems.

■ The Windows platform is not supported.

■ A static IP address is required for a VIP.

■ NFS protocol versions 2 and 3 are supported.

ACFS Snapshots

ACFS snapshots are online, point-in-time copies of an ACFS file system that can be either read-only or read-write. ACFS uses a copy-on-write design so that new snapshots of a file system are ready immediately. Before a file extent is written or deleted, the original value is copied to the snapshot, thus preserving the integrity of the snapshot. *Thin cloning* is a popular term for storage systems that use this type of technology.

Snapshots have many different uses. One of the most popular is to instantly create a thin clone of a database. The source database is put in hot backup mode, a snapshot is taken, and the source database is taken out of hot backup mode. The clone database is in a "crashed" state, and after instance recovery, you have a complete thin copy of the source database. Creating backups is another use for snapshots. This may be a popular solution if the backup system is not able to integrate with RMAN. The same steps that are used to create a clone are used to create a backup.

With 12c is it now possible to take a snapshot of a snapshot, and up to 63 snapshots can exist in a given ACFS file system. For these features to be available, the ADVM diskgroup compatibility must be set to 12.1.

Other Enhancements

Among other notable new features for RAC in 12c is that it is now IPv6 compatible. IPv6 is gradually being deployed over the past few years and as the free address of IPv4 are quickly becoming used up so IPv6 deployment is picking up steam.

Another enhancement is in the area of Oracle Cluster Registry (OCR) backups. In earlier releases, OCR was backed up to a local file system. Now OCR is backed up to a diskgroup, thus simplifying the backup of OCR.

With the relatively new massive scalable platforms like Oracle Exadata and others, there is a growing trend to consolidate database servers. One issue with consolidation and RAC is the SCAN address in multisubnet networks. In pre-Oracle Database 12c clusters, if you are consolidating database servers that are on different subnets, you have to choose which subnet the SCAN address will be on. In order to have network database access for the other subnet, you have to create listeners and VIPs for the other subnet, but you won't be able to get a SCAN address for the other subnet. In Oracle Database 12c, you can now have more than one SCAN address bring the benefits of SCAN to multisubnet deployments on a single cluster.

End of Line

Oracle Grid Infrastructure 12c adds exciting new features like Flex Clusters, Flex ASM, ACFS improvements, and IPv6 support to continue to ensure Oracle is ready to support tomorrow's database needs. While new features are great, not every organization is ready to embrace everything that is new at once. Oracle 12c Grid Infrastructure is designed to allow shops to continue to use RAC the same way they do today while making it easy to move to new technologies seamlessly.

CHAPTER
5

Backup, Recovery, and
Data Guard New Features

Perhaps the foremost job of the DBA is to make sure that the database is always backed up and that the corresponding backups are recoverable. Reporting and OLTP applications are useless without their data. Without backups, it only takes the loss of a disk, or some other disaster, for all that data to be lost. In this chapter, we discuss the new features in Oracle Database 12c that are associated with backup, recovery, and high availability. Most of the backup-related new features revolve around RMAN, so the focus of this chapter will in large part be with RMAN. Then we will close out this chapter by taking a look at Oracle Data Guard new features.

RMAN-Related New Features

Oracle Database 12c contains a number of new features related to RMAN. This section introduces the following new features:

- Improvements in incremental and multisection backups

- Recovery of databases over the network using backup sets from a standby database

- Active database duplication improvements

- Cross-platform backup and recovery improvements

- Recovering tables and partitions with RMAN

- Miscellaneous RMAN new features

Improvements in Incremental and Multisection Backups

Multisection backups, introduced in Oracle Database 11g, provide the capability to split large database datafiles into smaller chunks. This new feature enables you to parallelize the backup of large database datafiles, which can make backups much faster. Oracle Database 12c provides two new features with respect to multisection backups:

- The capability to perform incremental multisection backups.

- The capability to create multisection image copies with RMAN.

Making Multisection Incremental Backups

You have been able to do multisection base backups (level 0) with RMAN since Oracle Database 11g. Oracle Database 12c now allows multisection backups when doing incremental (Level 1) backups with RMAN. When making incremental multisection backups, RMAN will try to make use of block change tracking and unused block compression when possible. To use incremental multisection backups, you must set the COMPATIBLE parameter correctly based on the level of the backup. For a level 0 multisection incremental base backup, the COMPATIBLE parameter must be set to 11.0 or higher. To take advantage of level 1 multisection incremental backups, the COMPATIBLE parameter must be set to 12.0 or higher.

NOTE
*When doing an incremental backup RMAN may adjust the **section size** parameter setting based on the size of the database datafile being backed up. First, if the database datafile is smaller than the section size, Oracle will back up the entire datafile, and will not divide it into different sections. Second, Oracle will determine if the datafile size divided by the section size would result in more than 256 sections. If the answer is yes, then RMAN will adjust the **section size** parameter setting for that datafile so that it will only end up with 256 total sections. This rule also applied to multisection image copies.*

To create a multisection incremental backup, you use the **section size** parameter of the RMAN **backup** command, as shown here:

```
backup section size 200m incremental level 0 database plus archivelog delete input;
```

Making Multisection Image Copies

In Oracle Database 12c, RMAN can now take advantage of multisection image copies, too. At first, this idea might seem strange to you, since an image copy, by definition, is an exact copy of a database datafile. What is different in this case is that each multisection backup will take a certain begin and end set of bytes and write them out to the final image copy, in parallel. At the end of the write operation, the final result will be a single physical image copy of the source database datafile. Thus, a multisection image copy is a way to parallelize the creation of an image copy. The final result is still the same as a non-section-sized image copy.

Here is an example of creating image copies of all the database datafiles using the **section size** parameter:

```
backup as copy section size 1000m database;
```

Recovery of Databases Over the Network Using Backup Sets from a Standby Database

You might already be aware that without any additional license you can use an Oracle Database for full database backups. When using Oracle Active Data Guard, you can actually implement an incremental backup strategy with a standby database. In previous versions of Oracle Database, if you wanted to use the backup sets created on the standby database, you had to have some way to physically access them. This might include putting the backup set pieces on a shared file system or copying them across to the server where you wanted to perform the restore. All of this takes time and effort, of course. It can also be a less than secure way of treating your backup images.

In this section, we will cover new features related to using Oracle networking and standby databases. First we will look at using your standby database to restore your production database. Then we will look at using Oracle networking services to update a standby database with a production database backup.

Restoring Your Production Database from a Standby Database

Oracle Database 12*c* allows you to connect to a given service name when performing a RMAN restore and recovery operation. You can then use the backup files associated with that service name for the restore and recovery of that database. For example, assume you are using a standby database as the main means to back up your primary database. Now, you can access the backups made on the standby database by using the **from service** parameter of the **restore** and **recover** commands.

You can test this new capability by using the **validate** parameter of the **restore** command. As an example, suppose that we have a database called DTGRD and that its standby database service is called SDTGRD. We use the SDTGRD standby database to do our backups. To validate that we can restore (or duplicate) the DTGRD primary database from the backups on SDTGRD, we can use the **restore** command along with the **validate** option, as shown here:

```
RMAN> restore database from service sdtgrd validate;
Starting restore at 07-SEP-13
using target database control file instead of recovery catalog
allocated channel: ORA_DISK_1
channel ORA_DISK_1: SID=36 device type=DISK
channel ORA_DISK_1: starting validation of datafile backup set
channel ORA_DISK_1: using network backup set from service sdtgrd
channel ORA_DISK_1: validation complete, elapsed time: 00:01:56
channel ORA_DISK_1: starting validation of datafile backup set
channel ORA_DISK_1: using network backup set from service sdtgrd
channel ORA_DISK_1: validation complete, elapsed time: 00:00:15
channel ORA_DISK_1: starting validation of datafile backup set
channel ORA_DISK_1: using network backup set from service sdtgrd
```

```
channel ORA_DISK_1: validation complete, elapsed time: 00:01:25
channel ORA_DISK_1: starting validation of datafile backup set
channel ORA_DISK_1: using network backup set from service sdtgrd
channel ORA_DISK_1: validation complete, elapsed time: 00:00:07
channel ORA_DISK_1: starting validation of datafile backup set
channel ORA_DISK_1: using network backup set from service sdtgrd
channel ORA_DISK_1: validation complete, elapsed time: 00:00:03
Finished restore at 07-SEP-13
```

You will want to ensure that your password files on the primary database and the standby database are synced up; if they are not, it's possible that RMAN may not be able to connect to the standby database. If the password files are out of sync, copy the password file from the primary database to the standby database, shut down and restart the standby database (putting it in recovery mode if you wish), and then retry the operation.

Updating a Standby Database Quickly with a Production Backup

If your standby database falls far behind in the application of changes from the production database (perhaps your standby database server has been down for a day or two), the quickest way to get the standby database caught up might be to apply an incremental backup to the standby database. This has been supported since Oracle Database 11g Release 2, but now, in Oracle Database 12c, you can perform this refresh directly from a service, just as in the previous section's example of restoring the primary database.

NOTE
If you have a license to use Oracle Advanced Security, you can enable encryption from the RMAN prompt when moving any data across the network. The RMAN command to do this would look like this:

```
RMAN> SET ENCRYPTION ALGORITHM 'AES128';
```

To perform this restore, you first need to have the standby database mounted and not in recovery application mode. You also need to ensure that there is a service to the primary database, which in our example we will call DTGRD. Then, you simply issue the **recover database** command in RMAN. This will start an incremental backup of the primary database and send the results of that backup, over the network, to be applied to the database. In our example, we are using a compressed backup to reduce the amount of data that is transmitted over the network. Here is an example of such a restore:

```
RMAN> startup force mount
Oracle instance started
database mounted
```

```
Total System Global Area    1035534336 bytes
Fixed Size                     2268232 bytes
Variable Size                276825016 bytes
Database Buffers             750780416 bytes
Redo Buffers                   5660672 bytes
RMAN> recover database from service dtgrd using compressed backupset;
Starting recover at 07-SEP-13
allocated channel: ORA_DISK_1
channel ORA_DISK_1: SID=30 device type=DISK
channel ORA_DISK_1: starting incremental datafile backup set restore
channel ORA_DISK_1: using compressed network backup set from service DTGRD
destination for restore of datafile 00001:
/u01/app/oracle/oradata/dtgrd/system01.dbf
channel ORA_DISK_1: restore complete, elapsed time: 00:00:25
channel ORA_DISK_1: starting incremental datafile backup set restore
channel ORA_DISK_1: using compressed network backup set from service DTGRD
destination for restore of datafile 00002:
/u01/app/oracle/oradata/dtgrd/example01.dbf
channel ORA_DISK_1: restore complete, elapsed time: 00:00:07
channel ORA_DISK_1: starting incremental datafile backup set restore
channel ORA_DISK_1: using compressed network backup set from service DTGRD
destination for restore of datafile 00003:
/u01/app/oracle/oradata/dtgrd/sysaux01.dbf
channel ORA_DISK_1: restore complete, elapsed time: 00:00:55
channel ORA_DISK_1: starting incremental datafile backup set restore
channel ORA_DISK_1: using compressed network backup set from service DTGRD
destination for restore of datafile 00004:
/u01/app/oracle/oradata/dtgrd/undotbs01.dbf
channel ORA_DISK_1: restore complete, elapsed time: 00:00:15
channel ORA_DISK_1: starting incremental datafile backup set restore
channel ORA_DISK_1: using compressed network backup set from service DTGRD
destination for restore of datafile 00006:
/u01/app/oracle/oradata/dtgrd/users01.dbf
channel ORA_DISK_1: restore complete, elapsed time: 00:00:03
starting media recovery
archived log for thread 1 with sequence 20 is already on disk as file
/u01/app/oracle/archive/dtgrd/1_20_811287053.dbf
archived log file name=/u01/app/oracle/archive/dtgrd/1_20_811287053.dbf thread=1
sequence=20
media recovery complete, elapsed time: 00:00:00
Finished recover at 07-SEP-13
RMAN> alter database recover managed standby database disconnect;
Statement processed
```

NOTE
*The preceding example demonstrates another RMAN-related new feature—we didn't have to use the SQL command when we issued the **alter database** command at the end to start the database in managed recovery mode.*

Active Database Duplication Improvements

If you use active database duplication, you will be happy to know that Oracle Database 12c now enables you to perform this operation with existing database backup sets. This reduces the load on the active instance during the duplication process. RMAN will use unused block compression during the duplication process, which can result in reduced network throughput. You can also use regular compression, and encrypt the data being transported over the network between the target server/database and the destination server/database. Active database duplication also supports the use of multisection backups.

Cross-Platform Backup and Recovery Improvements

Oracle Database 12c offers the following improvements with respect to RMAN and cross-platform backup and recovery:

- Cross-platform data transport using backup sets

- Cross-platform movement of read-only tablespaces using backup sets

Cross-Platform Data Transport Using Backup Sets

In Oracle Database 12c, RMAN adds the capability to transport databases, datafiles, and tablespaces across platforms using RMAN backup sets. The process is similar to transportable tablespaces which you might be familiar with already. Just like moving transportable tablespaces, the tablespaces (or the database) that are (is) being backed up and moved need(s) to be taken offline first. Then the backup occurs, and the backup set pieces created for that backup are moved to the target server.

During the backup/restore process a conversion of those backup set pieces to the new platform needs to occur. This is true regardless of the platform to which the backup set is being restored. This can occur either during the backup on the source platform or during the restore on the target platform. Two options are available to control this conversion either **to platform** or **from platform**. If you use the **to platform** option of the RMAN **backup** command, then the conversion occurs on the source database platform. If you use the **from platform** option of the RMAN **restore** command on the destination database, then the conversion occurs on the destination database server. We will review these two options later in this section.

Using backup sets to transport data to other databases rather than transporting tablespaces or using Oracle Data Pump has several benefits. First, since you are using RMAN, you can take advantage of the various RMAN features, such as compression and encryption, during the platform movement. Second, moving an RMAN backup across the network is likely to be faster than moving tablespace datafiles or Oracle Data Pump export dump files across the network. Finally, restoring an RMAN physical backup on another database server is much less complex than trying to restore objects from an Oracle Data Pump export file. (I always seem to have annoying issues when doing large-scale Data Pump imports!)

So let's take a look at the following topics related to cross-platform data transport using RMAN backup sets:

- Restrictions on cross-platform data transport using backup sets

- Backup sets are implicitly usable across cross platforms

- Creating cross-platform transportable backup sets directly

- Restoring cross-platform transportable backup sets on a destination server

- What you can do with this new functionality

Restrictions and Requirements on Cross-Platform Data Transport Using Backup Sets There are some restrictions and requirements that apply if you wish to use cross-platform data transport using RMAN backup sets or image copies. These restrictions include

- The **compatible** parameter of the source and the destination database must be set to 12.0 or higher.

- The source database must be open in read-only mode.

- The results of the PL/SQL stored procedure **dbms_tdb.check_db** must indicate the source database is transportable to the target database server.

- The source and destination platform must be of the same endian byte format.

- Of course, you need to have an instance up and running already on the destination database server. You can easily accomplish that by using the Oracle Database Configuration Assistant (DBCA).

If all these requirements and restrictions are met, you can use backup sets to perform cross-platform restore using RMAN backup sets.

NOTE
If you need to move your database across endian byte format platforms, you can now use RMAN and transportable tablespaces, as covered in the next section, "Cross-Platform Movement of Read-Only Tablespaces Using Backup Sets."

Backup Sets Are Implicitly Usable Across Cross Platforms   Backup sets will implicitly be available as a cross-platform usable backup, as long as those backups meet the requirements listed in the previous section, and that no parameters used to create the backup command conflict with cross-platform usability. For example, the following backup is available for cross-platform movement because it meets those requirements:

```
shutdown immediate;
startup mount;
alter database read only;
backup database open;
```

Note that this backup uses the fast recovery area (FRA) for the location of the backup set pieces. While this is acceptable, it would be easier to use the **format** clause to create the backup set pieces in a directory specifically allocated for the purpose of the cross-platform movement of the database (such as an NFS mount that is accessible by both databases).

Creating Cross-Platform Transportable Backup Sets   When you create cross-platform backups in RMAN, there are some new clauses and options that you can use when issuing the RMAN **backup** command: **for transport**, **to platform**, and **datapump**. When you use these clauses, RMAN will create the backup sets as cross-platform transportable backup sets.

NOTE
Tablespace cross-platform movement is covered in the next section.

When you use the **for transport** clause, RMAN will create a backup set that can be transported across any platform as long as the endian byte format is the same. The conversion of the data will occur on the destination platform.

When you use the **to platform** clause, RMAN will do the database conversion on the source database. The use of the **to platform** clause requires that the transported platform be listed in the V$TRANSPORTABLE_PLATFORM view. You must list the platform name in the **to platform** clause exactly as it appears in the V$TRANSPORTABLE_PLATFORM view.

Example of Creating a Cross-Platform Transportable Backup Using Backup Sets   The process of creating a cross-platform transportable backup using backup sets in RMAN is fairly simple. In the following example, the source database is called source and the target database is called target. Here are the basic instructions:

1. Ensure that all restrictions and requirements listed earlier in this chapter have been met. You should check the most current Oracle documentation for any additional restrictions or requirements that might have been added since this book was written.

2. Determine where you want to create the backup set pieces. While you can use the FRA, Oracle recommends that you create a special directory for the purposes of creating backup sets that will be transported to other platforms. This makes working with those files easier. You use the RMAN **format** parameter of the **backup** command to define the location you want RMAN to write these files to. In this example, we will create and use a directory called /u01/app/oracle/cross_platform.

3. Start RMAN, using the source database as the target:

```
rman target=\"backup\"
connect target "backup@source as sysbackup"
```

4. From RMAN, place the database in read-only mode:

```
shutdown immediate;
startup mount;
alter database open read only;
```

5. Back up the database using either the **to platform** option or the **for transport** option of the **backup** command. In this case, we will use the **for transport** option. Note that we have also compressed this backup, which is optional:

```
backup as compressed backupset for transport
format '/u01/app/oracle/cross_platform/sourcedb_%U' database;
```

The backup we have just made in the previous example will not be converted until it is restored on the platform it is destined to. If we had used the **to platform** option, then the conversion would have happened on the source platform. Note that the use of **for transport** and **to platform** are mutually exclusive options. Here is an example of using the **to platform** option:

```
backup to platform='Linux x86 64-bit'
format '/u01/app/oracle/cross_platform/linux_sourcedb_%U' database;
```

NOTE
*If you use the **to platform** option instead of the **for transport** option, the backup takes longer and consumes more CPU and IO resources because the platform conversion takes place on the source server.*

You will notice that we did not back up the archived redo logs. This is because we are essentially transporting tablespaces across platforms, so there will be no application of redo from any archived redo logs. Thus, this backup and the associated restore is to the point in time that the source database was put in read-only mode.

When crafting this backup statement, we first would have needed to query the V$TRANSPORTABLE_PLATFORM view to get the correct platform name, as shown in this example:

```
column  platform_name format a60
set pages 30
select platform_name from v$transportable_platform;
PLATFORM_NAME
-------------------------------------------------------------------------
Solaris[tm] OE (32-bit)
Solaris[tm] OE (64-bit)
Microsoft Windows IA (32-bit)
Linux IA (32-bit)
AIX-Based Systems (64-bit)
HP-UX (64-bit)
HP Tru64 UNIX
HP-UX IA (64-bit)
Linux IA (64-bit)
HP Open VMS
Microsoft Windows IA (64-bit)
IBM zSeries Based Linux
Linux x86 64-bit
Apple Mac OS
Microsoft Windows x86 64-bit
Solaris Operating System (x86)
IBM Power Based Linux
HP IA Open VMS
Solaris Operating System (x86-64)
Apple Mac OS (x86-64)
```

 CAUTION
Entering the platform name incorrectly, even by having a small case error or something obnoxious like a space in front of the name (those spaces can be hard to see!) that gets copied and pasted, will cause the backup to fail.

6. If you try to perform a migration to a database that does not support the migration method (for example, its endian byte format is different), RMAN returns the following error:

```
backup to platform='AIX-Based Systems (64-bit)'
format '/u01/app/oracle/cross_platform/linux_sourcedb_%U' database;
Starting backup at 06-SEP-13
using channel ORA_DISK_1
RMAN-00571: ===========================================================
RMAN-00569: =============== ERROR MESSAGE STACK FOLLOWS ===============
RMAN-00571: ===========================================================
RMAN-03002: failure of backup command at 09/06/2013 12:04:24
RMAN-06921: Convert database check failed
```

In this case, you would need to explore the use of RMAN to do a database migration using transportable tablespaces. This is a new feature in Oracle Database 12*c*, discussed later in this chapter.

7. Exit RMAN and move the backup set pieces that you just created in the /u01/ app/oracle/cross_platform directory to the destination host (for example, use the **scp** or **sftp** command). In our example, we will move the RMAN backup set pieces we need to the directory /u01/app/oracle/cross_platform on the machine we want to restore the tablespace to.

Restoring a Cross-Platform Transportable Backup Using Backup Sets   Restoring a cross-platform transportable backup using backup sets is about as simple as the backup process itself. After moving the backup set piece that is created to the destination server, you need to shut down the target database. Then you use RMAN to restore the tablespaces that are contained in the backup.

Which version of the RMAN command you use to restore the database depends on whether the backup was converted on the source database or needs to be converted on the destination database. We describe the difference in more detail in the next section.

Example of Restoring a Cross-Platform Transportable Backup Using Backup Sets
Now that you have created the backup and transported it to the destination database server, you are ready to restore the backup. There are a few things you need to be aware of before you can start the restore:

1. The restore process is a lot like using transportable tablespaces except that you are using and moving RMAN backup sets rather than using and moving tablespace datafiles. First you need to determine which database you want to restore the backup sets to. Optionally, you can restore the database or specific tablespaces to a newly created database. In our case, we have created a database called MYDB.

2. On the source DB, you need to determine which platform you are moving from. In our case, we issue the following query against the V$TRANSPORTABLE_PLATFORM view, which tells us which platform we are on (notice that we ran this query in RMAN!):

```
RMAN> SELECT PLATFORM_NAME FROM V$TRANSPORTABLE_PLATFORM
2> WHERE PLATFORM_ID =( SELECT PLATFORM_ID FROM V$DATABASE );
PLATFORM_NAME
-----------------------------------------------------------------------
Linux x86 64-bit
```

3. Set your environment for the new database and start RMAN, connecting to the database on the destination server. For example:

```
[oracle@DTGRD cross_platform]$ . oraenv
ORACLE_SID = [DTGRD] ? mydb
```

4. Now, let's start the restore. Of course, we will use the RMAN **restore** command. In the case of the backup set we are restoring from in this example, we did not convert the backup to the new platform version, so we will use the **from platform** option of the **restore** command.

   We will also use a new option of the RMAN **restore** command here, the **foreign database to new** option. This indicates that the restore is being done using a backup set that is from a different database. It also indicates that the backup set needs to be converted during the restore process because it was not converted during the backup.

   Finally, we will use the **from backup** set option to indicate the location of the backup set that is to be restored. Here is the full **restore** command for this example:

```
restore from platform 'Linux x86 64-bit'
foreign database to new
from backupset '/u01/app/oracle/cross_platform/sourcedb_17o5tcsp_1_1';
```

   If we had already done the conversion during the backup, we would have used the **all foreign datafiles** option instead of the **foreign database to new** option:

```
restore from platform 'Linux x86 64-bit'
all foreign datafiles
from backupset '/u01/app/oracle/cross_platform/sourcedb_17o5tcsp_1_1';
```

   The end result of either command is that the source database on the source database server will be restored to the destination database on the target database server.

5. Here is a complete run of the database restore on the remote server.

```
RMAN> restore from platform 'Linux x86 64-bit'
2>foreign database to new
3>from backupset '/u01/app/oracle/cross_platform/sourcedb_17o5tcsp_1_1';
Starting restore at 06-SEP-13
allocated channel: ORA_DISK_1
channel ORA_DISK_1: SID=21 device type=DISK
channel ORA_DISK_1: starting datafile backup set restore
channel ORA_DISK_1: specifying datafile(s) to restore from backup set
channel ORA_DISK_1: restoring all foreign files in backup piece
channel ORA_DISK_1: reading from backup piece
/u01/app/oracle/cross_platform/sourcedb_17o5tcsp_1_1
channel ORA_DISK_1: restoring foreign file 1 to
/u01/app/oracle/oradata/MYDB/datafile/o1_mf_system_8ok5zpst_.dbf
channel ORA_DISK_1: restoring foreign file 3 to
/u01/app/oracle/oradata/MYDB/datafile/o1_mf_sysaux_8ok5zq08_.dbf
channel ORA_DISK_1: restoring foreign file 2 to
/u01/app/oracle/oradata/MYDB/datafile/o1_mf_example_8ok5zq4g_.dbf
channel ORA_DISK_1: restoring foreign file 4 to
/u01/app/oracle/oradata/MYDB/datafile/o1_mf_undotbs1_8ok5zq8v_.dbf
channel ORA_DISK_1: restoring foreign file 6 to
/u01/app/oracle/oradata/MYDB/datafile/o1_mf_users_8ok5zqf1_.dbf
channel ORA_DISK_1: foreign piece
handle=/u01/app/oracle/cross_platform/sourcedb_17o5tcsp_1_1
channel ORA_DISK_1: restored backup piece 1
channel ORA_DISK_1: restore complete, elapsed time: 00:01:56
Finished restore at 06-SEP-13
```

You might have noticed that we didn't open the database after the restore. The reason for that leads us to the next section.

So...What Do You Do Now with the Backup Sets? You will notice that in the examples we did in the previous section, we didn't issue a **recover** command from RMAN. This is because this is not really a complete backup. We are missing a few critical pieces of the puzzle, such as a control file.

One thing you can do with this backup set is use it to re-create the database on the platform itself. To do this, you re-create the control file so that it points to the new database datafiles that were restored, as follows:

1. Use the **alter database backup controlfile to trace** command to create a trace file that contains the **create controlfile** command in it.

2. Modify the **create controlfile** command so that it points to the new database datafiles that were just restored.

3. Shut down the database, and then restart the database in nomount mode (**startup nomount**).

4. Once the database instance has started, run the new **create controlfile** command.

5. Issue the **alter database open resetlogs** command to open the database.

At this point, Oracle creates new online redo logs and then opens the database using the new datafiles you are pointing to. Note that once you do this, you will not be able to switch over to the old database datafiles that previously belonged to the database, meaning this is truly a cross-platform database move.

You can also use the method of creating a cross-platform backup to move tablespaces for transport. This method adds a few more steps to this process which we will discuss in the next section.

Cross-Platform Movement of Read-Only Tablespaces Using Backup Sets

Now, let's build on what we learned in the previous sections. Perhaps the most useful function of the new cross-platform features of RMAN involves the movement of tablespaces between platforms. The principle new feature here is that you can move tablespaces across platforms regardless of the endian byte format of the source and destination platforms. One restriction is that the tablespaces that are to be moved must be in read-only mode when they are backed up by RMAN. This section explains how to back up the tablespaces on the source database server, convert them on either the source or target side, and then restore them on the target database server.

If your source database is running Oracle Database Release 10.2 or Oracle Database 11g, you can still take advantage of this feature. To do so, first create the backup sets of the tablespaces to be transported in RMAN, just as you normally would, and then manually create the Oracle Data Pump metadata export dump file that will be used during the restore. You then follow the steps demonstrated in the "Restoring the Tablespace on the Target" section to restore the backup on an Oracle Database 12c database.

NOTE
While the backup can occur on a non–Oracle Database 12c database, the restore must occur on an Oracle Database 12c database.

Backing Up Tablespaces for Transport: Converting at the Source   The first step is to back up the tablespaces on the source system that are to be moved to the destination system. In this example, we will move the EXAMPLE tablespace from our source system to our destination system. Follow these steps:

1. Make the EXAMPLE tablespace to be moved read-only with the **alter tablespace** command:

   ```
   alter tablespace example read only;
   ```

2. Back up the tablespace. In this case we want to do the conversion of the tablespace on the source database server, so we use the **to platform** option of the RMAN **backup** command. Also, since we are using Oracle's transportable tablespace feature, an export of the metadata associated with that tablespace needs to occur. Fortunately, RMAN will perform this export for us.

   This export is accomplished via the datapump **format** parameter of the **backup** command. As we did before, we include the **format** parameter to indicate where the backup set pieces and the Oracle Data Pump export file should be written to. Note that RMAN will perform the tablespace transport check for you. Here is the **backup** command:

   ```
   backup to platform='Linux x86 64-bit'
   format '/u01/app/oracle/cross_platform/linux_sourcedb_%U'
   datapump format '/u01/app/oracle/cross_platform/linux_expdp.dmp'
   tablespace example;
   ```

3. Once the backup is complete, check the /u01/app/oracle/cross_platform directory. You should find the RMAN backup set piece and the Oracle Data Pump export file. Here is an example of the directory listing:

   ```
   [oracle@server12c cross_platform]$ ls -al
   total 1331452
   drwxr-xr-x  2 oracle oinstall       4096 Sep  6 16:21 .
   drwxr-xr-x 17 oracle oinstall       4096 Sep  6 11:46 ..
   -rw-r-----  1 oracle oinstall   76185600 Sep  6 12:12 linux_expdp.dmp
   -rw-r-----  1 oracle oinstall 1287208960 Sep  6 12:12 linux_sourcedb_18o5trh1_1_1
   ```

   In this listing you can see the database backup file (*sourcedb*) and the Oracle Data Pump export file (*linux*).

4. Make the tablespace read-write with the **alter tablespace** command.

5. Now that the backup is complete, move these files to the target server so that you can restore them.

We will discuss restoring and plugging in the tablespace later in this section.

Backing Up Tablespaces for Transport: Converting at the Target The process of backing up a tablespace for transport but deferring the conversion for the target server is much like the process presented in the previous section. The only difference is that you use the **for transport** option of the RMAN **backup** command, which defers the conversion until the restore on the destination platform. Note that RMAN will perform the tablespace transport check for you. Here's an example:

```
backup for transport
format '/u01/app/oracle/cross_platform/linux_sourcedb_%U'
datapump format '/u01/app/oracle/cross_platform/linux_expdp.dmp'
tablespace example;
```

As was the case in the example in the previous section, the backup will create two files in the /u01/app/oracle/cross_platform directory. You then would copy the backup files and the Data Pump export files to the destination database server to prepare for the tablespace transport. We will convert the files on the destination server.

Restoring the Tablespace on the Target: Converted at the Source Having copied the RMAN backup files to the destination directory called /u01/app/oracle/cross_platform, you are ready to restore the tablespace and import the tablespace metadata. As with the previous examples, you have two options: one that performs the platform conversion, and one that does not. When you issue the RMAN **restore** command, the tablespace will be restored and then RMAN will automatically import the Oracle Data Pump metadata into the database, attaching the tablespace.

When restoring the database, you will use several parameters that are new in Oracle Database 12c. In this example we are looking at a restore and import of a database tablespace that does not require conversion, like we had to do earlier in this chapter. Here are some of the parameters we would use:

- The **foreign tablespace** parameter, which is followed by the list of tablespaces you wish to restore.

- The **from backupset** parameter, which lists the location and name of the backup set to be restored.

- The **dump file from backupset** parameter, which lists the location and name of the Oracle Data Pump dump file that was created when the backup was previously executed.

Here is the RMAN **restore** command that we would use to restore the backup taken earlier:

```
restore foreign tablespace example to new
from backupset
'/u01/app/oracle/product/cross_platform/linux_sourcedb_1eo5u3qj_1_1'
dump file from backupset
'/u01/app/oracle/product/cross_platform/linux_expdp.dmp';
```

Restoring the Tablespace on the Target: Converted at the Target   In this section we will discuss transporting tablespaces using backup sets that were converted on the source platform, like we would need for our second **backup tablespace** example above. To do this we use the following parameters:

- The **from platform** parameter of the **restore** command indicates the platform that the backup sets were converted from.

- The new parameter **foreign tablespace** indicates the tablespace or tablespaces to be transported into the database.

- The **format** parameter indicates the location where the datafiles associated with the backup set will be restored.

- The **backupset** parameter indicates the location of the backup set piece file that will be restored.

- The **data file datapump destination** parameter indicates the location that the Oracle Data Pump export should be extracted from.

- The last **from backupset** parameter indicates the location of the backup set piece that contains the export file created by RMAN during the backup.

Here is an example of using the **restore** command to transport the tablespace(s) and apply the Data Pump metadata:

```
RMAN> restore from platform='Linux x86 64-bit'
2> foreign tablespace example
3> format '/scratch/psharman/test/linux_sourcedb_%U.%n'
4> from backupset
5> '/scratch/psharman/test/linux_sourcedb_03o6th6t_1_1'
6> dump file datapump destination '/scratch/psharman/test'
7> from backupset
8> '/scratch/psharman/test/linux_expdp2.dmp';

Starting restore at 07-SEP-13
using channel ORA_DISK_1

channel ORA_DISK_1: starting datafile backup set restore
channel ORA_DISK_1: specifying datafile(s) to restore from backup set
```

```
channel ORA_DISK_1: restoring all files in foreign tablespace EXAMPLE
channel ORA_DISK_1: reading from backup piece /scratch/psharman/test/linux_
sourcedb_03o6th6t_1_1
channel ORA_DISK_1: restoring foreign file 19 to /scratch/psharman/test/linux_
sourcedb_data_D-TEST_I-2727559136_TS-EXAMPLE_FNO-19_c9o6tii9.TESTxxxx
channel ORA_DISK_1: foreign piece handle=/scratch/psharman/test/linux_
sourcedb_03o6th6t_1_1
channel ORA_DISK_1: restored backup piece 1
channel ORA_DISK_1: restore complete, elapsed time: 00:00:02
channel ORA_DISK_1: starting datafile backup set restore
channel ORA_DISK_1: specifying datafile(s) to restore from backup set
channel ORA_DISK_1: restoring Data Pump dump file to /scratch/psharman/test/backup_
tts_MYDB_13162.dmp
channel ORA_DISK_1: reading from backup piece /scratch/psharman/test/linux_expdp2.dmp
channel ORA_DISK_1: foreign piece handle=/scratch/psharman/test/linux_expdp2.dmp
channel ORA_DISK_1: restored backup piece 1
channel ORA_DISK_1: restore complete, elapsed time: 00:00:02

Performing import of metadata...
    IMPDP> Master table "SYS"."TSPITR_IMP_MYDB_mzia" successfully loaded/unloaded
    IMPDP> Starting "SYS"."TSPITR_IMP_MYDB_mzia":
    IMPDP> Processing object type TRANSPORTABLE_EXPORT/PLUGTS_BLK
    IMPDP> Processing object type TRANSPORTABLE_EXPORT/POST_INSTANCE/PLUGTS_BLK
    IMPDP> Job "SYS"."TSPITR_IMP_MYDB_mzia" successfully completed at
Sat Sep 7 17:05:20 2013 elapsed 0 00:00:02
Import completed

Finished restore at 07-SEP-13
```

Recovering Tables and Partitions with RMAN

There are many scenarios in which tables (partitioned and non-partitioned) may need to be restored. For example, a data load failure might impact only certain tables. Or perhaps your database is subdivided into many schemas and you need to restore only the objects in one specific schema. These kinds of restores could be problematic since a physical database restore requires that you restore the entire database, and then roll it forward in its entirety.

A second option is to use Oracle Data Pump to restore individual tables and/or schemas. The problem with this option is that it is not possible to roll the data backed up in the Data Pump export forward in time after it has been restored. Thus, if your export was taken three days ago at 4 P.M., then that is the image of the data that you're going to see when you restore the export file to the database.

Yet another method that is sometimes used is to create a second database (often called a *stub* database) using the backup of the first database. In this situation, you restore the SYSTEM, SYSAUX, and UNDO tablespaces. Additionally, you restore the individual tablespaces that contain the data that you want to restore. After the restore is complete, you alter any tablespaces that you did not restore offline. You then apply the archived redo logs to the point in time that you want to restore the individual objects to. Having restored the database to the appropriate point in time, you then use Oracle Data Pump to export the objects, and then you import them into the original database, again using Oracle Data Pump. As you can probably tell, the problem with this option is that it is a fairly convoluted process to do manually. Fortunately, Oracle Database 12c introduces new functionality in RMAN that supports point-in-time restore of individual database tables and individual table partitions.

In this section we discuss

■ Prerequisites for restoring and recovering tables and partitions

■ Restrictions on restoring and recovering database tables and partitions

■ Options to consider when restoring tables and table partitions

■ How RMAN implements the restore and recovery of tables and partitions

■ Using RMAN to restore and recover a database table—an example

Prerequisites for Restoring and Recovering Database Tables and Partitions

If you want to take advantage of RMAN's ability to restore tables and table partitions then there are a few rules we need to follow. The following are the prerequisites to be able to restore tables or table partitions:

■ The database was in ARCHIVELOG mode when it was backed up, and it remained in ARCHIVELOG mode up until the point in time that you want to restore the database to.

■ If you want to recover individual partitions, the COMPATIBLE parameter must be set to 11.1.0 or later.

■ An RMAN backup of the SYSTEM, SYSAUX, and UNDO tablespaces must be available, and this backup must have been completed before the point in time that you want to restore the object(s) to.

■ There must be a backup (backups) of the tablespace(s) that contain the available objects that you want to restore. This backup (or backups) must have been completed before the time that you want to restore the objects to.

■ All tablespaces in the restore set must be restored to the same point in time.

■ You must have all the archived redo logs generated from the point of the start of the backup that is being used to recover the objects until the point in time that you are trying to restore the object(s) to.

■ The database you are restoring to (the target database) must be open in read-write mode.

■ The target database must also be in ARCHIVELOG mode.

As with any point-in-time recovery, you will need to know either the time, the log sequence number, or the SCN that you want to restore the table or partitions to. Having met these prerequisites, you are ready to perform a restore of tables or table partitions using RMAN. First, though, take a look at some of the restrictions related to restoring and recovering database tables and table partitions.

Restrictions on Restoring and Recovering Database Tables and Partitions

As always, there are a few restrictions that you need to be aware of. First, you cannot restore tables that belong to the SYS schema. Also, you can't restore tables that are stored in the SYSTEM and SYSAUX tablespaces, and you can't restore tables and table partitions in standby databases.

Also, Oracle provides a **remap** option for the **recover table** command (discussed in the next section) that allows you to restore tables to a different name. If the table has a NOT NULL constraint, you can't use the **remap** option.

Options to Consider When Restoring Tables and Partitions

When you're recovering tables and table partitions, there are a number of options that you might want to take advantage of. The following table provides a list of these parameters and describes the purpose of each.

Parameter Name	Purpose
AUXILIARY DESTINATION	The location that the **recover** command will use to create the auxiliary instance–related files. By default, the files are created in the directory $ORACLE_HOME/dbs.
DUMP FILE	The name of the Data Pump export file.
DATAPUMP DESTINATION	The location where the Data Pump export file should be created.
NOTABLEIMPORT	Indicates that the export file should be created but that the contents should not be imported into the target database. This is helpful if you want to complete the restore into another schema or another database.
REMAP TABLE	Provides the ability to rename the table in the target database when it's created.
REMAP TABLESPACE	Provides the ability to create the tables in a different tablespace of the target database.

How RMAN Implements the
Restore and Recovery of Tables and Partitions

The process of restoring individual tables and partitions with RMAN is started with the execution of the RMAN **restore** command. RMAN first creates an auxiliary database and then restores to that database all the tablespaces that it needs from the physical backups that were previously taken. RMAN restores only the SYSTEM, SYSAUX, UNDO, and the tablespaces that contain the specific objects that are being restored. RMAN does not restore other tablespaces and associated datafiles.

After RMAN restores the auxiliary database, it rolls that database forward to the point in time that you indicated in the **restore** command. RMAN then creates an Oracle Data Pump export of the objects to be restored. After it has created that export, RMAN will then, optionally, import the objects into the target database. You can instruct RMAN to not import the objects into the target database, leaving this task to complete yourself. RMAN will clean up the auxiliary database once the operation is completed.

Now that you know the gory details, let's look at an example next.

Using RMAN to Restore and Recover a Database Table: An Example

This example uses a database called ORCL, which includes a schema named SCOTT. This example assumes that an RMAN backup of that database exists, and that all of the database's archived redo logs are either backed up by RMAN or available on disk. You are going to restore the tables owned by the SCOTT schema by using the RMAN **restore file** command, after making some changes to those tables. First, take a look at the current time before any changes were made:

```
SQL> alter session set nls_date_format='mm/dd/yyyy hh24:mi:ss';

Session altered.
SQL> select sysdate, current_scn from v$database;

SYSDATE              CURRENT_SCN
------------------   -----------
09/08/2013 19:15:09    2074999
```

The SCOTT schema has four tables, as shown in this query:

```
SQL> select table_name from dba_tables where owner='SCOTT';
TABLE_NAME
-----------------------------------------------------------------------
DEPT
EMP
BONUS
SALGRADE
```

The row counts in the table are shown here:

```
SQL> select count(*) from DEPT;
  COUNT(*)
----------
         4

SQL> select count(*) from EMP;
  COUNT(*)
----------
        14

SQL> select count(*) from BONUS;
  COUNT(*)
----------
         0

SQL> select count(*) from SALGRADE;
  COUNT(*)
----------
         5
```

For the purposes of this example, assume that something terribly bad happened when developers were testing. Instead of deleting individual rows, the new bulk update application, lacking an appropriate **where** clause in the **delete** statement, managed to remove all the records in all the tables instead of removing unique ones. After the run of the application, this is what the row counts looked like:

```
SQL> select count(*) from DEPT;
  COUNT(*)
----------
         0
SQL> select count(*) from EMP;
  COUNT(*)
----------
         0
SQL> select count(*) from BONUS;
  COUNT(*)
----------
         0
SQL> select count(*) from SALGRADE;
  COUNT(*)
----------
         0
```

It's a shame, but the developers also forgot to do an export of their test schema before the test. It's not a good day for the developers: not only did they lose their data, but they also know that the whole database will probably have to be restored instead of just the SCOTT schema (and lots of good and important data exists in the other schemas).

The developers call you, their brilliant DBA, and ask how they can get their data restored. Fortunately for you, the database is running Oracle Database 12c. You tell them to hang tight and you will take care of the problem for them. After asking them what time they started their testing, you tell them you will restore SCOTT to the second before testing, and that you'll get back to them when you are done. One important bit of information that the developers were able to give you is the specific point in time that you need to recover the table objects to. Assume that it's the same time and date that the query against V$DATABASE provided earlier in this section.

Sitting down at your laptop, you set your Oracle environment for the correct database and you start RMAN. Next, you use the RMAN **recover** command to recover the tables in the SCOTT schema. Knowing that you can't recover a specific schema, but only the tables in it, you specify in your **recover** command the schema and table names of the tables you need to restore.

NOTE
Recovery of any object with RMAN implies that you have completed a successful backup of the tablespace the object is in, and have all of the archived redo logs and online redo logs generated since the beginning of that backup.

Before you start the restore, you need to decide where you want the auxiliary database–related files to be stored. For this example, assume you have chosen to use the directory /u01/app/oracle/aux. So, you first make sure the directory exists.

Additionally, you will want to decide if you want to use the same object names as before, or if you want to remap the newly restored objects to different names. Once you decide these things, you log into RMAN and enter the following:

```
recover table scott.emp, scott.dept, scott.bonus, scott.salgrade
until time "to_date('09/08/2013 19:15:09','mm/dd/yyyy hh24:mi:ss')"
auxiliary destination '/u01/app/oracle/aux'
remap table scott.emp:rest_emp, scott.dept:rest_dept,
scott.bonus:rest_bonus, scott.salgrade:rest_salgrade;
```

Once you press ENTER, RMAN will start the restore. The output of the restore is quite lengthy, so we've decided not to waste trees by printing it here. In summary, you will see the following in the output:

- Allocation of channels
- Creation of the auxiliary instance
- Restore of the control file for the auxiliary instance

- A list of datafiles that will be restored, followed by their restore and recovery in the auxiliary instance

- Export of tables from the auxiliary instance via Oracle Data Pump

- Import of tables, constraints, indexes, and other dependent objects into the target database from the Data Pump export file

- Clean-up of the auxiliary instance

NOTE
If the tables you are trying to move are already in the schema, you will get an error. You need to rename or drop those tables before you restore them via RMAN. You can also use the RMAN REMAP parameter to recover the table to a different schema and/or table name.

Miscellaneous RMAN New Features

We have covered most of the significant RMAN new features thus far in this chapter, but there are several other RMAN new features that also deserve mention:

- Support for container databases and pluggable databases

- The SYSBACKUP privilege

- Storage snapshot optimization

- SQL commands from the RMAN prompt

- Duplicate database enhancements

Support for Container Databases and Pluggable Databases

Chapter 3 describes Oracle's Multitenant architecture including Container Databases (CDBs) and Pluggable Databases (PDBs) in detail. As noted in Chapter 2, in Oracle Database 12c, the Oracle RMAN backup and recovery utility fully supports the backup and restore/recovery of both CDBs and PDBs. Refer to Chapter 2 for complete information on new RMAN features with respect to CDBs and PDBs in Oracle Database 12c.

The SYSBACKUP Privilege

As in prior versions of Oracle Database, in Oracle Database 12c, RMAN by default logs into the database automatically using the SYSDBA privilege. SYSDBA has a number of high-level privileges, including **select any table**, so it's a good idea to limit access to this privilege and the number of people who are granted access to it.

To make limiting access to SYSDBA easier, Oracle Database 12c provides a new access privilege called SYSBACKUP that is specifically designed for logins that need to have the ability to back up the database.

To grant SYSBACKUP privileges, use the **grant** command:

```
grant sysbackup to scott;
```

Now, the SCOTT user can start RMAN using the SYSBACKUP privileges, as shown here:

```
rman target=\'scott/robert as sysbackup\'
```

If you wish to connect to the target database from the RMAN prompt, you would issue the following command:

```
RMAN> connect target "scott as sysbackup"
```

NOTE
You must use a password file in order to use the SYSBACKUP privileges.

Storage Snapshot Optimization

In Oracle Database 12c, if you are using storage snapshots to back up your database, you no longer need to put the database tablespaces in hot backup mode. You can simply execute the snapshot snap. For this to work, the vendor of the snapshot technology must guarantee that its technology meets the following requirements:

- The database is crash consistent during the snapshot.

- The snapshot preserves write order for each file.

- The snapshot technology stores the time at which the snapshot is completed.

If the vendor can guarantee these requirements, then you can perform your database storage snapshots without putting the database in hot backup mode.

NOTE
You should carefully test and validate any changes to your backup and recovery processes, even if your storage software vendor says it supports Oracle's new storage snapshot optimization technologies.

To restore the database using a restored snapshot backup, you can use either RMAN or SQL*Plus. A new **recover database** command parameter called **snapshot time** has been added to both the RMAN and SQL*Plus. When issuing the **recover**

database command with the **snapshot time** parameter, you indicate the time at which the snapshot was taken.

When issuing the **snapshot time** parameter, it is recommended that you add a few seconds to the actual snapshot time value, to account for any discrepancies. You don't want to make the snapshot time any earlier than the time that you created the snapshot, but it's okay if your setting for snapshot time is later than that of the snapshot. So, always err on the side of caution and make the snapshot time a little later than the actual time of the snapshot. Also, do your best to keep the database server time and the backup software media server time synchronized.

So, if your snapshot was taken at 9/1/2013 at 14:00 hours, you would want to issue the **recover database** command including the **snapshot time** parameter with a setting of 5/1/2013 at a time of 14:30 or so. The command would look like this:

```
RECOVER DATABASE UNTIL TIME '9/1/2013 14:00:00'
SNAPSHOT TIME '9/1/2013 14:00:30';
```

SQL Commands from the RMAN Prompt

In Oracle Database 12c, most SQL commands issued at the RMAN prompt no longer need to be prefixed with the SQL command, nor do they need to be enclosed in quotes. For example, now you can issue this command directly from the RMAN prompt:

```
RMAN> select name from v$database;
NAME
---------
ORCL
```

Also, RMAN now supports the SQL*Plus **describe** (or **desc**) command, as shown here:

```
RMAN> desc v$tablespace
 Name                               Null?    Type
 ---------------------------------- -------- -------------------
 TS#                                         NUMBER
 NAME                                        VARCHAR2(30)
 INCLUDED_IN_DATABASE_BACKUP                 VARCHAR2(3)
 BIGFILE                                     VARCHAR2(3)
 FLASHBACK_ON                                VARCHAR2(3)
 ENCRYPT_IN_BACKUP                           VARCHAR2(3)
 CON_ID                                      NUMBER
```

Duplicate Database Enhancements

A new clause, **noopen**, is available in Oracle Database 12c to let you indicate that the duplicated database should not be opened using **resetlogs** after the database duplication is complete. This clause can be useful if you want to change specific parameters in the duplicated database parameter file before it's opened, or if you want to make sure that certain services and jobs are adjusted before you open the database.

Oracle Data Guard New Features

Oracle Data Guard in Oracle Database 12c has a number of new features associated with it, including:

- The SYSDG privilege

- The Far Sync instance

- Cascaded redo transport destinations

- Fast-sync mode

- Other new standby database and Data Guard features

The SYSDG Privilege

Oracle Database 12c introduces the new SYSDG privilege, which is used to handle Oracle Data Guard administrative duties. This privilege provides only the minimum privilege level required to administer the Data Guard standby database. You can still administer the Data Guard standby database with the SYSDBA privilege.

The Far Sync Instance

A new option called the Far Sync instance is available in Oracle Database 12c. The purpose of the Far Sync instance is to facilitate the processing of redo between a primary database and one or more standby databases that are far away. The main purpose of the Far Sync instance is to reduce the network latency between the primary and the standby instances. Network latency increases the farther apart the primary and the standby instances are. Latency makes it more difficult to use Data Guard options that provide for zero data loss failover, because of the synchronous nature of these options.

When enabled, the Far Sync instance will collect the redo generated from the primary database. The Far Sync instance will acknowledge the receipt of that redo, which allows the primary instance to continue processing while the Far Sync instance ensures that the redo will be delivered to the standby database(s) as required.

The Far Sync instance requires that you possess a license for the Oracle Active Data Guard option.

Cascaded Redo Transport Destinations

Cascading redo enables a standby database to forward (or cascade) redo information to other standby databases. In doing so, the primary database that initially generated the redo forwards the redo to a standby database, as it normally would. In Oracle Database 12c, the standby database can then ship the redo either in real time or in non-real time, depending on the latency requirements and the network bandwidth that is available. In Oracle Database 12c, you can cascade in real time to all destinations, and you can only cascade to up to ten destinations in non-real time. You need a license for Oracle Active Data Guard to use real-time cascading.

Fast-Sync Mode

A new mode of operation called fast-sync mode is available in Oracle Database 12*c*. This mode allows you to combine the **sync** and **noaffirm** (as opposed to **sync** and **affirm**) attributes. This provides for reduced latency for synchronous processing of the redo stream between the primary database and the standby database, thus allowing for operations between the primary database and the standby database at a farther distance.

The main difference between when you are using fast-sync mode is that when **noaffirm** is configured, the primary database will wait for an acknowledgement that the redo has been received by the standby database. It will not, however, wait for an acknowledgement that the redo has actually been written to disk, which does occur when you have instead configured the **affirm** attribute. Note that using the **noaffirm** option does present a slight risk of data loss (for example, if there is a major disk subsystem failure on the standby system), but this risk can be mitigated by enabling normal hardware redundancy measures such as disk mirroring, multiple disk controllers, and disk multipathing.

Other New Standby Database and Data Guard Features

There are a number of other new features and changes you will want to investigate in Oracle Data Guard, including the following:

- The use of the **using current logfile** clause is no longer needed to start real-time apply.

- You can create a physical or logical standby database based on a container database.

- DML operations are now allowed on standby databases that are configured for Oracle Active Data Guard.

- You can now use sequences in a database using Oracle Active Data Guard.

- When performing a switchover from an Oracle RAC primary database to an Oracle Data Guard physical standby database, you no longer need to shut down all but one primary database instance.

- New SQL commands are available for switchover and failover operations to a physical standby database:

    - `alter database switchover to ... verify`

    - `alter database switchover to ... force`

- The Extended Datatype Support (EDS) feature enables the SQL Apply process to replicate changes made to tables that contain data types that are not natively supported by the Oracle database.

- A local standby database can accept archived redo logs while a rolling upgrade is taking place.

- If you are running Oracle Active Data Guard, a new automated rolling upgrade feature is available in Oracle Database 12c. This feature automates the processes that are used to perform rolling upgrades of the database and planned maintenance.

- Oracle SQL Apply now supports many new data types, including:

    - XMLType

    - Oracle Spatial

    - Oracle Multimedia

    - Oracle Text

    - Objects and collections (including VARRAYs and nested tables)

    - DBFS

    - XDB

    - De-duplication of Oracle SecureFiles

    - User-defined types

End of Line

As you have seen, there are some great new backup and recovery features in Oracle Database 12c. The ability to easily restore a file from an RMAN backup is just great, and the ability to move an entire Oracle Database across almost any platform without respect to byte format is terrific. The new Oracle Data Pump features also bring terrific new functionality to that product.

Now we move on to Chapter 6, in which we present you with new SQL and PL/SQL features to be found in Oracle Database 12c.

CHAPTER
6

Oracle Database 12c SQL
and PL/SQL New Features

S tarting with *Oracle9i New Features* more than a decade ago, this is the fourth book in the Oracle Database New Features series that I've authored (either on my own or with contributors). When I write these books, I always enjoy writing certain chapters more than others. I usually look forward to the backup and recovery new features chapter (largely given that I'm the "RMAN guy" for Oracle Press). I also usually look forward to writing the SQL and PL/SQL new features chapter, because it's in those new features that I often find things that are exciting and fun! Oracle Database 12*c* is no exception.

In this chapter you will find information on the following topics:

- Oracle Database 12*c* DML features

- Oracle Database 12*c* DDL features

- Oracle Database 12*c* PL/SQL features

There is a lot to cover here, so let's get started!

Oracle Database 12*c* DML New Features

Oracle Database 12*c* adds a lot of new features to DML. These include the following:

- Row pattern matching

- Enhancements to the Oracle native left outer join syntax

- Top-n Query new features

- Concurrent execution of union and union all branches

Let's take a look at each of these in some more detail.

Row Pattern Matching

Sometimes, you may want to search data in a table to see if a particular pattern exists in that data. For example, you might want to look at patterns of dollar sales for a particular department to see when that department sells the most parts, and when it sells the least. Note that this kind of pattern matching is different from that which occurs with matching clauses such as the **like** clause. The **like** clause looks for a pattern match within a single column of a single row. In this case, we are looking for pattern matches within a single column but across more than one row.

Now, this kind of pattern matching is pretty uncommon, and you might not have had a reason to do it. But just because something is uncommon does not mean it's

> **Tom Says**
>
> To me, this is the number one enhancement to SQL in Oracle Database 12*c*! It is almost like when analytic windowing functions were introduced in Oracle8*i*. Prior to analytic functions, a **where** clause was limited to looking left and right in a row. With the introduction of analytic functions, we could look left and right in a row and look "up and down" in a result set. Among dozens of other analytic functions, functions like LAG and LEAD let us look backward and forward in a set of rows. The new **match recognize** clause introduced in this section takes this one step further, allowing us to look for regular expressions in a partitioned, ordered set of data.

not useful! Very often we find great uses for new features once we figure out what they are useful for. Consider aggregate functions, for example. At first, I wasn't sure why they were supposed to be a big deal, but after I actually looked at the things and started to actually use them, I discovered this feature is really one of the slickest new features in Oracle Database 12*c*.

Keeping that in mind, Oracle Database 12*c* offers the ability to do pattern matching of columns across a set of rows using the new **pattern_matching_clause** clause (yes, that sounds redundant). Pattern matching provides the ability to recognize patterns in a sequence of rows in a projection called the *row pattern input table*. This can be helpful in finding outliers in trend analysis, for example. It can also be helpful in actually identifying patterns within large data sets that might otherwise be missed just because of the sheer volume of data. This feature is also useful in quality control processing, where you might be looking for true anomalies in the processing data.

Another place where such analysis is handy is in market analysis, such as a stock market. There are often patterns in markets, such as the "double dip," that identify possible trends and can provide classic buy or sell signals. Complex analytic packages can often pick up these kinds of trends now, but the ability to do row pattern matching will simplify this process quite a bit.

Oracle didn't just decide to add this feature to the database without applying any standards to it. Row pattern matching in Oracle Database 12*c* is fully compliant with the SQL/RPR:2012 standard.

In this section, we look at row pattern matching in a bit more detail. First, we establish what patterns are exactly. Then we look at an example of the pattern matching features present in Oracle Database 12*c*, with some sample code that reveals the pattern we are looking for. Then we take that code and break it into smaller pieces so that you can understand what's actually going on, step by step. Finally, I provide you with some parting words on pattern matching. Let's get moving!

What Are Patterns?

No doubt you have some familiarity with patterns. Patterns are all around us. We use patterns in IT a lot, with respect to processes, procedures, and standards. We use patterns when we build code, when we design databases, and when we build systems. Data has patterns as well, and often we look to those patterns to identify trends, identify outlier conditions, and perform other kinds of analysis.

As an example, let's look at a simple set of patterns that we are all familiar with: dates and their association with months. First, to cover the basic concepts, we are going to explore this example without any SQL. Then, we will add some SQL to the conversation to examine how pattern matching works.

For our example, let's assume that we have a table with three columns: YEAR, MONTH, and DAY. The MONTH column contains the shorthand name of the month. (I know, I know, you're probably asking why I'm not using a timestamp or date data type...work with me here for the sake of an example.) The YEAR and DAY columns are numeric representations of the year and day. So, for January 1, 2013, our data would look like 2013, JAN, 1 and would repeat until the end of January, which would look like 2013, JAN, 31.

In our example we want to look for a pattern in this data that will tell us what year is a leap year. As such, our pattern will span several years' worth of data until the pattern is found. Now, what pattern could we identify to indicate that a given year is a leap year? Of course, we look for a month of February with 29 days in it. The year associated with that data is the pattern we are looking for. Usually, we will find that pattern once in every four years' worth of data.

When we execute our query we will define the pattern. The first thing we will do is define a *partition*. The partition we define is a logical construct that tells the query how to group the data (it's kind of like a **group by** clause). If you have used SQL analytical functions, you have used partitioning. If you have not, don't worry, you will catch up here.

In our example, we are going to logically *partition* our data by YEAR and MONTH. This defines the logical search structure that we want to look for in our pattern searches. As a result, our searches occur individually within each partition. Each partition will translate into one output row that will be processed by the remainder of the query.

Here is an example. Suppose we have a table with 365 days in it, all with the year 2013. The result is a table with 365 rows in it, one row for every day in 2013. Now, assume that in our query we partition by YEAR and MONTH. We end up with 12 partitions. Table 6-1 provides a look at what this partition would look like.

Along with defining our partitions, we want to define how those partitions are ordered. In this case, they are ordered by YEAR, MONTH, and DATE. This will serve to order the output of the partitions. In our case, we are ordering on the partition key, and then adding the date to the sort order.

YEAR	MONTH	DAY
2013	JAN	31
2013	FEB	28
2013	MAR	31
2013	APR	30
2013	MAY	31
2013	JUN	30
2013	JUL	31
2013	AUG	31
2013	SEP	30
2013	OCT	31
2013	NOV	30
2013	DEC	31

TABLE 6-1. *Partitioned 2013 Data*

Within each partition (or the whole set of data), patterns will repeat. For example, if you had a table with each day of the month, you would see several repeating patterns: one with 28 days (for February), an occasional pattern of 29 days (leap years), patterns for 30 days, and patterns for 31 days. So now, we have defined our partitions and ordered them. Our query will then search the partitions for those with 29 days in them. We have then identified the pattern for leap year (any month with 29 days in it) and our query will display that year.

Now that we have defined what we are looking for and in general how we are going to go about finding it, let's craft a SQL statement to get to the results we want.

Row Pattern Matching: An Example

Row pattern matching is not for the faint of heart at first. We will spend several pages really digging into it, and I hope by the time we are done you will have a good start on understanding this new feature. First, let's set up the example that we are going to use. It's a pretty simple example, but I've always found that it's best to start learning with the easy stuff, and then build on that over time. After we have set up the example, we will discuss the pattern we are looking for in a bit more detail. I will also show you the SQL that we will be using to do the pattern matching and demonstrate its output. Finally, we will break down the SQL into smaller atomic units and discuss what these units of SQL code are doing.

Setting Up Our Example   For our example, we need to create a table with a lot of data in it, so let's start by creating the table:

```
create table calendar_MYD
( YEAR            CHAR(4),
  MONTH           CHAR(3),
  DAY             NUMBER);
```

Now, we need to populate the table with some data. We will populate it with ten years' worth of data so that we have a leap year (or two) in there somewhere. Here is the PL/SQL we will use to populate the table:

```
truncate table calendar_myd;
declare
        v_start_year        date;
        v_proc_year         date;
        v_end_year          date;
        v_stop              char(1):=NULL;
begin
        v_start_year:=to_date('01/01/2010','mm/dd/yyyy');
        v_proc_year:=v_start_year;
        v_end_year:=to_date('01/01/2020','mm/dd/yyyy');
        while v_stop is NULL
        loop
            insert into calendar_MYD values(
                to_char(v_proc_year, 'yyyy'),
                to_char(v_proc_year, 'mon'),
                to_char(v_proc_year, 'dd') );
            commit;
            v_proc_year:=v_proc_year+1;
            if v_proc_year=v_end_year
            then
                v_stop:='Y';
            end if;
        end loop;
end;
/
```

Now that we have our table, let's look at the SQL that we will use to do our pattern matching.

Finding Our Pattern   To find the years that are leap years, we need to find the years where February has 29 days in it. This is a pretty simple pattern, and since we have ten years' worth of dates in the table, the pattern should repeat twice if we do our work right. Here is the SQL that I crafted to find this pattern:

```
select year, o_month as month, o_day as day
    from calendar_myd
    match recognize
```

```
( partition by year order by month, day
measures
b.month as o_month,
c.day as o_day
one row per match
after match skip to next row
pattern (b c)
define
    b as b.month='feb',
    c as ( max(c.day)=29)
) MR
order by year, o_month, o_day;
```

And here is the output we would get:

```
P1   P2    P3
---- --- ----------
2012 feb   29
2016 feb   29
```

The preceding SQL might seem complex at first, and to be honest, it is. However, if you think about it, this SQL is the same as

```
select year, month, max(day)
from calendar_myd
where month = 'feb'
group by year, month
having max(day) = 29;
```

That makes it seem a bit simpler! Many pattern matching queries cannot be resolved as easily with SQL or even PL/SQL. I used this simple example not only to make it easier to understand exactly what we are doing but also so that you can relate it to a SQL statement that you already understand. I'll show where you can go to find a number of additional examples of pattern matching shortly. There are many different ways of doing pattern matching, so lots of examples are really handy to have.

Breaking Down the SQL   First we have the **select** list:

```
select year, o_month as month, o_day as day
    from calendar_myd
```

Now, this might look like a normal **select** list to you, but it's really not. The main thing you need to realize right off the bat is that you are *not* selecting columns out of a table. Rather, you are selecting columns that are going to be in the *output stream*, or *row pattern output table*, of this query.

Also note that we are pulling data from a table called CALENDAR_MYD—this is called the *row pattern input table*. The row pattern input table is the source of the data that is being matched. In this case, the row pattern input table is the physical table CALENDAR_MYD. The row pattern output table is going to be the result set that is finally presented to the user. The row pattern output table, then, is the projection of this SQL statement.

Note that we could have used the splat (*) in the SELECT clause. However, in my opinion, listing the column names explicitly is a best practice. It's important to note here (if you have not noticed already) that the YEAR, MONTH, and DAY columns are not the columns in the row pattern input table (or, in other words, the table in the **from** clause). I'll explain why that is in just a second, so don't let it confuse you just yet.

Next we have the **match recognize** clause. This is where things start to get a bit murky, so stick with me. In our example we have the following:

```
match recognize
    ( partition by year order by month, day
    measures
    b.month as o_month,
    c.day as o_day
```

The **partition by** clause defines how the data is logically partitioned. Each partition is processed as a logical unit. In our case, the data will be partitioned by year. We then use the **order by** clause and order the data in each partition by month and day. This is the order that the pattern matching will occur in. The data first will be partitioned by year and then ordered by month and day, and pattern matching will occur in that order. As you can imagine, selecting the right partition and data ordering can impact the **pattern matching** clause significantly.

The **measures** clause defines the relationship between the row pattern input table and the row pattern output table and, therefore, the output that will be returned to the user issuing the query. You will also see that the order of the columns in the **measures** clause is important for more than just display purposes. We will discuss that in more detail in a second, so for now just keep that in mind. For now what you need to understand about this statement is that the MONTH column in the row pattern input table will be associated with a column called O_MONTH. The same applies for the column DAY, which is associated with O_DAY.

Next, we have the **row_pattern_rows_per_match** clause (the part that says **one row per match**) and the **after match skip to next row** option, which is part of the **row_pattern_skip_to** clause.

```
one row per match
after match skip to next row
```

The **one row per match** option does what it says—displays only one row per match. There is another option, **all rows per match**, that displays all matching rows. So, if we replaced the **one row per match** clause with **all rows per match**, the output would look like this:

```
YEAR MON        DAY
---- --- ----------
2012 feb         29
2012 feb
2012 feb
2016 feb         29
2016 feb
2016 feb
```

In this case, each row that matches any of the matching criteria will be displayed. We see the two rows that were presented earlier. Then we see something from the 27th of February. Why would we see that row? Because one of the matching criteria is that the month should be "feb"; since the row meets that criteria, the row is displayed. When we indicate to display **one row per match**, we are indicating that all of the matching criteria need to be met to actually display a row.

Also note the **after match skip to next row** clause. This indicates where the cursor should resume the pattern matching after a match has been found. Other options allow you to move the cursor pointer to various places as required.

Next comes the **pattern** clause, which indicates which pattern variables need to be matched, the sequence in which they need to be matched, and the number of rows that need to be matched for the various pattern variables. That is a fancy way of saying the **pattern** clause is the magic by which the pattern searches are defined. Here is our **pattern** clause:

```
pattern (b c)
define
    b as b.month='feb',
    c as ( max(c.day)=29)
```

Note that after the **pattern** keyword we have (**b c**), which is called the *row pattern*. The values within the row pattern (**b** and **c**) are called *row pattern terms*. The order of the row pattern terms is very important. The pattern terms correlate with each column listed in the **measures** clause that we already discussed. Recall that our **measures** clause looked like this:

```
measures
    b.month as o_month,
    c.day as o_day
```

Recall too that the left side of each row is essentially the input and the right side is the output. Notice that there are three measures, and the pattern clause has three patterns defined (**a**, **b**, and **c**). So, there is a one-to-one correlation between the rows listed in the **measures** clause and each of the row pattern terms. Oracle automatically associates each row pattern term, in order, with the **measures** term, starting at the top of the **measures** term. In other words, row pattern term **a** is associated with the **measures** line **a.year as output_year**. Row pattern term **b** is associated with the

measures line **b.month as output_month**. Finally, row pattern term **c** is associated with the last **measures** line, **c.day as output_day**. This association of the row pattern terms to the lines of the **measures** clause is automatic; you don't need to do anything to make it happen.

Let's look at our **pattern** clause once more:

```
pattern (b c)
define
     b as b.month='feb',
     c as ( max(c.day)=29)
) MR
  order by year, o_month, o_day;
```

The **define** keyword indicates that we are going to define the patterns that we are looking for. The patterns we are searching for are pretty simple, but they give you a good idea of the power of pattern searching.

The first line in the **define** clause is **b as b.month='feb'**. This is the pattern for the **b** row pattern term, and it correlates with the MONTH column up in the **measures** clause and the MONTH column in the source table. This filter takes every row and compares the month to see if it has a value of **'feb'**. If it does, then that row passes the test and will be displayed (subject to other filters that might be in the **define** clause, and to other filtering that might appear in the body of the SQL statement, such as the **one row per match** clause).

The next line in the **define** clause is the filter statement **c as (max(c.day)=29)**. This statement is associated with the **c** row pattern term. It is also correlated, then, with the DAY column that appears in the **measures** clause.

Finally, we need to close out our SQL statement. We give the whole row pattern matching clause an alias **MR** and then we order it by the first column:

```
) MR
order by output_year;
```

Pattern Matching...Only the Beginning

As you can imagine, pattern matching can get very complex. The example we have used is a pretty basic introduction to the use of the **match recognize** clause. I could easily fill several chapters on pattern matching in Oracle SQL. There is a lot of additional functionality that you may find useful. You can find a number of examples in the *Oracle SQL Language Reference*, as well as in the syntax guide. In addition, the *Oracle Database Data Warehouse Guide for Oracle Database 12c* provides a number of different examples for you to borrow from.

This new pattern matching feature can be frustrating at first. When I was writing this book, I had only a few examples to learn from. By the time you are reading this, the Web likely will be full of great examples that will help you to further your understanding and use of this feature.

Enhancements to the Oracle Native Left Outer Join Syntax

I find that the ANSI outer join syntax tends to be harder to work with than the Oracle Database native join syntax (denoted with a (+) in the join of two tables). However, there are times when using the ANSI outer join syntax just ends up being clearer code and, once you get used to the new syntax, it really isn't that difficult.

In the past, there have been some cases where Oracle's outer join syntax could not do the job. For example, if you wanted to join two tables to a null-generated table, the (+) syntax would not support this.

Oracle Database 12c has tried to correct some of the missing pieces of the (+) puzzle by making the native outer join syntax (using the (+) parameter) more versatile.

In previous versions of Oracle Database, if you wanted to join the null-generated table to more than one table using the Oracle native outer join syntax, an Oracle error would occur, as shown here:

```
select count(*)
from emp a, dept b, bonus c
where a.deptno(+)= b.deptno
and a.ename(+)=c.ename;
ERROR at line 3:
ORA-01417: a table may be outer joined to at most one other table
```

Now, in Oracle Database 12c, this kind of query is supported using the Oracle native outer join syntax:

```
select count(*)
from emp a, dept b, bonus c
where a.deptno= b.deptno (+)
and a.ename=c.ename (+);

    COUNT(*)
----------
        14
```

The Oracle Optimizer can take advantage of this new functionality and perform join-reordering operations that will provide for a more efficient SQL statement, and better execution plans.

Top-n Query New Features

When using an application, you may want to return a certain number of rows, starting at a specific point (or offset) in the result set. This might be useful, for example, when paging out results. You might want to get the first ten rows of the result set, then the next ten rows of the result set, and so on. You also might want to return just a percentage of the rows that were queried.

Oracle Database 12*c* offers new syntax that enables you to easily limit the result set to a specific number or percentage of rows. The syntax used is fully ANSI SQL compliant, which is also a positive. The new clause that is used is called **row_limiting_clause**.

One of the things you can do with the **row_limiting** clause is start the resulting output from a query based on a specific row offset. This is done using the **offset n rows** option of the **row_limiting** clause. Here is an example of using the new feature to return the result set starting with row number 8:

```
select count(*) from emp;
  COUNT(*)
----------
        14

select empno, hiredate from emp order by hiredate offset 8 rows;

     EMPNO HIREDATE
---------- ---------
      7839 17-NOV-81
      7900 03-DEC-81
      7902 03-DEC-81
      7934 23-JAN-82
      7788 19-APR-87
      7876 23-MAY-87

6 rows selected.
```

Additionally, you can use the **percent** option of the **row_limiting** clause to fetch a certain percentage of rows:

```
select empno, hiredate from emp
order by hiredate fetch first 25 percent rows only;

     EMPNO HIREDATE
---------- ---------
      7369 17-DEC-80
      7499 20-FEB-81
      7521 22-FEB-81
      7566 02-APR-81
```

Tom Says

I've been looking forward to this clause for a long time. I've written more than one column in *Oracle Magazine* and answered hundreds, if not thousands, of questions on asktom.oracle.com regarding "how to get the first N rows" or "how to paginate through a result set." The new **row limiting** clause makes this so easy now.

Note what happens when we try to fetch the next 25 percent of the rows:

```
select empno, hiredate from emp
order by hiredate fetch next 25 percent rows only;

    EMPNO HIREDATE
---------- ---------
      7369 17-DEC-80
      7499 20-FEB-81
      7521 22-FEB-81
      7566 02-APR-81
```

Did you notice that even when we used the **next 25 percent** keywords we got the same number of rows. That's because, as odd as it sounds, the keywords **first** and **next** are synonymous. If we wanted to fetch the next 25 percent of the rows, we would need to include an offset value as seen here:

```
select empno, hiredate from emp order by hiredate offset 4 rows fetch
next 25 percent rows only;
SQL> select empno, hiredate from emp order by hiredate offset 4 rows
fetch next 25 percent rows only;

    EMPNO HIREDATE
---------- ---------
      7521 22-FEB-81
      7566 02-APR-81
      7698 01-MAY-81
      7782 09-JUN-81
```

Now, suppose two records have the same value and we want both those records to display, but we want them to be considered one record for the purposes of the

Tom Says

You will probably see the same result every time! If you were to scale the EMP table up, loading thousands of records, you might not see the exact same 25 percent every time. The reason: HIREDATE is not unique. If you do not order by something unique, your query is not deterministic using the **row limiting** clause. You could see a different 25 percent each time, depending on how much memory is available for your query at runtime. Next, Robert will introduce the **with ties** syntax as a solution to this.

calculation of the number of rows or percentage of records returned. For example, let's say we issued this query:

```
select ename, sal from emp
order by sal
fetch first 25 percent rows only;

ENAME          SAL
---------- ----------|
SMITH          800
JAMES          950
ADAMS          1100
WARD           1250
```

What might be the problem with this query? Well, let's look at the result of this next query and you might notice the problem:

```
select ename, sal from emp
where sal=1250;

ENAME          SAL
---------- ----------
WARD           1250
MARTIN         1250
```

We have two records with a salary value of 1250, but only one of those records showed up in our 50 percent query. So, what do we do if we want to make sure that all the records that have the same value as the last record actually show up. We replace the **with rows** syntax with the **with ties** syntax, as shown here:

```
select ename, sal from emp
order by sal
fetch first 25 percent rows with ties;

ENAME          SAL
---------- ----------
SMITH          800
JAMES          950
ADAMS          1100
WARD           1250
MARTIN         1250
```

Now we have both records with a SAL amount of 1250 appearing in our row set. That does mean, though, that we are getting slightly more than 25 percent of the rows back.

Concurrent Execution of Union and Union All Branches

If you run SQL statements with a number of **union** and/or **union all** branches, you may find that these statements run even faster now. Oracle can now execute several branches of these statements in parallel, instead of running them in a serial manner. You can enable or disable this feature with new hints: PQ_CONCURENT_UNION and NO_PQ_CONCURENT_UNION.

Oracle Database 12*c* DDL New Features

Now it's time to talk about some of the new DDL features present in Oracle Database 12*c*. Before we get started, I should mention that this section does not cover every DDL new feature. Instead, it covers the DDL features that didn't really fit well into any of the other chapters. For example, Chapter 7 introduces partitioning new features and the DDL associated with those features, Chapter 9 presents online-related DDL, and so on.

So, this section is kind of like the Island of Misfit Toys in *Rudolph the Red-Nosed Reindeer*—it's where the features that really didn't have a home anywhere else came to live. However, just like those toys on the island, these features really do have an important place in the Oracle world, so don't overlook them or you will miss something exciting and important!

In this section we will discuss

- Increased size limits for VARCHAR2, NVARCHAR2, and RAW data types (see, I said that you would miss something important if you skipped this section!)

- Identity columns

- Cascading **truncate** statements

- Invisible columns

- Default values for columns based on sequences

- Default values for columns when NULLs are inserted

- Creating multiple indexes with the same column list (I don't think this feature currently is nearly as cool as it sounds, but it has some promise in the future)

- With (subquery factoring clause) query new features

Wow, that's a lot of miscellaneous stuff! It almost deserves its own chapter, but I packed it all in here for you. Let's have at it!

Increased Size Limits for VARCHAR2, NVARCHAR2, and RAW Data Types

Oracle Database 12c introduces a new feature called *extended data types*, enabling you to now store up to 32,767 bytes in VARCHAR2, NVARCHAR2, and RAW data types. This section introduces you to extended data types, starting with a description of how to enable the use of extended data types. Then we will discuss some of the impacts of using extended data types. Finally, we will talk about some issues with extended data types and indexes in Oracle Database 12c.

Enabling Extended Data Types

After you upgrade to Oracle Database 12c, you enable this new feature by setting the MAX_STRING_SIZE parameter. By default, the value of MAX_STRING_SIZE is set to STANDARD, which continues to limit VARCHAR2, NVARCHAR2, and RAW data types to the limits that were set in Oracle Database 11g Release 2.

NOTE
Setting MAX_STRING_SIZE to EXTENDED will prevent you from rolling back to a previous version of Oracle Database 12c directly.

Setting MAX_STRING_SIZE to a value of EXTENDED will allow you to store up to 32,767 bytes in these different data types. After you set the MAX_STRING_SIZE parameter to EXTENDED, you need to run a script in $ORACLE_HOME/rdbms/admin called utl32k in upgrade mode. After you run this script, you will find that some objects have been invalidated. So, when you make this change, you probably should schedule it at a time when users are not on the system. You will also want to run the ?/rdbms/admin/utlrp.sql script to recompile any objects that might be invalidated.

When MAX_STRING_SIZE is set to EXTENDED, any data stored in a VARCHAR2, NVARCHAR2, or RAW data type that is greater than 4000 bytes in size will be stored in an Oracle LOB. This LOB is allocated internally by Oracle, and you should not try to manipulate the LOBs that are associated with the extended data type columns.

Impacts of the Use of Extended Data Types

Using extended data types has impacts in a number of different areas. When MAX_STRING_SIZE is set to EXTENDED:

- The creation and use of indexes is impacted (as covered in the next section in more detail).

- The limit of the combined length of concatenated character strings is increased.

- The length of the collation key returned by the NLSSORT function is increased.

- The size of some of the attributes of the XMLFormat objects is increased.

- The size of some expressions in some XML functions is adjusted.

Extended Data Types and Indexes

The biggest impacts of the use of extended data types may be on indexes. For example, if you try to create an index on a column that is defined with an extended data type, you might not be able to get that index to create successfully, or worse yet, the index will create successfully but an **insert** or **update** operation will fail. This limitation is based on the maximum key length supported by a B*tree index in Oracle, which is dependent on the database block size. Currently, a database with an 8k block size can have a maximum length index key of around 6400 bytes. So, you might not be able to index the column if you are going to store data in it. Note that this is a function of the size of the data in the column, not the size of the column itself. Oracle provides a few options to work around this:

- Create a function-based index using the **substr** function or the **standard_ hash** function to reduce the size of the column.

- Create a virtual column that restricts the value in the column using **substr** and then create an index on that virtual column.

Because primary key and unique key constraints involve indexes, the restrictions and solutions related to indexes also apply if you are using primary keys or unique key on columns using extended data types. In most cases, the use of a virtual column with the hash value of the data in the column is probably the best solution in these cases. This will require some adjustment of SQL code against these tables, of course.

Identity Columns

I hate surrogate keys. I know they are sometimes the only solution to certain design issues, but I hate them anyway. I just thought that we should be clear on that. So, for those of you who are stuck with surrogate keys, you will be happy to know that Oracle Database 12c provides a new column type called the *identity column*.

About Identity Columns

An identity column is perfectly suited for a database model that uses surrogate keys. An identity column will assign an increasing and decreasing integer value from a sequence generator for each row that is inserted.

By default, Oracle will always create the value in the column from the sequence by using the ALWAYS option. If you try to insert or update a value in the column, an error will be raised. You can optionally indicate that assignment of the sequence number is the default setting for the column, but any **insert** or **update** statement can assign a value to that column instead.

You define the sequence generator using the **identity_options** clause in the **create table** command or **alter table** command. The **identity_options** clause parameters are pretty much the same as those in the **create sequence** command. I'll show you an example in a moment.

Identity Columns and Rules

As you might expect, there are some rules associated with identity columns. There are always rules. Some of the rules to keep in mind are

- You can only have one identity column per table.

- An identity column has to be defined as a **number** data type.

- You cannot have a **default** clause specified for the identity column that you define.

- NOT NULL and NOT DEFERRABLE constraint states are implicitly defined when you create an identity column. Inline constraints that conflict with these constraint states will raise an error.

- Identity columns can be encrypted.

- If you issue a **create table as select** command, the resulting table that is created will not inherit the **identity** property on a column. Instead, the column will simply be a column that is a **number** type.

Creating and Using Identity Columns

Creating identity columns and using them is a pretty easy thing to do. First, here is an example of the creation of an identity column when using the **create table** command:

```
create table robert
(s_key number generated as identity primary key, data varchar2(30));
insert into robert (data) values ('Robert');
commit;
select * from robert;
     S_KEY DATA
---------- ------------------------------
         1 Robert
-- let's add another value
insert into robert (data) values ('Carrie');
select * from robert;
```

```
     S_KEY DATA
---------- ------------------------------
         1 Robert
         2 Carrie
```

Now, let's see what happens when we update a column in the table:

```
update robert set data='Amelia' where s_key=1;
commit;

select * from robert;
     S_KEY DATA
---------- ------------------------------
         1 Amelia
         2 Carrie
```

Now, let's see what happens when we try to insert our own key into the S_KEY column:

```
insert into robert values(3,'Vic');
insert into robert values(3,'Vic')
            *
ERROR at line 1:
ORA-32795: cannot insert into a generated always identity column
```

As you can see, by default we can't enter data into the identity column. However, we can redefine the table in such a way that we can enter data into the identity column, as shown here:

```
alter table robert modify (s_key number generated by default as identity);
insert into robert values (10, 'Bennett');
commit;
insert into robert (data) values ('Lizzie');
select * from robert;

     S_KEY DATA
---------- ------------------------------
         1 Amelia
         2 Carrie
        10 Bennett
         3 Lizzie
```

By modifying the column, we can now insert or update the key data either by choosing to use the sequence by default or by defining our own key value. Note that we didn't define the column as unique or as a primary key.

An interesting problem can arise if you define the column as a primary key or a unique key but do not enforce the use of the sequence when inserting or updating data: an insert might fail. A word of caution. It is possible that if you both use a sequence to assign the number sometimes and sometimes you manually insert a value not using the sequence that you can have a uniqueness conflict. It could be that if you manually insert a value into the table, and then later on you insert a value using the sequence, that a duplicate value might exist that will cause an error.

Cascading Truncate Statements

In prior versions of Oracle Database, you could not truncate a table with foreign key constraints to other tables. Now, in Oracle Database 12c, you can issue a **truncate table** statement that cascades down to the child tables of the parent table being truncated. To indicate that you want the truncate to cascade through the child records, you issue the **truncate table** command with the **cascade** command. One requirement is that you have to create the foreign key using the **on delete cascade** option.

Here is an example where we create two tables, define the foreign key relationship, and then truncate the tables with the **cascade** option:

```
drop table child;
drop table parent;
create table parent(id number primary key);
create table child(cid number primary key, pid number);
alter table child add constraint fk_parent_child
foreign key (pid)
references parent(id) on delete cascade;
insert into parent values (1);
insert into parent values (2);
insert into child values (1,1);
insert into child values (2,1);
insert into child values (3,2);
commit;

select a.id, b.cid, b.pid
from parent a, child b
where a.id=b.pid;
        ID        CID        PID
---------- ---------- ----------
         1          1          1
         1          2          1
         2          3          2

Truncate table parent cascade;

select a.id, b.cid, b.pid
from parent a, child b
where a.id=b.pid;

no rows selected
select count(*) from parent;
```

```
  COUNT(*)
----------
         0
select count(*) from child;
  COUNT(*)
----------
         0
```

In this example, we created the tables PARENT and CHILD, established the foreign key relationship, and loaded data. Then, we queried the table to make sure our data is in there. We then truncated the table using the **cascade** command. Finally, we executed the same query again and confirmed that the data in both the PARENT and CHILD tables has been removed.

Invisible Columns

Oracle Database 12c introduces the notion of invisible columns. When a column is made invisible, statements that do not directly call that column (called generic statements) will not see that column. Examples of the kinds of operations that would not see a column set to invisible include the following:

- A statement with a wildcard character, such as **select * from employee**

- The SQL*Plus **desc** command

- A PL/SQL **%rowtype** declaration

- An **insert into select *** statement

Any SQL statement that explicitly references the column will still be able to see and manipulate the column. Invisible columns can be used as the partition key or as part of an index and you can make regular and virtual columns invisible.

Columns can be made invisible when using the **create table**, **create view**, **alter view**, and **alter table** commands. Here is an example of creating a table with an invisible column:

```
drop table hasinvisiblecolumn;
create table hasinvisiblecolumn (id number, goodbye_column number invisible);
desc hasinvisiblecolumn
 Name                                      Null?    Type
 ----------------------------------------- -------- -------------------------
 ID                        NUMBER
```

Let's use the **alter table** command to make an existing visible column invisible:

```
drop table needsinvisiblecolumn ;

create table needsinvisiblecolumn
(id number, goodbye_column number);
```

```
desc needsinvisiblecolumn
SQL>  Name                                          Null?     Type
     ----------------------------------------- -------- -----------------
  ID                                                      NUMBER
  GOODBYE_COLUMN                                          NUMBER
alter table needsinvisiblecolumn modify (goodbye_column invisible);

desc needsinvisiblecolumn
 Name                                          Null?     Type
     ----------------------------------------- -------- -----------------
  ID                                                      NUMBER
```

Next, let's use the data dictionary to find all tables with invisible columns. In this case we will use the HIDDEN_COLUMN column of the DBA_TAB_COLS view to find tables with columns that are hidden. Then, we will use the **alter table** command to make a column visible.

```
column owner format a30
column table_name format a30
column owner format a20
column table_name format a20
column column_name format a20
select owner, table_name, column_name, hidden_column
from dba_tab_cols
where hidden_column='YES'
and owner='SCOTT';

OWNER                    TABLE_NAME           COLUMN_NAME           HID
------------------- -------------------- -------------------- ---
SCOTT                    HASINVISIBLECOLUMN   GOODBYE_COLUMN        YES
SCOTT                    NEEDSINVISIBLECOLUMN GOODBYE_COLUMN        YES

alter table hasinvisiblecolumn modify (goodbye_column visible);

select owner, table_name, column_name, hidden_column
from dba_tab_cols
where hidden_column='YES'
and owner='SCOTT';

OWNER                    TABLE_NAME           COLUMN_NAME           HID
------------------- -------------------- -------------------- ---
 SCOTT                    NEEDSINVISIBLECOLUMN GOODBYE_COLUMN        YES
```

NOTE
Making a column invisible will change the column order in the table.

Tom Says

The implication of changing the column order by making a column invisible can be profound. If you've ever wanted to add a column to the middle of a table so that it shows up in the middle of a **describe** or **select ***, you can. You would just add the column (it'll go to the bottom) and then make all of the columns that should come after it invisible (the new column will be the last column still). As you make visible the columns you just hid, the new column will retain its ordinal position in the table and the newly visible columns will follow it!

Default Values for Columns Based on Oracle Sequences

Oracle Database 12c allows you to define a sequence and then declare that sequence as the default expression for a given column. You can then use the sequence pseudocolumns CURRVAL and NEXTVAL in the default clause of that column. This is different from an identity column in these ways:

- There are no restrictions on how many columns can be defined.

- The sequence must be manually created before the column default is defined.

- If the sequence is dropped, errors will be raised with any subsequent **insert** operation.

- The owner of the table, and any user of the column that is assigned the default value, must have **select** privilege on the sequence.

- The column that the sequence is built on can always have a value inserted into it, in which case the sequence will not be used. The same rule applies to updates of that column as well.

Following is an example of the creation of a table that uses a sequence in the default clause. First we create the sequence, then we create the table that uses the sequence, and then we insert data into the table.

```
drop sequence test_seq;
create sequence test_seq start with 1;
drop table sequence_test_tab;
create table sequence_test_tab(id number default test_seq.nextval);
insert into sequence_test_tab values (null);
insert into sequence_test_tab values (default);
```

```
insert into sequence_test_tab values (default);
insert into sequence_test_tab values (10000);
commit;
select nvl(id, 0) as ID from sequence_test_tab;
      ID
----------
       0
       1
       2
   10000
alter table sequence_test_tab add (col_2 number);
insert into sequence_test_tab (col_2) values (20);
select * from sequence_test_tab;
        ID       COL_2
---------- ----------
         1
         2
     10000
         3          20
```

As you can see, if we insert NULL values (converted to a value of 0 in our query so you can easily see the NULL), then the sequence is not used (recall it starts with a value of 1). If we insert into the table using the **default** clause, then the sequence is used. Also note that we can insert a literal value into the column as well and the sequence is not used. Finally, we added a new column, and we inserted a value only into that column. We used the default sequence NEXTVAL in that case.

Note that, as with identity columns, you can run into uniqueness problems here if the column is a primary key or a unique key. So, you want to be careful about your database model and your application design.

> **NOTE**
> *If I were designing a database and had to use surrogate keys, I'd use an identity column configured as a primary key or a unique key by using the **generated as identity primary key** clause when creating the table.*

Tom Says
I agree with Robert on this—use the identity type in the future for tables with surrogates. And consider going back to your existing applications and default the existing primary key to the sequence you have been using, and DROP any and all triggers that exist solely to populate this value. Any feature that can help us get rid of triggers is a good feature!

Default Values for Columns on Explicit NULL Insertion

Some people just do not like NULL values. Personally, I think they are great, and *not* using them can sometimes really mess up some of the Optimizer statistics (but that's for another book…or a visit to http://asktom.oracle.com). If you don't want NULL values in your database for some reason, you can create tables that will assign default values to columns when an attempt is made to insert or update that column with a NULL value. Here is an example where we have a table:

```
drop table sales_information;
create table sales_information (
store_id number,
sales_date date default on null to_date('12/31/2099', 'mm/dd/yyyy') not null,
sale_number number,
product_id number,
quantity number default on null 0 not null,
constraint pk_sales_information primary key (product_id, sales_date, sale_number) );
```

In this case, we have indicated that two columns, SALES_DATE and QUANTITY, should take on default values if the user or application tries to make them NULL. SALES_DATE will take on a default date of 12/31/2099, and QUANTITY will take on a value of 0. We can see the results when we issue this **insert** and the subsequent query:

```
insert into sales_information values (1,NULL, 01,12345, NULL);
select * from sales_information;

  STORE_ID SALES_DAT SALE_NUMBER PRODUCT_ID   QUANTITY
---------- --------- ----------- ---------- ----------
         1 31-DEC-99           1      12345          0
```

Finally, a new column in the *_TAB_COLUMNS views called DEFAULT_ON_NULL provides information on whether a NULL default is assigned to the column, as shown in this query:

```
select table_name, column_name, default_on_null
from user_tab_columns
where table_name='SALES_INFORMATION';

TABLE_NAME                       COLUMN_NAME                     DEF
-------------------------------- ------------------------------- ---
SALES_INFORMATION                QUANTITY                        YES
SALES_INFORMATION                PRODUCT_ID                      NO
SALES_INFORMATION                SALE_NUMBER                     NO
SALES_INFORMATION                SALES_DATE                      YES
SALES_INFORMATION                STORE_ID                        NO
```

Sequence-Related New Features

If you use Global Temporary Tables (GTTs) and sequences, you may have on occasion come across a design issue. This is because the scope of the GTT is aligned with a session (or a transaction in a session) while the scope of a sequence is global across the database—at least, it was until Oracle Database 12c. Now, in Oracle Database 12c, you can create a sequence in which the scope of the values allocated for that sequence is only for a given session.

Let's look at an example where we define a sequence as a session-level sequence so that we can see how that impacts the use of a sequence (to conserve space, I've removed some lines of feedback that aren't required to demonstrate this new feature):

```
--First, create the GTT:
connect scott/robert
drop table gtt;
create global temporary table gtt (id number, seq_number number);
grant all on gtt to tiger;
drop sequence seq_session;
create sequence seq_session start with 1 session;
grant all on seq_session to tiger;
insert into gtt values (1, seq_session.nextval);
insert into gtt values (2, seq_session.nextval);
 select * from scott.gtt;
        ID    SEQ_NUMBER
---------- ----------
         1          1
         2          2
commit;
select * from scott.gtt;
no rows selected
insert into gtt values (1, seq_session.nextval);
insert into gtt values (2, seq_session.nextval);
select * from scott.gtt;
        ID SEQ_NUMBER
---------- ----------
         1          1
         2          2
connect tiger/robert
-- This account needs connect, create synonym privileges.
drop synonym gtt;
drop synonym seq_session;
create synonym gtt for scott.gtt;
create synonym seq_session for scott.seq_session;
select * from gtt;
no rows selected
insert into gtt values (1, seq_session.nextval);
insert into gtt values (2, seq_session.nextval);
```

```
select * from gtt;
        ID SEQ_NUMBER
---------- ----------
         1          1
         2          2
commit;
select * from gtt;
no rows selected

connect scott/robert
insert into gtt values (1, seq_session.nextval);
insert into gtt values (2, seq_session.nextval);
select * from scott.gtt;

        ID SEQ_NUMBER
---------- ----------
         1          1
         2          2
commit;
select * from scott.gtt;
no rows selected
```

Did you see what happened? When the GTT is cleared in a given session (via a **commit**), the sequence does not get reset. Instead, the next input into the GTT will use the next value of the sequence. Once the session ends (in our case by a **connect** command), the sequence gets reset to the value that was defined in the sequence's **start with** parameter.

Also, sequences in Oracle Database 12c have the **keep** and **nokeep** clauses added. These clauses control whether the NEXTVAL pseudocolumn returns the same value during Oracle Replay.

Creating Multiple Indexes on the Same Column Set

With Oracle Database 12c, you can create multiple indexes on the same column list, though the index types have to be different. For example, suppose you have a table called EMP and you have a B*tree index on columns HIRE_DATE and RETIRED_STATUS. You can create both the B*tree index and, say, a bitmap index as shown in this example:

```
drop table emp_tab;
create table emp_tab (empno number, hire_date date, retired_status char(1) );
create index emp_tab_ix_01 on emp_tab(hire_date, retired_status);
-- make the first index invisible so we can create the second index.
alter index emp_tab_ix_01 invisible;
create bitmap index emp_tab_bit_01 on emp_tab(hire_date, retired_status);
```

Tom Says

This feature is excellent for availability purposes. Suppose you need to take an unpartitioned index and partition it. Or, suppose that you have marching orders to convert a B*tree index into a bitmap index in the reporting system. Or that you need to convert an index into a unique index suddenly. What would you have to do to accomplish any of these tasks? Schedule downtime. You would need to first drop the old index, then build the new one, and then invite everyone back in. Now, with invisible same type indexes, you can build the new index online and then simply drop the old index and make the new one visible.

Oracle supports creating indexes with the same set of columns or the same set of column expressions, or both, if one of the following conditions has been met *and* only one of the indexes is visible at any given time:

- The indexes are of different types.

- The indexes use different partitioning.

- The indexes have different uniqueness properties.

With Clause New Features

I'm amazed at how many places I go where I mention the **with** clause (known as the subquery factoring clause) and nobody has heard about it. The **with** clause provides a way to pre-materialize results of queries before the statement executes. This is much more efficient than, say, using subqueries all over creation. Consider this query, for example:

```
select a.empno, b.dname
from emp a, dept b
where a.deptno=b.deptno
and b.deptno < (select avg(deptno) from dept);
```

This query likely will be much more efficient if we use the **with** clause instead of the subquery on the last line:

```
with temp_table as (select avg(deptno) dept_result from dept)
select a.empno, b.dname
from emp a, dept b, temp_table c
where a.deptno=b.deptno
and b.deptno < c.dept_result;
```

```
    EMPNO DNAME
---------- --------------
     7369 RESEARCH
     7566 RESEARCH
     7782 ACCOUNTING
     7788 RESEARCH
     7839 ACCOUNTING
     7876 RESEARCH
     7902 RESEARCH
     7934 ACCOUNTING
8 rows selected.
```

Pretty slick, eh? It can make a huge performance difference, especially with queries that contain a lot of subqueries. Now, you can have PL/SQL functions within the **with** clause. These functions can then be executed within the SQL statement itself. Here is an example:

```
drop table test_table;
create table test_table (id number);
insert into test_table values (1);
insert into test_table values (2);
commit;

with
function f_robert(p_id number) return number is
begin
     return p_id+1;
end;
select f_robert(id) from test_table;
/
F_ROBERT(ID)
------------
           2
           3
```

Instead of using a stored PL/SQL function, we have included the body of the function in the SQL query. One of the potential benefits (according to Oracle) of defining the

Tom Says

There is currently a limitation in the first release of Oracle Database 12c that will be resolved in a subsequent patch set. This new feature allows you to embed PL/SQL in SQL, but if you try to take that SQL with PL/SQL query and embed it in PL/SQL, it will not work! The PL/SQL parser will not recognize this new capability. Until it does, you have to either use dynamic SQL in PL/SQL to access this capability or create a view that hides the PL/SQL from PL/SQL.

function in the body of the SQL statement is that it might run faster than the call of a function by the same statement. Also, if you are using read-only databases (like a Data Guard database open read-only), then this can be very useful.

Oracle Database 12c PL/SQL New Features

In the final section, we look at PL/SQL new features in Oracle Database 12c that you will want to be aware of. These new features include the following:

■ The ability to indicate whether a function in a view definition should be executed based on the privileges of the owner or the privileges of the invoker of the view

■ Using white lists when creating PL/SQL programs, to enhance security

■ Using PL/SQL data types across the SQL interface

■ Changes to security privileges on invoker rights PL/SQL program units

■ Granting roles to PL/SQL packages and stand-alone subprograms

■ Miscellaneous PL/SQL new features

Using the Bequeath Clause on Views

Oracle Database 12c provides the ability to indicate if a function that is included in the definition of a view should be executed using the privileges of the owner of the view or the privileges of the invoker of the view. This is supported through the use of the **bequeath** clause of the **create view** command.

PL/SQL Subprogram White Lists

There are often cases where a given PL/SQL package (and API interface) will call additional helper packages. In such cases, it is preferable to restrict access to the helper packages only to the API calling package. In other words, you don't want clients to be able to call these other packages. While Oracle has offered a certain level of security in the past through grants, context, and the like. Oracle Database goes a step further by providing an interface that improves the grain at which you can secure a PL/SQL unit.

There is a number of varying security-related patterns that one could follow, but they often tend to get complex. However, there is one pattern that can be followed that is pretty straightforward and secure without being complex. This is known as the white list.

The idea behind the white list is pretty simple. You use a new clause called **accessible by** to define the PL/SQL program units that have access to your PL/SQL code unit. The white list augments other security features of Oracle Database 12*c*, such as the **grant** command, so those privileges need to be in place as well.

Let's look at an example of a PL/SQL program unit that is secured with a white list:

```
create or replace function helper (v_input  number)
return number
accessible by (api)
is
begin
     return v_input+1;
end;
/
```

The white list is generated by our use of the **accessible by** clause. In this case, we defined a PL/SQL program unit called **api** to be on the white list. Note that we have not created **api** yet. Oracle Database 12*c* will only check the syntax of the **accessible by** clause. Validation of the white list occurs at run time. This makes sense, because otherwise we'd have a major "chicken-and-the-egg" problem if it tried to validate the PL/SQL program unit that would be referencing it.

So, what would happen if we were to try to access the function that we just created? Keep in mind, we are still connected as the owner of this function. In previous versions of Oracle Database, we would be able to just run the thing from the owning account—no more. Here is what happens:

```
select helper(1) from dual;
select helper(1) from dual
       *
ERROR at line 1:
ORA-06552: PL/SQL: Statement ignored
ORA-06553: PLS-904: insufficient privilege to access object HELPER
```

This has major implications for code distribution, as you can imagine. You could wrap your PL/SQL, including the white list, and thereby have the ability to control who can call the various program units.

So now, let's create our **api** function that will call the code just shown:

```
create or replace function api (v_input  number)
return number
is
     v_return   number;
begin
     v_return:=helper(v_input);
     return v_return;
end;
/
```

Let's see if this code runs:

```
select api(1) from dual;

    API(1)
----------
         2
1 row selected.
```

Using PL/SQL-Specific Data Types Across the PL/SQL-to-SQL Interface

In previous versions of Oracle Database, there were PL/SQL-only data types (such as BOOLEAN, associative arrays, and records) that could not be bound from client programs, both static SQL or dynamic SQL. These restrictions have been relaxed somewhat in Oracle Database 12c. Now it is possible to bind values with PL/SQL-only data types to anonymous blocks, PL/SQL function calls in SQL queries, call statements, and the **table** operator in SQL queries.

Still, some restrictions remain:

- The PL/SQL-only data type must have been predefined or it must have been declared in a package specification.

- If you are using associative arrays in PL/SQL, then those array must be indexed by the **pls_integer** data type.

- A PL/SQL function cannot return a PL/SQL-only data type to SQL.

- A **boolean** literal cannot be an argument to a PL/SQL function called from a static SQL query.

- Within the context of SQL, you can't use a function whose return type was declared in a package specification.

Here is an example of using a PL/SQL-only data type as a part of an **execute immediate** call from a PL/SQL anonymous block:

```
create or replace procedure answer_me (p_r boolean)
is
begin
    if p_r then
        dbms_output.put_line('Answer is TRUE');
    else
        dbms_output.put_line('Answer is FALSE');
    end if;
```

```
end;
/
-- Let's test the code
set serveroutput on
declare
     v_sql          varchar2(1000);
     v_boolean      boolean:=TRUE;
begin
     v_sql:='BEGIN answer_me(:x); END;';
     execute immediate v_sql using v_boolean;
end;
/
Answer is TRUE
```

Changes to Security Privileges on Invoker Rights PL/SQL Program Units

Oracle Database 12*c* introduces a new privilege. If you intend to create PL/SQL programs and you intend to use invokers' privileges when creating those procedures, then you will need to make sure that the owner of the PL/SQL program unit has either the **inherit any privilege** or **inherit privilege** privileges on the invoker of the PL/SQL unit. You issue the **grant** statement in any of the following three ways:

```
grant inherit privileges on user scott to public;
grant inherit privileges on user scott to tiger;
grant inherit any privileges to tiger;
```

Tom Says

By default, a **grant inherit any privileges to public** is issued for each user. This makes Oracle Database 12*c* work just like any other release of Oracle Database with respect to invokers' rights. That said, I suggest you consider revoking that privilege from public, especially for privileged accounts such as DBA accounts, Application Server connection pool accounts, and the like. These accounts should explicitly grant the **inherit privileges** privilege only to those accounts that need it and can be trusted not to abuse it. Remember, if a DBA runs an invokers' rights routine, that routine runs with DBA privileges. You want to make sure you run only trusted code. With things like SQL Injection bugs rife in applications, privilege escalation is something to take seriously. The fewer schemas that can inherit your privileges, the better.

Granting Roles to PL/SQL Packages and Stand-Alone Subprograms

In Oracle Database 12c, you can grant roles to individual PL/SQL packages and to stand-alone PL/SQL subprograms. Instead of defining these stored procedures with definer's rights, you can define them with invokers' rights, and then you can grant the PL/SQL program a role that contains the additional privileges that the package would need to execute. The result is that the privileges associated with the use of the PL/SQL program unit (such as access to the underlying tables that the PL/SQL program requires) are narrowed to only those absolutely needed to execute the package, plus any additional rights that the invoker might own.

To grant roles, you first create the role or roles that you want to use. Then, use the **grant** command to grant the roles to the PL/SQL program unit. First, we will log into the SCOTT account and create a function called **get_new_value**:

```
connect scott/robert
drop table need_privs;
create table need_privs(id number);
insert into need_privs values (1);
commit;
create or replace function get_new_value(v_input in number)
return number
authid definer
as
    v_number      number:=0;
begin
    select id+v_input into v_number from scott.need_privs;
    return v_number;
end;
/
```

Note that our function has been set for **definer** execution privileges. This means that this function will run with the privileges of the person who executed the PL/SQL routine. We have an application that is role heavy, and instead of granting a specific user execute privilege to the function, we want to grant a role privilege to execute the PL/SQL. In doing so, any user granted that role will be able to execute the function.

To make this happen, we first grant **execute** privileges on the function to the TIGER user:

```
grant execute on get_new_value to tiger;
select get_new_value(1) from dual;

GET_NEW_VALUE(1)
----------------
       2
```

Next, let's see what happens when we try to run it in the SCOTT account:

```
connect tiger/robert
select scott.get_new_value(1) from dual;
select scott.get_new_value(1) from dual
          *
ERROR at line 1:
ORA-00942: table or view does not exist
ORA-06512: at "SCOTT.GET_NEW_VALUE", line 7
```

Well, that does not work. Normally, we would need to grant TIGER privileges to the SCOTT.NEED_PRIVS table for that account to be able to execute the function. Now, in Oracle Database 12*c*, we can just create a role and grant it the privileges we need, as shown here:

```
connect scott/robert
drop role run_get_new_value;
create role run_get_new_value;
grant select on need_privs to run_get_new_value;
grant run_get_new_value to function get_new_value;
```

Most of this probably looks familiar to you, except that last line. What the heck is going on there? We are granting a role to a function? Bizarre! Really, though, it makes sense. What we are doing is localizing the security needed to execute that function *to* that function. We don't have to give anyone direct access to anything but the right to execute the function.

The function now owns its own security. Pretty slick! Now let's see if our query executes:

```
connect tiger/robert
select scott.get_new_value(1) from dual;

SCOTT.GET_NEW_VALUE(1)
--------------------
                   2
```

Bravo! Our query is now executing from the TIGER account. So, in summary, to take advantage of this feature, you do the following:

- Create the PL/SQL stored program unit.

- Create a role that will contain the privileges that the PL/SQL program unit needs.

- Grant all the privileges to the role that the PL/SQL program unit will need. This might include **select**, **insert, delete**, and other privileges.

- Grant the role to the PL/SQL program unit.

- Grant **execute** on the PL/SQL program unit to whoever you want to be able to execute the PL/SQL program unit.

It's that simple!

A Final Word on PL/SQL New Features

This section introduces some miscellaneous PL/SQL–related new features that really don't warrant their own individual sections, but do merit some attention.

First, you should be aware that invoker's rights functions can now be result-cached, through the use of the **result_cache** clause in the function definition. There are a number of restrictions to be aware of, though:

- The function can't be defined in an anonymous block; can't be a pipelined table function; and can't reference data dictionary tables, temporary tables, sequences, or nondeterministic SQL functions (such as **sysdate**).

- The function can't have any **out** or **in out** parameters.

- The **in** parameter and the return type can't contain a BLOB, CLOB, NCLOB, reference cursor, collection, object, or record. There is an exception here for the return type, which can be a record or PL/SQL collection, but that collection cannot contain an unsupported return type.

I mentioned the **fetch first** clause earlier in this chapter in the context of DML new features. This clause is also available in PL/SQL program units. This helps to limit the number of rows returned by a SQL statement.

Pluggable databases were discussed in depth in Chapter 2. You can create event triggers on the root of the pluggable CDB, or within any of the PDBs. You will need to use the new **pluggable** keyword if you're creating an event trigger in a PDB if that trigger type is specific to a pluggable database (**clone** or **unplug**). Otherwise, a **create database** trigger will work just fine and will create the trigger in whichever PDB you are in, or in the root if you are in the root of the CDB.

Another new feature in PL/SQL associated with pluggable databases is that you can use the following two new database events to build an event trigger on. If you are creating a pluggable database trigger, it will be created on the PDB that you are connected to, so be careful there.

- **before unplug** Executes before Oracle unplugs a database. The trigger is fired and then is deleted. If the trigger fails, the unplug operation will fail in totality.

- **after clone**   Fires after a PDB has been cloned. The trigger is fired in the newly cloned PDB, and then the trigger is deleted. If the trigger fails, the clone operation will fail.

Finally, there are two new PL/SQL directives that can be helpful in debugging your PL/SQL code:

- **$$PLSQL_UNIT_OWNER**   Provides the name of the owner of the current PL/SQL unit. If the unit is an anonymous block, the value of the directive will be NULL.

- **$$PLSQL_UNIT_TYPE**   Provides a literal value that contains the type of the current PL/SQL program unit. This type can be ANONYMOUS BLOCK, FUNCTION, PACKAGE, PACKAGE BODY, PROCEDURE, TRIGGER, TYPE, or TYPE BODY.

End of Line

In this chapter we have discussed a number of SQL and PL/SQL features that are new in Oracle Database 12*c*. As you can see, there are a number of changes. As time goes on and as additional releases of Oracle Database 12*c* are made available, you will no doubt see even more functionality released. Oracle continues to be competitive and innovative in a very fast-moving market. It's important to keep up with these new features so you can be as efficient and productive on the job.

In some cases, we have just scratched the surface on these features and their power. For example, there is a whole host of functionality in pattern matching that we could dedicate three to four chapters, perhaps more, to. This book and this chapter are just a launching point from which to start your quest for understanding. So get out there and do just that! Write blogs and participate in user groups and share what you have learned with the whole world.

CHAPTER
7

Partitioning Enhancements

racle Database 12*c* continues to improve partitioning in the areas of partitioning manageability, performance, and availability. In this chapter we will address the enhancements to partitioning in Oracle Database 12*c*. These new features include

- Moving partitions online

- Interval-reference partitioning

- Cascade functionality

- Partition maintenance

- Partial indexes

- Global index maintenance

- Improved statistics

Let's take a deeper look at each of these new partitioning features.

Moving Partitions Online

In Oracle Database 12*c*, you can now move partitions and subpartitions online. The capability to move partitions to lower-costing or lower-performing storage should be part of your information lifecycle management plan. When moving partitions online, you should seriously consider compression as an option. In addition to moving partitions online, you can move datafiles online. Being able to move partitions and/or datafiles online provides increased flexibility that you can take advantage of when new storage is purchased.

Let's look at an example of this new feature in action. Assuming that we have already logged into the database as a user who has the appropriate privileges, first we will create a small tablespace. Then we will create an interval-partitioned table and insert some records. Finally, we will move a partition online into the newly created tablespace.

First, we create the tablespace:

```
create tablespace target_ts datafile
'/u01/app/oracle/oradata/target_ts_01.dbf'
size 10M;
```

Now let's create a partitioned table called FRIENDS with the following DDL:

```
create table friends
( fname varchar2(10)  not null
, lname varchar2(10)  not null
```

```
, dob    date           not null)
partition by range (dob)
interval (NUMTODSINTERVAL(7,'day'))
( partition p_before_01_JAN_1971 values
  less than (to_date('01-01-1971','dd-mm-yyyy')))
enable row movement;
```

Next, we will insert some records into the FRIENDS table. Since the FRIENDS table is an interval-partitioned table, new partitions are automatically created when data is inserted. You might have noticed in the preceding **create table** statement that the partitions created have the granularity of one week. Let's insert ten records, which will cause the automatic creation of three additional partitions:

```
Insert into friends values
('Alice'   , 'Abad'    , to_date('12-15-1970','mm-dd-yyyy'));
Insert into friends values
('Bob'     , 'Abad'    , to_date('12-15-1970','mm-dd-yyyy'));
Insert into friends values
('Cathy'   , 'Abad'    , to_date('12-15-1970','mm-dd-yyyy'));
Insert into friends values
('Kathy'   , 'Kawabata', to_date('12-31-1970','mm-dd-yyyy'));
Insert into friends values
('Dave'    , 'Drew'    , to_date('01-01-1971','mm-dd-yyyy'));
Insert into friends values
('Michelle', 'Morton'  , to_date('01-02-1971','mm-dd-yyyy'));
Insert into friends values
('Michelle', 'Miyaki'  , to_date('01-14-1971','mm-dd-yyyy'));
Insert into friends values
('Eric',    'Yen'    , to_date('09-20-1971','mm-dd-yyyy'));
Insert into friends values
('Carlie',  'Rose'    , to_date('09-20-1971','mm-dd-yyyy'));
Insert into friends values
('Emma',    'Rose'    , to_date('09-20-1971','mm-dd-yyyy'));
commit;
```

We want to understand how many rows there are per partition, so we gather fresh statistics on the FRIENDS table (adjust as necessary for your environment):

```
exec DBMS_STATS.gather_table_stats('HR', 'FRIENDS');
```

After fresh statistics are gathered, we can determine which partition has the most rows:

```
select partition_name, num_rows, TABLESPACE_NAME
from user_tab_partitions
where table_name = 'FRIENDS'
order by 2 desc;
```

```
PARTITION_NAME        NUM_ROWS TABLESPACE_NAME
--------------------  -------- --------------------
P_BEFORE_01_JAN_1971         4 EXAMPLE
SYS_P326                     2 EXAMPLE
SYS_P327                     1 EXAMPLE
SYS_P328                     3 EXAMPLE
```

Besides the number of rows shown in the NUM_ROWS column, notice the names of the partitions in the PARTITION_NAME column. The partitions that were automatically created have system-generated names of SYS_P###. This is why your results will be different from the results shown here.

Now that we know our first partition has more rows (4) than the rest of the partitions, let's move it to a different tablespace, the one we previously created, tablespace TARGET_TS:

```
ALTER TABLE FRIENDS
MOVE PARTITION P_BEFORE_01_JAN_1971 COMPRESS BASIC
TABLESPACE TARGET_TS
UPDATE INDEXES ONLINE;
```

Rerun the previous query and check your results:

```
select partition_name, num_rows, TABLESPACE_NAME
from user_tab_partitions
where table_name = 'FRIENDS'
order by 1;
```

```
PARTITION_NAME        NUM_ROWS TABLESPACE_NAME
--------------------  -------- --------------------
P_BEFORE_01_JAN_1971         4 TARGET_TS
SYS_P326                     2 EXAMPLE
SYS_P327                     1 EXAMPLE
SYS_P328                     3 EXAMPLE
```

Take a look at the **alter table** command that was used above to move the P_BEFORE_01_JAN_1971 partition. The **compress basic** option was added to compress the tablespace as part of the move. Compression is another reason to move partitions. The compression options are **compresss basic** and **compresss for oltp**. If you are using ZFS Storage, Pillar Axiom Storage, or Exadata, then you can use Hybrid Columnar Compression (HCC) options: **compresss for query low** or **high** (default is **high**) and **compresss for archive low** or **high** (default is **low**).

Interval-Reference Partitioning

Prior to Oracle Database 12c, reference partitioning had some restrictions, one of which was related to using interval partitioning for the parent table. Oracle Database 12c removes that restriction, so now the parent table can be created using interval partitioning and have a referencing child table. In the following example we create a parent and child table using interval-reference partitioning.

First we create the parent table, CUSTOMER ORDERS:

```
create table customer_orders
( customer_id   number,
  order_id      number constraint customer_orders_pk PRIMARY KEY,
  order_date    date    not null)
partition by range (order_date)
interval (NUMTODSINTERVAL(7,'day'))
( partition p_before_1_jan_2013 values
  less than (to_date('01-01-2013','dd-mm-yyyy')) )
enable row movement;
```

Next we create the child table, CUSTOMER_ORDER_ITEMS:

```
create table customer_order_items
( order_id       number not null
, product_id     number not null
, quantity       number not null
, sales_amount number not null
, constraint customer_order_items_orders_fk
  foreign key (order_id) references
  customer_orders(order_id) on delete cascade )
partition by reference (customer_order_items_orders_fk)
enable row movement;
```

This child table is created with a foreign key constraint that references the parent table. The **partition by reference** clause references the foreign key constraint as the partition key. Then the child table uses the foreign key as its partition key. So, the parent table defines the partition key of the child table.

Once the tables are created, we can check the reference and partitioning between the two tables:

```
select up.table_name, up.partitioning_type,
       uc.table_name ref_table
from user_part_tables up,
```

```
(select r.table_name, r.constraint_name
from user_constraints uc, user_constraints r
where uc.constraint_name=r.constraint_name
and uc.owner=r.owner) uc
where up.ref_ptn_constraint_name = uc.constraint_name(+)
and up.table_name
in ('CUSTOMER_ORDERS','CUSTOMER_ORDER_ITEMS')
order by 1;

TABLE_NAME            PARTITION REF_TABLE
-------------------- --------- ----------------------
CUSTOMER_ORDERS       RANGE
CUSTOMER_ORDER_ITEMS REFERENCE CUSTOMER_ORDER_ITEMS
```

Cascade Functionality

The truncate table command is now improved in Oracle Database 12c. The **cascade** operation is also an option for the **truncate partition** command and the **exchange [sub] partition** command when used with reference partitioning. Recall that to be able to perform a cascading truncate operation, the parent and child tables have to have at least one constraint that has **on delete cascade** defined and enabled. When the constraint is enabled, then the **truncate table cascade** command will truncate both the parent and the child tables.

Let's use the CUSTOMER_ORDERS and CUSTOMER_ORDER_ITEMS tables from the previous examples. If we were to create a foreign key between the two tables that forced a **cascade delete** operation, we could truncate a specific partition of CUSTOMER_ORDERS, and the equivalent partition in CUSTOMER_ORDER_ITEMS would be truncated as well.

Tom Says

This cascade functionality is nice for three reasons. First, it makes maintaining rolling windows of data easier; a single command removes all old data, instead of multiple commands as in the past. Second, it is an all-or-nothing operation: either the parent and child (and any other children) are truncated or none are truncated. Last, it is an atomic operation. In earlier releases, you would truncate the child table and then truncate the parent table, in two (or more) steps. That could lead to inconsistent results, as the parent table would have data for which the child table had been truncated. Using the cascade option mitigates all of this.

Partition Maintenance Operations on Multiple Partitions

Now you can get more work done per command when performing partition maintenance in Oracle Database 12c. The following partition maintenance commands can be applied over multiple partitions:

- alter partition add

- alter partition truncate

- alter partition drop

- alter partition split

- alter partition merge

Let's look at some examples of these commands in use. First, we will create a partitioned table called SALES888:

```
CREATE TABLE SALES888 (
    PRODUCTID      NUMBER,
    SALEDATE       DATE,
    CUSTID         NUMBER,
    TOTALPRICE     NUMBER   )
PARTITION BY RANGE (SALEDATE)
(
    PARTITION PART_2009 VALUES LESS THAN
      (TO_DATE('01-JAN-2010','DD-MON-YYYY')),
    PARTITION PART_2010 VALUES LESS THAN
      (TO_DATE('01-JAN-2011','DD-MON-YYYY')),
    PARTITION PART_2011 VALUES LESS THAN
      (TO_DATE('01-JAN-2012','DD-MON-YYYY')),
    PARTITION PART_2012 VALUES LESS THAN
      (TO_DATE('01-JAN-2013','DD-MON-YYYY')),
    PARTITION P_Q1_2013 VALUES LESS THAN
      (TO_DATE('01-APR-2013','DD-MON-YYYY')),
    PARTITION P_Q2_2013 VALUES LESS THAN
      (TO_DATE('01-JUL-2013','DD-MON-YYYY'))
)
ENABLE ROW MOVEMENT;
```

Now, we can perform several partition maintenance operations across the individual partitions. Most of the partition maintenance operations we will perform will modify the table partitions in some way. You can run the following command after many of the examples to see how the partitions in the table have been changed by that operation:

```
SELECT TABLE_NAME, PARTITION_NAME, PARTITION_POSITION
FROM USER_TAB_PARTITIONS
WHERE TABLE_NAME = 'SALES888'
ORDER BY PARTITION_POSITION;
```

First, let's extend the SALES888 table by adding two partitions for the next two quarters:

```
ALTER TABLE SALES888 ADD
    PARTITION P_Q3_2013 VALUES LESS THAN
      (TO_DATE('01-OCT-2013','DD-MON-YYYY')),
    PARTITION P_Q4_2013 VALUES LESS THAN
      (TO_DATE('01-JAN-2014','DD-MON-YYYY'));
```

Next, we truncate two partitions in one simple **alter table truncate partitions** command, and then drop those same partitions in one **alter table drop partitions** command:

```
ALTER TABLE SALES888 TRUNCATE PARTITIONS PART_2009, PART_2010;
ALTER TABLE SALES888 DROP PARTITIONS PART_2009, PART_2010;
```

Finally, we split one of the partitions in SALES888, called PART_2011, into three partitions using the **alter table split partition** command:

```
ALTER TABLE SALES888 SPLIT PARTITION PART_2011 INTO
(PARTITION P_1ST_Q_2011 VALUES LESS THAN
   (TO_DATE('01-APR-2011','DD-MON-YYYY')),
 PARTITION P_2nd_Q_2011 VALUES LESS THAN
   (TO_DATE('01-JUL-2011','DD-MON-YYYY')),
 PARTITION P_2011_LAST_HALF);
```

Tom Says

Using this split and subsequent merge operation is particularly nice. Prior to Oracle Database 12c, in order to split a partition into three, you had to split the partition into two and then split one of the remaining partitions into two again. That is a lot of reading and rereading and writing and rewriting that can now be avoided.

Should you decide that what you did in the preceding steps was a mistake, you can roll it back using the **alter table merge partitions** command:

```
ALTER TABLE SALES888
MERGE PARTITIONS  P_1ST_Q_2011,
                  P_2nd_Q_2011,
                  P_2011_FIRST_HALF
INTO PARTITION PART_2011;
```

Again, the new multipartition feature reduces the total number of SQL statements that you need to execute.

Partial Indexes

In previous versions of Oracle Database, a given index had to span all partitions of a partitioned table. However, you might find that you often want to mix and match local and global indexes at a partition level. Oracle Database 12c provides the capability to do this, with the new partial-indexing capabilities.

Full indexing is what we are normally used to when working with partitioned tables. In full indexing, all partitions are indexed. Now, with partial indexing, we can identify the partitions that should or should not be indexed.

Using partial indexing, you save space by not indexing unused partitions. This can improve the performance of index maintenance operations (for example, global maintenance operations on nonindexed partitions would be faster). Partial indexing can also improve performance by not indexing in environments such as Exadata. Also, for large objects, you may reduce the impacts of sort operations on index creation by creating the index partitions in separate operations.

In this section we will discuss partial indexing. First we will discuss turning indexing on or off on the partitions of a partitioned table. Then we will demonstrate the creation of partial indexes.

Tom Says
You could have partial indexes in Oracle Database 11g, but the functionality was limited and hard to administer. To create a partial index in the earlier releases, you had to create the entire index unusable. Then you could rebuild individual partitions. This was clumsy, and if someone were to rebuild the index, it would rebuild *all* index partitions, not just the ones you wanted. This new capability in Oracle Database 12c allows you to mark partitions permanently so that subsequent rebuilds and such do not attempt to touch certain partitions.

Creating Partitions With or Without Indexing

To enable partial indexes, we first need to define which columns should not have indexes created on them. We do so by turning indexing on or off on a given partition. If indexing is turned off for a given partition, then that partition will not have usable index partitions if the index is created as a partial index (as discussed in the next section). Also, all global indexes created as partial indexes (again, discussed in the next section), whether partitioned or not, will not have data for any partition that has indexing turned off.

By default, all partitions of a table have indexing enabled. If we want to create a partitioned table and take advantage of partial indexes, we have two different options for how to do that. First, we can create the table with a default setting that indicates how any partition should be configured for indexing. Second, we can explicitly define the indexing attribute for specific partitions when they are created with either **indexing on** (the default) or **indexing off**.

The following example demonstrates disabling and enabling indexing on partitions and setting the default for indexing for the table. Note that indexing is enabled through the use of the **indexing off** and **indexing on** clauses.

```
CREATE TABLE PRODUCTS (
   MFGID NUMBER,
   PRODUCTID NUMBER,
   RECEIVED_DATE DATE)
INDEXING OFF
PARTITION BY RANGE (RECEIVED_DATE)
(
   PARTITION PART_2011 VALUES LESS THAN
     (TO_DATE('01-JAN-2012','DD-MON-YYYY')) INDEXING OFF,
   PARTITION PART_2012 VALUES LESS THAN
     (TO_DATE('01-JAN-2013','DD-MON-YYYY')) INDEXING ON,
   PARTITION PART_2013 VALUES LESS THAN
     (TO_DATE('01-JAN-2014','DD-MON-YYYY'))
)
ENABLE ROW MOVEMENT;
```

The first **indexing off** option indicates the default for indexing of partitions assigned to the table that do not have the **indexing** clause specified. In this example, partition PART_2013 would be assigned the attribute of **indexing off** because that is the default for the table.

The preceding example has further occurrences of **indexing off** and **indexing on** attributes assigned to specific partitions. Once the table is created, you can confirm which partitions have indexing on or off with the following script:

```
SELECT TABLE_NAME, PARTITION_NAME, INDEXING
FROM USER_TAB_PARTITIONS
```

```
WHERE TABLE_NAME = 'PRODUCTS'
ORDER BY PARTITION_POSITION;

TABLE_NAME      PARTITION_NAME          INDEXING
------------    -------------------     --------
PRODUCTS        PART_2011               OFF
PRODUCTS        PART_2012               ON
PRODUCTS        PART_2013               OFF
```

Note that you can use the **alter table** command to modify the indexing attributes of a given table. Now that we have created the table with the necessary indexing on and indexing off syntax, we can move on to actually creating the partial indexes.

Partial Indexing of Partitions Within a Partitioned Table

Partial indexing involves the use of the **create index** command and then the keyword **partial**. Without the **partial** keyword, the index being created will not consider the state of the individual partitions with respect to indexing or no indexing. Thus, full indexing always overrides the indexing instructions defined when we create a partitioned table. So, the following statement would create a complete global index on our PRODUCTS table, across every partition, even though some are marked no index:

```
CREATE INDEX PRODUCTS_FULL
ON PRODUCTS (MFGID)
GLOBAL INDEXING FULL;
```

We need to add the **partial** keyword to take advantage of the indexing instructions defined when we created the PRODUCTS table. Note here that we have included the **partial** keyword instead of the **full** keyword:

```
CREATE INDEX PRODUCTS_PARTIAL
ON PRODUCTS (PRODUCTID)
GLOBAL INDEXING PARTIAL;
```

You can confirm the indexing type with this script:

```
SELECT TABLE_NAME, INDEX_NAME, INDEXING
FROM   USER_INDEXES
WHERE  TABLE_NAME = 'PRODUCTS'
ORDER BY 2 DESC;
TABLE_NAME      INDEX_NAME              INDEXING
------------    -------------------     --------
PRODUCTS        PRODUCTS_PARTIAL        PARTIAL
PRODUCTS        PRODUCTS_FULL           FULL
```

As you can see, using partial indexes requires two separate processes. The first is to define the indexing attributes of the partitions of the table, and the second is the actual creation of the partial indexes using the **partial** keyword.

Global Index Maintenance

Global indexes become stale after specific maintenance operations. The operations that cause global indexes to become stale are

- **DROP PARTITION**

- **TRUNCATE PARTITION**

- **MODIFY PARTITION INDEXING OFF**

You can identify these stale statistics in the column ORPHANED_ENTRIES in the views DBA/ALL/USER_INDEXES and DBA/ALL/USER_IND_PARTITION. The values for ORPHANED_ENTRIES are

- **YES**   There are orphaned entries.

- **NO**   There are no orphaned entries.

- **N/A**   Does not apply. The index is local or is on a nonpartitioned table.

There is an automatically scheduled job, SYS.PMO_DEFERRED_GIDX_MAINT_JOB, that can be used to clean up all global indexes at the default time of 2:00 A.M. Another method is to use **alter index rebuild [partition]** or **alter index coalesce partition cleanup**.

The new method in Oracle Database 12c to clean up orphaned entries is to use the **dbms_part.cleanup_gidx** procedure. This procedure identifies and cleans up the global indexes that have orphaned entries. The parameters for the **dbms_part.cleanup_gidx** procedure are **schema_name** and **table_name**. Regardless of the method you use to clean up the orphaned entries, the index maintenance is a metadata update. Updating the metadata is a fast process as compared to removing the actual orphaned entries.

Automatic Global Statistics

In Oracle Database 12c you can control how the database determines if statistics are stale for the partition or subpartition. For tables that have **incremental** set to **true**, any DML activity causes stale statistics. These stale statistics aggregate into inaccurate

global statistics, causing the need for statistics to be regathered. The unnecessary regathering of statistics for a small percentage change is a performance overhead that should be avoided.

You can avoid this problem by adjusting the table preference **incremental_ staleness**. Setting **incremental_staleness** to a different value will adjust how and when the database considers statistics to be stale. This is in essence setting a tolerance level for stale statistics. This new setting has three values:

- **NULL** The default value. Any DML activity will cause the partition or subpartition to be stale. Think of this as a strict interpretation.

- **USED_LOCKED_STATS** Statistics for locked partitions or subpartitions are not stale. This is the opposite end of the spectrum from the NULL setting.

- **USE_STALE_PERCENT** The default value is 10 percent. If DML causes more than 10 percent of the rows to change, then the table is stale. You can also set the "sweet spot," as shown next.

The following list shows how to set INCREMENTAL_STALENESS using the SALES table from the SH example schema.

- Set INCREMENTAL_STALENESS to NULL, which is the normal Oracle Database 11*g* behavior:

```
exec DBMS_STATS.SET_TABLE_PREFS ('SH', 'SALES', -
'INCREMENTAL_STALENESS' ,   NULL);
```

- Set INCREMENTAL_STALENESS to USE_LOCKED_STATS. This will ensure that statistics are never considered stale:

```
exec DBMS_STATS.SET_TABLE_PREFS ('SH', 'SALES', -
'INCREMENTAL_STALENESS' , 'USE_LOCKED_STATS');
```

- Setting INCREMENTAL_STALENESS to USE_STALE_PERCENT allows for some tolerance of DML activity without causing statistics to be stale:

```
exec DBMS_STATS.SET_TABLE_PREFS ('SH', 'SALES', -
'INCREMENTAL_STALENESS' , 'USE_STALE_PERCENT');
```

- USE_STALE_PERCENT can also take STALE_PERCENT as input:

```
exec DBMS_STATS.SET_TABLE_PREFS ('SH', 'SALES', -
'STALE_PERCENT', '15');
```

End of Line

There have been a lot of exciting changes related to partitioning in Oracle Database 12c. These new features have increased our ability to maintain higher uptimes, ease administration, and improve on performance. Take a break now and grab some coffee before jumping into the next chapter. The next chapter is about the Business Intelligence and Data Warehousing in Oracle Database 12c.

CHAPTER
8

Business Intelligence and Data Warehousing

This chapter explores new features and improvements in Oracle Database 12c related to Business Intelligence (BI) and Data Warehousing (DW). This chapter explores the following topics:

- Advanced analytics

- Online analytical processing (OLAP)

- Information lifecycle management (ILM)

- Temporal History (TH)

- Performance enhancements

Advanced Analytics

Oracle Database 12c improves analytic capabilities in these areas:

- New algorithms

- New data types and search capabilities

- Prediction and cluster functions

New Algorithms

Oracle Database 12c introduces three additional algorithms used in Oracle Data Mining (ODM):

- Expectation Maximization (EM)

- Singular Value Decomposition (SVD)

- Generalized Linear Models (GLM) algorithm

A description follows for each new algorithm.

Expectation Maximization

EM is composed of the following two steps, the end goal of which is to determine the optimal number of clusters needed to model the data:

1. **Expectation** Parameter values are used to compute the likelihood of the current model having the optimal number of clusters.

2. **Maximization** Parameter values derived from the Expectation step are used to recompute the model.

These two steps continue until the optimal number of clusters is determined.

A possible usage of EM is to determine target clusters for an advertising campaign, with the initial input being a list of customers that have bought a particular product. The output would be the optimal number of clusters. From the output, a target cluster would be identified for the advertising campaign.

Singular Value Decomposition

Oracle Database 12c introduces SVD, a technique for doing large matrix math manipulations. SVD is typically used to sort through large amounts of variables (for example, unstructured data/text tokens or big data) to find the "signals" where there are some patterns, correlations, and so forth. Text mining is one of the domains in which SVD projections have wide application.

Generalized Linear Models Algorithm

Feature selection reduces the number of predictors used by a model. This allows for smaller, faster scoring, and more meaningful Generalized Linear Models (GLM). The use of feature selection with GLM can then be done in a faster, iterative process.

Search Capabilities

ODM now supports additional numeric datatypes of BINARY_DOUBLE and BINARY_FLOAT. Native Text Support also is integrated into ODM. Native Text Support simplifies and improves performance of text searches in ODM. Searching for text in unstructured CLOB, BLOB and BFILE data is easier than ever. Furthermore, ODM can now use the Decision Tree algorithm for text mining.

Prediction Detail Functions

Prediction details are XML strings that provide additional details about the score of the attribute. There are three details functions: CLUSTER_DETAILS, FEATURE_DETAILS, and PREDICTION_DETAILS. The detail functions return the value and the relative importance of the attributes used in determining the score.

OLAP

Oracle Database 12c provides additional performance and support related to cubes. Performance enhancements for Oracle OLAP queries take advantage of Oracle shared cursors, dramatically reducing memory requirements with the goal of reducing I/O. Cubes created with Oracle Business Intelligence Enterprise Edition (OBIEE) Plug-in for Analytic Workspace Manager can be exported to OBIEE.

Administration of cube statistics is easier with Oracle Database 12c. Cube statistics are now part of Oracle statistic and metadata repositories. This allows for administration of cube statistics that are within Automatic Workload Repository (AWR), Active Session History (ASH), and Automatic Database Diagnostic Monitor (ADDM).

Information Lifecycle Management

When the topic of ILM comes up, a normal response might be, "storage is cheap." Let's pause for a moment and think about the previous statement. Is storage really cheap? Consider the following:

- More storage does not mean more performance.

- Databases grow; rarely do they get smaller.

- Data growth rates are accelerating.

- The value of data ages over time.

The simple goal of ILM is to assign values to the data based on business rules. As the value of the data lowers over time, the related data should be moved to less costly storage. More valuable data can then use the higher-performing storage once occupied by the aged data.

Oracle Database 12c makes ILM easier. Improvements include

- In-Database Archiving (IDA)

- Temporal Validity

- Automatic Data Optimization (ADO)

Each of these improvements will be covered in detail.

NOTE
IDA, Temporal Validity, ADO, and Temporal History can be used only in noncontainer databases.

In-Database Archiving and Temporal Validity

Archiving data can be a daunting task. Some companies are not able to allocate the time and resources necessary to properly analyze, plan, and implement archiving of data. Such companies often determine that it is easier to simply keep all the data in place and declare themselves in compliance for data retention. In-Database

Archiving (IDA) makes data archiving easier by breaking down data archiving into a smaller step and with less risk. IDA allows for data to be marked as "archived" or "active." When data is marked as "archived," it becomes invisible to the application and is compressed. Due diligence still must take place to plan which data to mark and when to do the actual marking. What IDA provides is an intermediate step of marking the data as "archived" before deleting or moving the data off.

The following two sections provide an IDA example and a Temporal Validity example, respectively. For the IDA example, a limited clone of the HR.EMPLOYEE table will be used, called HR.EMPLOYEES_ARCHIVE_TEST. The example for Temporal Validity will also use a limited clone of the HR.EMPLOYEE table, called HR.EMPLOYEES_TEMPORAL_TEST. All work will be done as the HR sample schema.

NOTE
The following examples for IDA and Temporal Validity use the HR demo schema. Connect as the HR user when working through these two examples. The SQL and results have been formatted for readability.

In-Database Archiving

To illustrate how IDA works, the following example leads you through creating a table and archiving some rows. First, create the table:

```
CREATE TABLE EMPLOYEES_ARCHIVE_TEST AS
SELECT EMPLOYEE_ID, FIRST_NAME, LAST_NAME
FROM EMPLOYEES WHERE EMPLOYEE_ID IN (200, 201, 202, 203, 204, 205);
Table created.
```

Next, enable archiving with the following **alter** command:

```
ALTER TABLE EMPLOYEES_ARCHIVE_TEST ROW ARCHIVAL;
```

Enabling archiving will add hidden columns that are used to indicate whether a row of data is visible or invisible. Archiving can be enabled during the creation of a table, as shown in this example:

```
CREATE TABLE ARCHIVE_TEST2 (COL1 VARCHAR2(5)) ROW ARCHIVAL;
```

Notice that when archiving is enabled, there are no changes to the normal describes table command:

```
DESC EMPLOYEES_ARCHIVE_TEST;
```

```
Name              Null?      Type
--------------    ---------  ----------------------
EMPLOYEE_ID                  NUMBER(6)
FIRST_NAME                   VARCHAR2(20)
LAST_NAME         NOT NULL   VARCHAR2(25)
```

Querying USER_TAB_COLS and including the new additional columns of COLUMN_ID and HIDDEN_COLUMN shows the state of the columns:

```
SELECT TABLE_NAME, COLUMN_NAME, COLUMN_ID,
HIDDEN_COLUMN FROM USER_TAB_COLS WHERE
TABLE_NAME = 'EMPLOYEES_ARCHIVE_TEST'
ORDER BY COLUMN_ID;
TABLE_NAME                 COLUMN_NAME          COLUMN_ID  HID
-------------------------  -------------------  ---------  ---
EMPLOYEES_ARCHIVE_TEST     EMPLOYEE_ID                  1  NO
EMPLOYEES_ARCHIVE_TEST     FIRST_NAME                  2  NO
EMPLOYEES_ARCHIVE_TEST     LAST_NAME                   3  NO
EMPLOYEES_ARCHIVE_TEST     SYS_NC00004$                   YES
EMPLOYEES_ARCHIVE_TEST     ORA_ARCHIVE_STATE              YES
```

When you query the EMPLOYEES_ARCHIVE_TEST table, as shown next, the results are as expected—all six records are returned:

```
SELECT EMPLOYEE_ID, FIRST_NAME ||' '|| LAST_NAME as
FULL_NAME, ORA_ARCHIVE_STATE
FROM EMPLOYEES_ARCHIVE_TEST ORDER BY EMPLOYEE_ID;
EMPLOYEE_ID FULL_NAME            ORA_ARCHIVE_STATE
----------- -------------------- --------------------
        200 Jennifer Whalen                         0
        201 Michael Hartstein                       0
        202 Pat Fay                                 0
        203 Susan Mavris                            0
        204 Hermann Baer                            0
        205 Shelley Higgins                         0
6 rows selected.
```

Now let's use In-Database Archiving. Assume that employees Jennifer and Michael (listed in the preceding results) have decided that today is the day to run off to Alaska and live in the wild frontier. We have decided to use IDA to archive their records, both for performance reasons and for ease of administration. After all, we expect they will come back after their first Alaskan winter. To set archiving for the records, we need to flip the bit from 0 (visible) to 1 (invisible). However, this isn't as easy as simply changing the value of the ORA_ARCHIVE_STATE column. (If it were that easy, you wouldn't be making the big bucks and buying cool books like this one.)

To flip the bit for **ora_archive_state**, you must use the **archivestatename** procedure of the **dbms_ilm** package as part of the **update** statement, as shown here:

```
UPDATE EMPLOYEES_ARCHIVE_TEST
SET ORA_ARCHIVE_STATE=DBMS_ILM.ARCHIVESTATENAME(1)
WHERE EMPLOYEE_ID IN (200, 201);
2 rows updated.
COMMIT;
Commit complete.
```

Now when you requery the EMPLOYEES_ARCHIVE_TEST table, the records for Jennifer Whalen and Michael Hartstein do not appear, because the ora_archive_state column is set to 1, invisible:

```
SELECT EMPLOYEE_ID, FIRST_NAME ||' '|| LAST_NAME
as FULL_NAME, ORA_ARCHIVE_STATE
FROM EMPLOYEES_ARCHIVE_TEST ORDER BY EMPLOYEE_ID;
EMPLOYEE_ID FULL_NAME                     ORA_ARCHIVE_STATE
----------- ------------------------- --------------------
        202 Pat Fay                                      0
        203 Susan Mavris                                 0
        204 Hermann Baer                                 0
        205 Shelley Higgins                              0
4 rows selected.
```

You can change the session to show all data as follows:

```
ALTER SESSION SET ROW ARCHIVAL VISIBILITY = ALL;
Session altered.
```

Requerying again shows all the records, with Jennifer and Michael restored to the ORA_ARCHIVE_STATE column:

```
SELECT EMPLOYEE_ID, FIRST_NAME ||' '|| LAST_NAME
as FULL_NAME, ORA_ARCHIVE_STATE
FROM EMPLOYEES_ARCHIVE_TEST
ORDER BY EMPLOYEE_ID;

EMPLOYEE_ID FULL_NAME                     ORA_ARCHIVE_STATE
----------- ------------------------- --------------------
        200 Jennifer Whalen                              1
        201 Michael Hartstein                            1
        202 Pat Fay                                      0
        203 Susan Mavris                                 0
        204 Hermann Baer                                 0
        205 Shelley Higgins                              0
6 rows selected.
```

Switch back to show only active data and rerun the query:

```
ALTER SESSION SET ROW ARCHIVAL VISIBILITY = ACTIVE;
Session altered.
SELECT EMPLOYEE_ID, FIRST_NAME ||' '|| LAST_NAME
as FULL_NAME, ORA_ARCHIVE_STATE
FROM EMPLOYEES_ARCHIVE_TEST
ORDER BY EMPLOYEE_ID;
EMPLOYEE_ID FULL_NAME                          ORA_ARCHIVE_STATE
----------- -------------------------  --------------------
        202 Pat Fay                                       0
        203 Susan Mavris                                  0
        204 Hermann Baer                                  0
        205 Shelley Higgins                               0
4 rows selected.
```

Here is something interesting and important to remember: just because a row is archived does not mean it is not *really* there. For instance, add a primary key constraint to the EMPLOYEES_ARCHIVE_TEST table and then try to insert a row that would violate the PK constraint:

```
ALTER TABLE EMPLOYEES_ARCHIVE_TEST ADD PRIMARY KEY (EMPLOYEE_ID);
COMMIT;
INSERT INTO EMPLOYEES_ARCHIVE_TEST values (200, 'I want', ' in ');
```

As you might expect, this causes an "ORA-00001: unique constraint (HR.SYS_C0011591) violated" violation. The row is not visible but that does not mean the constraints aren't enforced for the invisible record(s).

Drop the EMPLOYEES_ARCHIVE_TEST table:

```
DROP TABLE EMPLOYEES_ARCHIVE_TEST;
Table dropped.
```

IDA can be used as an intermediate step before moving off data. The appropriate data can be marked "archived." Later, the "archived" data can be moved to a separate tablespace where the datafile is on lower-tiered storage.

Temporal Validity

Temporal Validity (TempVal) adds the dimension of time to determine which data can be viewed. The best way to understand any new feature is to go through an example. The example for TempVal is based on a limited clone of the HR.EMPLOYEE table, called HR.EMPLOYEES_TEMPORAL_TEST. For the TempVal scenario, various employees will have different start and end dates. These dates will be used to determine if data can be viewed.

Let's look at an example of using these new temporal features. As shown next, first we use the **create table** command to create our example table, EMPLOYEES_TEMPORAL_TEST, and then we alter the table to add Temporal Validity:

```
CREATE TABLE EMPLOYEES_TEMPORAL_TEST
AS SELECT EMPLOYEE_ID, FIRST_NAME, LAST_NAME , SALARY
FROM EMPLOYEES
WHERE EMPLOYEE_ID IN (200, 201, 202, 203, 204, 205);
Table created.

ALTER TABLE EMPLOYEES_TEMPORAL_TEST ADD PERIOD FOR VALID_TIME;
Table altered.
```

Now when you look at the table, as shown next, you see that some hidden columns have been added after enabling Temporal Validity: VALID_TIME_START, VALID_TIME_END, and VALID_TIME. These columns are used to determine when a row of data is valid.

```
SELECT COLUMN_NAME, HIDDEN_COLUMN, DATA_TYPE
FROM USER_TAB_COLS WHERE TABLE_NAME = 'EMPLOYEES_TEMPORAL_TEST'
ORDER BY COLUMN_ID, COLUMN_NAME DESC;

COLUMN_NAME              HIDDEN_COLUMN    DATA_TYPE
------------------       ---------------  ---------------------------
EMPLOYEE_ID              NO               NUMBER
FIRST_NAME               NO               VARCHAR2
LAST_NAME                NO               VARCHAR2
SALARY                   NO               NUMBER
VALID_TIME_START         YES              TIMESTAMP(6) WITH TIME ZONE
VALID_TIME_END           YES              TIMESTAMP(6) WITH TIME ZONE
VALID_TIME               YES              NUMBER
7 rows selected.
```

The initial value of valid_time_start and valid_time_end columns is NULL:

```
select EMPLOYEE_ID, FIRST_NAME, LAST_NAME
 , SALARY, to_char(valid_time_start,'ddmonyyyy') "Start"
 , to_char(valid_time_end,'ddmonyyyy') "End"
from EMPLOYEES_TEMPORAL_TEST;

EMPLOYEE_ID FIRST_NAME LAST_NAME  SALARY      Start  End
----------- ---------- ---------- ----------  ------ ------
        200 Jennifer   Whalen           4400
        201 Michael    Hartstein       13000
```

```
        202 Pat        Fay            6000
        203 Susan      Mavris         6500
        204 Hermann    Baer          10000
        205 Shelley    Higgins       12008
6 rows selected.
```

To really show the effects of temporal validity, update a couple of rows, giving each set of two records the same VALID_TIME_START and VALID_TIME_END date. There are three sets:

```
UPDATE EMPLOYEES_TEMPORAL_TEST SET
VALID_TIME_START = TO_DATE('01JAN2012','DDMONYYYY'),
VALID_TIME_END = TO_DATE('15FEB2013','DDMONYYYY')
WHERE EMPLOYEE_ID IN (200, 201);
2 rows updated.

UPDATE EMPLOYEES_TEMPORAL_TEST SET
VALID_TIME_START = TO_DATE('16FEB2013','DDMONYYYY'),
VALID_TIME_END = TO_DATE('21MAR2013','DDMONYYYY')
WHERE EMPLOYEE_ID IN (202, 203);
2 rows updated.

UPDATE EMPLOYEES_TEMPORAL_TEST SET
VALID_TIME_START = TO_DATE('20MAR2013',' DDMONYYYY')
WHERE EMPLOYEE_ID IN (204, 205);
2 rows updated.

COMMIT;
Commit complete.
```

Now let's take a look at the results of the updates. Pay particular attention to the values for the START and END columns of each record. Afterward, the next set of queries will show Temporal Validity in action.

```
SELECT EMPLOYEE_ID, FIRST_NAME, LAST_NAME
 , SALARY, TO_CHAR(VALID_TIME_START,'DD-MON-YYYY') "START"
 , TO_CHAR(VALID_TIME_END,'DD-MON-YYYY') "END"
FROM EMPLOYEES_TEMPORAL_TEST ORDER BY EMPLOYEE_ID;
EMPLOYEE_ID FIRST_NAME LAST_NAME SALARY START       END
----------- ---------- --------- ------ ----------- -----------
        200 Jennifer   Whalen      4400 01-JAN-2012 15-FEB-2013
        201 Michael    Hartstein  13000 01-JAN-2012 15-FEB-2013
        202 Pat        Fay         6000 16-FEB-2013 21-MAR-2013
        203 Susan      Mavris      6500 16-FEB-2013 21-MAR-2013
        204 Hermann    Baer       10000 20-MAR-2013
        205 Shelley    Higgins    12008 20-MAR-2013
6 rows selected.
```

TempVal in action is all about using the new syntax. The following is the syntax to find employees who have a valid date of January 10, 2013. Being valid in this case means the date falls between the employee's START value and END value.

```
SELECT EMPLOYEE_ID, FIRST_NAME,
TO_CHAR(VALID_TIME_START,'DD-MON-YYYY') "START",
TO_CHAR(VALID_TIME_END,'DD-MON-YYYY') "END"
FROM EMPLOYEES_TEMPORAL_TEST
AS OF PERIOD FOR VALID_TIME TO_DATE('10-JAN-2013') ORDER BY 2;
EMPLOYEE_ID FIRST_NAME LAST_NAME SALARY START       END
----------- ---------- --------- ------ ----------- -----------
        200 Jennifer   Whalen      4400 01-JAN-2012 15-FEB-2013
        201 Michael    Hartstein  13000 01-JAN-2012 15-FEB-2013
2 rows selected.
```

Show employees that have a valid date between February 17, 2013 and February 24, 2013:

```
SELECT EMPLOYEE_ID,FIRST_NAME,
TO_CHAR(VALID_TIME_START,'DD-MON-YYYY') "START",
TO_CHAR(VALID_TIME_END,'DD-MON-YYYY') "END"
FROM EMPLOYEES_TEMPORAL_TEST
VERSIONS PERIOD FOR VALID_TIME
BETWEEN TO_DATE('17FEB2013') AND TO_DATE('24FEB2013')
ORDER BY 1;
EMPLOYEE_ID FIRST_NAME LAST_NAME SALARY START       END
----------- ---------- --------- ------ ----------- -----------
        202 Pat        Fay         6000 16-FEB-2013 21-MAR-2013
        203 Susan      Mavris      6500 16-FEB-2013 21-MAR-2013
2 rows selected.
```

To show employees who are currently valid, use DBMS_FLASHBACK_ARCHIVE .ENABLE_AT_VALID_TIME set to 'CURRENT':

```
EXEC DBMS_FLASHBACK_ARCHIVE.ENABLE_AT_VALID_TIME('CURRENT');
PL/SQL procedure successfully completed.
```

Rerunning the query now shows only records that are "current" as of the date the query is run (which was March 20, 2013 in this example):

Tom Says

You can avoid the use of the DBMS_FLASHBACK package altogether by using the as of period clause in your SQL statement. For example, **select * from employees_temporal_test as of period for valid_time sysdate** would show you current data as well.

```
SELECT EMPLOYEE_ID, FIRST_NAME, LAST_NAME
  , SALARY, TO_CHAR(VALID_TIME_START,'DD-MON-YYYY') "START"
  , TO_CHAR(VALID_TIME_END,'DD-MON-YYYY') "END"
FROM EMPLOYEES_TEMPORAL_TEST order by EMPLOYEE_ID;

EMPLOYEE_ID FIRST_NAME LAST_NAME SALARY START       END
----------- ---------- --------- ------ ----------- -----------
        204 Hermann    Baer       10000 20-MAR-2013
        205 Shelley    Higgins    12008 20-MAR-2013
2 rows selected.
```

To see all the records, simply use DBMS_FLASHBACK_ARCHIVE.ENABLE_AT_ VALID_TIME again with 'ALL' and run the query again:

```
EXEC DBMS_FLASHBACK_ARCHIVE.ENABLE_AT_VALID_TIME('ALL');
PL/SQL procedure successfully completed.
SELECT EMPLOYEE_ID, FIRST_NAME, LAST_NAME
  , SALARY, TO_CHAR(VALID_TIME_START,'DD-MON-YYYY') "START"
  , TO_CHAR(VALID_TIME_END,'DD-MON-YYYY') "END"
FROM EMPLOYEES_TEMPORAL_TEST order by EMPLOYEE_ID;

EMPLOYEE_ID FIRST_NAME LAST_NAME SALARY START       END
----------- ---------- --------- ------ ----------- -----------
        200 Jennifer   Whalen      4400 01-JAN-2012 15-FEB-2013
        201 Michael    Hartstein  13000 01-JAN-2012 15-FEB-2013
        202 Pat        Fay         6000 16-FEB-2013 21-MAR-2013
        203 Susan      Mavris      6500 16-FEB-2013 21-MAR-2013
        204 Hermann    Baer       10000 20-MAR-2013
        205 Shelley    Higgins    12008 20-MAR-2013
6 rows selected.
```

CURRENT and ALL are the extremes in our time travel adventures when using TempVal. To have greater control, there is a third way to travel in time: use DBMS_ FLASHBACK_ARCHIVE. That third option is to use DBMS_FLASHBACK_ARCHIVE to be specific and use the concept of "AS OF".

```
EXEC DBMS_FLASHBACK_ARCHIVE.ENABLE_AT_VALID_TIME('ASOF', TO_
TIMESTAMP('02-Jan-12'));
```

The previous code example shows moving in time to '02-Jan-12' for Jennifer and Michael is valid. Now go ahead and try using "AS OF" with different date values to only show records for the set of data for Pat and Susan. Then try it again to show records for the set of data for Hermann and Shelley.

Once you are comfortable using TempVal, clean up by dropping the demo table that was used:

```
DROP TABLE EMPLOYEES_TEMPORAL_TEST;
Table dropped.
```

Automatic Data Optimization

Oracle Database 12*c* ADO needs to be aware of what is going on with the data at the segment and row levels. At these levels, access and modification of data is tracked with Heat Map. Figure 8-1 shows the concept of a heat map. The legend for Figure 8-1 is

* Represents high/hot levels of access and modification of data

+ Represents medium/moderate levels of access and modification of data

− Represents low/cold levels of access and modification of data

Heat Map is used by ADO to decide which actions to take, and when, based off of the access and modification of data. The more the data is accessed and/or modified, the hotter the data is.

We'll look at two ADO examples in this section. The first ADO example is a table that is moved from one tablespace to another due to it increasing past a size threshold. The second example is a table being compressed after 30 days of no data modification.

NOTE
For the following two examples, use a privileged account such as SYS or SYDBA. Instructions are provided on when to use the HR account.

ADO Table Movement

As SYSDBA, activate and confirm that Heat Map is turned on (continue to use a privileged account until you are instructed to use the HR account):

```
ALTER SYSTEM SET HEAT_MAP=ON SCOPE=BOTH;
System altered.
SELECT NAME, VALUE FROM V$PARAMETER
```

*	*	*	*		*	14
+	+	+	*	*	+	10
−	*	−	+	*	−	6
−	*	+	+	*		30
+	+	+	−	+		
*	−	*	−	*		

FIGURE 8-1. *Simple heat map*

```
WHERE NAME LIKE 'heat%';
NAME                  VALUE
-------------------- ------
heat_map              ON
```

Create two tablespaces to represent a fast disk and a slow disk, as shown next. The tablespace T1_ILM_TBS is the faster tablespace and T2_ILM_TBS is the slower tablespace. Then confirm the creation and size of each of the tablespaces.

```
create tablespace t1_ilm_tbs datafile '/opt/oracle/oradata/noncdb/t1_ilm_tbs.dbf'
size 10m reuse autoextend off extent management local;
Tablespace created.

create tablespace t2_ilm_tbs datafile '/opt/oracle/oradata/noncdb/t2_ilm_tbs.dbf'
size 10m reuse autoextend off extent management local;
Tablespace created.

SELECT TABLESPACE_NAME , FILE_NAME
FROM DBA_DATA_FILES
WHERE TABLESPACE_NAME LIKE '%ILM%'
ORDER BY 1;
TABLESPACE_NAME FILE_NAME
-------------- ---------------------------------------------
T1_ILM_TBS      /opt/oracle/oradata/noncdb/t1_ilm_tbs.dbf
T2_ILM_TBS      /opt/oracle/oradata/noncdb/t2_ilm_tbs.dbf

SELECT DF.TABLESPACE_NAME "TABLESPACE",
    DF.BYTES / (1024 * 1024) "SIZE (MB)",
    SUM(FS.BYTES) / (1024 * 1024) "FREE (MB)",
    NVL(ROUND(SUM(FS.BYTES) * 100 / DF.BYTES),1) "% FREE",
    ROUND((DF.BYTES - SUM(FS.BYTES)) * 100 / DF.BYTES) "% USED"
FROM DBA_FREE_SPACE FS,
(SELECT TABLESPACE_NAME,SUM(BYTES) BYTES
FROM DBA_DATA_FILES
GROUP BY TABLESPACE_NAME) DF
WHERE    FS.TABLESPACE_NAME (+) = DF.TABLESPACE_NAME
AND      DF.TABLESPACE_NAME LIKE 'T%ILM%TBS'
GROUP    BY DF.TABLESPACE_NAME, DF.BYTES
ORDER BY 1;
TABLESPACE    SIZE (MB) FREE (MB)  % FRE  % USED
------------- --------- ---------- ------ ------
T1_ILM_TBS           10         9     90      10
T2_ILM_TBS           10         9     90      10
```

The HR account is used for this example. If you have not already done so, set up the HR account with the following script. Connect to the database as an administrative user (SYS or SYSDBA).

```
ALTER USER HR IDENTIFIED BY hr;
ALTER USER HR ACCOUNT UNLOCK;
ALTER USER HR QUOTA UNLIMITED ON T1_ILM_TBS;
ALTER USER HR QUOTA UNLIMITED ON T2_ILM_TBS;
GRANT ALTER TABLESPACE, SELECT ANY DICTIONARY TO HR;
```

```
GRANT ALL ON TS$ TO HR;
GRANT ALL ON DBA_SEGMENTS TO HR;
```

In this example, we will create the HR.ILM_MOVE_TEST table and populate it. We are creating the table in the faster tablespace, T1_ILM_TBS. Later, we'll add an ILM policy to the table that will move the table to the slower, T2_ILM_TBS tablespace. The policy is activated when tablespace T1_ILM_TBS approaches less than 95 percent of free space available.

```
CREATE TABLE HR.ILM_MOVE_TEST TABLESPACE T1_ILM_TBS
AS SELECT * FROM HR.EMPLOYEES;
Table created.
```

The following procedure will help us quickly load the table HR.ILM_MOVE_ TEST. This causes the tablespace T1_ILM_TBS to fill up to a point where there is less than 95 percent of free space available.

```
DECLARE
STOP_LOOP PLS_INTEGER := 6;
SQL_TEST CLOB;
BEGIN
FOR I IN 1..STOP_LOOP LOOP
SQL_TEST := 'INSERT /*+ APPEND */ INTO HR.ILM_MOVE_TEST
SELECT * FROM HR.ILM_MOVE_TEST';
EXECUTE IMMEDIATE SQL_TEST;
COMMIT;
END LOOP;
END;
/
PL/SQL procedure successfully completed.
```

Next, gather fresh statistics for the table; confirm which tablespace is being used and the record count of the table. The record count of the table should be 6848. This confirms that the table is in the proper tablespace and that the records were inserted correctly.

```
EXEC DBMS_STATS.GATHER_TABLE_STATS('HR', 'ILM_MOVE_TEST');
PL/SQL procedure successfully completed.

SELECT OWNER, TABLE_NAME, TABLESPACE_NAME
FROM DBA_TABLES
WHERE OWNER = 'HR'
AND TABLE_NAME = 'ILM_MOVE_TEST';

OWNER                TABLE_NAME           TABLESPACE_NAME
-------------------- -------------------- --------------------
HR                   ILM_MOVE_TEST        T1_ILM_TBS
```

```
SELECT COUNT(*) FROM HR.ILM_MOVE_TEST;
COUNT(*)
----------
      6848
```

ADO requires Heat Map to be active. Confirm that Heat Map is active for ILM_MOVE_TEST:

```
SELECT OBJECT_NAME, SEGMENT_READ_TIME,
FROM DBA_HEAT_MAP_SEGMENT
WHERE OWNER ='HR'
AND OBJECT_NAME='ILM_MOVE_TEST';
OBJECT_NAME    SEGMENT_READ_TIME
------------- -----------------

ILM_MOVE_TEST           27-APR-13
```

The column SEGMENT_READ_TIME indicates the last timestamp on which the segment was read. This also indicates that Heat Map is active for the table.

Next, we'll add the policy to the table. The policy that we are adding to the HR.ILM_MOVE_TEST table will cause the table to be moved once the T1_ILM_TBS free space is below 95 percent.

```
ALTER TABLE HR.ILM_MOVE_TEST
ILM ADD POLICY TIER TO T2_ILM_TBS;
Table altered.
```

Once the table is altered, confirm that the policy is attached. Your policy name will be different from the one in the exam. In this example, policy_name is P102. The first query, shown next, confirms that the table will be moved to the slow tablespace, T2_ILM_TBS. The second query confirms that the policy is applied to the table ILM_MOVE_TEST.

```
SELECT CAST(POLICY_NAME AS VARCHAR2(30)) POLICY_NAME,
ACTION_TYPE, SCOPE, COMPRESSION_LEVEL, CAST(TIER_TABLESPACE AS
VARCHAR2(30)) TIER_TBS, CONDITION_TYPE, CONDITION_DAYS
FROM DBA_ILMDATAMOVEMENTPOLICIES
ORDER BY POLICY_NAME;
POLICY_NAME:    P102              ACTION_TYPE: STORAGE
SCOPE:          SEGMENT           COMPRESSION_LEVEL:
TIER_TBS:       T2_ILM_TBS        CONDITION_TYPE:
CONDITION_DAYS: 0

SELECT * FROM DBA_ILMOBJECTS;
POLICY_NAME:    P102              OBJECT_OWNER: HR
OBJECT_NAME:    ILM_MOVE_TEST     SUBOBJECT_NAME:
OBJECT_TYPE:    TABLE             INHERITED_FROM: POLICY NOT INHERITED
ENABLED: YES
```

The default thresholds for the ILM parameters are shown next. Changing the thresholds will cause the policy on the table to be run during the next default nightly maintenance window.

```
SELECT * FROM DBA_ILMPARAMETERS
WHERE NAME LIKE 'TBS%PERCENT%';
NAME                    VALUE
-------------------- ----------
TBS PERCENT USED      85
TBS PERCENT FREE      25

EXEC DBMS_ILM_ADMIN.CUSTOMIZE_ILM(DBMS_ILM_ADMIN.TBS_PERCENT_FREE,95)
PL/SQL procedure successfully completed.

EXEC DBMS_ILM_ADMIN.CUSTOMIZE_ILM(DBMS_ILM_ADMIN.TBS_PERCENT_USED,5)
PL/SQL procedure successfully completed.

SELECT * FROM DBA_ILMPARAMETERS
WHERE NAME LIKE 'TBS%PERCENT%';
NAME                    VALUE
-------------------- ----------
TBS PERCENT USED          5
TBS PERCENT FREE         95
```

As shown next, use DBMS_ILM.EXECUTE_ILM instead of waiting for the nightly maintenance window to move the table. *Use the HR user until we reset the environment at the end of this example.*

```
DECLARE
V_EXECUTIONID NUMBER;
BEGIN
DBMS_ILM.EXECUTE_ILM (ILM_SCOPE => DBMS_ILM.SCOPE_SCHEMA,
                      EXECUTION_MODE => DBMS_ILM.ILM_EXECUTION_OFFLINE,
                      TASK_ID => V_EXECUTIONID);
END;
/
PL/SQL procedure successfully completed.
```

Check the job with the following script. The job should run successfully and be the first row of the results.

```
SELECT UIT.TASK_ID, UIR.JOB_NAME, UIR.JOB_STATE
, TO_CHAR(UIT.CREATION_TIME, 'DD/MM/YYYY HH24:MI:SS')
  CREATION_TIME
, TO_CHAR(UIT.START_TIME, 'DD/MM/YYYY HH24:MI:SS')
  START_TIME
```

```
, TO_CHAR(UIR.COMPLETION_TIME,'DD/MM/YYYY HH24:MI:SS')
  COMPLETION
, TO_CHAR((UIR.COMPLETION_TIME - UIT.START_TIME), 'HH24:MI:SS')
  "ELAPSED TIME"
FROM USER_ILMTASKS UIT, USER_ILMRESULTS UIR
WHERE UIT.TASK_ID = UIR.TASK_ID
ORDER BY UIT.CREATION_TIME DESC;
TASK_ID:  1332
JOB_NAME:   ILMJOB2888
JOB_STATE:   COMPLETED SUCCESSFULLY
CREATION_TIME:  27/04/2013 06:07:02
START_TIME:  27/04/2013 06:07:02
COMPLETION:  27/04/2013 06:07:05
ELAPSED TIME:  +000000000 00:00:02.341728
```

Confirm that the table has moved from the T1_ILM_TBS tablespace to the
T2_ILM_TBS tablespace:

```
SELECT TABLE_NAME, TABLESPACE_NAME
FROM USER_TABLES
WHERE TABLE_NAME = 'ILM_MOVE_TEST';
TABLE_NAME               TABLESPACE_NAME
-------------------- --------------------

ILM_MOVE_TEST            T2_ILM_TBS
```

As SYSDBA, reset the environment by changing the ILM threshold parameter to
its default, and then drop the table and tablespaces:

```
EXEC DBMS_ILM_ADMIN.CUSTOMIZE_ILM(DBMS_ILM_ADMIN.TBS_PERCENT_FREE,25);
PL/SQL procedure successfully completed.

EXEC DBMS_ILM_ADMIN.CUSTOMIZE_ILM(DBMS_ILM_ADMIN.TBS_PERCENT_USED,85);
PL/SQL procedure successfully completed.

SELECT * FROM DBA_ILMPARAMETERS;
NAME                     VALUE
----------------     ----------
TBS PERCENT USED           85
TBS PERCENT FREE           25
DROP TABLE HR.ILM_MOVE_TEST PURGE;
Table dropped.
DROP TABLESPACE T1_ILM_TBS
INCLUDING CONTENTS AND DATAFILES;
Tablespace dropped.
DROP TABLESPACE T2_ILM_TBS
INCLUDING CONTENTS AND DATAFILES;
Tablespace dropped.
```

ADO Table Compression

This second example of ADO demonstrates automatic compression, where a table is compressed if no modification of the data has occurred for 30 days. The compression used is segment-level compression. Row-level compression is covered in the next section, "Compression."

Instead of having to wait for 30 days to elapse for this demo, we are going to create a procedure, ADJ_TIME, to accelerate the "aging" of the data. This procedure essentially inserts a record into the Heat Map statistics that fools ADO into thinking the data has not been modified for 30 days. (This is something that you probably would not do in a production environment.) Create the ADJ_TIME procedure as shown next. Use a privileged account such as SYS or SYDBA until you are instructed to switch to using the HR account.

```
CREATE OR REPLACE PROCEDURE ADJ_TIME (OBJECT_ID NUMBER,
DATA_OBJECT_ID NUMBER,
N_DAYS NUMBER,
P_TS# NUMBER,
P_SEGMENT_ACCESS NUMBER)
AS
BEGIN
INSERT INTO SYS.HEAT_MAP_STAT$ (OBJ#, DATAOBJ#, TRACK_TIME,
SEGMENT_ACCESS, TS#) VALUES
(OBJECT_ID, DATA_OBJECT_ID, SYSDATE - N_DAYS,
P_SEGMENT_ACCESS, P_TS# );
COMMIT;
END;
/
Procedure created.
```

If you have not already enabled Heat Map from the previous example, enable it with the following script. When Heat Map is enabled, access and modification of data is tracked at the segment and row level. We need the tracking to be turned on so that Oracle Database knows that the data has not been modified for 30 days.

```
ALTER SYSTEM SET HEAT_MAP=ON SCOPE=BOTH;
System altered.
```

The example table for this demo is a copy of HR.EMPLOYEES, HR.ILM_ COMPRESSION_TEST. We will also add some data to the table and check the size after the data is added. A policy will then be added to the table so ADO can evaluate when to compress the table. By using the procedure ADJ_TIME, we "age" the data causing ADO to then compress the data that has not been modified.

```
CREATE TABLE HR.ILM_COMPRESSION_TEST TABLESPACE USERS
AS SELECT * FROM HR.EMPLOYEES;
Table created.
```

To increase the size of HR.ILM_COMPRESSION_TEST, use the following script to insert additional records. Confirm the record count after the additional records are inserted.

```
DECLARE
STOP_LOOP PLS_INTEGER := 6;
SQL_TEST CLOB;
BEGIN
FOR I IN 1..STOP_LOOP LOOP
SQL_TEST := 'INSERT /*+ APPEND */ INTO
HR.ILM_COMPRESSION_TEST
SELECT * FROM HR.ILM_COMPRESSION_TEST';
EXECUTE IMMEDIATE SQL_TEST;
COMMIT;
END LOOP;
END;
/
PL/SQL procedure successfully completed.

SELECT COUNT(*) FROM HR.ILM_COMPRESSION_TEST;
COUNT(*)

----------
      6848
```

Confirm that the size of the table is .6875MB, as shown next. At the competition of this example, the compressed size of the table will be 0.5MB.

```
SELECT SEGMENT_NAME, BYTES/1024/1024 MB
FROM DBA_SEGMENTS
WHERE OWNER = 'HR'
AND SEGMENT_NAME = 'ILM_COMPRESSION_TEST';
SEGMENT_NAME                    MB
----------------------- ----------
ILM_COMPRESSION_TEST        .6875
```

Make sure that the table is being tracked by Heat Map:

```
SELECT OBJECT_NAME, FULL_SCAN
FROM DBA_HEAT_MAP_SEGMENT
WHERE OWNER ='HR'
AND OBJECT_NAME='ILM_COMPRESSION_TEST';
OBJECT_NAME            FULL_SCAN
-------------------- ---------
ILM_COMPRESSION_TEST 27-APR-13
```

Next, we apply the compression policy to the table. The options for compression policy are related to time and activity. For time, increments are designated in number of days (as in the following example), months, or years. For activity, the possible conditions are **low access**, **no access**, **no modification**, and **creation**. The activity for creation is a time period after the table is created. Again, in this example, after 30 days of no modification, the table will be compressed.

```
ALTER TABLE HR.ILM_COMPRESSION_TEST
ILM ADD POLICY ROW STORE COMPRESS
ADVANCED SEGMENT AFTER 30 DAYS OF NO MODIFICATION;
Table altered.
```

Confirm that the advanced compression policy is created and applied to the table, as shown next. Your policy name will be different. Make sure that the policy name for the next two queries are the same.

```
SELECT CAST(POLICY_NAME AS VARCHAR2(30)) POLICY_NAME,
ACTION_TYPE, SCOPE, COMPRESSION_LEVEL, CAST(TIER_TABLESPACE AS
VARCHAR2(30)) TIER_TBS, CONDITION_TYPE, CONDITION_DAYS
FROM DBA_ILMDATAMOVEMENTPOLICIES
ORDER BY POLICY_NAME;
POLICY_NAME: P122
ACTION_TYPE: COMPRESSION
SCOPE: SEGMENT
COMPRESSION_LEVEL: ADVANCED
TIER_TBS:
CONDITION_TYPE: LAST MODIFICATION TIME
CONDITION_DAYS: 30


SELECT * FROM DBA_ILMOBJECTS;
POLICY_NAME: P122
OBJECT_OWNER:HR
OBJECT_NAME: ILM_COMPRESSION_TEST
SUBOBJECT_NAME:
OBJECT_TYPE: TABLE
INHERITED_FROM: POLICY NOT INHERITED
ENABLED: YES
```

At the beginning of this example, we created ADJ_TIME to adjust SYS.HEAT_MAP_STAT$ so that it appears that there has been no modification to the data for the ILM_COMPRESSION_TEST table. Now, execute ADJ_TIME to modify the data SYS.HEAT_MAP_STAT$:

```
DECLARE
    V_OBJECT_ID NUMBER;
    V_DATAOBJ_ID NUMBER;
    V_TS_NUM NUMBER;
BEGIN
  SELECT OBJECT_ID, DATA_OBJECT_ID INTO V_OBJECT_ID, V_DATAOBJ_ID
  FROM ALL_OBJECTS
```

```
WHERE OBJECT_NAME = 'ILM_COMPRESSION_TEST'
AND OWNER = 'HR';
SELECT TS# INTO V_TS_NUM
FROM SYS.TS$ A,
DBA_SEGMENTS B
WHERE A.NAME = B.TABLESPACE_NAME
AND B.SEGMENT_NAME = 'ILM_COMPRESSION_TEST';
COMMIT;
  SYS.ADJ_TIME
  (OBJECT_ID => V_OBJECT_ID,
   DATA_OBJECT_ID => V_DATAOBJ_ID,
   N_DAYS => 30,
   P_TS# => V_TS_NUM,
   P_SEGMENT_ACCESS => 1);
END;
/
PL/SQL procedure successfully completed.
```

Currently there is no compression for the ILM_COMPRESSION_TEST table because the 30 days have not passed:

```
SELECT COMPRESSION, COMPRESS_FOR FROM DBA_TABLES
WHERE OWNER = 'HR' AND TABLE_NAME = 'ILM_COMPRESSION_TEST';
COMPRESS COMPRESS_FOR
-------- ------------
DISABLED
```

To view the updated statistics right away, you need to restart the database:

```
-- AS SYSDBA
-- BOUNCE THE INSTANCE
```

Check the statistics after restarting the database. The SEGMENT_WRITE_TIME value should be 30 days in the past.

```
SELECT OWNER, OBJECT_NAME, SEGMENT_WRITE_TIME
FROM DBA_HEAT_MAP_SEGMENT
WHERE OBJECT_NAME='ILM_COMPRESSION_TEST';
OWNER   OBJECT_NAME             SEGMENT_WRITE_TIME
------  --------------------    -------------------
HR      ILM_COMPRESSION_TEST         28-MAR-13
```

Instead of waiting the normal nightly maintenance window, force the execution of ADO. *Use the HR account for the next five commands, until we reset the environment.*

```
declare
v_executionid number;
begin
```

```
    dbms_ilm.execute_ILM (ILM_SCOPE => dbms_ilm.SCOPE_SCHEMA,
    execution_mode => dbms_ilm.ilm_execution_offline,
    task_id => v_executionid);
end;
/
PL/SQL procedure successfully completed.
```

Check to make sure that the latest job completes successfully:

```
SELECT UIT.TASK_ID, UIR.JOB_NAME, UIR.JOB_STATE
, TO_CHAR(UIT.CREATION_TIME, 'DD/MM/YYYY HH24:MI:SS')
  CREATION_TIME
, TO_CHAR(UIT.START_TIME, 'DD/MM/YYYY HH24:MI:SS')
  START_TIME
, TO_CHAR(UIR.COMPLETION_TIME,'DD/MM/YYYY HH24:MI:SS')
  COMPLETION
, TO_CHAR((UIR.COMPLETION_TIME - UIT.START_TIME), 'HH24:MI:SS')
  "ELAPSED TIME"
FROM USER_ILMTASKS UIT, USER_ILMRESULTS UIR
WHERE UIT.TASK_ID = UIR.TASK_ID
ORDER BY UIT.CREATION_TIME;
TASK_ID: 1383
JOB_NAME: ILMJOB3050
JOB_STATE: COMPLETED SUCCESSFULLY
CREATION_TIME: 27/04/2013 14:46:25
START_TIME: 27/04/2013 14:46:25
COMPLETION: 27/04/2013 14:46:28
ELAPSED TIME: +000000000 00:00:03.184412
```

Gather fresh statistics on the HR.ILM_COMPRESSION_TEST table:

```
EXEC DBMS_STATS.GATHER_TABLE_STATS('HR','ILM_COMPRESSION_TEST');
PL/SQL procedure successfully completed.
```

HR.ILM_COMPRESSION_TEST now has advanced compression. Confirm this with this script:

```
SELECT COMPRESSION, COMPRESS_FOR
FROM USER_TABLES
WHERE TABLE_NAME = 'ILM_COMPRESSION_TEST';
COMPRESS COMPRESS_FOR
-------- -------------
ENABLED  ADVANCED
```

Now confirm that the size of HR.ILM_COMPRESSION_TEST has been reduced to 0.5MB:

```
SELECT SEGMENT_NAME, BYTES/1024/1024 MB
FROM USER_SEGMENTS
```

```
WHERE SEGMENT_NAME = 'ILM_COMPRESSION_TEST';
SEGMENT_NAME                        MB
------------------------ ----------
ILM_COMPRESSION_TEST               .5
```

If you did get the expected results, reset the environment and try this example again. Reset the environment and remove the demo by using a privileged account such as SYS or SYSDBA:

```
ALTER TABLE HR.ILM_COMPRESSION_TEST
ILM DELETE_ALL;
Table altered.
SELECT * FROM USER_ILMPOLICIES;
no rows selected
SELECT * FROM USER_ILMDATAMOVEMENTPOLICIES;
no rows selected
DROP TABLE HR.ILM_COMPRESSION_TEST PURGE;
Table dropped.
DROP PROCEDURE SYS.ADJ_TIME;
Procedure dropped.
```

Compression

There are two new compression algorithms that can be used in ADO. We used the first one in the previous section for the example of ADO automatic compression. We added a policy to the HR.ILM_COMPRESSION_TEST table that used segment-level compression after 30 days of no data modification. The other compression technique uses row-level compression. The following is a direct comparison of the two methods.

Segment-level compression:

```
ALTER TABLE HR.ILM_COMPRESSION_TEST
ILM ADD POLICY ROW STORE
COMPRESS ADVANCED   SEGMENT AFTER 30 DAYS
OF NO MODIFICATION;
```

Row-level compression:

```
ALTER TABLE HR.ILM_COMPRESSION_TEST
ILM ADD POLICY ROW STORE
COMPRESS ADVANCED   ROW AFTER 30 DAYS
OF NO MODIFICATION;
```

Go ahead and try the ADO automatic compression again with row-level compression instead of segment-level compression. Just make the changes shown above to the policy by using the **alter table** command for row-level compression. Also, increase the STOP_LOOP PLS_INTEGER to a greater number.

NOTE
Refer to Oracle Database SQL Language Reference
12c Release 1 (12.1) E17209-12 *for complete syntax
options related to ILM compression.*

Temporal History

Oracle Database 11*g* offered Total Recall. Total Recall was the branding name for a
feature called Flashback Data Archive (FDA). FDA enables you to take a portion of a
tablespace and define a size and retention time to record changes in data for
particular tables, as demonstrated in the following list.

- Create a tablespace that will be partially used for FLASHBACK DATA
  ARCHIVE:

  ```
  create tablespace fda_ts datafile
  '/u01/app/oracle/oradata/fda_ts_01.dbf'
  size 15m;
  ```

- Create the FLASHBACK ARCHIVE using the tablespace just created:

  ```
  CREATE FLASHBACK ARCHIVE DEFAULT
  fla001 TABLESPACE fda_ts
  QUOTA 10G RETENTION 1 YEAR;
  ```

- Create the table that will use FLASHBACK ARCHIVE:

  ```
  CREATE TABLE hr.test123 (col1 varchar2(10),
                           col2 VARCHAR2(10))
  FLASHBACK ARCHIVE fla001;
  ```

- Remove the table from FLASHBACK ARCHIVE and drop the table:

  ```
  ALTER TABLE hr.test123 NO FLASHBACK ARCHIVE;
  DROP TABLE hr.test123;
  ```

In-Database Archiving, Temporal Validity, and Temporal History

Deciding when to use In-Database Archiving, Temporal Validity, and Temporal
History can be a little tricky. Here are some guidelines:

Feature	Usage Example
In-Database Archiving	Records are either visible or invisible.
Temporal Validity	Records are visible during a specific period of time.
Temporal History	Histories of the records are always recorded while the table is in FLASHBACK ARCHIVE.

Performance Enhancements

Oracle Database 12c comes with built-in performance enhancements (PEs) that are specific to Business Intelligence and Data Warehousing. The following PEs are grouped in the broad categories of Materialized Views (MVs) and Parallelism. Since these PEs do not require any configuration, this table provides only a brief description of each and notes its benefit.

Grouping	Performance Enhancement	Description	Benefit
Materialized Views	Out-of-place materialized view refresh	Stale MVs are now refreshed by out-of-place MVs. This increases availability by "swapping" the stale MV with a fresh MV.	Faster refresh of MV
	Synchronous materialized view refresh	MVs and base tables can be refreshed simultaneously.	Faster refresh of MV
Parallelism	Enhanced parallel statement queuing	Provides the ability to bypass parallel statement queue.	Increased visibility into parallel queue allows prioritizing by business rules
	Improved automatic degree of parallelism (Auto DOP)	The database has better evaluation of when to use Auto DOP based on more database and statement characteristics.	Better performance

End of Line

Oracle Database 12c introduces a number of new features directly related to BI and DW. Improvements in analytic capabilities, better statistics, ILM, and performance continue to make Oracle's flagship product an excellent choice for BI and DW. Our next chapter covers the topic of security.

CHAPTER
9

Security New Features

T his chapter describes the new features in Oracle Database 12*c* that are related to security. In this chapter, we cover the following features and topics:

- Auditing
- Privilege Analysis
- Data Redaction
- Miscellaneous security improvements
- Mixing and matching security features

NOTE
You can find the name and description of each Oracle Database process in Appendix F of the Oracle Database Reference.

Auditing

The need to audit database activities varies depending on the specific industry. Industries in the areas of healthcare, finance, and government (local, state, and federal) are required to audit for legal and regulatory compliance. Regardless of the reasons for auditing, many DBAs are required to audit at some level.

Changes in the SGA

Oracle Database 12*c* introduces Unified Audit Trail (UAT) to simplify auditing. In order to support UAT, the SGA now has two additional named queues. These queues are used to record the audit activity in memory. Audit activity is stored in one queue at a time, and the second queue is used once the first queue is filled. When the first queue becomes full, the background process GEN0 (General Task Execution Process) flushes the records in memory to the read-only AUDSYS table. The GEN0 process essentially writes the records to disk.

The default size of the queues is 1MB each. The size of the queues can be increased to 30MB depending on how much auditing is set up in your database and the need to flush the audit activities to disk. Resizing the queues requires shutting down the database and changing the parameter **unified_audit_sga_queue_size**. Plan the sizing of this parameter when you first enable UAT. The default value should generally be sufficient.

Enabling UAT

UAT is not enabled by default in this release of Oracle Database 12c (12.1.0.1.0). In order to enable UAT, you need to relink Oracle Database. After relinking Oracle Database, all instances that run from the relinked ORACLE_HOME will have UAT enabled. The process to relink Oracle Database to enable UAT is simple:

1. Stop all Oracle processes running from ORACLE_HOME (listener and database).

2. Relink the Oracle Database binaries using the **uniaud_on** parameter.

3. Restart the Oracle processes.

The following example shows how to relink the Oracle binaries (in step 2):

```
[oracle@localhost lib]$ cd $ORACLE_HOME/rdbms/lib
[oracle@localhost lib]$ make -f ins_rdbms.mk uniaud_on ioracle ORACLE_
HOME=$ORACLE_HOME
```

This process may take a couple of minutes, depending on your hardware. Once relinking is complete, restart the Oracle processes (listener and database) and log into the database, as shown next. Look for "and Unified Auditing" at the end of the login banner.

```
SQL*Plus: Release 12.1.0.1.0 Production on Thu May 2 22:43:14 2013
Copyright (c) 1982, 2012, Oracle.  All rights reserved.
Connected to:
Oracle Database 12c Enterprise Edition Release 12.1.0.1.0 - 64bit Production
With the Partitioning, OLAP, Advanced Analytics, Real Application Testing
and Unified Auditing options
```

NOTE
If you want to reduce the outage time your database would experience while relinking to enable UAT, you can create a new ORACLE_HOME. You can then relink the Oracle Executable there. Move the database SPFILE and password file to the new ORACLE_HOME. Then shut down your database, point it to the new ORACLE_HOME directory, and restart the database.

Tom Says
The audit trail is also flushed on a timed basis, about every 3 seconds, depending on the load on the system. So, you won't have audit trail records sitting in the SGA for long periods of time; they'll safely be on disk on a regular basis regardless of the queue size.

Forcing Immediate Writes

If you are in an environment that does not allow for a buffering of audit activities, you can use the following code to require that audit activity be written immediately to disk as it is created:

```
EXEC DBMS_AUDIT_MGMT.SET_AUDIT_TRAIL_PROPERTY(
  DBMS_AUDIT_MGMT.AUDIT_TRAIL_UNIFIED,
  DBMS_AUDIT_MGMT.AUDIT_TRAIL_WRITE_MODE,
  DBMS_AUDIT_MGMT.AUDIT_TRAIL_IMMEDIATE_WRITE);
```

Separation of Duties

UAT provides better security and reporting through the use of two specific roles, AUDIT_ADMIN and AUDIT_VIEWER. Users who have been granted the role of AUDIT_ADMIN can set up and administer audit policies. Users who have been granted the role of AUDIT_VIEWER can review the audit results. Having these two separate roles follows the concept of separation of duties (SoD), which requires the participation of more than one person to complete a specified task. By splitting the task, an internal control is created that prevents a prohibited activity from being committed by one person. In this case, the prohibited activity would be one person creating and reviewing audits. The concept of SOD being applied to auditing does not allow for one person to be the audit admin and the review of the audit logs.

Basic Audit Information

In this example of basic audit information (BAI), MR_SMITH is the auditor who will create the audit policies, and AUDITMAN will review the audit results. We will audit activity on the HR.CC_INFO table, created with the following code. Use a privileged account such as DBA to create the HR.CC_INFO table, MR_SMITH, and AUDITMAN. This example was created in a pluggable database.

NOTE
UAT is part of both container and pluggable databases.

```
CREATE TABLE HR.CC_INFO (
    FNAME    VARCHAR2(30),
    LNAME    VARCHAR2(30),
    CCNUM    VARCHAR2(30),
    CCCODE   VARCHAR2(10),
    ZIP_CODE VARCHAR2(10)
) TABLESPACE EXAMPLE;
```

Create MR_SMITH as the AUDIT_ADMIN user who creates the audit policies:

```
CREATE USER MR_SMITH IDENTIFIED BY sunglasses
DEFAULT TABLESPACE USERS;
GRANT CONNECT, RESOURCE TO MR_SMITH;
ALTER USER MR_SMITH QUOTA 10M ON USERS;
GRANT AUDIT_ADMIN TO MR_SMITH;
```

Create AUDITMAN as the auditor who reviews the BAI:

```
CREATE USER AUDITMAN IDENTIFIED BY auditme
DEFAULT TABLESPACE USERS;
GRANT CONNECT, RESOURCE TO AUDITMAN;
ALTER USER AUDITMAN QUOTA 10M ON USERS;
GRANT AUDIT_VIEWER TO AUDITMAN;
```

Now, as MR_SMITH, create and enable the policy T001 on the HR.CC_INFO table:

```
CREATE AUDIT POLICY T001 ACTIONS SELECT, INSERT,
UPDATE, DELETE ON HR.CC_INFO;
AUDIT POLICY T001;
```

We want the UAT to be immediately written to disk:

```
EXEC DBMS_AUDIT_MGMT.SET_AUDIT_TRAIL_PROPERTY(
DBMS_AUDIT_MGMT.AUDIT_TRAIL_UNIFIED,
DBMS_AUDIT_MGMT.AUDIT_TRAIL_WRITE_MODE,
DBMS_AUDIT_MGMT.AUDIT_TRAIL_IMMEDIATE_WRITE);
```

Use the following query to confirm that the policy is enabled, before you run any DML:

```
SELECT * FROM AUDIT_UNIFIED_ENABLED_POLICIES
WHERE POLICY_NAME = 'T001';
```

The results of this query should be as follows:

```
USER_NAME   POLICY_NAME   ENABLED_OPT   SUC FAI
----------  ------------  ------------  --- ---
ALL USERS   T001          BY            YES YES
```

As HR, run the following DML to create audit activity:

```
INSERT INTO HR.CC_INFO VALUES('TOM',    'LEE',    '123456789',
'1234', '91729');
INSERT INTO HR.CC_INFO VALUES('CHUCK', 'SMITH',  '234567891',
'2345', '91730');
```

```
INSERT INTO HR.CC_INFO VALUES('DAVID', 'KIM',        '345678912',
'3456', '91731');
INSERT INTO HR.CC_INFO VALUES('VIKI',  'MICHELLE', '456789123',
'4567', '91732');
INSERT INTO HR.CC_INFO VALUES('FOCUS', 'VISION',    '567891234',
'5678', '91733');
COMMIT;
UPDATE HR.CC_INFO SET ZIP_CODE = '99999'
WHERE ZIP_CODE = '91733';
COMMIT;
DELETE FROM HR.CC_INFO
WHERE ZIP_CODE = '99999';
COMMIT;
```

All of the above code was just the setup so that AUDITMAN can determine which DML activity occurred on HR.CC_INFO. As AUDITMAN, run this query to show the table creation and DML activity on HR.CC_INFO:

```
SELECT EVENT_TIMESTAMP,
       OBJECT_SCHEMA || '.' || OBJECT_NAME AS "AUDIT_OBJECT",
       SQL_TEXT
FROM UNIFIED_AUDIT_TRAIL
WHERE  OBJECT_NAME = 'CC_INFO'
AND    OBJECT_SCHEMA = 'HR'
AND    OBJECT_SCHEMA IS NOT NULL
ORDER BY EVENT_TIMESTAMP;
```

Disable and drop the policy as MR_SMITH:

```
NOAUDIT POLICY T001;
DROP AUDIT POLICY T001;
```

Then change the write policy back to the default:

```
EXEC DBMS_AUDIT_MGMT.SET_AUDIT_TRAIL_PROPERTY(
DBMS_AUDIT_MGMT.AUDIT_TRAIL_UNIFIED,
DBMS_AUDIT_MGMT.AUDIT_TRAIL_WRITE_MODE,
DBMS_AUDIT_MGMT.AUDIT_TRAIL_QUEUED_WRITE);
```

Extended Audit Information

Extended audit information (EAI) allows the auditing of the following Oracle Database 12c components:

- Fine Grained Auditing (FGA)
- Data Pump export/imports
- RMAN activity

- Oracle Label Security (OLS)

- Database Vault

- Real Application Security (RAS)

For the EAI example, we'll audit Data Pump activity. This example picks up from the BAI example using the same HR.CC_INFO table. The activity to be audited is expdp.

In this example, use a privileged account such as SYSDBA to create the directory for the export, and grant the necessary permissions:

```
CREATE OR REPLACE DIRECTORY UAT_DEMO AS '/u01/app/oracle/
product/12.1.0.1/demo/unified_audit_trail';
GRANT READ, WRITE ON DIRECTORY UAT_DEMO TO HR;
```

Now, as MR_SMITH, create and enable the policy AUDIT_DP_ACTIVITY:

```
CREATE AUDIT POLICY AUDIT_DP_ACTIVITY
ACTIONS COMPONENT=DATAPUMP ALL;
AUDIT POLICY AUDIT_DP_ACTIVITY;
```

Now, as HR, use Data Pump to export the HR.CC_INFO table:

```
expdp hr/hr@localhost:1521/pdb1 tables=CC_INFO
directory=UAT_DEMO
dumpfile=UAT_DEMO.dmp
logfile=expdp_UAT_DEMO.log
```

Once the export is completed, use AUDITMAN to look at the audit activity:

```
SELECT EVENT_TIMESTAMP,
       DP_TEXT_PARAMETERS1,
       DP_BOOLEAN_PARAMETERS1
FROM UNIFIED_AUDIT_TRAIL
WHERE  DP_TEXT_PARAMETERS1 IS NOT NULL
ORDER BY EVENT_TIMESTAMP;
```

Disable and drop the policy as MR_SMITH:

```
NOAUDIT POLICY AUDIT_DP_ACTIVITY;
DROP AUDIT POLICY AUDIT_DP_ACTIVITY;
```

Then change the write policy back to the default:

```
EXEC DBMS_AUDIT_MGMT.SET_AUDIT_TRAIL_PROPERTY(
DBMS_AUDIT_MGMT.AUDIT_TRAIL_UNIFIED,
DBMS_AUDIT_MGMT.AUDIT_TRAIL_WRITE_MODE,
DBMS_AUDIT_MGMT.AUDIT_TRAIL_QUEUED_WRITE);
```

Privilege Analysis

Oracle Database 12c Privilege Analysis (PA) is used to determine if there are users or roles that have excessive privileges. It has, in the past, been common practice to overallocate privileges for the sake of simplicity rather than take the time and due diligence needed to create users and roles properly. No doubt, by now, you have recognized this as a (very) bad practice. Now you need some tool to analyze legacy accounts and the privileges granted to them (because you will never again overallocate privileges to user accounts, right?) Oracle Database 12c introduces Privilege Analysis (PA) to help with this task. PA is the tool to use after the fact to determine which privileges users and roles use.

Privilege Analysis Overview

The Oracle Database 12c PA process is composed of the following steps:

1. Create the analysis capture process (ACP). You can choose one of four options: capture the entire database, capture by role(s), capture by context (SYS_CONTEXT), or capture by a combination of role and context.

2. Enable the ACP.

3. Wait for a period of time to allow the ACP to record privilege usage activity.

4. Disable the ACP.

5. Generate the results of the ACP.

6. Analyze the results of the ACP.

The following section provides an example of this process.

Privilege Analysis Example

Referring to the previous six steps that comprise PA, use the HR account during step 3 and use a privileged account for the rest of the steps. Once again, we will use the HR.CC_INFO table for this example. First, drop the HR.CC_INFO table:

```
DROP TABLE HR.CC_INFO PURGE;
```

For step 1, you need to decide on which analysis capture method to use. The choice depends on the scope of your analysis needs. All four methods are shown next for the sake of completeness. The first three are for reference only and are not part of the example. The fourth is the capture by context (SYS_CONTEXT) method, which is what we will use in this example.

You would use the following if you wanted to create a database-wide analysis capture:

```
BEGIN
 DBMS_PRIVILEGE_CAPTURE.CREATE_CAPTURE(
 NAME => 'PRIV_ANALYSIS_DB',
 DESCRIPTION => 'ANALYZE ALL PRIVILEGES IN DB',
 TYPE => DBMS_PRIVILEGE_CAPTURE.G_DATABASE);
END;
```

Capturing by ROLE would be accomplished with this statement:

```
BEGIN
 DBMS_PRIVILEGE_CAPTURE.CREATE_CAPTURE(
 NAME => 'PRIV_ANALYSIS_RESOURCE',
 DESCRIPTION => 'RECORD PRIVILEGE USE BY PUBLIC',
 TYPE => DBMS_PRIVILEGE_CAPTURE.G_ROLE,
 ROLES => ROLE_NAME_LIST('RESOURCE'));
END;
```

This is the combination of analysis capturing with ROLE and CONTEXT information:

```
BEGIN
 DBMS_PRIVILEGE_CAPTURE.CREATE_CAPTURE(
 NAME => 'PRIV_ANALYSIS_HR_USER_RESOURCE',
 DESCRIPTION => 'RECORD PRIVILEGE USE BY HR USER WITH RESOURCE',
 TYPE =>  DBMS_PRIVILEGE_CAPTURE.G_ROLE_AND_CONTEXT,
 ROLES =>  ROLE_NAME_LIST('RESOURCE'),
 CONDITION => 'SYS_CONTEXT(''USERENV'', ''SESSION_USER'') = ''HR''');
END;
```

The following method is the one that we are using in this PA example. It creates an analysis capture for a particular user, 'PRIV_ANALYSIS_HR_USER'. We then immediately enable the capture, which is step 2.

```
BEGIN
 DBMS_PRIVILEGE_CAPTURE.CREATE_CAPTURE(
 NAME => 'PRIV_ANALYSIS_HR_USER',
 DESCRIPTION => 'RECORD PRIVILEGE USE BY HR USER',
 TYPE =>  DBMS_PRIVILEGE_CAPTURE.G_CONTEXT,
 CONDITION => 'SYS_CONTEXT(''USERENV'', ''SESSION_USER'') = ''HR''');
END;
/

EXEC DBMS_PRIVILEGE_CAPTURE.ENABLE_CAPTURE(NAME =>
'PRIV_ANALYSIS_HR_USER')
```

Note the NAME of this capture, as you will use it during steps 4 and 5.

Now that we have the capture 'PRIV_ANALYSIS_HR_USER' created, we need to create the table and some DML activity to be captured in step 3. Now, connect to the

HR account (starting a new session) or start a new SQL*Plus session. Now we want to create the HR.CC_INFO table and insert some data using the following SQL statements:

```
CREATE TABLE HR.CC_INFO
(FNAME     VARCHAR2(30),
 LNAME     VARCHAR2(30),
 CCNUM     VARCHAR2(30),
 CCCODE    VARCHAR2(10),
 ZIP_CODE VARCHAR2(10)
) TABLESPACE EXAMPLE;

INSERT INTO HR.CC_INFO VALUES('TOM',    'LEE',      '123456789',
  '1234', '91729');
INSERT INTO HR.CC_INFO VALUES('CHUCK', 'SMITH',     '234567891',
  '2345', '91730');
INSERT INTO HR.CC_INFO VALUES('DAVID', 'KIM',       '345678912',
  '3456', '91731');
INSERT INTO HR.CC_INFO VALUES('VIKI',   'MICHELLE', '456789123',
  '4567', '91732');
INSERT INTO HR.CC_INFO VALUES('FOCUS', 'VISION',    '567891234',
  '5678', '91733');
COMMIT;

UPDATE HR.CC_INFO SET ZIP_CODE = '99999'
WHERE ZIP_CODE = '91733';
COMMIT;

DELETE FROM HR.CC_INFO
WHERE ZIP_CODE = '99999';
COMMIT;
```

To complete steps 4 and 5, use the privileged account to disable the capture and generate the results:

```
EXEC DBMS_PRIVILEGE_CAPTURE.DISABLE_CAPTURE(NAME =>
  'PRIV_ANALYSIS_HR_USER')
EXEC DBMS_PRIVILEGE_CAPTURE.GENERATE_RESULT(NAME =>
  'PRIV_ANALYSIS_HR_USER')
```

The final step, the analysis of privileges, involves querying a handful of DBA_* tables. Table 9-1 lists these tables and provides a description of what type of analysis you can perform on each.

The following list shows the query that you would use for each type of analysis:

- Analyze which system privileges were used:

```
SELECT USERNAME, USED_ROLE , SYS_PRIV
FROM DBA_USED_SYSPRIVS
WHERE USERNAME = 'HR';
```

Table Name	Description
DBA_USED_SYSPRIVS	Analyze which system privileges were used.
DBA_USED_OBJPRIVS	Analyze which object privileges were used.
DBA_USED_PRIVS	Analyze which system and object privileges were used.
DBA_USED_OBJPRIVS_PATH	Analyze how privileges were acquired.
DBA_UNUSED_PRIVS	Analyze which system and object privileges were not used.

TABLE 9-1. *Views related to Privilege Analysis*

- Analyze which object privileges were used:

```
SELECT USERNAME, OBJECT_OWNER,
OBJECT_NAME, OBJECT_TYPE, OBJ_PRIV
FROM DBA_USED_OBJPRIVS
WHERE USERNAME = 'HR';
```

- Analyze which system and object privileges were used:

```
SELECT USERNAME , SYS_PRIV, OBJ_PRIV,
       OBJECT_OWNER, OBJECT_NAME
FROM   DBA_USED_PRIVS
WHERE  USERNAME = 'HR';
```

- Analyze how privileges were acquired:

```
SELECT USERNAME, OBJ_PRIV,
       OBJECT_NAME, PATH
FROM   DBA_USED_OBJPRIVS_PATH
WHERE  USERNAME = 'HR';
```

- Analyze which system and object privileges were not used:

```
SELECT USERNAME , SYS_PRIV, OBJ_PRIV,
       OBJECT_OWNER, OBJECT_NAME
FROM   DBA_UNUSED_PRIVS
WHERE  USERNAME = 'HR';
```

Once your analysis is complete, you can disable and drop the capturing of PA. One thing to consider is that dropping the capture of PA also means dropping the related data that is used for analysis. So, before you execute the **drop** command, make sure that you really want to drop the capture and have completed all of your analyses. Since we only enabled and disabled 'PRIV_ANALYSIS_HR_USER', we can now drop all the captures using a DBA account and the package that follows.

```
EXEC DBMS_PRIVILEGE_CAPTURE.DROP_CAPTURE(NAME =>
'PRIV_ANALYSIS_HR_USER')
```

Data Redaction

Oracle Database 12c introduces Data Redaction as a new feature. Data Redaction is different from Data Masking. Data Masking is used to change the actual data that is being moved from a production environment to a lower development and test environment. With Data Redaction, just the display of the data is changed, not the data itself.

Limiting the ability of customer service representatives (CSRs) to see credit card numbers is an example of where Data Redaction would be useful. CSRs do not and should not see the entire credit card number. Data Redaction can be used to redact all but the last four numbers of the credit card number. CSRs can still complete their work without knowing the full credit card number.

NOTE
Oracle Data Redaction has also been made available in Oracle Database Release 11.2.0.4!

NOTE
Data Redaction is part of the Oracle Advanced Security option.

Data Redaction Scenario

The following Data Redaction sample shows the values of four columns (LAST_NAME, SALARY, EMAIL, and PHONE_NUMBER) before and after one of the various redaction methods has been applied to each. Table 9-2 explains the redaction method used on each (relative) column.

> **Tom Says**
> Note that Data Redaction is not a method to hide information from authorized end users. Data Redaction is used solely to protect sensitive information displayed on the screen or in a printed report. It does not prevent an authorized user from interacting with the data. For example, suppose the LAST_NAME field in a table was redacted so that it displayed ******* when retrieved. An authorized user would be able to query **select * from employees where last_name = 'Kyte'** and see all of the records that match 'Kyte'. Even though the LAST_NAME field would display ********, the authorized user would know what the last name is. If your goal is to limit access to sensitive information, you would want to explore the Oracle Virtual Private Database (VPD) feature.

Redaction Method	Column Applied To	Description
PARTIAL	LAST_NAME	Determine start and end position along with replacement redaction character.
FULL	SALARY	Numeric values redact to 0. Characters redact to a single blank (" "). Date redacts to 01-JAN-01.
RANDOM	EMAIL	Redaction uses randomly generated characters.
REGULAR EXPRESSION	PHONE_NUMBER	Use of regular expression pattern matching and replacement for redaction.

TABLE 9-2.   *Redaction Plan*

Before Data Redaction:

```
EMPLOYEE_ID FIRST_NAME   LAST_NAME     SALARY EMAIL         PHONE_NUMBER
----------- -----------  -----------  ---------- ------------  ---------------
        205 Shelly       Higgins       12008 SHIGGINS      515.123.8080
        206 William      Gietz          8300 WGIETZ        515.123.8181
```

After Data Redaction:

```
EMPLOYEE_ID FIRST_NAME   LAST_NAME     SALARY EMAIL         PHONE_NUMBER
----------- -----------  -----------  ---------- ------------  --------------------
        205 Shelly       H******           0 ,T"/&        ***.***.****
        206 William      G****             0 1ii4rw>N     ***.***.****
```

Our example will implement Data Redaction as shown in Table 9-2. We will also create the role of CLERK and allow that role to view the plain-text data as it is stored in the database (without redaction). Remember that the data in the database is not changed. Data Redaction is about controlling how the data is presented. We will also create a special view to allow PHONE_NUMBER to be shown in plain text.

We will be using the DBMS_REDACT package for this example. Use an account with SYSDBA privilege to execute this example.

First set up the table:

```
CREATE TABLE HR.RDTEST1 AS SELECT * FROM HR.EMPLOYEES;
```

Next, create the CLERK role, grant it to SCOTT, and then grant select access to HR.RDTEST1 to SCOTT:

```
CREATE ROLE CLERK;
GRANT CLERK TO SCOTT;
GRANT SELECT ON HR.RDTEST1 TO SCOTT;
```

So, SCOTT will be able to see the data in plain text because he has the role of CLERK. The HR user will see the redacted data. The security requirement fulfilled by this measure could be as simple as not allowing the schema owner to make direct queries on sensitive columns. We will see how this is accomplished in a moment.

Creating Redaction Policies

In this example we show full Data Redaction on the SALARY column. Pay attention to the EXPRESSION—if the session has the ROLE of CLERK, then Data Redaction does not apply. Also, make sure that you choose a POLICY_NAME and POLICY_DESCRIPTION wisely, because a table or view can have only one policy at this time. The policy can (and will for this example) be altered to add additional Data Redaction.

```
BEGIN
DBMS_REDACT.ADD_POLICY(
OBJECT_SCHEMA      => 'HR',
OBJECT_NAME        => 'RDTEST1',
COLUMN_NAME        => 'SALARY',
POLICY_NAME        => 'REDACT_RDTEST1',
POLICY_DESCRIPTION => 'REDACT RDTEST1 PII',
FUNCTION_TYPE      => DBMS_REDACT.FULL,
EXPRESSION =>
'SYS_CONTEXT(''SYS_SESSION_ROLES'',''CLERK'') = ''FALSE''');
END;
/
```

Check the Data Redaction as HR and as SCOTT. Make sure that you log in with a new session for HR and a new session for SCOTT. Run this script after each alteration of the policy:

```
SELECT EMPLOYEE_ID, FIRST_NAME, LAST_NAME, SALARY,
EMAIL, PHONE_NUMBER
FROM HR.RDTEST1 WHERE EMPLOYEE_ID IN (205, 206);
```

After the SALARY redaction is in place, the HR user should see the following after running the preceding query:

```
EMPLOYEE_ID FIRST_NAME LAST_NAME  SALARY EMAIL    PHONE_NUMBER
----------- ---------- ---------- ------ -------- ------------
    205     Shelley    Higgins         0 SHIGGINS 515.123.8080
    206     William    Gietz           0 WGIETZ   515.123.8181
```

Since SCOTT has the role of CLERK and sees the results in plain text, no query result will be shown for the SCOTT user.

Next we redact the last name but leave the first initial in plain text. This is a partial Data Redaction.

```
BEGIN
DBMS_REDACT.ALTER_POLICY(
OBJECT_SCHEMA        => 'HR',
OBJECT_NAME          => 'RDTEST1',
COLUMN_NAME          => 'LAST_NAME',
POLICY_NAME          => 'REDACT_RDTEST1',
POLICY_DESCRIPTION   => 'REDACT RDTEST1 PII',
ACTION               => DBMS_REDACT.ADD_COLUMN,
FUNCTION_TYPE        => DBMS_REDACT.PARTIAL,
FUNCTION_PARAMETERS =>
'VVVVVVVVVVVVVVVVVVV,VVVVVVVVVVVVVVVVVVVV,*,2,25',
EXPRESSION =>
'SYS_CONTEXT(''SYS_SESSION_ROLES'',''CLERK'') = ''FALSE''');
END;
/


EMPLOYEE_ID FIRST_NAME LAST_NAME  SALARY EMAIL    PHONE_NUMBER
----------- ---------- ---------- ------ -------- ------------
205         Shelley    H******         0 SHIGGINS 515.123.8080
206         William    G****           0 WGIETZ   515.123.8181
```

We will use random Data Redaction on the email address:

```
BEGIN
DBMS_REDACT.ALTER_POLICY(
OBJECT_SCHEMA        => 'HR',
OBJECT_NAME          => 'RDTEST1',
POLICY_NAME          => 'REDACT_RDTEST1',
POLICY_DESCRIPTION  => 'REDACT RDTEST1 PII',
ACTION               => DBMS_REDACT.ADD_COLUMN,
COLUMN_NAME          => 'EMAIL',
FUNCTION_TYPE        => DBMS_REDACT.RANDOM,
EXPRESSION =>
'SYS_CONTEXT(''SYS_SESSION_ROLES'',''CLERK'') = ''FALSE''');
END;
/


EMPLOYEE_ID FIRST_NAME LAST_NAME  SALARY EMAIL    PHONE_NUMBER
----------- ---------- ---------- ------ -------- ------------
205         Shelley    H******         0 OaDVUjPl 515.123.8080
206         William    G****           0 B#$0[9   515.123.8181
```

Since the ALTER_POLICY is using DBMS_REDACT.RANDOM, your results will be different.

The Data Redaction of U.S. phone numbers is accomplished through a regular expression:

```
BEGIN
DBMS_REDACT.ALTER_POLICY(
OBJECT_SCHEMA          => 'HR',
OBJECT_NAME            => 'RDTEST1',
POLICY_NAME            => 'REDACT_RDTEST1',
POLICY_DESCRIPTION     => 'REDACT RDTEST1 PII',
ACTION                 => DBMS_REDACT.ADD_COLUMN,
COLUMN_NAME            => 'PHONE_NUMBER',
FUNCTION_TYPE          => DBMS_REDACT.REGEXP,
EXPRESSION =>
'SYS_CONTEXT(''SYS_SESSION_ROLES'',''CLERK'') = ''FALSE''',
REGEXP_PATTERN => '(\d\d\d).(\d\d\d).(\d\d\d\d)',
REGEXP_REPLACE_STRING  => '***.***.****',
REGEXP_POSITION        => 1,
REGEXP_OCCURRENCE      => 0,
REGEXP_MATCH_PARAMETER => 'i');
END;
/


EMPLOYEE_ID FIRST_NAME LAST_NAME  SALARY EMAIL    PHONE_NUMBER
----------- ---------- ---------- ------ -------- ------------
205         Shelley    H******         0 )Df4Uj,t ***.***.****
206         William    G****           0 Q(K9yR   ***.***.****
```

After the use of DBMS_REDACT.REGEXP, the phone number is replaced with asterisks *if* the phone number format is area code and phone number as indicated by the REGEXP_PATTERN. If the REGEXP_PATTERN is a match, then it will be replaced with the REGEX_REPLACE_STRING, which in this case are the asterisks. Notice also that the results for EMAIL are different. That's because DBMS_REDACT .RANDOM is executed for each query.

NOTE
When you check the results after adding the phone number Data Redaction, if there are phone numbers that do not match the regular expression pattern, a null will be the result for the column.

Data Redactions and Views

If an underlying table has data-redacted columns, we can create a view on top of the table that undoes the Data Redaction. Create the view HR.V1 with the following script:

```
CREATE OR REPLACE VIEW HR.V1 AS SELECT
EMPLOYEE_ID, FIRST_NAME, LAST_NAME,
SALARY, EMAIL, PHONE_NUMBER
FROM HR.RDTEST1;
```

Then create a "no Data Redaction" policy on the view HR.V1 that undoes the redaction on the PHONE_NUMBER column:

```
BEGIN
DBMS_REDACT.ADD_POLICY(
OBJECT_SCHEMA => 'HR',
OBJECT_NAME => 'V1',
COLUMN_NAME => 'PHONE_NUMBER',
POLICY_NAME => 'NO_RD_PHONE_NUM',
FUNCTION_TYPE => DBMS_REDACT.NONE,
EXPRESSION => '1=1');
END;
/
```

Now, as the HR user, enter the following query to confirm that the policy does undo the Data Redaction:

```
SELECT EMPLOYEE_ID, FIRST_NAME,
       LAST_NAME,  SALARY,
       EMAIL, PHONE_NUMBER
FROM HR.V1
WHERE EMPLOYEE_ID IN (205, 206);
```

EMPLOYEE_ID	FIRST_NAME	LAST_NAME	SALARY	EMAIL	PHONE_NUMBER
205	Shelley	H******	0	:@%J%2Gv	515.123.8080
206	William	G****	0	1-,OT{	515.123.8181

CAUTION
*You should strongly restrict the usage of the DBMS_
REDACT package. A quick use of DBMS_REDACT
.ADD_POLICY with FUNCTION_TYPE => DBMS_
REDACT.NONE can bypass Data Redaction.*

Miscellaneous Security Improvements

This section covers the additional security improvements for Oracle Database 12c that do not neatly fall into a category. As such, you will find in this section each feature is mentioned and then followed by a short description. While some of these features are automatic and are enabled, others will need some sort of minor configuration and planning.

In the area of encryption, Oracle Database 12c provides additional support for the SHA-2 algorithm. SHA-2 is now used in the password verifier. Also, SHA-2 is an option for the PL/SQL DBMS_CRYPTO package. Encryption key management has been simplified with an updated Key Management Framework (KMF) along with the new SYSKM database administration privilege, which is used for management of keystore operations. SYSKM is just one of the new database administration privileges introduced in Oracle Database 12c to support separation of duties (SoD).

Prior to Oracle Database 12c, DBAs usually used an account with the SYSDBA and SYSASM privileges. With Oracle Database 12c, new database administration privileges of SYSBACKUP, SYSDG, and SYSKM (previously mentioned) create greater SoD and support the concept of least-privileged accounts. SYSBACKUP is for RMAN-related tasks, and SYSDG provides privileges for Data Guard–related tasks.

When you create databases using the Database Configuration Assistant (DBCA), you now have the option to enable password complexity for accounts. By enforcing password complexity, accounts are more secure.

The problem of the UNLIMITED TABLESPACE privilege being part of the RESOURCE role has been corrected. The RESOURCE role no longer has UNLIMITED TABLESPACE privilege. The SELECT ANY DICTIONARY privilege also has been improved to no longer have access to the following security-related data dictionary tables: DEFAULT_PWD$, ENC$, LINK$, USER$, USER_HISTORY$, and XS$VERIFIERS. Finally, when users log into SQL*Plus, they will also see the last successful login time in the banner, as shown here:

```
Last Successful login time: Wed May 08 2013 23:11:43 +00:00
```

Tom Says

This is big...this is huge! Most DBAs should not have the SYSDBA privilege, and the introduction of these new SYSxxxx privileges will help us get to that point. Imagine that you can have a DBA that can back up the database, but cannot see the data they are backing up, cannot alter the users in the database, and so on. That is what the SYSBACKUP role permits. I suggest reading the *Oracle Database Security Guide 12c Release 1* from cover to cover to get an in-depth look at all of the new security-related features!

These incremental changes, mentioned directly above, in security are improvements that many DBAs have been asking for years.

Code-Based Access Control (CBAC) is when database roles are assigned to PL/SQL code. Now PL/SQL packages, procedures, and functions no longer are run with the owner's or definer's rights. Using the appropriately defined "PL/SQL" role and attaching it to PL/SQL code provides the proper privileges to the code.

Transparent Sensitive Data Protection (TSDP) is used to protect sensitive data at the column, table, or database level. TSDP is combined with Data Redaction or Virtual Private Database (VPD) to identify the sensitive data and then design and apply a protection policy. The protection policy is designed once and applied to the sensitive data located in various tables throughout the database.

VPD evaluates context-sensitive policy (CSP) with greater efficiency. Before Oracle Database 12c, VPD would always evaluate CSP for any context change of any attribute. Now the evaluation of CSP happens when a context attribute changes the associated application. This reduces the number of times the CSP needs to be evaluated.

In Oracle Database 12c, controlling access to the database is enhanced across three security features: Oracle Label Security (OLS), VPD, and Database Vault (DV). OLS and VPD are now installed by default and are enabled at the command line. Another enhancement to OLS is the capability to import and export the metadata of the LBACSYS schema. This enables you to move policies and protected tables between databases. DV enhancements include mandatory realms that protect objects even from the objects' owners and DBAs. DV protection is now persisted when a database is moved to a new ORACLE_HOME or server.

Restricting access to Oracle Real Application Clusters can be accomplished through the Oracle Listener, which is under the control of the Oracle Grid Infrastructure. Configuration of the Oracle Listener would contain only valid IP addresses or subnets.

Oracle Database 12c introduces Real Application Security (RAS), which provides a database-centric, end-to-end authorization solution. Security control that was once at the application layer is now moved to the database layer where the data resides. Since the security control is at the database layer, it is created once and used multiple times at the application layer. This reduces the application's complexity and development time.

Mixing and Matching Security Features

When contemplating the topic of IT security, many broad concepts come to mind: the CIA triad (confidentiality, integrity, and availability), defense in depth, separation of duties, compartmentalization … and the list goes on and on. Choosing the right combination of technologies to fulfill the legal, regulatory, and company requirements is a daunting task. Oracle Database 12c introduces many new security features.

Combining these security features successfully is the task of either the DBA or, in some organizations, the data security officer. A delicate balance must be achieved between often-competing interests of business, performance, availability, and security requirements. The combinations of various Oracle Database 12c security features listed here are intended to provoke thought and discussion with your peers about how to develop a more robust security profile:

- Transparent Tablespace Encryption with Transparent Sensitive Data Protection

- Transparent Sensitive Data Protection with Data Redaction or Virtual Private Database

- Network Data Encryption with Secure Oracle Listener allowing access from a White List of IP addresses

- Database Vault with Data Redaction

- Unified Audit Trail with Oracle Data Mining for anomaly detection

These are only some of the combinations that can be used to secure your database. As each set of requirements are specific, the general guideline is to use only what is needed to secure your database to the specific requirements. Any security product or feature that is used entails some performance overhead.

End of Line

This chapter has covered the new security features found in Oracle Database 12c. Of these new features, Auditing, Privileges Analysis, and Data Redaction were covered in greater depth. That by no means suggests that any of the other new security features are not just as important. Each new security feature should be seen as a resource that can be used, in combinations, to help secure your database.

CHAPTER
10

Oracle Database 12c Manageability New Features

racle Database 12c offers a large number of new features related to database manageability. In this chapter we will review a number of these new features, grouped as follows:

- Online operations

- Database monitoring and administration

- Miscellaneous manageability features

Each of the features discussed in this chapter will make your job as a DBA a little easier, so let's get started!

Online Operations

When trying to perform some administrative operation, nothing is worse than having an error occur because the database is busy (such as a lock with NOWAIT condition). Online operations are designed to reduce this frustration. They enable you to execute the operation and then let Oracle Database take care of the rest for you. New online operations have been added in Oracle Database 12c! These features include

- Enhanced online DDL capabilities

- Lock timeout available for online redefinitions

- Moving a datafile online

- A single command to redefine certain table or partition storage-related definitions

- Support for redefinition of tables with Oracle Virtual Private Database (VPD) policies

Let's look at each of these features in turn so that you can put them to use as soon as you upgrade to Oracle Database 12c.

Enhanced Online DDL Capabilities

Oracle Database 12c has added additional online DDL capabilities. If you have ever tried to drop an index on a busy system, you will appreciate that you can now drop indexes online. In fact, there are several DDL commands that can now be completed online:

- **drop index**

- **drop constraint**

- **set unused column**

- **alter index unusable**

- **alter index visible**

- **alter index invisible**

All of these commands now include the **online** keyword to indicate that the operation is an online operation. For example, to drop an index online, you would use the **drop index online** command, as shown here:

```
drop index test_idx_01 online;
```

The index will not actually be able to drop until any other DDL or DML operations have released all locks associated with that index. For example, during a long-running **update** command, you cannot drop the index until the **update** command has completed.

Lock Timeout Available for Online Redefinitions

When you are completing an online redefinition of a table, the **finish_redef_table** procedure of **dbms_redefinition** is executed. One of the things this procedure does is take out locks on the source table briefly as the redefinition completes. Sometimes the procedure cannot acquire the locks in a timely manner; for example, a long-running **update** statement might be holding up the acquisition of the locks, or an **insert** might not have been committed. Normally in cases like this, the **finish_redef_table** procedure will simply wait until it can acquire the locks and complete the redefinition process.

Now, in Oracle Database 12*c*, you can use the **ddl_lock_timeout** parameter to indicate how long the **finish_redef_table** procedure will wait to acquire those locks. If it cannot acquire those locks in the time allotted, then the procedure will exit with an Oracle error.

Move a Datafile Online

There are several reasons why you might want to move a database datafile. For example, you might want to move it to another file system or to an Oracle Automatic Storage Management (ASM) disk group that has more space. Perhaps you have added storage and you want to move the datafile (or datafiles) to the new file system.

Until now, if you wanted to move or rename a database datafile, at a minimum you would need to take the datafile offline and then rename it or move it. You would then need to recover the datafile and bring it back online. During this operation, anyone who tried to access the data in the datafile would find that their query had failed because the datafile was offline. This had a rather negative impact on uptime and availability and required such operations to be scheduled at odd hours with associated outages.

Oracle Database 12c enables you to move or rename Oracle Database datafiles online, without requiring an outage. You do so through the **alter database** command using the new **move datafile** option. When you execute the **alter database move datafile** command, Oracle Database 12c will rename or move the database datafile online as appropriate. This functionality is supported in both ARCHIVELOG mode and NOARCHIVELOG mode.

The basic format of the **alter database move datafile** command is shown here:

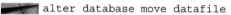

```
alter database move datafile
'/u01/app/oracle/oradata/NEW12C/datafile/o1_mf_users_01.dbf' to
'/u01/app/oracle/oradata/NEW12C/datafile/o1_mf_users.dbf';
```

This command will rename the users01.dbf datafile to users01_orcl.dbf. This command would fail if the users01_orcl.dbf file already existed. This command will take longer to complete than a simple file rename because the file itself is actually being copied to the new filename.

Also note that if you are moving an Oracle Managed File (OMF) to a non-OMF file, you will lose the benefits of OMF. You cannot move a non-OMF file to an OMF file with this command.

NOTE
While a file copy is occurring, you will see waits in v$session_wait on db file single write and db file sequential read. You will also see the move in v$session_longops with an OPNAME of Online datafile move.

When copying a file or renaming it, Oracle will, by default, clean up the source file. You can override this behavior by using the **keep** parameter:

```
alter database move datafile '/u01/app/oracle/oradata/orcl/users01.dbf' to
'/u01/app/oracle/oradata/orcl/users01_orcl.dbf' keep;
```

It's possible that a datafile with the same name will already be in place and you will want to overwrite that file. In this case you can use the **reuse** parameter:

```
alter database move datafile '/u01/app/oracle/oradata/orcl/users01.dbf' to
'/u01/app/oracle/oradata/orcl/users01_orcl.dbf' reuse;
```

This command also works with ASM, allowing you to move files between ASM disk groups easily:

```
alter database move datafile '/u01/app/oracle/oradata/orcl/users01.dbf' to
'+data_dg';
```

NOTE
This might seem like a minor feature, but being able to easily move database datafiles online, with minimal impact to the database, is a big deal. Clearly, there will be some performance impacts during the file move, but that certainly beats an outage!

Tom Says
I agree 100 percent. This new feature will allow you to migrate to new storage or new storage methods, such as ASM, without having to take a full outage. DBAs migrating to ASM storage will truly appreciate this capability.

Single Command to Redefine Certain Table or Partition Storage-Related Definitions

Oracle Database 12c now allows you to perform in a single step certain online table or partition storage-related redefinitions. These changes include

■ Tablespace changes

■ Compression changes

■ Changing LOB columns to a SecureFile or BasicFile storage

For other kinds of changes, you will still need to use the traditional multistep process. This new feature is supported with a new procedure called **dbms_ redefinition.redef_table** that has been added to the **dbms_redefinition** package. Here is a description of that procedure:

```
PROCEDURE REDEF_TABLE
 Argument Name                   Type                    In/Out Default?
 ------------------------------  ----------------------  ------ --------
 UNAME                           VARCHAR2                IN
 TNAME                           VARCHAR2                IN
 TABLE_COMPRESSION_TYPE          VARCHAR2                IN     DEFAULT
 TABLE_PART_TABLESPACE           VARCHAR2                IN     DEFAULT
 INDEX_KEY_COMPRESSION_TYPE      VARCHAR2                IN     DEFAULT
 INDEX_TABLESPACE                VARCHAR2                IN     DEFAULT
 LOB_COMPRESSION_TYPE            VARCHAR2                IN     DEFAULT
 LOB_TABLESPACE                  VARCHAR2                IN     DEFAULT
 LOB_STORE_AS                    VARCHAR2                IN     DEFAULT
```

In this example we are going to redefine the tablespace for the EMP table in the SCOTT schema:

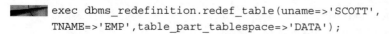

```
exec dbms_redefinition.redef_table(uname=>'SCOTT',
TNAME=>'EMP',table_part_tablespace=>'DATA');
```

Support for Redefinition of Tables with VPD Policies

If you are using Virtual Private Database (VPD) policies, you will be happy to hear that Oracle has improved the **dbms_redefinition.start_redef_table** procedure such that VPD policies will be automatically copied from the original table to the new table during the redefinition. A new parameter, **copy_vpd_opt**, is available in **dbms_redefinition.start_redef_table** that indicates how you want the redefinition to handle VPD policies. The **copy_vpd_opt** parameter takes one of three options:

- **dbms_redefinition.cons_vpd_none**   Indicates that there are no VPD policies on the original table. This is the default value. If there are VPD policies on this table, an error will be raised.

- **dbms_redefinition.cons_vpd_auto**   Indicates that the VPD policies should be copied over to the new table from the original table automatically. You would use this option if there are VPD policies and only if the column names and types between the original table and the interim table will remain the same. If you use this setting, the column mapping string between the original table and the interim table must be either NULL or *. Note that if you use this option, only the table owner and the user invoking the redefinition will be able to access the interim table during the online redefinition.

- **dbms_redefinition.cons_vpd_manual**   Indicates that the VPD policies will be manually copied from the original table to the new table during the redefinition process. You would use this option when you can't meet the restrictions for the use of the option **dbms_redefinition.cons_vpd_auto**. Also, you would use this option if you wanted to add or modify VPD policies during the table redefinition of the table.

Tom Says
This new feature makes moving tables across tablespaces and performing other maintenance operations almost trivial from the perspective of the DBA. To be able to online move an entire table with a single command is very powerful.

Database Monitoring and Administration

There are changes and new features in Oracle Database 12c that will impact how you monitor and administer the Oracle database. In this section we will talk about these in some detail. The topics we will cover include

- Oracle Enterprise Manager Database Express

- Real-time database operations monitoring

- Real-time Automatic Database Diagnostic Monitor (ADDM) monitoring

Oracle Enterprise Manager Database Express

Oracle Enterprise Manager Database Express (EM Database Express) is a replacement for Oracle Enterprise Manager Database Control. It is much easier to manage and administer than Database Control because it has no middleware components to manage. Some functionality has been lost in this new version, but it is much more lightweight, performant, and server friendly with respect to resource utilization. So, Oracle has made a trade-off between form and functionality in this product. Some of the new features in the database (such as Container Databases) and some of the older features (such as ASM) are not present in EM Database Express, but that's okay, because you really should be using Oracle Enterprise Manager Cloud Control 12c anyway.

To connect to EM Database Express, you need to know what port it's listening on. When you create the database with the Oracle Database Configuration Assistant (DBCA), the application will tell you what the port is after it has created the database. Another way to find out what port the database is listening on is to run the following query:

```
select dbms_xdb_config.gethttpsport() from dual;
DBMS_XDB_CONFIG.GETHTTPSPORT()
------------------------------
                5501
```

Once you know the port, getting to EM Database Express is as simple as opening your web browser and typing in the URL. The format of the URL is

https://*database-hostname*:*portnumber*/em/

Here is an example of the URL on an actual machine:

```
https://server12c:5501/em/
```

With so much material to cover in this book, we are not going to fill it up with a bunch of screenshots of EM Database Express, but we do want to discuss the four main focus areas of EM Database Express:

- **Database configuration** Initialization parameters, memory, database feature usage, and current database properties

- **Storage** Tablespaces, undo management, redo log groups, archived redo logs, and control files

- **Security** Users, roles, and profiles

- **Performance** Performance Hub and SQL Tuning Advisor

After you start EM Database Express, you are prompted to log in to the database. Then, you see the Database Home Page, which provides a summary of various database-related information. It also provides links to the pages that are associated with the different focus areas that EM Database Express supports.

Most of the different focus areas in the preceding list are self-explanatory, with the exception of the Performance Hub. I mentioned it a bit in Chapter 1, but I wanted to discuss it a bit further here. Performance Hub enables you to view database activity and perform various SQL tuning activities, as shown in Figure 10-1.

Figure 10-1 is representative of the functionality that EM Database Express provides. The Summary tab shows you the load of the system over time. The other tabs provide information on processes, memory, active sessions, and I/O.

Additional functionality provides information on database activity (such as user sessions, waits, and SQL). You can look at the overall workload of the system, including top SQL, current logons, user calls, and open cursors. One of the nicest features of Oracle Database 12c is SQL Monitoring. It's so nice, in fact, that the Performance Hub provides an interface into Oracle Database SQL Monitoring. The Performance Hub also provides access to ADDM and the SQL Tuning Advisor.

All in all, EM Database Express 12c is a nice management tool, but it really is no competition for Enterprise Manager Cloud Control 12c, nor is it meant to be. If you want to get the most out of Oracle Database 12c and its rich feature set, you really need to set up Enterprise Manager Cloud Control 12c.

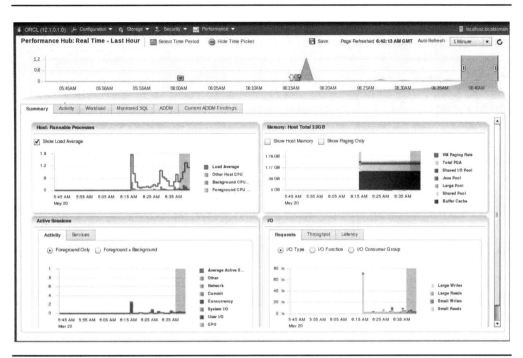

FIGURE 10-1. *Performance Hub page*

Real-Time Database Operations Monitoring

Real-time SQL Monitoring was introduced in Oracle Database 11g. Oracle Database 12c has added additional functionality to this feature. Real-time SQL monitoring in Oracle Database 12c will start monitoring SQL parallel execution and DDL statements as soon as execution begins. Other SQL statements are monitored in real time after they have consumed 5 seconds of CPU or I/O time in a single execution.

In Oracle Database 12c, the Oracle database will monitor composite operations automatically. Composite operations are logically grouped sets of related SQL statements. In Oracle Database 12c, a composite database operation is considered to be the activity of one session between two points in time. All of the SQL and PL/SQL operations running in that session are considered part of the composite operation. Examples of composite operations include things like SQL*Plus scripts, batch jobs, and ETL processing operations.

The Oracle database will identify these composite database operations through various means, including specific user-created names assigned to the jobs or the database execution ID (which can be database- or user-generated through the

dbms_sql_monitor package). The database then identifies the SQL and PL/SQL operations that are to be monitored within the context of the operation, and starts SQL monitoring on those statements.

You can observe SQL statements that are being monitored by the Oracle database from EM Database Express or Enterprise Manager Cloud Control 12c.

Real-Time ADDM Monitoring

Real-Time (sometimes called Spot) ADDM is a new feature of ADDM. When certain problems occur, such as high CPU load or I/O loads becoming significant, Oracle will trigger the execution of an ADDM run to try to help spot the current performance issue. Looking at the EM Database Express screen in Figure 10-1, introduced a bit earlier in this chapter, you can see that a Real-Time ADDM run was run, as noted above the graph at the top of the Performance Hub screen. Notice the little icon there that looks like a calculator? That indicates the execution of a Real-Time ADDM run. If you go to the ADDM tab on the EM Database Express Performance Hub page, you will see the Real-Time ADDM report runs, and the reason for those runs. Click the report to view additional information about the ADDM findings.

Miscellaneous Manageability Features

This final section of the chapter introduces a host of other new features that you can use to manage your Oracle Database 12c database. We will also discuss a few things that have changed between Oracle Database 12c and earlier versions of the database that you will want to be aware of with respect to management of the database. That being said, we will cover the following topics in this section:

- PGA size limits
- New administrator privileges
- Real application testing changes

PGA Size Limits

Occasionally, the PGA may consume an inordinate amount of memory on the Oracle Database servers, leading to problems. A new database parameter called PGA_AGGREGATE_LIMIT has been added to Oracle Database 12c to provide a hard limit on the amount of PGA that can be consumed by a given instance. When PGA_AGGREGATE_LIMIT has been reached, sessions that have the largest amount of untunable memory allocations will start to be aborted. Any Oracle process other than job queue processes will not be subject to these measures.

Tom Says

There are two types of PGA memory used by processes: tunable and untunable. Tunable PGA memory is the memory used by sort, hash, bitmap merge, and similar areas. We call it *tunable* because we allocate larger or smaller work areas based on the current concurrent user load. Few users = larger sort areas; lots of users = smaller areas. We "tune" that memory. *Untunable* memory, on the other hand, is memory we cannot control; only the developer who wrote the program we are running can control it.

PL/SQL variables are a large consumer of these untunable memory allocations. If a programmer decides to populate a PL/SQL index-by table of VARCHAR2(4000) strings with millions of entries, we will try to accommodate that in memory—possibly using gigabytes or more of memory.

By default, the PGA_AGGREGATE_LIMIT is set to the greater of 2GB, 200 percent of the value of PGA_AGGREGATE_TARGET, or 3MB times the setting of the PROCESSES database parameter. It will never exceed 120 percent of the total physical memory available on the system less the total SGA size of the database. The parameter cannot be set below its default limit, but it can be set above that limit, so essentially there is no difference between changing the value of the parameter or leaving it set to the default.

New Administrator Privileges

Oracle Database 12*c* adds additional privileges that provide a greater degree of granularity in the administration of the Oracle database. New privileges with respect to RMAN backup and recovery, Oracle Data Guard, and Transparent Data Encryption grant only the minimum privileges required to administer these database tasks.

The following table lists and describes these new privileges:

Privilege	Description
SYSBACKUP	Provides all the operations that are required to perform backup and recovery operations on the database.
SYSDG	Provides all the operations required to perform Data Guard operations. This privilege can be used with Data Guard Broker or the DGMGRL command-line interface.
SYSKM	Provides all the operations required to perform Transparent Data Encryption administration operations.

Tom Says

This is really important. We have to get away from giving every DBA the SYSDBA privilege. These fine-grained privileges are just what we need. With SYSBACKUP, for example, a DBA can back up and manage the database but cannot see what is in the database. You might say, "Oh, if they can back it up, they can steal it," but that is where encryption comes into play. They might be able to steal it, but it won't give them anything because the data is encrypted. If a DBA who is responsible for backup has SYSDBA, they can do anything they want to the data; if they have SYSBACKUP, the only thing they can do is back it up.

Real Application Testing Changes

Oracle Real Application Testing (RAT) has changed in Oracle Database 12c. These changes include

- Removal of Oracle Database Control
- Data masking changes
- Oracle Database Replay new features
- Addition of Oracle Database Replay Workload Intelligence
- Queryable Patch Inventory
- Oracle Direct NFS (dNFS) new features
- Database cloning
- Advanced Network Compression new parameters
- Very large network buffers
- Multiprocess, multithreaded Oracle
- Database Smart Flash Cache support for multiple flash drives
- New Oracle Scheduler script jobs

That's a lot of stuff to tackle, so let's get at it!

Removal of Oracle Database Control

Perhaps one of the biggest changes to using the features of RAT is the removal of Oracle Database Control, which provided an interface into RAT. Of course, if you are running Oracle Enterprise Manager Cloud Control 12c (and you really should be!), then this isn't a problem for you. If you are not using Enterprise Manager Cloud Control 12c, then you will need to use the manual methods of performing RAT operations. Using the manual methods is well documented, and there is really nothing new in the steps of the process that you will use (though there are some new features) overall. If you want a good introduction, my book, *Oracle Database 11g New Features*, has information on using RAT.

Data Masking Changes

Oracle Data Masking is a useful tool that will mask your database data based on your definition of what needs to be masked. Masking is based on the creation of masking templates that define how the masking occurs. In the past, you had to make a duplicate copy of your database before you could actually proceed to mask the data. Because of the sensitive nature of data, this "staging" area often had to be on the production database system. Once you duplicated the database, you had to mask the data in the staging database, and then move the database to the testing environment either via RMAN or Oracle Data Pump.

Oracle Database 12c, in concert with Enterprise Manager Cloud Control 12c, provides some new data masking functionality via data subsetting. Data subsetting has been available prior to Oracle Database 12c, but now you can subset data at the column level. Also, Oracle Database 12c enables you to mask data inline as it's being exported to an Oracle Data Pump dump file.

Let's look at inline data masking and subsetting in some more detail, followed by a look at the different kinds of data masking scenarios that are possible now in Oracle Database 12c.

Inline Data Masking and Subsetting   Previous to Oracle Database 12c, Oracle Data Masking provided the ability to subset data. This means that you can subdivide the data that is moved and masked. The end result is that the test database can be much smaller than the production database, because you can eliminate tables and specific rows from tables, based on rules that you define, from the final testing image.

Oracle data subsetting can occur either inline, by piping the subsetted data to an export file, or on the target (or cloned) database, through the removal of data in the target database. The only problem with subsetting of data prior to Oracle Database 12c was that you could not mask the data until it was present in the target database. Thus, any export file or cloned database would still contain sensitive data.

NOTE
Oracle data subsetting is actually available for Oracle Database 10.1 and later if you use Enterprise Manager Cloud Control version 12.1 or higher.

Oracle Database 12c (when Enterprise Manager Cloud Control 12c is included) enhances data subsetting and masking by adding two new features:

■ The ability to remove specific columns in a table from the subsetted data

■ The ability to mask inline as the Data Pump export file is written

The ability to remove specific column data provides a way to further reduce the size of the testing image that you create. For example, if you have tables with long VARCHAR2 columns that contain data that is not important to your testing process (perhaps they have freeform comments in them), you can choose not to include those columns as a part of the overall subsetting process.

With inline masking, the data in the database is masked on the fly, in real time, as it's being written to the Data Pump dump file. Inline masking eliminates the need for an interim database at all. Instead, the data is masked on the fly, and the resulting masked data is exported via the Data Pump utility. You can then import the masked data to one or more target databases as needed.

Now that we have discussed these new features, let's see how they can be used to create your testing databases with masked data.

Data Masking Scenarios   There are different scenarios that you can use when taking advantage of the inline masking and subsetting features of Oracle Enterprise Manager Cloud Control 12c. These different possible combinations of operations include the following:

■ Mask and export production data inline

  ■ Resulting data is masked inline and stored in an Oracle Data Pump dump file.

■ Mask, export, and subset production data inline

  ■ Resulting data is masked and subsetted on the target system, and stored in an Oracle Data Pump dump file.

  ■ Subsetting can also include the removal of rows and columns in the database.

- Mask data on the target database

    - The target database is cloned from the production database.

    - Masking occurs on the target database.

    - The target database is backed up using RMAN or Oracle Data Pump, and that backup is used to create other test databases.

- Mask data and subset on the target database

    - The target database is cloned from the production database.

    - Masking occurs on the target database.

    - Data subsetting occurs on the target database.

    - Subsetting can also include the removal of rows and columns in the database.

    - The target database is backed up using RMAN or Oracle Data Pump, and that backup is used to create other test databases.

Database Replay

Oracle Database Replay is an exciting feature that has been available in Oracle Database for a little while now. Oracle Database 12c provides some new features for Database Replay:

- Consolidated Database Replay

- Database Replay user remapping

- Database Replay ASH Data Comparison Report

Consolidated Database Replay   Oracle Database 12c introduces the concept of Consolidated Database Replay, which enables you to take multiple workload captures from one or more sources and replay them concurrently on a single test system. This can be helpful in many cases:

- **Database consolidation**   Database consolidation seems to be something that is happening more and more. If you find yourself consolidating databases onto a single system, then Consolidated Database Replay can help you to estimate the overall load that the consolidated databases will have on the hardware that you have assigned to the consolidation environment.

    With Consolidated Database Replay, you can determine how your system will perform before it's actually turned over as a production database system.

You can also use this testing to determine if resource management is properly set up and tuned in the consolidated environment before the system is made a production database system.

Also, if your consolidated environment is a RAC environment and the current production system is not a RAC environment, you can determine if the RAC infrastructure that you have configured will handle the workloads you expect.

■ **Stress testing** Stress testing is a common way of determining how heavy of a workload a given system can take before it starts to suffer significant performance degradation that impacts the user experience. With Consolidated Database Replay, you can add additional stress on a given system by replaying double the workload, or even more.

■ **Scale-up testing** Scale-up testing is similar to consolidation testing in that your goal is to see how the addition of additional workload will impact a given system. For example, you might want to determine how the workload will change should you add existing HR functions in one database to your existing financial system on another database.

This feature is possible through the introduction of the ability to manipulate workloads by filtering workloads on dimensions such as time, services, and module names. You can also schedule workloads to run at a specific time, which enables you to coordinate the start of the various workloads across the database server. Additionally, you can characterize workload capture based on attributes such as request types, activity, access, transaction patterns, and application-defined attributes.

Database Replay User Remapping   Now, in Oracle Database 12c, when you execute a database workload replay, you can remap the capture user to a different user on the replay. For example, suppose that your production database captured changes done by the user SCOTT and the object resides in the SCOTT schema. Now you want to replay those transactions on another database, with a similar schema with similar data (assume only the name of the schema is different, say TIGER). You can do this in Oracle Database 12c by remapping the SCOTT schema to the TIGER schema, either through OEM or by using the **dbms_workload_repository** PL/SQL-supplied package using the **set_user_mapping** procedure.

Database Replay ASH Data Comparison Report   A new report comparing ASH data across the capture and replay runs is now available in Oracle Database 12*c*. The report contains several sections:

- **Summary**   A summary of the activity of the capture and replay runs based on DB Time (that is, Total DB, CPU, Wait, and IO times) and wait time (for example, log file synch waits, IO waits, and so on) distributions.

- **Top SQL**   Provides a comparative report of ASH top SQL statements from both capture and replay runs.

- **Long Running SQL**   Provides a report of ASH long-running SQL statements for both the capture and replay runs.

- **Common SQL**   Extracted SQL statements that are common for both capture and replay runs. Filtering could change which SQL statements are common between the two runs. Top SQL statements are compared by variance in average response time and total database time.

- **Top Objects**   Report of total wait times for top objects used in both the capture and replay runs.

Database Replay Workload Intelligence

A new feature of Oracle Database Replay is Workload Intelligence (WI). Workload Intelligence is a collection of external Java programs that is distributed with the Oracle Database product that provides the ability to analyze the capture files generated during database capture and determine various patterns and trends present in the workload. You can also analyze and model the workload, and use the capture files to analyze what was running on the system during workload capture.

Workload Intelligence functionality can be used to better understand what is happening on your database, during the time that the database is being captured. This can be helpful when you are trying to solve performance problems. This would be particularly true when your database is supporting applications from one or more vendors, and you are not privy to the execution code base. Additionally, complex applications written in-house can be very difficult to tune, and the modeling provided by Workload Intelligence can assist in these efforts as well. Finally, Workload Intelligence will combine similar SQL statements into a single execution pattern within the model. Thus, if you have 10,000 similar SQL statements, differing because of the use of bind variables or values of literals, they will be combined into one modeled SQL statement. This can help identify patterns that are harder to find via tools such as the Automatic Workload Repository (AWR).

Workload Intelligence does not require a connection to the database that the workload was recorded on. It does, however, require a database to operate. Often this can just be a database set up in a test or development environment. Still, consideration should be given to the fact that the workload contents could conceivably contain personally identifiable information or other confidential information. Thus, carefully consider the choice of system that you use when using Workload Intelligence.

Preparing to Run Workload Intelligence   Before you can analyze captured workloads with Workload Intelligence, you need to do a bit of preparation work. You first need to make sure that the system is set up to find the Java JAR files that are required to run the Workload Intelligence framework. Then, you need to select the database that you will use when you are analyzing the captured workloads with Workload Intelligence.

When you install Oracle Database 12c, the Java code that contains the classes needed to invoke the Workload Intelligence code are installed automatically. These classes are packed in the following Java JAR file: $ORACLE_HOME/rdbms/jlib/dbrintelligence.jar. You also need to make sure that CLASSPATH includes $ORACLE_HOME/rdbms/jlib/dbrparser.jar and $ORACLE_HOME/jdbc/lib/ojdbc6.jar.

As mentioned earlier, Workload Intelligence does require the use of a database, but it does not need to be the database that you captured the workload from. As such, Workload Intelligence will require access to some of the SYS tables and views in the database that will be used.

You will want to ensure that your system has sufficient storage space to hold the workload capture files. An alternative to storing them locally is to create some sort of NFS (or dNFS) file system on which to store the capture files so that they can be shared across the enterprise without having to be moved all over creation. Of course, you will want to consider the security issues related to this kind of architecture.

There are five main steps that you will follow as you analyze the captured workloads. These are summarized here:

1. Configure the system to support the use of Workload Intelligence.

2. Create the new Workload Intelligence job.

3. Generate a workload model that describes the workload.

4. Identify patterns in the workload.

5. Generate reports.

Let's look at each of these steps in more detail next. In the examples that accompany these steps, we will assume the captured workload is in a directory called /u01/app/oracle/capture/orcl. Note that we will be running the Workload

Intelligence operations on the same machine and database that we ran the workload capture on. This is completely okay in our case, but not required. We could have easily used another database.

Configure the System to Support the Use of Workload Intelligence   We are using a database called new12c. We need to create a user that we will use for our Workload Intelligence operations. We will call this user WIUSER and give it the password robert. We will need to give it several privileges, as shown in the following example code:

```
create user wiuser identified by robert;
grant create session to wiuser;
grant select,insert,alter on WI$_JOB to wiuser;
grant insert,alter on WI$_TEMPLATE to wiuser;
grant insert,alter on WI$_STATEMENT to wiuser;
grant insert,alter on WI$_OBJECT to wiuser;
grant insert,alter on WI$_CAPTURE_FILE to wiuser;
grant select,insert,alter on WI$_EXECUTION_ORDER to wiuser;
grant insert,update,delete,alter on WI$_FREQUENT_PATTERN to wiuser;
grant insert,delete,alter on WI$_FREQUENT_PATTERN_ITEM to wiuser;
grant insert,delete,alter on WI$_FREQUENT_PATTERN_METADATA to wiuser;
grant select on WI$_JOB_ID to wiuser;
grant execute on DBMS_WORKLOAD_REPLAY to wiuser;
```

We will also make sure the CLASSPATH is set correctly. In our case, we will set the CLASSPATH thusly:

```
export CLASSPATH=$ORACLE_HOME/rdbms/jlib/dbrintelligence.jar:
$ORACLE_HOME/rdbms/jlib/dbrparser.jar:$ORACLE_HOME/jdbc/lib/ojdbc6.jar
```

Once the CLASSPATH is set correctly, we can test the Workload Intelligence Java program and ensure that it works correctly by using the **-version** parameter. Here is an example:

```
java oracle.dbreplay.workload.intelligence.LoadInfo -version
Workload Intelligence Load Information, version 1.0.0
```

Note that we used the **LoadInfo** program here to make sure everything was set up correctly. Let's look at **LoadInfo** just a bit more before we create our new Workload Intelligence job.

The **LoadInfo** program is the central program that is used to create and manage the tasks that parse the data in the capture files. **LoadInfo** then determines what is relevant and stores it in tables within the database schema you created earlier.

Before we get started generating the Workload Intelligence job, just in case you ever need to know, you can also check the parameters available for use with the **LoadInfo** program as shown here:

```
java oracle.dbreplay.workload.intelligence.LoadInfo -usage
Usage:
  java LoadInfo -cstr <connection-string> -user <username> -job <job-name> -cdir
<capture-directory>
connection-string: JDBC connection string to the Database
(jdbc:oracle:thin:@hostname:portnum:ORACLE_SID).
username: Database username.
job-name: A name that uniquely defines the new workload-intelligence job.
capture-directory: OS path of the capture directory.
```

The **LoadInfo** program parameters are listed and described in the following table:

Parameter	Description
-cstr	Defines the JDBC connection string to the database that will be used by WI. An example would be jdbc:oracle:thin@robert.com:1521:orcl. This is a required parameter to get the data to load into the database, which also implies that the database listener must be up and running.
-user	This is the database user that you created earlier to process the WI information.
-job	This is a job name that will be assigned to the WI job.
-cdir	This is the directory that contains the capture file.
-version	Provides the version number of the **LoadInfo** program.
-usage	Provides usage information on the **LoadInfo** program.

Create the New Workload Intelligence Job   Now that we know a bit more about the **LoadInfo** program, let's use it to generate the Workload Intelligence job that we discussed earlier. Here is an example of using the **LoadInfo** program to load our workload capture data:

```
java oracle.dbreplay.workload.intelligence.LoadInfo
-job wijobsales
-cdir /u01/app/oracle/capture/new12c
-cstr jdbc:oracle:thin:@server12c:1521:new12c
-user wiuser
```

NOTE
This code (and other code) is broken out into multiple lines only for book formatting purposes. You can run the code with no carriage returns or line feeds. If you prefer to format your code, similar to what's shown here, you can use continuation characters (like the Linux \ character).

Note that if you don't want to set the CLASSPATH variable, you could execute your code this way:

```
java -classpath $ORACLE_HOME/rdbms/jlib/dbrintelligence.jar:
$ORACLE_HOME/rdbms/jlib/dbrparser.jar:
$ORACLE_HOME/jdbc/lib/ojdbc6.jar:
oracle.dbreplay.workload.intelligence.LoadInfo -job wijobsales
-cdir /u01/app/oracle/capture/new12c
-cstr jdbc:oracle:thin:@server12c:1521:new12c
-user wiuser
```

NOTE
And thus, I ran into a bug in the GA release of Oracle Database 12c (12.1.0.1).
If you have executed a workload capture on a system with many CPUs, and the database is not very busy, then you might get the following error:
LoadInfo: *ORA-00054: resource busy and acquire with NOWAIT specified or timeout expired.*
I have opened a service request with Oracle and this has been acknowledged as a bug in the Workload Intelligence code. It should be corrected soon. If you run into this bug, check with Oracle Support and see if there is a patch available.

The program will prompt you for the password for the user listed in the **-user** parameter. The code does not indicate whether or not it was successful, but if you don't get any error messages, you can assume it was.

Generate a Workload Model That Describes the Workload   Now that we have populated the repository, we are ready to generate a workload model. The model describes the workload and can be used to identify patterns that occur in the workload. To generate the workload, we use another Java program called **BuildModel**. The **BuildModel** program is pretty basic and has the following syntax:

Parameter	Description
-cstr	Defines the JDBC connection string to the database that will be used by WI. An example would be jdbc:oracle:thin@robert.com:1521:orcl. This is a required parameter to get the data to load into the database, which also implies that the database listener must be up and running.
-user	This is the database user that you created earlier to process the WI information.
-job	This is a job name that will be assigned to the WI job.
-version	Provides the version number of the **BuildModel** program.
-usage	Provides usage information on the **BuildModel** program.

The **BuildModel** program requires the same CLASSPATH environment parameter be set as did the **LoadInfo** program. Here is an example of the execution of the **BuildModel** program:

```
java oracle.dbreplay.workload.intelligence.BuildModel -cstr
jdbc:oracle:thin:@server12c:1521:new12c -user wiuser -job wijobsales
```

As with **LoadInfo**, you are prompted for the password for the user, and no output appears to indicate whether or not it was successful (errors will appear if it's not successful). The end result is that the Workload Intelligence model will be created in the database. Once that is done, we can have Oracle identify the patterns, which we will discuss next.

Identify Patterns in the Workload   As mentioned earlier, one of the main uses of WI is to identify patterns in the workload. As such, we will use the **FindPatterns** Java program to read the captured workload and use the associated workload model (both of which we created earlier in this section on WI). The **FindPatterns** program will then identify the frequent patterns that occur in the workload. Here is an example of the execution of the **FindPatterns** program:

```
java oracle.dbreplay.workload.intelligence.FindPatterns -cstr
jdbc:oracle:thin:@server12c:1521:new12c -user wiuser -job wijobsales -t .2
```

The parameters for the **FindPatterns** program are similar to those for the **LoadInfo** and **BuildModel** programs, as shown in the following table:

Parameter	Description
-cstr	Defines the JDBC connection string to the database that will be used by WI. An example would be jdbc:oracle:thin@robert .com:1521:orcl. This is a required parameter to get the data to load into the database, which also implies that the database listener must be up and running.
-user	This is the database user that you created earlier to process the WI information.
-job	This is a job name that will be assigned to the WI job.
-t	This is the threshold probability that defines when a translation from one template to the next is part of the same pattern, or that it borders between two patterns. Valid values are real numbers between 0 and 1. The default is .5. In English, this threshold is used to define when patterns change. As the value reaches 0, the WI pattern program will be more likely to associate similar SQL within the same pattern. As the threshold moves away from 0, WI will be more discriminating about pattern matching.
-version	Provides the version number of the **FindPatterns** program.
-usage	Provides usage information on the **FindPatterns** program.

Again, as with the previous programs, you will be prompted for the user password. No output will be returned to indicate whether or not it was a successful run.

Generate Reports   Having done all of the work of processing the workload capture, generating models, and looking for patterns, we are ready to generate reports to see the fruits of our labors. This is done through the reporting function, which is surfaced through the **GenerateReport** program. Here is an example of the execution of **GenerateReport**:

```
java oracle.dbreplay.workload.intelligence.GenerateReport -cstr
jdbc:oracle:thin:@server12c:1521:new12c -user wiuser -job wijobsales  -out
/tmp/wireport.html
```

The parameters of the **GenerateReport** program are listed and described here:

Parameter	Description
-cstr	Defines the JDBC connection string to the database that will be used by WI. An example would be jdbc:oracle:thin@robert.com:1521:orcl. This is a required parameter to get the data to load into the database, which also implies that the database listener must be up and running.
-user	This is the database user that you created earlier to process the WI information.
-job	This is a job name that will be assigned to the WI job.
-top	This is a number value that indicates how many patterns you want to have displayed in the report. Patterns are ordered by different criteria in the report. This value defaults to a value of 10 and is optional.
-version	Provides the version number of the **GenerateReport** program.
-usage	Provides usage information on the **GenerateReport** program.

Again, you will be prompted to enter the password for the user that you have defined using the **-user** parameter. The resulting output, if all goes well, should contain a HTML file that presents a report of patterns that you are interested in.

NOTE
As I did earlier, I ran into a bug with the ***GenerateReport*** *program at the time we went to press, so I can't provide an example of the output file with any patterns listed. I've filed a bug report and hopefully this problem will be corrected soon.*

Queryable Patch Inventory

When you install Oracle Database 12c, one of the first things that gets created is the Oracle inventory. The Oracle inventory is a metadata repository of the software, patches, and other information related to the Oracle installations on your system. Until now, the only way to query the Oracle inventory was to use the **opatch** utility. The returned data was very difficult to deal with, and you could not use SQL or PL/SQL to process it.

In Oracle Database 12c, you can now use the **dbms_qopatch** package to view the Oracle Database inventory in real time. You can fetch this information for a single server configuration or even for each node in a RAC configuration. Most of the subprograms of the **dbms_qopatch** package return the information in an XMLTYPE data type format. Thus, you can use XQuery to further process the data that is being returned by the **dbms_qopatch** package. Let's look at an example:

```
set long 1000000
with all_output as
(select dbms_qopatch.get_opatch_lsinventory as patch_output from dual)
select xmlquery(
'for $i in InventoryInstance/oracleHome
return $i'
passing by value patch_output
returning content) xmldata from all_output;

XMLDATA
--------------------------------------------------------------------
<oracleHome><UId>
OracleHome-0dcd4366-cdf9-48e0-88de-7a75f7b2f259</UId>
<targetTypeId>oracle_home</targetTypeId>
<patchingModel>oneoff</patchingModel>
<path>/u01/app/oracle/product/12.1.0.1/dbhome_1</path>
<targetTypeId>oracle_home</targetTypeId>
<inventoryLocation>/u01/app/oraInventory</inventoryLocation>
<isShared>false</isShared></oracleHome>
```

Oracle dNFS New Features

A new database parameter, dNFS_BATCH_SIZE, controls the number of asynchronous I/O requests that a given Oracle process can queue up when a Direct NFS Client is enabled. This helps situations in which the NFS server cannot handle a large number of outstanding asynch I/O requests reliably. If you are using dNFS, Oracle recommends that you start with the parameter set at 128k and then increase or decrease the parameter as required for optimal NFS server performance.

You can also use the NFS_VERSION parameter to specify the NFS protocol that is to be used by the dNFS Client. Valid values are **nfsv3** (the default), **nfsv4**, and **nfsv4.1**.

Database Cloning

While database cloning is not a new feature, as it was available in Oracle Database 11*g* Release 2 (though not very well documented), we thought it worth mentioning that Oracle Database now has the ability to do database cloning. This kind of cloning is different from database duplication done by RMAN. Cloning is provided through the use of a script called clonedb.pl and is only available when you are using dNFS. You can also choose to clone your database manually should you run into a problem with the clonedb.pl script.

The clone is built off of a static copy of the source database (such as an RMAN image copy or a snapshot). The resulting image of the cloned database is usually much smaller than that of the source database, because the database datafiles are not copied over to the clone. Instead, Oracle Database uses a copy-on-write technology. As a result, only blocks that are modified in the cloned database will require any additional storage. So, over time as you modify the cloned database, you will see its storage utilization grow.

Advanced Network Compression

The following two new parameters are available with Advanced Network Compression, providing for enhanced compression services at the network layer:

- SQLNET.COMPRESSION

- SQLNET.COMPRESSION_LEVELS

These new parameters can be set at the connection layer, the service level, or the database level.

Very Large Network Buffers

Oracle has added support for larger network packets. The session data unit (SDU) size can now range from 512 bytes all the way up to 2MB. In Oracle Database 12c, the default SDU for a client and a dedicated server is 8,192 bytes. The default SDU for a shared server environment is 65,535 bytes.

Multiprocess, Multithreaded Oracle

Oracle Database 12c introduces a new model for processes called the *multithreaded Oracle Database*. The previous mode, called *process mode*, is still the default setting for Oracle Database 12c. However, you can put the Oracle database into a mode called *threaded execution mode*. In this mode, some Oracle background processes will continue to run as processes, but many of the older Oracle processes will now run as threads instead. In fact, when we ran the database in this mode, we went from a count of 47 processes to just 6 processes for our non-RAC Oracle 12c Database. Clearly, this should result in better use of system resources overall.

To run in threaded execution mode, you need to set the THREADED_EXECUTION parameter to a value of TRUE (the default is FALSE). If you choose to use threaded execution mode, you need to be aware of a couple of things:

- You will no longer be able to use operating system authentication. If you try, an ORA-01031 or ORA-01017 error will be raised.

- You need to set the parameter DEDICATED_THROUGH_BROKER_listener-name=ON in the listener.ora file on the database server. This allows the server to spawn threads when connections to the database are requested through the listener.

Database Smart Flash Cache Support for Multiple Flash Drives

Oracle Database 12c now provides the ability to access and combine multiple flash devices for Database Smart Flash Cache without the need for a volume manager. You will still need a volume manager if you wish to share a flash file among more than one instance. To add multiple flash cache devices, simply list the path for each device in the DB_FLASH_CACHE_FILE parameter. Before Oracle Database 12c, you could add only one device, but now you can add up to 16 devices. You would also need to add the associated size of the cache in the DB_FLASH_CACHE_SIZE parameter.

New Oracle Scheduler Script Jobs

Oracle Database 12c has made it easier to run certain types of jobs from the Oracle Scheduler by adding new script jobs. These new script jobs support custom user scripts within specific functional realms. You still use the DBMS_SCHEDULE package to create the script jobs. In the **job_type** parameter, you find that three new script job types are defined:

- **SQL_SCRIPT**   These jobs use the SQL*Plus interpreter to run the job. So, within the job, you can use SQL*Plus commands to format the output. Authentication is supported either inline, passed in as part of the JOB_ACTION parameter or indicating to the scheduler which connect credential should be used.

- **EXTERNAL_SCRIPT**   This kind of script job is used to execute the OS shell interpreter, and thus you can use it to execute command shell scripts. For Unix, the default shell is the **sh** shell, but you can override this in the shell script itself.

- **BACKUP_SCRIPT**   This job provides a direct way to specify RMAN commands within the context of a script to perform various RMAN operations.

NOTE
Scheduler programs can also use these new job types.

Many of these jobs will require the use of credentials. You can use the PL/SQL-supplied program **dbms_credential.create_credential** to define the credentials for the jobs. You then have to give the job execute privileges on the credential that you have created. Credentials are specific to individual schemas, so if you have jobs running in different schemas, you will need to create the credential in each schema that a given job will be running from.

Finally, a *_CREDENTIALS view is provided so that you can see the list of credentials in the database.

End of Line

Oracle Database 12c has added a number of new features that impact the management and monitoring of the Oracle 12c database. Anything that can make the DBA's job easier and that can reduce the outage time required to complete maintenance operations is most welcome and helpful.

Something to keep in mind with all of the new features in this book (and those we don't cover too): The fact is that there can be unseen operational impacts when you implement these features. For example, you might wish to start using multiprocess, multithreaded Oracle. However, if you have a monitoring process that looks for the LGWR or DBWR processes, you will find they are no longer there in the multithreaded model. As a result, your monitoring process will need to be refactored. These are the subtle kinds of things that get missed when using new features, so plan carefully.

CHAPTER
11

Oracle Database 12c
Performance New Features

Oracle Database 12c offers several new features with respect to improving the performance of the database, tuning bad SQL statements, and monitoring database performance. In this chapter we will cover each of these topics in some detail. First we will look at statistics-related new features, and then we will dive into Optimizer-related new features—only two sections, true, but there is oh so much packed into these two sections!

Statistics-Related New Features

I don't have statistics to prove my theory, and it is highly theoretical at that ... but I believe that a large percentage of SQL performance problems are the result of slow query performance. Mull over that theory for a minute or two before you start reading about statistics-related new features in Oracle Database 12c. In this section, we dive into the following exciting topics:

- Automatic column group detection

- Concurrent statistics gathering

- Enhancements to incremental statistics

- Online statistics gathering for bulk loads

- Session-private statistics for global temporary tables

- Running statistics gathering options in reporting mode

- Running reports on previously executed statistics runs

Automatic Column Group Detection

Extended statistics were introduced in Oracle Database 11g Release 2. Extended statistics are collected using the **dbms_stats** PL/SQL-supplied package. Extended statistics provide two features:

- **Column group statistics**   A collection of statistics on two or more columns in a given table. These statistics provide cardinality estimates for the Oracle Optimizer to use when SQL queries use the columns that the extended statistics are collected on.

- **Expression statistics**   Provides additional statistics to the Optimizer to use for SQL statements that use expressions in their predicates.

While Oracle Database 12c does not introduce any new features with regard to expression statistics, there is something new to be aware of with column group statistics. Previously, you had to guess which columns you should create column group statistics on. The Oracle database did not provide any intelligence to help you decide which tables and columns would benefit from the creation of column group statistics. Now, in Oracle Database 12c, the database can actually detect column combinations that would benefit from column group statistics and then the database will automatically create those column group statistics. This is facilitated through SQL plan directives, which are discussed later in this chapter. A SQL plan directive can automatically trigger the creation of column group statistics.

You can also use the **dbms_stats.seed_col_usage** and **dbms_stats.report_col_usage** PL/SQL programs to help determine which columns you should create column group statistics on. Using the output of the **report_col_usage** function, you can decide which columns to create extended statistics on. This output has even more usefulness, as you will see shortly. In the next example we will look at how we get the output and then what we can do with it.

First, let's set up our test environment. In this example we will use a copy of the SCOTT.EMP table called COPY_EMP. In the following code, we do just that, connecting to the SCOTT schema and creating the COPY_EMP table. We then analyze the table with **dbms_stats**.

```
connect scott/robert
drop table copy_emp;
create table copy_emp as select * from emp;
alter table copy_emp add constraint pk_copy_emp primary key (empno);
create index ix_copy_emp_01 on copy_emp (mgr, job);
exec dbms_stats.gather_table_stats('SCOTT','COPY_EMP', cascade=>TRUE);
```

Let's also quickly look at column group statistics on the COPY_EMP table:

```
SELECT COLUMN_NAME, NUM_DISTINCT, HISTOGRAM
FROM USER_TAB_COL_STATISTICS
WHERE TABLE_NAME ='COPY_EMP'
order by 1;

COLUMN_NAME                            NUM_DISTINCT HISTOGRAM
-------------------------------------- ------------ ---------------
COMM                                              4 NONE
DEPTNO                                            3 NONE
EMPNO                                            14 NONE
ENAME                                            14 NONE
HIREDATE                                         13 NONE
JOB                                               5 NONE
MGR                                               6 NONE
SAL                                              12 NONE
```

Tom Says
It is interesting to note that **seed_col_usage** and **report_col_usage** first appeared in Oracle Database 11*g* Release 2. It is "official" in Oracle Database 12*c* Release 1, but it can be used before that release.

Next, we want to collect column usage information so that the Oracle database can suggest some columns that we might want to create column group statistics on. To do this we use the **dbms_stats.seed_col_usage** PL/SQL stored procedure. We have two options as to how to collect column usage information when using this program:

- Have it populate the column usage statistics based on an existing SQL tuning set

- Have it monitor the current workload for a given period of time

In our case, let's use the second option and have the program monitor the given workload for an hour. As such, we will start the process with the following command:

```
-- note that the robert account here has DBA and SYSDBA privileges.
connect robert/password as sysdba
exec dbms_stats.seed_col_usage(null, null, 3600);
```

Note that the execution of the **dbms_stats.seed_col_usage** program returns quickly. It does not hold up the SQL*Plus session for the whole hour.
Now that we have started monitoring, let's run some SQL statements. Here is our first one:

```
connect scott/robert
set autotrace on
select empno, ename, job, mgr, hiredate
from copy_emp
where job='CLERK' and mgr=7902 and hiredate<sysdate;

    EMPNO ENAME      JOB            MGR HIREDATE
---------- ---------- --------- ---------- ---------
      7369 SMITH      CLERK         7902 17-DEC-80
```

Let's look at the execution plan for this statement:

```
--------------------------------------------------------------------------
| Id | Operation          | Name    | Rows | Bytes | Cost (%CPU)| Time     |
--------------------------------------------------------------------------
|  0 | SELECT STATEMENT   |         |    1 |    30 |     3   (0)| 00:00:01 |
|* 1 |  TABLE ACCESS FULL | COPY_EMP|    1 |    30 |     3   (0)| 00:00:01 |
--------------------------------------------------------------------------
```

Next, we will run a query that performs a **group by** operation:

```
select mgr, job, count(*)
from copy_emp
where job='CLERK' and mgr=7902 and hiredate<sysdate
group by mgr, job;
```

Here is the resulting explain plan:

```
---------------------------------------------------------------------------
| Id  | Operation           | Name     | Rows  | Bytes | Cost (%CPU)| Time     |
---------------------------------------------------------------------------
|   0 | SELECT STATEMENT    |          |     1 |    20 |     3   (0)| 00:00:01 |
|   1 |  SORT GROUP BY NOSORT|         |     1 |    20 |     3   (0)| 00:00:01 |
|*  2 |   TABLE ACCESS FULL | COPY_EMP |     1 |    20 |     3   (0)| 00:00:01 |
---------------------------------------------------------------------------
```

Now, let's look at a report of the column relationships that the database has discovered. To do this we will use the **dbms_stats.report_col_usage** function:

```
set long 10000
select dbms_stats.report_col_usage('SCOTT','COPY_EMP') from dual;
DBMS_STATS.REPORT_COL_USAGE('SCOTT','COPY_EMP')
-------------------------------------------------------------------------------
LEGEND:
.......
EQ          : Used in single table EQuality predicate
RANGE       : Used in single table RANGE predicate
LIKE        : Used in single table LIKE predicate
NULL        : Used in single table is (not) NULL predicate
EQ_JOIN     : Used in EQuality JOIN predicate
NONEQ_JOIN  : Used in NON EQuality JOIN predicate
FILTER      : Used in single table FILTER predicate
JOIN        : Used in JOIN predicate

DBMS_STATS.REPORT_COL_USAGE('SCOTT','COPY_EMP')
-------------------------------------------------------------------------------
GROUP_BY    : Used in GROUP BY expression
...............................................................................
###############################################################################
COLUMN USAGE REPORT FOR SCOTT.COPY_EMP
.......................................
1. HIREDATE                         : RANGE
2. JOB                              : EQ
3. MGR                              : EQ

DBMS_STATS.REPORT_COL_USAGE('SCOTT','COPY_EMP')
-------------------------------------------------------------------------------
4. (JOB, MGR)                       : FILTER GROUP_BY
###############################################################################
```

There is some great information in this report! We can see that the HIREDATE column was used in a range predicate (the **hiredate<sysdate** part of our first query

predicate). At first glance, this output might well be a hint that we should look further to see if the creation of an index on the HIREDATE column (if one does not already exist) might be warranted. Of course, this report isn't telling us to create such an index (and that's an important distinction here), but looking at the fact that HIREDATE is used in a rage predicate might cause us to investigate the possibility further.

We can also see that the JOB and MGR columns were used in Equality predicates. This harbors back to our first query again, where our predicates included the JOB and MGR columns (**where job='CLERK' and mgr=7902**). Finally, we see that the JOB and MGR columns were used in a **group by** clause, which is true in our second SQL statement. The JOB and MGR columns, then, are considered candidates for extended column group statistics.

Once the monitoring window has ended, we can create extended statistics on the columns the database has identified by using the **dbms_stats.create_extended_stats** function, as shown here:

```
connect robert/password as sysdba
SELECT DBMS_STATS.CREATE_EXTENDED_STATS('SCOTT','COPY_EMP') FROM DUAL;

DBMS_STATS.CREATE_EXTENDED_STATS('SCOTT','COPY_EMP')
--------------------------------------------------------------------------------
################################################################################
EXTENSIONS FOR SCOTT.COPY_EMP
...........................
1. (JOB, MGR)                          : SYS_STULPA1A#B6YL4KQ59DQO3OADQ created
################################################################################
```

After we have created the extended statistics on the table, we need to re-collect the object statistics on the object:

```
exec dbms_stats.gather_table_stats('SCOTT','COPY_EMP',cascade=>TRUE);
```

Now, let's look at our column listing again:

```
connect scott/robert
SELECT COLUMN_NAME, NUM_DISTINCT, HISTOGRAM
FROM USER_TAB_COL_STATISTICS
WHERE TABLE_NAME ='COPY_EMP'
order by 1;
COLUMN_NAME                     NUM_DISTINCT HISTOGRAM
------------------------------- ------------ ---------------
COMM                                       4 NONE
DEPTNO                                     3 NONE
EMPNO                                     14 NONE
ENAME                                     14 NONE
HIREDATE                                  13 FREQUENCY
JOB                                        5 FREQUENCY
MGR                                        6 FREQUENCY
SAL                                       12 NONE
SYS_STULPA1A#B6YL4KQ59DQO3OADQ             8 FREQUENCY
```

It appears that we have had a new column added! This actually represents the presence of an extended column statistic, and on the right we see that there is a frequency-based histogram that has been created on that statistic and that the expected cardinality is 8. Let's see how this new functionality can impact our queries.

First, I've modified the COPY_EMP table so that it now contains 2.7 million rows. I've also ensured that all of the EMPNO values are distinct. You can see the result in these queries:

```
connect scott/robert
SELECT COLUMN_NAME, NUM_DISTINCT, HISTOGRAM
FROM USER_TAB_COL_STATISTICS
WHERE TABLE_NAME ='COPY_EMP'
order by 1;
COLUMN_NAME                        NUM_DISTINCT HISTOGRAM
--------------------------------   ------------ ---------------

COMM                                          4 NONE
DEPTNO                                         3 NONE
EMPNO                                    2752512 NONE
ENAME                                         14 NONE
HIREDATE                                      13 FREQUENCY
JOB                                            5 FREQUENCY
MGR                                            6 FREQUENCY
SAL                                           12 NONE
SYS_STULPA1A#B6YL4KQ59DQO3OADQ                 8 FREQUENCY
```

Note the number of distinct records for EMPNO and also for the row that starts with SYS_. This last row is the extended statistic for the MGR and JOB columns, and it tells us that the cardinality for those columns is 8. So, right now, it appears that JOB and MGR, when combined, are not terribly selective.

Let's look at this query again:

```
select mgr, job, count(*)
from copy_emp
where job='CLERK' and mgr=7902 and hiredate<sysdate
group by mgr, job;
```

Here is the resulting explain plan:

```
---------------------------------------------------------------------------
| Id | Operation             | Name     | Rows | Bytes | Cost (%CPU)| Time     |
---------------------------------------------------------------------------
|  0 | SELECT STATEMENT      |          |    1 |    20 |     3   (0)| 00:00:01 |
|  1 |  SORT GROUP BY NOSORT |          |    1 |    20 |     3   (0)| 00:00:01 |
|* 2 |   TABLE ACCESS FULL   | COPY_EMP |    1 |    20 |     3   (0)| 00:00:01 |
---------------------------------------------------------------------------
```

Note that the Optimizer has selected a full table scan for the execution plan. This is driven, in part, because of the non-selectiveness of the MGR and JOB column values. Let's see what happens when this selectivity changes.

First, we update the MGR column so that, essentially, each employee becomes his or her own manager. Then we will re-collect statistics and look at how selectivity has changed.

```
update copy_emp set mgr=empno;
commit;
exec dbms_stats.gather_table_stats('SCOTT','COPY_EMP',cascade=>TRUE);
SELECT COLUMN_NAME, NUM_DISTINCT, HISTOGRAM
FROM USER_TAB_COL_STATISTICS
WHERE TABLE_NAME ='COPY_EMP'
order by 1;
COLUMN_NAME                           NUM_DISTINCT HISTOGRAM
------------------------------------- ------------ ---------------

COMM                                            4 NONE
DEPTNO                                          3 NONE
EMPNO                                     2752512 NONE
ENAME                                          14 NONE
HIREDATE                                       13 FREQUENCY
JOB                                             5 FREQUENCY
MGR                                       2752512 NONE
SAL                                            12 NONE
SYS_STULPA1A#B6YL4KQ59DQO3OADQ            2751232 NONE
```

Let's rerun our query and see how our execution plan might have changed:

```
select mgr, job, count(*)
from copy_emp
where job='CLERK' and mgr=10011 and hiredate<sysdate
group by mgr, job;
```

```
--------------------------------------------------------------------------------
----------
| Id  | Operation                    | Name          | Rows  | Bytes | Cost (%CPU)|
Time     |
--------------------------------------------------------------------------------
----------
|   0 | SELECT STATEMENT             |               |     1 |    22 |     4   (0)|
00:00:01 |
|   1 |  SORT GROUP BY NOSORT        |               |     1 |    22 |     4   (0)|
00:00:01 |
|*  2 |   TABLE ACCESS BY INDEX ROWID| COPY_EMP      |     1 |    22 |     4   (0)|
00:00:01 |
|*  3 |    INDEX RANGE SCAN          | IX_COPY_EMP_01 |    1 |       |     3   (0)|
00:00:01 |
--------------------------------------------------------------------------------
----------
```

You can see how the extended statistics have switched the execution plan from a full table scan to an index range scan!

Concurrent Statistics Gathering

Concurrent statistics collection can be very helpful if you have a schema with multiple tables, or a table with multiple partitions. Oracle has enhanced the **dbms_stats** procedure with a new preference called **concurrent**. When **concurrent** is set, Oracle Database 12c will use the Oracle Scheduler, Oracle Database Advanced Queuing, and the Oracle Database Resource Manager, respectively to schedule, manage, and execute concurrent statistics gathering. The job scheduler will determine the level of concurrency, which you can control by defining the **job_queue_processes** parameter to throttle the total number of scheduler jobs that are allowed.

The **concurrent** preference can have the following values:

- **MANUAL**   Concurrent statistics gathering only occurs for manual statistics collection efforts.

- **AUTOMATIC**   Concurrent statistics gathering only occurs for automatic statistics gathering efforts.

- **ALL**   Concurrent statistics gathering is enabled for both manual and automatic statistics gathering efforts.

- **OFF** (default value)   Concurrent statistics gathering is completely disabled.

There are other requirements if you want to use concurrent statistics. First, the account that is going to be creating the statistics must have the normal privileges for gathering statistics and must also have the following privileges:

- **create job**

- **manage scheduler**

- **manage any queue**

Additionally, the SYSAUX tablespace must be online and available. The parameter JOB_QUEUE_PROCESSES must be set to a value greater than 3. Finally, the Database Resource Manager must be enabled (by default it is disabled).

After the gather statistics operation runs, it generates a statistics collection process for each object to be analyzed. Tables, indexes, and partitioned and subpartitioned objects can all be analyzed this way. This creates the first level of parallelism. In this level of parallelism, the degree of parallelism is constrained by the setting of JOB_QUEUE_PROCESSES and, optionally, the Database Resource Manager (which you will have enabled).

The second level of parallelism occurs when the query coordinator jobs that were spawned off on the first level spawn off analyze jobs for all partitions and subpartitions to be analyzed. This degree of parallelism is determined by the Oracle database.

Here is an example of enabling and collecting concurrent statistics. First, we will enable the Database Resource Manager by using the default resource plan, and then we will make sure that the JOB_QUEUE_PROCESSES parameter is set high enough:

```
show parameter resource_manager_plan
NAME                                 TYPE     VALUE
------------------------------------ -------- ----------------------------
resource_limit                       boolean  FALSE
resource_manager_cpu_allocation      integer  6
resource_manager_plan                string

alter system set resource_manager_plan='DEFAULT_PLAN';

show parameter job_queue
NAME                                 TYPE     VALUE
------------------------------------ -------- ----------------------------
job_queue_processes                  integer  1000
```

Next, we can enable concurrent statistics by using the **dbms_stats** procedure **set_global_prefs**:

```
exec dbms_stats.set_global_prefs('CONCURRENT','ALL');
```

We can check to verify that the change was completed by calling the **dbms_stats** function **get_prefs**:

```
select dbms_stats.get_prefs('CONCURRENT') from dual;
DBMS_STATS.GET_PREFS('CONCURRENT')
----------------------------------------------------------------
ALL
```

Finally, we can generate statistics for a schema in parallel:

```
exec dbms_stats.gather_schema_stats('SCOTT', cascade=>TRUE);
```

When this job is executed, Oracle Database 12c will create a job for each object (tables, partitions, indexes, and so forth) in the schema. Each of those gather operations can itself operate in parallel.

We can query the view DBA_OPTSTAT_OPERATION_TASKS to see the completed jobs, as shown here:

```
select target, target_type, job_name, to_char(start_time, 'dd-mon-yyyy
hh24:mi:ss')
from dba_optstat_operation_tasks
```

```
where status = 'COMPLETED'
and opid = (select max(id)
from dba_optstat_operations
where operation = 'gather_schema_stats');
```

```
TARGET                        TARGET_TYPE     JOB_N TO_CHAR(START_TIME,
----------------------------- --------------- ----- --------------------
SCOTT.BONUS                   TABLE                 01-jun-2013 22:55:32
SCOTT.CHILDREN                TABLE                 01-jun-2013 22:55:32
SCOTT.COPY_EMP                TABLE                 01-jun-2013 22:55:33
SCOTT.DEPT                    TABLE                 01-jun-2013 22:55:33
SCOTT.PK_DEPT                 INDEX                 01-jun-2013 22:55:33
SCOTT.ECOM_DETAIL             TABLE                 01-jun-2013 22:55:33
SCOTT.PK_ECOM_DETAIL          INDEX                 01-jun-2013 22:55:33
SCOTT.ECOM_HEADER             TABLE                 01-jun-2013 22:55:33
SCOTT.SYS_C0010207            INDEX                 01-jun-2013 22:55:33
SCOTT.EMP                     TABLE                 01-jun-2013 22:55:33
SCOTT.PK_EMP                  INDEX                 01-jun-2013 22:55:33
SCOTT.PARENTS                 TABLE                 01-jun-2013 22:55:33
SCOTT.SALGRADE                TABLE                 01-jun-2013 22:55:33
SCOTT.TESTING_C               TABLE                 01-jun-2013 22:55:34
SCOTT.IX_TESTINGC_01          INDEX                 01-jun-2013 22:55:34
SCOTT.IX_TESTINGC_02          INDEX                 01-jun-2013 22:55:34
SCOTT.IX_TESTINGC_03          INDEX                 01-jun-2013 22:55:34
SCOTT.TESTING_P               TABLE                 01-jun-2013 22:55:34
SCOTT.IX_TESTINGP             INDEX                 01-jun-2013 22:55:34
SCOTT.TEST_TABLE              TABLE                 01-jun-2013 22:55:34
SCOTT.TEST_TABLE_TWO          TABLE                 01-jun-2013 22:55:36
```

Note that several of the job start times are at the exact same time, indicating that the jobs were started concurrently in parallel.

Tom Says

Before you use concurrent statistics, make sure that doing so makes sense! Parallel operations are inherently nonscalable; they are designed for a single thing (such as gathering statistics) to use as much of the machine resources as possible. While that sounds good, consider what it means for a single task, like statistics gathering, to consume all of the machine resources; it means nothing else can be running. So, unless you are running statistics in isolation, as you might be in a warehouse environment, beware of highly concurrent statistics gathering. Your OLTP users might not appreciate your consuming all of the CPU, memory, and IO resources. Also, remember that the default setting of JOB_QUEUE_PROCESSES is 1,000. Unless you have a machine with tons of small disks and around 500 or so CPUs, 1,000 is far too high. Make sure you use reasonable values for this setting (start with two or four times the number of CPUs!).

Enhancements to Incremental Statistics

The purpose of incremental statistics is to avoid the overhead of full statistics collection on a given partitioned table by deriving the global statistics for that partitioned object from only the partitions that have changed. In Oracle Database 12c, Oracle has introduced new functionality to incremental statistics that performs statistics collection as part of partition maintenance operations.

Incremental Statistics for Partition Maintenance Operations

In Oracle Database 12c, if a partition maintenance operation forces statistics gathering, the database can reuse the synopses that were associated with the old segments that are a part of that partition maintenance operation.

Now, **dbms_stats** can create a synopsis on a nonpartitioned table. This enables you to maintain incremental statistics during a partition exchange operation, removing the requirement to gather statistics on the partition after the exchange operation has completed. You are probably already aware of the **incremental** preference, which is set to TRUE or FALSE depending on your desire to collect incremental statistics. Oracle Database 12c adds the **incremental_level** preference, which controls which synopses are collected and when.

You can set **incremental_level** to either TABLE or PARTITION (the default). When set to PARTITION, the synopses are only gathered at the partition level of a partitioned table. If the preference is set to TABLE, then the synopses are generated on the table. The **incremental_level** preference can only be set to TABLE at the table level using **dbms_stats.set_table_prefs**; it cannot be set at the schema, database, or global level.

For example, suppose we have an empty partition called EMPTY_GRADES_ Q1_2013 in a partitioned table called GRADES. We want to exchange that partition with a new one, called NEW_GRADES_Q1_2013, that contains complete grade data. We would first need to set the table preferences on the new partition like this:

```
exec dbms_stats.set table_prefs('SCOTT', 'NEW_GRADES_Q1_2013',
'INCREMENTAL', 'true');
exec dbms_stats.set_table_prefs('SCOTT', 'NEW_GRADES_Q1_2013',
'INCREMENTAL_LEVEL', 'table');
```

Next, we need to gather the statistics on the NEW_GRADES_Q1_2013 table that we will be exchanging shortly:

```
exec dbms_stats.gather_table_stats('SCOTT','NEW_GRADES_Q1_2013');
```

Now, we need to set the preferences for the GRADES partitioned table:

```
exec dbms_Stats.set_table_prefs('SCOTT','GRADES','INCREMENTAL','TRUE');
```

Having changed the GRADES table to use an incremental statistics collection strategy, we need to gather statistics on the partition that we will be changing:

```
exec dbms_stats.gather_table_stats('SCOTT','GRADES','EMPTY_GRADES_Q1_20
13',granularity=>'partition');
```

We can now perform the partition exchange operation:

```
alter table grades exchange partition emprty_grades_q1_2013 with table
new_grades_q1_2013;
```

As a result of the new features in Oracle Database 12c, the synopses for the nonpartitioned table (and the statistics as well) will be moved over to the partitioned table and the global statistics will be updated. Thus, there is no need to reanalyze the GRADES partitioned table after a partition swap.

Incremental Statistics for Tables with Stale or Locked Partition Statistics

In previous versions of Oracle Database and by default in Oracle Database 12c, a partition or subpartition is considered stale if any DML changes have occurred in that partition or subpartition. To gather complete statistics for a partitioned table, including the global statistics of that table, you need to run **dbms_stats** to gather complete statistics again after a DML operation on a partition or subpartition. Additionally, if the statistics on a given partition are locked, **dbms_stats** cannot re-collect statistics on that partition if that partition is considered stale. The result is that a full table scan is the only way to collect global statistics on a partitioned table.

In Oracle Database 12c, a preference called **incremental_staleness** is available that enables you to control the staleness percentage that is allowed on a given partition before it's considered actually stale. **incremental_staleness** can be set to the following values:

- **USE_STALE_PERCENT** (can be used with USE_LOCKED_STATS)   Oracle will use the default STALE_PERCENT setting when determining if a partition or subpartition is stale.

- **USE_LOCKED_STATS** (can be used with USE_STALE_PERCENT)   If a given partition or subpartition is locked, then it will not be considered stale regardless of how much it changes as a result of DML operations.

- **NULL**   This is the default value and the behavior is the same as in Oracle Database 11g. A partition or subpartition will be considered stale if any DML operation occurs in that partition or subpartition. Incrementally updated statistics will be the same as those statistics gathered in nonincremental mode. If this mode is not used, then it is possible that the statistics gathered in incremental mode will not be as accurate as those gathered in a nonincremental fashion.

Here is an example of setting these table preferences using the PL/SQL procedure **dbms_stats.set_table_prefs**:

```
exec dbms_stats.set_table_prefs('SCOTT','EMP','incremental_
staleness','use_stale_percent,use_locked_stats');
```

Online Statistics Gathering for Bulk Loads

Oracle Database 12c automatically collects statistics after a bulk load operation. A bulk load operation in this context means one of the following SQL statements:

- **create table as select**

- **insert into .. select when using the direct path mode (/*+APPEND */ hint)**

- **parallel inserts**

When inserting into an empty partitioned table using direct path mode, the database will collect global statistics as the operation is occurring. Partition-level information is not collected during the operation, however. If you are using the extended partition syntax and inserting directly into an empty partition, then statistics will be collected for that partition. Global statistics are not collected in that case.

If the **incremental** preference (discussed earlier in this chapter) is enabled, then the statistics will be available as soon as the **insert** statement is complete. Of course, if the **insert** statement is rolled back, then the statistics will be deleted too.

When inserting into a nonempty object, check the DBA_TAB_COL_STATISTICS view. That view has a column called NOTES that will show a value of STATS_ON_LOAD if column statistics are to be gathered during a bulk load.

Note that statistics for indexes are not created in this mode, nor are histograms. If you need either of these, then you will want to run the normal **dbms_stats** programs to gather table statistics or index statistics as required. If you run **dbms_stats.gather_table_stats** with the **options** parameter set to GATHER AUTO, the program will only gather missing and stale statistics. In this case, statistics on indexes would be generated, as

Tom Says
Remember, though, that since Oracle Database 10g, statistics are "automagically" computed on indexes whenever you create them or rebuild them. So, if your steps are either a) **create table as select**, b) build indexes; or a) **insert /*+ APPEND */ into** an empty table b) rebuild indexes, you are probably done, with the exception of some histograms. Your indexes will already have statistics computed on them!

would histograms. Table and column statistics information would not need to be collected. It may be helpful to set table-level defaults for the **options** parameter to GATHER AUTO for tables that are often bulk loaded into, to reduce statistics collection times.

The hint NO_GATHER_OPTIMIZER_STATISTICS will disable this functionality. There is also a hint, GATHER_OPTIMIZER_STATISTICS, that you can use to explicitly enable the feature in a given statement.

This feature will not work on any objects owned by SYS. It will not work on nested tables, index-organized tables, external tables, or global temporary tables that are defined as **on commit delete rows**. This feature will also not work on tables with virtual columns, or tables with the **publish** preference set to FALSE. Finally, if the table is partitioned, the **incremental** preference is set to FALSE, and you do not use the extended syntax, then the feature cannot be used.

The following example shows an empty, nonpartitioned table being created from another table. We can see that, after the bulk load, the table has been analyzed.

```
create table test_dba_table as select * from dba_users;
select count(*) from test_dba_table;

  COUNT(*)
----------
        43

select owner, table_name, num_rows from dba_tables
where owner='SCOTT'
and table_name='TEST_DBA_TABLE';

OWNER      TABLE_NAME                       NUM_ROWS
---------- -------------------------------- ----------
SCOTT      TEST_DBA_TABLE                         43
```

Session-Private Statistics for Global Temporary Tables

Starting with Oracle Database 12*c*, global temporary tables can now have their own set of statistics for each individual session. By setting the statistics preference GLOBAL_TEMP_TABLE_STATS to SESSION, you can make statistics on a global temporary table session specific. The default value is SESSION PRIVATE, which means all statistics are shared across users of that global temporary table.

If you set the statistics to be session specific, then you can gather the statistics of the global temporary table within the session that is using that table, and those statistics will be unique to only that session. Other users can either use session-specific statistics or share statistics at the same time, depending on their need.

Tom Says

Be careful with this new capability! If you have a batch program that uses a global temporary table in a few concurrent jobs once a month, session-private statistics will be great. However, if you have an OLTP application that is using a global temporary table to hold in-list values (or something similar) and you execute queries against this global temporary frequently, session-private statistics will cause excessive hard parsing because each session will have its own unique set of statistics. For most cases, assuming batch operations, session-private statistics will work well.

When the Optimizer generates an execution plan for a SQL statement that includes a global temporary table, it will check to see if session-specific statistics exist. If they do not, then the Optimizer will use shared statistics (or do dynamic sampling).

The dictionary views related to statistics have been modified to include a SCOPE column that indicates whether the statistics for a global temporary table are session specific or shared. These views include DBA_TAB_STATISTICS, DBA_IND_STATISTICS, DBA_TAB_HISTOGRAMS, and DBA_TAB_COL_STATISTICS.

The **dbms_stats** programs have been altered so that they do not commit changes to transaction-specific global temporary tables. Thus, the collection of statistics does not have the nasty side effect of wiping out the data that is in the global temporary table.

The **dbms_stats** programs will collect statistics based on the setting of the preference GLOBAL_TEMP_TABLE_STATS. If it's set to SHARED, then the statistics collected by **dbms_stats** will be for the shared statistics. If the preference is set to SESSION then session statistics will be the statistics that **dbms_stats** will operate on.

These **dbms_stats** procedures have been written to operate on global temporary table session statistics (meaning they won't wipe out the session data in a global temporary table):

- GATHER_TABLE_STATS

- DELETE_TABLE_STATS

- DELETE_COLUMN_STATS

- DELETE_INDEX_STATS

- SET_TABLE_STATS

- SET_COLUMN_STATS

- SET_INDEX_STATS

- GET_TABLE_STATS

- GET_COLUMN_STATS

- GET_INDEX_STATS

Running Statistics Gathering Options in Reporting Mode

You can now opt to run statistics collections in what is called reporting mode. When statistics are collected in reporting mode, the statistics are not actually collected, but rather the database reports on the objects that would be analyzed should you actually gather statistics. New **dbms_stats** procedures are available to run the reporting function, and new **dbms_stats** functions have been added to produce the reports afterward.

Each **dbms_stat** statistics collection procedure now has a sibling procedure for statistics collection reporting. Each reporting function begins with the word **report_**. So, for example, for **dbms_stats.gather_table_stats**, there is now a **dbms_stats.report_ gather_table_stats** procedure too. The **report_gather_*_stats** procedures are as follows:

- **report_gather_table_stats**

- **report_gather_schema_stats**

- **report_gather_dictionary_stats**

- **report_gather_database_stats**

- **report_gather_fixed_obj_stats**

- **report_gather_auto_stats**

The procedures have the same parameters as their big brothers, as well as two additional ones you will want to know about:

- **detail_level** Valid detail levels include BASIC, TYPICAL, and ALL. Each level provides progressively more detailed information in the output. TYPICAL is the default value.

- **format** Three format levels are available: XML, HTML, and TEXT. TEXT is the default value.

Let's look at a quick example of the reports in action, using the procedure
dbms_stats.report_gather_schema_stats:

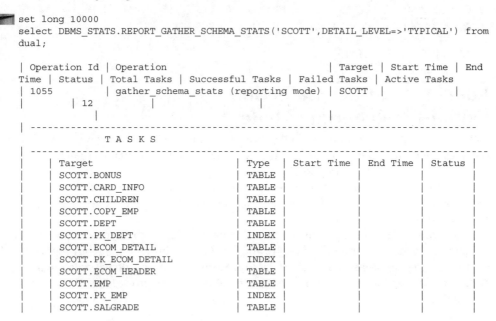

```
set long 10000
select DBMS_STATS.REPORT_GATHER_SCHEMA_STATS('SCOTT',DETAIL_LEVEL=>'TYPICAL') from
dual;

| Operation Id | Operation                          | Target | Start Time | End
Time | Status | Total Tasks | Successful Tasks | Failed Tasks | Active Tasks
| 1055         | gather_schema_stats (reporting mode) | SCOTT |            |
|         | 12 |             |                  |
|            |                                    |        |
| ----------------------------------------------------------------------------
|            T A S K S
| ----------------------------------------------------------------------------
|   | Target                | Type  | Start Time | End Time | Status |
|   | SCOTT.BONUS           | TABLE |            |          |        |
|   | SCOTT.CARD_INFO       | TABLE |            |          |        |
|   | SCOTT.CHILDREN        | TABLE |            |          |        |
|   | SCOTT.COPY_EMP        | TABLE |            |          |        |
|   | SCOTT.DEPT            | TABLE |            |          |        |
|   | SCOTT.PK_DEPT         | INDEX |            |          |        |
|   | SCOTT.ECOM_DETAIL     | TABLE |            |          |        |
|   | SCOTT.PK_ECOM_DETAIL  | INDEX |            |          |        |
|   | SCOTT.ECOM_HEADER     | TABLE |            |          |        |
|   | SCOTT.EMP             | TABLE |            |          |        |
|   | SCOTT.PK_EMP          | INDEX |            |          |        |
|   | SCOTT.SALGRADE        | TABLE |            |          |        |
```

This output shows the list of objects that would be analyzed (12) should you
execute the **dbms_stats.gather_schema_stats** PL/SQL procedure against the SCOTT
schema. There are certain cases where **dbms_stats.gather_schema_stats** would not
choose to analyze the object in question. There are certain cases where an object
would not be analyzed by **dbms_stats**. So, this set of reporting procedures can be
useful in determining if a given object that you feel needs to be analyzed would, in
fact, be analyzed.

Reports on Past Statistics Collection Operations

Just as it's nice to be able to see which objects a given call to a **dbms_stats** statistics
collection feature will analyze, it's nice to be able to generate reports on past
statistics collection efforts. There are two different functions within **dbms_stats** that
you will use for this reporting:

- **dbms_stats.report_stats_operations**   Produces a report that displays all
  statistics operations that occurred between two different points in time.
  Other parameters can be used to further refine the granularity of the report.

- **dbms_stats.report_single_stats_operation**   Produces a report for a specific
  statistics collection operation.

The procedures have the following parameters:

- **opid (report_single_stats_operation** only)   The operation ID for the statistics report run that you wish to report on.

- **detail_level**   Valid detail levels include BASIC, TYPICAL, and ALL. Each level provides progressively more detailed information in the output. TYPICAL is the default value.

- **format**   Three format levels are available: XML, HTML, and TEXT. TEXT is the default value.

- **LatestN (report_stats_operation** only)   Restricts the report to the last *N* number of operations.

- **Since (report_stats_operation** only)   Limits the report to only statistics collected since the timestamp indicated.

- **Until (report_stats_operation** only)   Limits the report to only statistics collected up until the timestamp indicated.

- **Auto_Only (report_stats_operation** only)   Only reports on automatic statistics collection operations (TRUE|FALSE).

- **Container_ids**   Container ID for a Container Database. This limits the reporting to just specific PDBs.

The following example shows how to generate a report of all statistics collection operations that were executed in the last day:

NOTE
Due to page width issues, I've omitted the output. It was simply way too wide!

```
select dbms_stats.report_stats_operations(since=>sysdate-1,
until=>sysdate,format=>'TEXT') REPORT_OUTPUT from dual;
```

Optimizer-Related New Features

When the *Victoria*, the last surviving ship of a five-ship Spanish expedition, returned to its harbor of departure after the first circumnavigation of the earth, only 18 of the original 237 men were on board. The rest died, probably painful and horrible deaths. What is the point here? The point is that there is always risk associated with something and when you open new doors, there is a price to be paid. But the reward, likewise, is huge and it can change your world!

Anyway, in this section we are going to be dealing with the heart of the Oracle Database, the Optimizer. There are some great new Optimizer features in Oracle Database 12*c*, and, like the *Victoria*, we are going to go on a journey of exploration and find out what these new features are and what they do. We will discuss adaptive query optimization and histogram-related new features. Now, that might not sound like a lot to cover, but trust me, this is meaty, heady, and really good stuff. So, carry on! And bring your life jacket!

Adaptive Query Optimization

If you are an experienced DBA, you know that in some cases, analyzing a table, even on a regular basis, just does not get the job done. Performance can still suffer. There are a lot of reasons for this, from data volatility, to a query reusing existing execution plans that are not really as efficient for that query as they could be (for example, if you are using bind variables), to a host of other issues (including, yes, really poorly written SQL). Often, the issue is not really the Optimizer's fault nor your fault as the DBA, but you have to deal with it because that's your job.

Oracle has in the past tried to help the database (and the DBA) deal with these issues with various features such as dynamic sampling, SQL Plan Baselines, and the like. In Oracle Database 12*c*, Oracle offers a new feature called Adaptive Query Optimization (AQO). AQO is a set of features that enables the Oracle database, through the Optimizer, to make run-time adjustments to execution plans, and also collect additional metadata that can help the Optimizer to create better execution plans in the future.

Oracle Database 12*c* adds the following features under the umbrella of Adaptive Query Optimization:

- Adaptive plans
- Adaptive statistics

We will look at each of these in the following sections in much more detail.

Adaptive Plans

In Oracle Database 12*c* an adaptive plan is a bit like a military's special forces unit. Its job is to adapt to and overcome potentially bad execution plans. With adaptive plans, the Optimizer can take a SQL statement and create an execution plan. Additionally, execution plans can be adjusted at run time by the Optimizer based on statistics collected during the actual execution of the SQL statement. The final, adapted plan will then be used for later executions of the query (based on its hash value). In this section we will look at the following topics related to adaptive plans in Oracle Database 12c:

- Mechanics of adaptive plans

- Configuring to use adaptive plans

- Viewing adaptive plans

- Adaptive plans involving join methods

- Adaptive plans involved with parallel processing methods

Mechanics of Adaptive Plans   Adaptive plans are only created for SQL that contain joins and distributed queries. Thus, a single table query will not be able to take advantage of adaptive plans. How do adaptive plans work? First, the SQL statement is parsed and the execution plan for that SQL statement is generated. At the same time, if the statement qualifies for adaptive plans, Oracle Database 12c will generate additional subplans for that SQL statement. These subplans are associated with a set of statistics collectors that are inserted into the plan. It's the job of the statistics collectors to buffer in a certain amount of data, analyze it, and determine if it is aligned with the existing table and column statistical metadata. Based on certain defined thresholds, the statistics collectors will determine which subplan to use at run time. The execution plan with its subplans and the associated statistics collectors are stored in the cursor for later use.

When Oracle Database 12c then executes the cursor, it executes the original plan. As it executes the plan, samples of data are collected, buffered, and analyzed by the statistics collector. If the sampled row thresholds are within those calculated for the original plan, then that plan will continue to be used. If the rows sampled fall outside the statistical threshold (for example, cardinality has been wildly skewed), then the Optimizer may choose to swap in the alternative subplan based on the precalculated thresholds of that plan and how they match the data that has been read. Thus, the execution plan can change dynamically during the query's execution, or any subsequent execution of the query.

Configuring to Use Adaptive Plans   When Oracle Database 12c is first configured, adaptive plans are enabled by default. Adaptive plans are enabled through the setting of these parameters:

- **OPTIMIZER_FEATURES_ENABLE**   Must be set to 12.1.0.01 or later.

- **OPTIMIZER_ADAPTIVE_REPORTING_ONLY**   Must be set to FALSE to use adaptive plans. FALSE is the default value. If you set this parameter to TRUE (it can be set at the system or session level), you will disable the use of adaptive plans.

NOTE
*The parameters OPTIMIZER_FEATURES_ENABLE
and OPTIMZER_ADAPTIVE_REPORTING_ONLY
will be set to the default values for a newly created
database. However, if you manually upgrade
to Oracle Database 12c from an older version
of Oracle Database, you will need to set the
OPTIMIZER_FEATURES_ENABLE parameter in order
for adaptive plans to work. OPTIMZIER_ADAPTIVE_
REPORTING_ONLY should default to FALSE in both
new and upgraded databases.*

You can choose to run your database in adaptive reporting mode only by setting
OPTIMIZER_ADAPTIVE_REPORTING_ONLY to a value of TRUE. In this case,
execution plans will not be adjusted at run time. The database will still collect and
store the information about the execution of the SQL query, however. OPTIMIZER_
ADAPTIVE_REPORTING_ONLY can be set through either the **alter session** command
or the **alter system** command. The parameter is a dynamic parameter, so you can
change it on-the-fly.

Now that you know about adaptive plans, the following section explains how
you can observe them in action!

Viewing Adaptive Plans   You can see the results of adaptive plans by using the
dbms_xplain.display_cursor PL/SQL function. You are probably already familiar with
this function, as it provides the ability to see the execution plan of cursors loaded in
the database cursor cache. This function contains a FORMAT argument that now has
a new value that can be used, called ADAPTIVE. Let's look at an example of its use
and what **dbms_xplan.display_cursor** will show us about a given SQL statement
with respect to adaptive plans:

```
select * from table(dbms_xplan.display_cursor(null, null, 'all +note
+adaptive'));
```

The following two sections will show adaptive plans in action and demonstrate
how to actually read the results of the output.

Adaptive plans can be generated when you execute a query with a join or when a
query with parallelism is involved. This implies that you will not get any benefit from
adaptive plans when executing a single-table query (and my testing confirms this).

The column IS_RESOLVED_DYNAMIC_PLAN in the V$SQL view can also help
you to determine if the SQL statement was resolved based on the original plan or
an adaptive plan. If IS_RESOLVED_DYNAMIC_PLAN is set to Y, the SQL statement
was resolved using one of the generated subplans (thus the final execution plan

has changed). If the column is set to N, then the original plan was used. Here is an example query that shows a case where the dynamic plan was used:

```
select sql_text, is_resolved_adaptive_plan from v$sql
where sql_text  like 'select count(*) from testing_P%'

SQL_TEXT
-------------------------------------------------------------------------
-------------------------------------------
select count(*) from testing_P a, testing_c b where a.id=b.id_p and a.id
between :"SYS_B_0" and :"SYS_B_1"
Y
select count(*) from testing_P a, testing_c b where a.id=b.id_p and a.id
between 500 and 501
Y
```

So, let's look next at how adaptive plans work when we issue queries with joins. Then, in the subsequent section, we will look at how adaptive plans work when we issue queries that use parallelism.

Join Methods   A goodly number of queries involve joins. The presence of joins also tends to complicate the work of the Optimizer because the number of access path permutations becomes greater and more complex. Thus, it seems understandable that as you add additional joins to a given SQL statement, and as the predicates become more complex, it's more likely that the Optimizer might choose a suboptimal plan from time to time. Then factor in things like stale statistics, the impacts of bind variables, and the impacts of data skewing, and you can see how things can sometimes get out of hand.

Let's look at an example of what an adaptive plan looks like. First let's create our test environment:

```
connect scott/robert
set autotrace off
set lines 200
set timing on
drop table testing_p;
create table testing_p (id number, the_value varchar2(30) );
create index ix_testingP on testing_p (id);
drop table testing_c;
create table testing_c (id_p number, id_t number, another_value
varchar2(30) );
create index ix_testingc_01 on testing_c (id_p);
create index ix_testingc_02 on testing_c (id_t);
create index ix_testingc_03 on testing_c (id_p, id_t);
```

In the test environment we have just created, we have two tables, TESTING_P and TESTING_C. Note that to keep this example simple, I have not created primary keys or foreign key references here, as you might normally do.

TESTING_P has two columns in it, ID (a **number** column) and THE_VALUE (a **varchar2** column). The second table, TESTING_C, has three columns: ID_P (a **number**), ID_T (another **number**), and ANOTHER_VALUE (a **varchar2**). While I have not created a foreign key, my intent is to have ID_T be the column that relates TESTING_P(ID) to TESTING_C(ID_T).

Now that we have our test environment set up, let's do some testing. First, notice that we don't have any data in our tables yet. Also, we have not analyzed them. Statistics were created on the indexes when they were created (which happens automatically), there are no table statistics as demonstrated here:

```
column table_name format a30
column index_name format a30
select a.table_name, a.index_name, b.num_rows table_rows, a.num_rows index_rows
from user_indexes a, user_tables b
where a.table_name=b.table_name
and a.table_name like 'TESTING%';


TABLE_NAME                     INDEX_NAME                     TABLE_ROWS INDEX_ROWS
------------------------------ ------------------------------ ---------- ----------
TESTING_C                      IX_TESTINGC_03                                      0
TESTING_C                      IX_TESTINGC_02                                      0
TESTING_C                      IX_TESTINGC_01                                      0
TESTING_P                      IX_TESTINGP                                         0
```

Now, let's run our first set of tests. We will run a query against these empty tables:

```
select count(*) from
(
select b.id_t, b.id_p, b.another_value
from testing_P a, testing_c b
where a.id=b.id_p
and a.id between 10001 and 10003
);
select * from table(dbms_xplan.display_cursor(null, null, 'all +note
+adaptive'));

SQL_ID      1k8t60hqsm4g4, child number 0
-------------------------------------
select count(*) from ( select b.id_t, b.id_p, b.another_value from
testing_P a, testing_c b where a.id=b.id_p and a.id between 10001 and 10003 )
Plan hash value: 2138458964
---------------------------------------------------------------------------
| Id  | Operation            | Name           | Rows  | Bytes | Cost (%CPU)|
---------------------------------------------------------------------------
|   0 | SELECT STATEMENT     |                |       |       |     1 (100)|
|   1 |  SORT AGGREGATE      |                |     1 |    26 |            |
|   2 |   NESTED LOOPS       |                |     1 |    26 |     0   (0)|
|*  3 |    INDEX RANGE SCAN  | IX_TESTINGP    |     1 |    13 |     0   (0)|
|*  4 |    INDEX RANGE SCAN  | IX_TESTINGC_01 |     1 |    13 |     0   (0)|
---------------------------------------------------------------------------

Note
----
   - dynamic statistics used: dynamic sampling (level=2)
```

First, notice that we generated the execution plan with the **dbms_xplan** PL/SQL function **display_cursor**. We used the new **adaptive** option, mentioned earlier. This is new in Oracle Database 12c, and it provides a directive for **dbms_xplan.display_cursor** to include adaptive plan information, which we are interested in.

Looking at the execution plan generated, notice that the Optimizer used dynamic sampling. This is because we don't have any table statistics at all, so there is no adaptive planning possible. The database just generates dynamic statistics at run time, generates a plan, and executes that plan.

So, let's put some data in our tables:

```
truncate table testing_p;
truncate table testing_c;
declare
begin
for tt in 1..1000
loop
    insert into testing_p values(tt, 'www.testing.com');
    commit;
end loop;
for tt in 1..1000
loop
    insert into testing_p values (10001,'www.testing.com');
    commit;
end loop;
end;
/

declare
begin
for aa in (select id from testing_p)
loop
    for zz in 1..3
    loop
        insert into testing_c values (aa.id, zz, 'www.testing.com');
    end loop;
end loop;
commit;

for zz in 4..1000
loop
    insert into testing_c values (1001, zz, 'www.testing.com');
end loop;
commit;
end;
/
```

Notice that we have not yet analyzed the tables. Let's see what happens when we issue our query again:

```
select count(*) from
(
select b.id_t, b.id_p, b.another_value
from testing_P a, testing_c b
where a.id=b.id_p
and a.id between 10001 and 10003
);
select * from table(dbms_xplan.display_cursor(null, null, 'all +note +adaptive'));

SQL_ID      1k8t60hqsm4g4, child number 1
-------------------------------------
select count(*) from ( select b.id_t, b.id_p, b.another_value from
testing_P a, testing_c b where a.id=b.id_p and a.id between 10001 and
10003 )

Plan hash value: 2138458964

-----------------------------------------------------------------------------------
| Id  | Operation          | Name         | Rows  | Bytes | Cost (%CPU)| Time     |
-----------------------------------------------------------------------------------
|   0 | SELECT STATEMENT   |              |       |       |   3 (100)|           |
|   1 |  SORT AGGREGATE    |              |     1 |    26 |          |           |
|   2 |   NESTED LOOPS     |              | 3000K |   74M |   3   (0)| 00:00:01 |
|*  3 |    INDEX RANGE SCAN| IX_TESTINGP  |  1000 | 13000 |   3   (0)| 00:00:01 |
|*  4 |    INDEX RANGE SCAN| IX_TESTINGC_01 | 3000 | 39000 |   0   (0)|         |
-----------------------------------------------------------------------------------

Note
-----
   - dynamic statistics used: dynamic sampling (level=2)
   - statistics feedback used for this statement
```

By this point, you must be asking yourself if I'm crazy. I have not analyzed the tables yet, so it's pretty obvious that we will still get dynamic sampling. But I wanted to point out a couple of things here:

■ Adaptive plans will not appear unless the tables have been analyzed. It does not matter whether the statistics are stale, are on an empty table, or are current; all that matters is that they exist. Since they don't exist in this case (yet), we are getting dynamic sampling.

■ Check out the "Note" about statistics feedback at the end of the output. We will be coming back to that Note later in this chapter, so file that information somewhere in the back of your mind for now.

■ Looking at the statistics, notice that we have done 58 consistent gets. That will come into play as an important factor in a moment.

So, let's create the statistics now. Trust me, things are about to get really interesting!

```
exec dbms_stats.gather_table_stats('SCOTT','TESTING_P',cascade=>TRUE);
exec dbms_stats.gather_table_stats('SCOTT','TESTING_C',cascade=>TRUE);
```

Now that we have analyzed our tables, let's rerun our test query. This time, we are going to enable **autotrace** first, and then we will use **dbms_xplan** afterward:

```
set autotrace on
select count(*) from
(
select b.id_t, b.id_p, b.another_value
from testing_P a, testing_c b
where a.id=b.id_p
and a.id between 10001 and 10003
);
set autotrace off


Execution Plan
----------------------------------------------------------
Plan hash value: 3242817927
---------------------------------------------------------------------------
------------------
| Id  | Operation            | Name           | Rows  | Bytes | Cost
(%CPU)| Time      |
---------------------------------------------------------------------------
------------------
|   0 | SELECT STATEMENT     |                |     1 |    10 |    19
(37)| 00:00:01 |
|   1 |  SORT AGGREGATE      |                |     1 |    10 |
|          |
|*  2 |   HASH JOIN          |                | 3000K|   28M|    19
(37)| 00:00:01 |
|*  3 |    INDEX FAST FULL SCAN| IX_TESTINGP  |  1000 |  5000 |     3
(0)| 00:00:01 |
|*  4 |    INDEX FAST FULL SCAN| IX_TESTINGC_01 |  3000 | 15000 |     9
(0)| 00:00:01 |
---------------------------------------------------------------------------
------------------
Predicate Information (identified by operation id):
---------------------------------------------------
   2 - access("A"."ID"="B"."ID_P")
   3 - filter("A"."ID">=10001 AND "A"."ID"<=10003)
   4 - filter("B"."ID_P">=10001 AND "B"."ID_P"<=10003)
Note
-----
   - this is an adaptive plan
```

Now, this is interesting: the Note stating "this is an adaptive plan" is new (both in our testing and in Oracle Database 12*c* period!). It appears that this query used something called an adaptive plan, and our plan has changed because of it.

If you want more information on the execution plan, you can use the **dbms_xplan.display_cursor** function as shown here:

```
select * from table(dbms_xplan.display_cursor(null, null, 'all +note
+adaptive'));
SQL> select * from table(dbms_xplan.display_cursor(null, null, 'all +note
+adaptive'));

PLAN_TABLE_OUTPUT
-----------------------------------------------------------------------------
-----------------------------------------------------------------
SQL_ID  1k8t60hqsm4g4, child number 1
---------------------------------
select count(*) from ( select b.id_t, b.id_p, b.another_value from
testing_P a, testing_c b where a.id=b.id_p and a.id between 10001 and
10003 )

Plan hash value: 3242817927


-----------------------------------------------------------------------------
------------------
|  Id | Operation             | Name          | Rows  | Bytes | Cost
(%CPU)| Time      |
-----------------------------------------------------------------------------
------------------
PLAN_TABLE_OUTPUT
-----------------------------------------------------------------------------
---------------------------------------------------------------
|   0 | SELECT STATEMENT      |               |       |       |     19
(100)|           |
|   1 |  SORT AGGREGATE       |               |     1 |    10 |
|     |           |
|*  2 |   HASH JOIN           |               | 3000K|   28M|     19
(37)| 00:00:01 |
|-  3 |    NESTED LOOPS       |               | 3000K|   28M|     19
(37)| 00:00:01 |
|-  4 |     STATISTICS COLLECTOR |            |       |       |
|     |           |
|*  5 |      INDEX FAST FULL SCAN| IX_TESTINGP | 1000 |  5000 |      3
(0)| 00:00:01 |
|- * 6 |     INDEX RANGE SCAN  | IX_TESTINGC_01 | 3000 | 15000 |      9
(0)| 00:00:01 |
|*  7 |     INDEX FAST FULL SCAN | IX_TESTINGC_01 | 3000 | 15000 |      9
(0)| 00:00:01 |
-----------------------------------------------------------------------------
------------------
```

```
Query Block Name / Object Alias (identified by operation id):

   1 - SEL$F5BB74E1
   5 - SEL$F5BB74E1 / A@SEL$2
   6 - SEL$F5BB74E1 / B@SEL$2
   7 - SEL$F5BB74E1 / B@SEL$2

Predicate Information (identified by operation id):
---------------------------------------------------
   2 - access("A"."ID"="B"."ID_P")
   5 - filter(("A"."ID">=10001 AND "A"."ID"<=10003))
   6 - access("A"."ID"="B"."ID_P")
       filter(("B"."ID_P">=10001 AND "B"."ID_P"<=10003))
   7 - filter(("B"."ID_P">=10001 AND "B"."ID_P"<=10003))

Column Projection Information (identified by operation id):
----------------------------------------------------------
   1 - (#keys=0) COUNT(*)[22]
   2 - (#keys=1)
   3 - "A"."ID"[NUMBER,22]
   4 - "A"."ID"[NUMBER,22]
   5 - "A"."ID"[NUMBER,22]
   7 - "B"."ID_P"[NUMBER,22]

Note
-----
   - statistics feedback used for this statement
   - this is an adaptive plan (rows marked '-' are inactive)
```

Yikes, look at the execution plan up there! Has the Optimizer lost its mind? Did I just cut and paste two execution plans together in some weird and crazy way? Not at all; in fact, the Optimizer has gotten smarter, and this is the evidence of that fact. What you see here is not only the actual execution plan, but also parts of the subplans that were considered but not executed. What you see is more than one execution plan that might have been used by Oracle Database 12c to retrieve the result set from the query.

Now, look again at the **autotrace** plan and the **dbms_stats**-generated execution plan presented earlier in this section. As expected, both execution plans are different since we generated statistics. The **dbms_stats** plan has more "stuff" in it. Notice these lines in particular:

```
|-   3 |    NESTED LOOPS          |               | 3000K|    28M|
19  (37)| 00:00:01 |
|-   4 |     STATISTICS COLLECTOR |               |      |       |
|       |
|- *  6 |      INDEX RANGE SCAN   | IX_TESTINGC_01 | 3000 | 15000 |
9   (0)| 00:00:01 |
```

Those dashes on the left side are new.

Now, looking at that Note down there at the bottom of both plans, there is something else new there too:

```
Note
-----
   - this is an adaptive plan (rows marked '-' are inactive)
```

So, the lines marked with dashes are inactive (there is no mention of dashes in the **autotrace** plan because they don't appear in the plan). The dashes, then, indicate that these rows in the execution plan (rows 3 and 6 in particular) are subplans that were considered but were found to be not optimal, and thus were not used.

Line 4 indicates where the statistics collector was executed. As mentioned earlier in the chapter, the statistics collector buffers rows, analyzes them, and then decides which access method in the execution plan is the best one to use. In this case, the Optimizer opted to use the index fast full scan over the index range scan.

Finally, notice that in this case the adaptive plan matches the plan that **autotrace** reports.

Now, let's see what happens to our plan when something changes, like the data in the tables:

```
truncate table testing_p;
truncate table testing_c;
set autotrace on
select count(*) from
(
select b.id_t, b.id_p, b.another_value
from testing_P a, testing_c b
where a.id=b.id_p
and a.id between 10001 and 10003
);

Execution Plan
----------------------------------------------------------
Plan hash value: 3242817927

---------------------------------------------------------------------------
--------------
| Id  | Operation           | Name         | Rows  | Bytes | Cost
(%CPU)| Time      |
---------------------------------------------------------------------------
--------------
|   0 | SELECT STATEMENT    |              |     1 |    10 |    19
(37)| 00:00:01 |
|   1 |  SORT AGGREGATE     |              |     1 |    10 |
|     |           |
|*  2 |   HASH JOIN         |              | 3000K|   28M|    19
(37)| 00:00:01 |
|*  3 |    INDEX FAST FULL SCAN| IX_TESTINGP |  1000 |  5000 |     3
(0)| 00:00:01 |
```

```
|*  4 |       INDEX FAST FULL SCAN|  IX_TESTINGC_01 |  3000 |  15000 |       9
(0)|  00:00:01 |
---------------------------------------------------------------------------
--------------
    - this is an adaptive plan
```

set autotrace off

Well, the **autotrace** plan isn't any different, is it? Let's look at what **dbms_xplan** has to say:

```
select * from table(dbms_xplan.display_cursor(null, null, 'all +note +adaptive'));
SQL_ID  1k8t60hqsm4g4, child number 1
-------------------------------------
select count(*) from ( select b.id_t, b.id_p, b.another_value from
testing_P a, testing_c b where a.id=b.id_p and a.id between 10001 and
10003 )
Plan hash value: 3921797721
-------------------------------------------------------------------------------
--------
| Id  | Operation                  | Name            | Rows  | Bytes | Cost (%CPU)|
Time     |
-------------------------------------------------------------------------------
--------
|   0 | SELECT STATEMENT           |                 |       |       |    19 (100)|
|
|   1 |  SORT AGGREGATE            |                 |     1 |    10 |            |
|
|-  * 2 |   HASH JOIN              |                 | 3000K|   28M|    19  (37)|
00:00:01 |
|   3 |    NESTED LOOPS            |                 | 3000K|   28M|    19  (37)|
00:00:01 |
|-  4 |     STATISTICS COLLECTOR   |                 |       |       |            |
|
|  * 5 |      INDEX FAST FULL SCAN| IX_TESTINGP      |  1000 |  5000 |     3   (0)|
00:00:01 |
|  * 6 |      INDEX RANGE SCAN     | IX_TESTINGC_01  |  3000 | 15000 |     9   (0)|
00:00:01 |
|-  * 7 |     INDEX FAST FULL SCAN | IX_TESTINGC_01  |  3000 | 15000 |     9   (0)|
00:00:01 |
-------------------------------------------------------------------------------
--------
Query Block Name / Object Alias (identified by operation id):
    1 - SEL$F5BB74E1
    5 - SEL$F5BB74E1 / A@SEL$2
    6 - SEL$F5BB74E1 / B@SEL$2
    7 - SEL$F5BB74E1 / B@SEL$2

Predicate Information (identified by operation id):
---------------------------------------------------
    2 - access("A"."ID"="B"."ID_P")
    5 - filter(("A"."ID">=10001 AND "A"."ID"<=10003))
    6 - access("A"."ID"="B"."ID_P")
        filter(("B"."ID_P">=10001 AND "B"."ID_P"<=10003))
    7 - filter(("B"."ID_P">=10001 AND "B"."ID_P"<=10003))
```

```
Column Projection Information (identified by operation id):
-------------------------------------------------------------
   1 - (#keys=0) COUNT(*)[22]
   2 - (#keys=1)
   3 - "A"."ID"[NUMBER,22]
   4 - "A"."ID"[NUMBER,22]
   5 - "A"."ID"[NUMBER,22]
   7 - "B"."ID_P"[NUMBER,22]

Note
-----
   - this is an adaptive plan (rows marked '-' are inactive)
```

First, note that the SQLID is the same for all the plans. This confirms that the SQL statement itself is the same. Then, look at the plan hash value; it is different in the last query execution (after truncating the tables) and the query before the table truncate. This indicates that the execution plan has, indeed, changed.

Now, the actual execution plan looks like this:

```
-------------------------------------------------------------------------
-----------------------
|   Id  | Operation               | Name          | Rows  | Bytes |
Cost (%CPU)| Time      |
-------------------------------------------------------------------------
-----------------------
|     0 | SELECT STATEMENT        |               |       |       |
19 (100)|           |
|     1 |  SORT AGGREGATE         |               |     1 |    10 |
        |           |
|     3 |   NESTED LOOPS          |               | 3000K|   28M|
19  (37)| 00:00:01  |
| *   5 |    INDEX FAST FULL SCAN| IX_TESTINGP    |  1000 |  5000 |
 3  (0)| 00:00:01  |
| *   6 |    INDEX RANGE SCAN     | IX_TESTINGC_01 |  3000 | 15000 |
 9  (0)| 00:00:01  |
-------------------------------------------------------------------------
----------------------

Note
-----
   - this is an adaptive plan
```

Notice that the execution plan generated by **dbms_xplan** output is different from the **autotrace** plan. This is because the **autotrace** output is the equivalent of the output of the **explain plan** command. Since the execution plan can change during the execution of a SQL statement, in real time, there is no way for the execution plan to really be properly reported until it has been executed. Even then, it's possible that Oracle Database has modified the execution plan in mid-execution based on the statistics collectors. The **autotrace** output simply does not report this information with respect to the execution plan.

The output from the **dbms_xplan.display_cursor** function is different, though. It reports on the plan that is actually cached in the database cursor cache. So, it will report on the actual plan that was executed at run time. It also reports on the subplan parts of the execution plan that were executed and that were not executed. This plan is also different from the one we ran earlier, when there was actually data in the tables. The plan with the data did an index fast full scan on IX_TESTING_01. Once we truncated the table, the adaptive plan performed an index range scan on the IX_TESTINGC_01 index. The Optimizer, during the execution of the query plan, sampled the data, and then, based on that operation, the plan was dynamically modified in-flight so that the best execution path would be utilized. This can result in significant performance improvements for queries against tables that are very volatile.

So, we can see the benefit of adaptive plans: the execution plans change as the data (and its cardinality) changes! This can have significant impacts on performance for a number of reasons such as cases where there is serious data skewing and more!

Parallel Distribution Methods   If you are familiar with parallel queries in Oracle Database, then you know that there are various ways of distributing the parallel processing. In some cases, the Optimizer may not be fully aware of which method would be the most appropriate. In such cases the Optimizer may choose to use a distribution technique called the *hybrid hash distribution technique*. When the Optimizer chooses to use this technique, it does not decide which distribution method to use until run time. As it generates the plan, the Optimizer will insert statistics collectors (discussed earlier in this chapter) in front of the parallel server processes on the producer side of the operation. By default, the execution plan will use a hash broadcast distribution method, but if the number of rows is less than two times the degree of parallelism, the execution plan will switch over the query to a broadcast distribution method.

Let's look at an example. In our example we will use the previous query, but we will add some hints to force it to execute in parallel:

```
set autotrace on
select count(*) from
(
select /*+ parallel(4) full(a) full(b) */
b.id_t, b.id_p, b.another_value
from testing_P a, testing_c b
where a.id=b.id_p
and a.id between 10001 and 10003
);
set autotrace off
```

Here is the **autotrace** execution plan:

```
------------------------------------------------------------------------------------
------------------------------------------------
| Id  | Operation                      | Name       | Rows  | Bytes | Cost (%CPU)|
Time      | TQ    |IN-OUT| PQ Distrib |
------------------------------------------------------------------------------------
------------------------------------------------
|   0 | SELECT STATEMENT               |            |     1 |    10 |   287  (91)|
00:00:01 |       |      |            |
|   1 |  SORT AGGREGATE                |            |     1 |    10 |            |
|         |       |      |            |
|   2 |   PX COORDINATOR               |            |       |       |            |
|         |       |      |            |
|   3 |    PX SEND QC (RANDOM)         | :TQ10002   |     1 |    10 |            |
| Q1,02 | P->S | QC (RAND)  |
|   4 |     SORT AGGREGATE             |            |     1 |    10 |            |
| Q1,02 | PCWP |            |
|*  5 |      HASH JOIN                 |            |  375M |  3576M|   287  (91)|
00:00:01 | Q1,02 | PCWP |            |
|   6 |       PX RECEIVE               |            | 15698 | 78490 |     9   (0)|
00:00:01 | Q1,02 | PCWP |            |
|   7 |        PX SEND HYBRID HASH     | :TQ10000   | 15698 | 78490 |     9   (0)|
00:00:01 | Q1,00 | P->P | HYBRID HASH|
|   8 |         STATISTICS COLLECTOR   |            |       |       |            |
| Q1,00 | PCWC |            |
|   9 |          PX BLOCK ITERATOR     |            | 15698 | 78490 |     9   (0)|
00:00:01 | Q1,00 | PCWC |            |
|* 10 |           TABLE ACCESS FULL    | TESTING_P  | 15698 | 78490 |     9   (0)|
00:00:01 | Q1,00 | PCWP |            |
|  11 |       PX RECEIVE               |            | 23893 |  116K |    19   (0)|
00:00:01 | Q1,02 | PCWP |            |
|  12 |        PX SEND HYBRID HASH (SKEW)| :TQ10001 | 23893 |  116K |    19   (0)|
00:00:01 | Q1,01 | P->P | HYBRID HASH|
|  13 |         PX BLOCK ITERATOR      |            | 23893 |  116K |    19   (0)|
00:00:01 | Q1,01 | PCWC |            |
|* 14 |          TABLE ACCESS FULL     | TESTING_C  | 23893 |  116K |    19   (0)|
00:00:01 | Q1,01 | PCWP |            |
------------------------------------------------------------------------------------
------------------------------------------------
```

The execution plan in this case is the same whether we generate it with **autotrace** or the **dbms_xplan.display_cursor** function. Notice the statistics collectors that were put in place. These collectors will analyze the data at run time and determine the distribution method to be used. Unlike the adaptive plans we saw earlier in this section, there is no real indication in the execution plan, beyond the presence of the statistics collector, that this is an adaptive plan.

Adaptive Statistics

Statistics are at the heart of getting good execution plans. Analyzing tables and indexes and creating histograms and extended statistics are all great, but sometimes it's just not enough. Sometimes the query becomes so complex that the Optimizer has a hard time generating the most efficient execution plan. Oracle Database 12*c* has added new features and augmented existing features that are designed to help the Optimizer generate better plans. These features are collectively called Adaptive Statistics in Oracle Database 12*c*.

In this section we will look at the following new or improved features in Oracle Database 12*c*:

■ Automatic reoptimization (statistics feedback)

■ SQL plan directives

■ Dynamic statistics enhancements

Automatic Reoptimization Adaptive plans have their limitations. For example, an inefficient join order might cause a suboptimal plan to be generated. Each time a SQL statement executes, the Optimizer will review statistics that are collected during the execution of the statement. It will compare those statistics to the statistics that it used when it generated the plan. If the statistics vary significantly, the Optimizer will generate a replacement plan for the next execution. This reoptimization can occur many times over the life of a given query in the cursor cache. Thus, the optimization is an iterative process.

There are two kinds of reoptimization that can occur:

■ Statistics feedback

■ Performance feedback

Statistics feedback was previously known as cardinality feedback. Basically, it improves plans that have issues with cardinality estimates. This isn't really a new feature, then, but a renamed one with some improvements thrown in! In essence, in certain cases the Optimizer will monitor the rows returned by a given SQL statement and compare them to the estimates that it made when it generated the execution plan. If the estimates are off, then the Optimizer will store the actual data for use later. In Oracle Database 11*g* these statistics were stored with the cursor, so they could be aged out. In Oracle Database 12*c* the Optimizer will create a SQL plan directive (a new feature, which we will discuss next) so that the statistics collected will be persisted for the benefit of other SQL statements.

Statistics feedback now includes join statistics as a part of the statistics collected. Statistics feedback can also work with adaptive cursor sharing to improve the performance of statements with bind variables. Oracle has added to the V$SQL and V$SQLAREA views a new column called IS_REOPTIMIZABLE that indicates if the SQL statement can be reoptimized.

Performance feedback assists in optimizing parallel queries. When you set the database parameter PARALLEL_DEGREE_POLICY to a value of ADAPTIVE, the Optimizer will determine if the query should be run in parallel, and if it chooses to run it in parallel, it will choose the degree of parallelism (DOP) to use for that query. The database will then monitor the performance of the query as it executes. After the query has completed its first execution, the Optimizer will compare the DOP chosen initially by the Optimizer and the DOP computed based on various performance statistics collected during statement execution. If the values differ, the database will mark the statement for later reparsing and the execution statistics that were collected will be stored as feedback. The feedback is used later, when the statement is parsed and a new DOP is calculated.

NOTE
Sometimes, you might see statistics feedback influence the DOP of a SQL statement, even though PARALLEL_DEGREE_POLICY is not set to ADAPTIVE.

SQL Plan Directives   SQL plan directives provide at the query expression level additional information that the Optimizer can use to better optimize other SQL statements. Thus, multiple queries with a similar **where** clause can take advantage of the SQL plan directive generated by a single query.

As we discussed earlier in this chapter, when a SQL statement is executed, the Optimizer checks the computed cardinality estimates against the real cardinality returned by the query. This information is stored in a SQL plan directive (newly created or already existing). Initially the SQL plan directive is stored in the cursor cache, but eventually it is stored persistently in the SYSAUX tablespace (the redo logs ensure the persistence of the directives in the database should it be restarted). You can use the **dbms_spd.flush_sql_plan_directive** procedure to flush the SQL plan directives that are in memory to persistent storage. Unless the directives are flushed, the directives may not show up in the data dictionary views. Thus, you should flush the SQL plan directives before you do any administrative activities that involve querying data dictionary views that have SQL plan directives in them.

During subsequent SQL compilation, the Optimizer will examine the query and the SQL plan directives and determine if there are any missing extended statistics or histograms. These missing statistics or histograms will be recorded and later collected. If the directive that has been created requires additional statistics, the Optimizer will use dynamic sampling to collect those statistics. This includes the creation of extended statistics on column groups. I will show you how to look at SQL plan directives in the data dictionary in the upcoming section "Adaptive Plan–Related Views and Columns."

SQL plan directives are also fed to the Optimizer as information that can be used to help determine if column groups need to be analyzed. If a SQL plan directive indicates that a column group needs to be created and analyzed, the Optimizer can now do this automatically.

The Oracle database will continue to use the SQL plan directives until conditions occur (such as re-collection of statistics) that make it no longer necessary to use them. SQL plan directives are automatically managed by the Oracle database. If a specific SQL plan directive is not used within 53 weeks, then it will be purged. You can manually drop a SQL plan directive with the **dbms_spd.drop_sql_plan_directive** procedure. You can change the retention period of the SQL plan directives by using the **dbms_spd.set_prefs** function, as shown in the following example where we change the retention period to 26 weeks:

```
exec dbms_spd.set_prefs('SPD_RETENTION_WEEKS','26');
```

Several new views are available in Oracle Database 12*c* to help you manage SQL plan directives:

- **DBA_SQL_PLAN_DIRECTIVES**   This view provides information on the SQL plan directives stored in the database. This view includes information on why the SQL plan directive was created, the date it was created, and when it was most recently used.

- **DBA_SQL_PLAN_DIR_OBJECTS**   This is a child view of DBA_SQL_PLAN_ DIRECTIVES that displays the objects that are contained in the SQL plan directive.

As previously mentioned, the new **dbms_spd** package is used to manage SQL plan directives. This package can also be used to import and export SQL plan directives, if so required.

Adaptive Plan–Related Views and Columns   As DBAs, we like facts. We like to know how database features actually work, not just that they work. So, in this section we'll look at some of the views and columns that show how adaptive plans work.

First, we need a query to work with. The query that we used earlier in this chapter in the "Join Method" section seemed to serve us well, so let's reuse it with a few slight modifications. We'll remove **select count(*)** from the top, so that this version will run longer and produce more output, and we'll use the **gather_plan_statistics** hint so that we can get some additional statistics:

```
select /*+ gather_plan_statistics */
b.id_t, b.id_p, b.another_value
from testing_P a, testing_c b
where a.id=b.id_p
and a.id between 10001 and 10003;
```

After running it, let's see what it looks like in the V$SQL view:

```
select sql_id, child_number, substr(sql_text, 1,40) sql_text, is_reoptimizable
from v$sql
where sql_text like 'select /*+ gather_plan_statistics */ b.id_t, b.id_p, b.another_
value%';

SQL_ID              CHILD_NUMBER SQL_TEXT                                 I
-------------       ------------ ---------------------------------------- -
1pazunuydtvac                  0 select /*+ gather_plan_statistics */ b.i Y
```

Right now, we are interested in the SQL_ID value so that we can look at the execution plan with the **dbms_xplan** PL/SQL function **display_cursor**, as we did earlier. Here is the query:

```
select * from table(dbms_xplan.display_cursor('1pazunuydtvac', null,
'allstats last'));
```

We did a few things different this time:

- We used the SQL_ID of the SQL statement that we queried about in the call, instead of just depending on the last SQL statement that was executed. This enables us to break the query execution with CTRL-C before it completes its run; otherwise, we would have to wait quite a while as the query returns its row set.

- We changed the parameters, using the **allstats** and **last** parameters for the first time. The **allstats** parameter is a shortcut for the parameters **iostats**, which provides IO-related information for each execution step of the plan cursor, and **memstats**, which provides memory-related information for each execution step of the plan. Each of these requires that you include the **gather_plan_statistics** hint in the SQL statement, as we have in this example. The **last** parameter indicates that we want results from the statistics from just the last execution of the cursor, not from all execution of the cursor.

Here is the output from our query:

```
PLAN_TABLE_OUTPUT
-------------------------------------------------------------------------- -- ----------------
-----------------------
SQL_ID  1pazunuydtvac, child number 0
---------------------------------------
select /*+ gather_plan_statistics */ b.id_t, b.id_p, b.another_value
from testing_P a, testing_c b where a.id=b.id_p and a.id between 10001
and 10003
Plan hash value: 2365402516
-------------------------------------------------------------------------------------
-------------------
| Id  | Operation                 | Name          | Starts | E-Rows | A-Rows |
```

```
A-Time   | Buffers |
---------------------------------------------------------------------------------
-------------------
|   0 | SELECT STATEMENT              |              |       1 |        | 86206
|00:00:09.70 |   12364 |
|   1 |   NESTED LOOPS               |              |       1 |        | 86206
|00:00:09.70 |   12364 |
|   2 |    NESTED LOOPS              |              |       1 |      1 | 86206
|00:00:03.00 |    6042 |
|*  3 |     INDEX RANGE SCAN         | IX_TESTINGP  |       1 |      1 |    20
|00:00:00.01 |      21 |
|*  4 |     INDEX RANGE SCAN         | IX_TESTINGC_01 |    20 |      1 | 86206
|00:00:01.11 |    6021 |
|   5 |    TABLE ACCESS BY INDEX ROWID| TESTING_C   | 86206 |      1 | 86206
|00:00:02.84 |    6322 |
---------------------------------------------------------------------------------
-------------------
```

This shows a significant difference in the expected number of rows returned and the actual number of rows returned! As a result, this statement would become a candidate for automatic reoptimization, discussed earlier in this section.

Recall from our earlier query against V$SQL that we queried a column called IS_REOPTIMIZABLE. This column enables us to see if the statement can actually be reoptimized. Thus, the statement will be reparsed on the next execution, and the Optimizer will use the actual run statistics instead of the collected statistics. A better execution plan would be the desired result.

Also, because of the large statistics difference, there should have been at least one SQL plan directive created. We can query the new views DBA_SQL_PLAN_DIRECTIVES and DBA_SQL_PLAN_DIR_OBJECTS to see what, if any, SQL plan directives were created:

```
column dir_id format a20
column owner format a5
column object_name format a12
column col_name format a10
column type format a10 wrap
column state format a10
column reason format a15 wrap
set lines 80
SELECT TO_CHAR(d.DIRECTIVE_ID) dir_id, o.OWNER, o.OBJECT_NAME,
o.SUBOBJECT_NAME col_name, o.OBJECT_TYPE, d.TYPE, d.STATE, d.REASON
FROM DBA_SQL_PLAN_DIRECTIVES d, DBA_SQL_PLAN_DIR_OBJECTS o
WHERE d.DIRECTIVE_ID=o.DIRECTIVE_ID
AND o.OWNER IN ('SCOTT')
AND o.OBJECT_NAME LIKE 'TESTING%'
ORDER BY 1,2,3,4,5;
DIR_ID     OWNER  OBJECT_NAME      COL_NAME   OBJECT TYPE    STATE
REASON
---------- ------ ---------------- ---------- ------ -------- -------------
-------------------------
```

```
1215148865 SCOTT  TESTING_C      ID_P      COLUMN DYNAMIC_ PERMANENT
SINGLE TABLE CARDINALITY
5796912769                                        SAMPLING
MISESTIMATE
1215148865 SCOTT  TESTING_C                TABLE  DYNAMIC_ PERMANENT
SINGLE TABLE CARDINALITY
5796912769                                        SAMPLING
MISESTIMATE
5350351742 SCOTT  TESTING_P      ID        COLUMN DYNAMIC_ PERMANENT
SINGLE TABLE CARDINALITY
389310867                                         SAMPLING
MISESTIMATE
5350351742 SCOTT  TESTING_P                TABLE  DYNAMIC_ PERMANENT
SINGLE TABLE CARDINALITY
389310867                                         SAMPLING
MISESTIMATE
```

It appears that two separate SQL plan directives have been created. Although four rows are returned by the query, there are only two unique DIR_ID values. This indicates that there are two distinct SQL plan directives. So, yeah, this view is a little denormalized.

In the preceding output, we see that the cardinality estimates generated for the TESTING_P and TESTING_C tables are misestimates because they differ from the actual cardinality returned in the sampling at run time. We then see child rows that indicate that the TESTING_C.ID_P and TESTING_P.ID columns are the offending columns in the SQL plan directives.

So, let's see what happens when we rerun the query:

```
select /*+ gather_plan_statistics */
b.id_t, b.id_p, b.another_value
from testing_P a, testing_c b
where a.id=b.id_p
and a.id between 10001 and 10003;
```

Let's see what's in our V$SQL view:

```
select sql_id, child_number, substr(sql_text, 1,40) sql_text, is_
reoptimizable
from v$sql
where sql_text like 'select /*+ gather_plan_statistics */ b.id_t, b.id_p,
b.another_value%';

SQL_ID       CHILD_NUMBER SQL_TEXT                                 I
------------ ------------ ---------------------------------------- -
1pazunuydtvac           0 select /*+ gather_plan_statistics */ b.i Y
1pazunuydtvac           1 select /*+ gather_plan_statistics */ b.i N
```

Now we have two different cursors for this SQL statement: the one that we saw earlier, and a second one that was just created. Let's look at the execution plan for this new cursor:

```
SQL_ID  1pazunuydtvac, child number 1
-------------------------------------
select /*+ gather_plan_statistics */ b.id_t, b.id_p, b.another_value
from testing_P a, testing_c b where a.id=b.id_p and a.id between 10001
and 10003
Plan hash value: 2879834597
---------------------------------------------------------------------
--------------------------------------------------
| Id  | Operation          | Name       | Starts | E-Rows | A-Rows |
A-Time    | Buffers |  OMem |  1Mem | Used-Mem |
---------------------------------------------------------------------
--------------------------------------------------
|   0 | SELECT STATEMENT   |            |      1 |        |  31111 |
|00:00:00.55 |      69 |       |       |          |
|*  1 |   HASH JOIN        |            |      1 |  2247K |  31111 |
|00:00:00.55 |      69 | 1696K| 1696K| 4593K (0)|
|*  2 |    INDEX RANGE SCAN | IX_TESTINGP |      1 |    500 |    500 |
|00:00:00.01 |       3 |       |       |          |
|*  3 |    TABLE ACCESS FULL| TESTING_C  |      1 |   4499 |     63 |
|00:00:00.01 |      66 |       |       |          |
---------------------------------------------------------------------
--------------------------------------------------
```

As you can see, the plan here has changed quite a bit, and the estimated and actual rows read are much more in line (though the estimated rows on the left are still quite a bit off on the hash join). Note that the estimated run time is much shorter on the later plan! Did you find that the query ran any faster when you tried this?

Dynamic Statistics Enhancements   The notion of dynamic statistics (previously called dynamic sampling) has been around for some time. Dynamic statistics come in handy when the statistics on a given table or other object are not collected.

Tom Says
Previously, the default behavior of dynamic sampling would come into play only if a segment was unanalyzed, due to the default setting of **dynamic_sampling**, at level 2. At levels 3–10 in prior releases, dynamic sampling would occur even if all segments had statistics. The difference between Oracle Database 12*c* versus older releases is that dynamic sampling of the type that happened at level 3 and above can happen automatically without adjusting this parameter.

Previously, dynamic statistics would occur only if statistics data was missing on one of the tables involved in the query. In that case, dynamic sampling would gather statistics on the tables before the cursor was optimized for that statement.

Now, in Oracle Database 12*c*, the Optimizer decides if the collection of dynamic statistics will be useful for all SQL statements and if dynamic sampling is the right approach. The primary deciding factor is if the Optimizer has enough information to generate an optimal plan. If the Optimizer chooses to use dynamic statistics, then it will determine what level to use. Dynamic statistics will also now be generated for **join** and **group by** clauses, if the Optimizer determines that they are needed.

Histograms

The Optimizer uses histograms to determine things like data distribution and the like. However, histograms traditionally have had issues with data that has a large number of distinct values that vary wildly. Some new features in Oracle Database 12*c* improve histograms and address some of the problems that they caused in the past. These features include

- Popular, unpopular, and almost popular values

- Top-frequency histograms

- Hybrid histograms

- Increase in the maximum number of histogram buckets

NOTE
The pre-Oracle Database 12c normal height-based histograms are no longer created by default. If you set the sampling percentage to AUTO_SAMPLE_SIZE, Oracle Database 12c will create either a height-balanced histogram (which might be a hybrid histogram) or a top-frequency histogram.

Popular, Unpopular, and Almost Popular Values

Oracle Database 12*c* introduces a new but simple histogram concept of popular, unpopular, and almost popular values. This concept applies to important things like cardinality and distribution. Understanding these terms is integral to understanding some of the new histogram features, so I thought I'd take a moment to introduce you to the terms.

Popular, unpopular, and almost popular values refer to columnar data and its cardinality (or frequency). Popular values are pretty much what they sound like: data points that occur as an endpoint of one or more buckets. The Optimizer determines if a given value is popular and will manage that value depending on the type of histogram. I will discuss what happens to popular values in the following sections on histograms.

Anything that is not popular is either unpopular or almost popular. With frequency histograms, there are only unpopular and popular values. With hybrid histograms, the idea of almost popular values comes into play. I will also discuss these values in more detail in the next few sections on histograms.

Top-Frequency Histograms

Prior to Oracle Database 12*c*, if you were analyzing a given table and indicated that you wanted a histogram to be created, the database would decide for you which kind of histogram to create, based on the distinct number of column values.

- **Fewer than 255 distinct values** In this case the database would create a *frequency histogram*. In a frequency histogram, the database creates a bucket for each distinct value in the database, along with information related to that value, like how many rows contain that value. A frequency histogram is considered the best type of histogram because it can provide accurate information to the Optimizer about the number and distribution of distinct values within that column.

- **Greater than 254 distinct values** In this case the database would create a *height-balanced histogram*. In a height-balanced histogram, the columnar metadata is somewhat (or very) summarized, since there are not enough buckets to provide a place to store information for each distinct value. This type of histogram can be problematic because the Optimizer does not have true statistics related to unique value distribution or cardinality. In effect, the Optimizer has to guess about the cardinality of a given value. Sometimes these guesses are good (if the data is not terribly skewed), but sometimes they are very bad (if the data is terribly skewed).

Now, in Oracle Database 12*c*, a new type of frequency histogram called the top-frequency histogram provides a modified approach to the frequency histogram. In cases where the number of distinct values exceeds the number of buckets, the database may create a top-frequency histogram instead of opting for a height-based histogram.

When creating a top-frequency histogram, the database ignores the distinct column values with lesser cardinality (as previously mentioned, these are called unpopular values) in favor of more popular (higher cardinality) column values. The result is a frequency histogram that records the most common values and their distribution. Oracle Database 12c will create a top-frequency histogram when the following is true:

- There are more distinct values than available buckets (by default, 254 buckets are available, but you can adjust this number, as described in the final section of this chapter).

- The percentage of rows occupied by the available buckets (n) is equal to or greater than the value of $(1 - (1 / n)) \times 100$. Thus, if you have 500 buckets, 99.8 percent of the rows must fit in the available buckets. So, if you have 1,000,000 rows, then 998,000 rows' worth of the column values must have sufficient cardinality to fit within the 500 buckets allocated to the histogram. That actually leaves quite a bit of room for values with very low cardinality (you could theoretically throw out 2,000 low-cardinality values in this case).

- The ESTIMATE_PERCENT parameter is set to AUTO_SAMPLE_SIZE when statistics are created through **dbms_stats**.

Also in Oracle Database 12c, the Optimizer will build histograms based off of a full table scan if ESTIMATE_PERCENT is set to AUTO_SAMPLE_SIZE, whereas in previous versions it sampled a percentage of data. This has the effect of detecting low-frequency values much more reliability than in previous versions. This change will improve selectivity estimates and the resulting execution plans.

We query the view DBA_TAB_COL_STATISTICS (or the USER_ or ALL_ versions of this view) to determine if we have a top-frequency histogram. Here is an example:

```
create table high_frequency_histogram(id number, the_column number);
insert into high_frequency_histogram values (1,1);
insert into high_frequency_histogram values (1,2);
insert into high_frequency_histogram values (1,3);
insert into high_frequency_histogram values (1,4);
insert into high_frequency_histogram values (1,51);
insert into high_frequency_histogram values (1,61);
insert into high_frequency_histogram values (1,71);
insert into high_frequency_histogram values (1,81);
exec dbms_stats.gather_table_stats(null,'HIGH_FREQUENCY_HISTOGRAM', method_opt=>'for
columns the_column size 7');

select table_name, column_name, num_distinct, histogram from user_tab_col_statistics
where table_name='HIGH_FREQUENCY_HISTOGRAM';
TABLE_NAME                      COLUMN_NAME           NUM_DISTINCT HISTOGRAM
------------------------------- --------------------- ------------ ----------------

HIGH_FREQUENCY_HISTOGRAM        THE_COLUMN                       8 TOP-FREQUENCY
```

In this case, we have inserted eight distinct values but have created a histogram with only seven buckets. Because we met all of the requirements for a top-frequency histogram, **dbms_stats** generously created one for us! We can see how the buckets were actually filled by issuing the following query:

```
select owner, table_name, column_name, endpoint_value
from dba_histograms
where owner='SCOTT' and table_name='HIGH_FREQUENCY_HISTOGRAM'
order by 1,2,3,4;
```

OWNER	TABLE_NAME	COLUMN_NAME	ENDPOINT_VALUE
SCOTT	HIGH_FREQUENCY_HISTOGRAM	THE_COLUMN	1
SCOTT	HIGH_FREQUENCY_HISTOGRAM	THE_COLUMN	2
SCOTT	HIGH_FREQUENCY_HISTOGRAM	THE_COLUMN	3
SCOTT	HIGH_FREQUENCY_HISTOGRAM	THE_COLUMN	4
SCOTT	HIGH_FREQUENCY_HISTOGRAM	THE_COLUMN	51
SCOTT	HIGH_FREQUENCY_HISTOGRAM	THE_COLUMN	61
SCOTT	HIGH_FREQUENCY_HISTOGRAM	THE_COLUMN	81

In this case the Optimizer threw out the value 71 as an unpopular value, and filled the remaining seven buckets.

In almost every case, a frequency histogram will be preferable to a height-based or hybrid histogram. However, there will be times when a height-based or hybrid histogram is what you need (or have to live with). Hybrid histograms are new, so let's look at those next.

Hybrid Histograms

As mentioned earlier, the normal height-based histograms that were created by default prior to Oracle Database 12*c* are no longer created by default. If the sampling percentage is set to AUTO_SAMPLE_SIZE, Oracle Database 12*c* will create either a height-balanced histogram (which might be a hybrid histogram) or a top-frequency histogram.

A *hybrid histogram* is an enhanced height-based histogram (as opposed to a frequency histogram) that combines the characteristics of a height-based histogram and a frequency histogram. A hybrid histogram distributes the column values so that no value will appear in more than one bucket. Additionally, the endpoint repeat count is stored in the bucket with the value to indicate the number of times that the endpoint value is repeated. The result is that the database can obtain measures for popular and almost popular values more accurately, which will lead to better execution plan generation. The hybrid histogram is more efficient than normal height-based histograms that do not store this additional endpoint information.

A hybrid histogram will be created by the database when the following is true:

■ The database sample percentage is set to AUTO_SAMPLE_SIZE.

■ The number of buckets is less than the number of distinct values in the table.

■ The database cannot otherwise create a frequency histogram.

Here is an example of the use of a hybrid frequency histogram:

```
drop table hybrid_histogram;
create table hybrid_histogram
(id number, the_column number);
insert into hybrid_histogram values (1,1);
insert into hybrid_histogram values (1,2);
insert into hybrid_histogram values (1,2);
insert into hybrid_histogram values (1,2);
insert into hybrid_histogram values (1,51);
insert into hybrid_histogram values (1,51);
insert into hybrid_histogram values (1,71);
insert into hybrid_histogram values (1,81);
insert into hybrid_histogram values (1,81);
insert into hybrid_histogram values (1,82);
insert into hybrid_histogram values (1,83);
insert into hybrid_histogram values (1,83);
commit;

exec dbms_stats.gather_table_stats(null,'HYBRID_HISTOGRAM', method_opt=>'for columns
the_column size 3');
select table_name, column_name, num_distinct, histogram from user_tab_col_statistics
where table_name='HYBRID_HISTOGRAM';
TABLE_NAME                          COLUMN_NAME              NUM_DISTINCT HISTOGRAM
------------------------------ -------------------- ------------ ---------------
HYBRID_HISTOGRAM                    THE_COLUMN                          7 HYBRID
select owner, table_name, column_name, endpoint_value, endpoint_repeat_count
from dba_histograms
where owner='SCOTT' and table_name='HYBRID_HISTOGRAM'
order by 1,2,3,4;


OWNER      TABLE_NAME         COLUMN_NAME        ENDPOINT_VALUE ENDPOINT_REPEAT_COUNT
--------   ------------------ -----------        -------------- ---------------------
SCOTT      HYBRID_HISTOGRAM   THE_COLUMN                      1                     1
SCOTT      HYBRID_HISTOGRAM   THE_COLUMN                     51                     2
SCOTT      HYBRID_HISTOGRAM   THE_COLUMN                     83                     2
```

Notice that this example is very similar to the previous example of a top-frequency histogram. The main difference here is that we created only three histogram buckets rather than the seven we created in the earlier example. As you can see, the column THE_COLUMN has seven distinct values, but we have only three buckets. Note the endpoint values listed in the buckets, and that the endpoint repeat counts match the number of repeating values for those endpoints.

Increases in the Maximum Number of Histogram Buckets

Oracle Database 12c has increased the maximum number of buckets that can be allocated to a given histogram. The default value remains 254, but now you can create histograms with up to 2,048 buckets. You can use the **dbms_stats.set_*_prefs** procedure to modify the default setting to something other than 254 buckets.

End of Line

This has been a long chapter. As you can see, Oracle Database 12*c* has introduced a number of new features to help improve not only the performance of SQL programs over the long run, but also to help them perform better in real time. Some of these features are right there for you out of the box, helping day one. Some of them might take some study and understanding before you can really use them to your best benefit. All of them have the ability to improve the performance of your database significantly.

The heart of the database is performance. All the memory, CPU, and storage in the world isn't going to make up for poor performance. (Well, it can, but do you really want to throw money at a problem that can be easily solved by some basic SQL tuning?)

As with much in this book, we have just touched on the basics here. There is a lot more in the details to understand. We have given you a launching pad to start your journey, now it's time for you to decide what features can help you, and to start learning more about them and actually using them.

Also, don't think this chapter is just for DBAs. Of all the chapters in this book, this might be the most beneficial to the developer, to the report writer, and even to the architect. So if you're a DBA, after you have read what is in this chapter and learned all you can about it, pass your knowledge on! Make sure everyone is the expert. It will make your job easier if others are doing things the right way in the first place.

Now, there is just one more chapter left for you to read. It's kind of the database new features catch-all chapter and it's full of new and interesting stuff to learn about. So, without further delay, let's move on to Chapter 12!

CHAPTER
12

Other Oracle Database
12c New Features

While the term "other" in this chapter's title might make this chapter sound like the dumping ground for all of the new features in Oracle Database 12c that are perhaps less important, nothing could be further from the truth. This chapter is full of exciting new stuff that you will want to know about! This chapter covers the following:

■ Oracle Data Pump Export and Import new features

■ Oracle SQL*Loader enhancements

■ Oracle External Table enhancements

■ Oracle Log Miner enhancements

■ ADR DDL and debug logs

■ Oracle SecureFiles enhancements

■ Oracle Database R, Hadoop, and MapReduce

■ CloneDB

■ SQL Translation Framework

Data Pump Export and Import New Features

Oracle Database 12c has added new features to Oracle Data Pump Export and Import. These features include

■ The **views_as_tables** parameter

■ Moving databases across platforms, regardless of byte format, with transportable tablespaces

■ **Transform** clause new features

■ Data Pump Export and Import fully supports Oracle's Multitenant Database technologies

■ Unified Auditing for Data Pump jobs

■ Miscellaneous enhancements to Data Pump

The views_as_tables Parameter

If you have ever wanted to convert a view into a table during an export or import process, then you will be interested in the new **views_as_tables** parameter. This parameter enables you to convert a view into a table during either an export to a dump file or an import from a dump file. The **views_as_tables** parameter is available with both the Oracle Data Pump Export and Data Pump Import utilities.

Oracle Data Pump Export and the views_as_tables Parameter

Have you ever wanted to export a view in the form of a table, with the data stored in the export dump file? Have you ever wanted to import a view from a Data Pump dump file, and have that view be created as a table instead? Now, Oracle Database 12c supports both these operations through the use of the **views_as_tables** parameter available in both Oracle Data Pump Import and Export utilities.

When you use the **views_as_tables** parameter with Oracle Data Pump Export, the views listed in the parameter will be converted into tables during the export process. Thus, the DDL for the object will not be a **create view** command but will instead be a **create table** command. Further, the data that is contained in that view will be physically exported to the dump file. Note that in this case, if the source objects are encrypted, the data exported will not be encrypted, so you will want to encrypt the Data Pump export itself.

Tom Says

It is interesting to note that Oracle Database has been able to "export" a view as a table for a while now, one view at a time, using just SQL. For example,

```
SQL> create table all_objects_unload
  2  organization external
  3  ( type oracle_datapump
  4    default directory TMP
  5    location( 'allobjects.dat' )
  6  )
  7  as
  8  select a.*, dbms_random.random rnd from stage a;
Table created.
```

allows me to take an arbitrary SQL statement and use Data Pump Export to export it as raw data. I can then use a **create table as select** command from this exported data either on this database or any other database to "import" the information.

In addition to the table DDL and the data itself, dependent objects such as grants will also be exported. The new table will be created in the same schema as the view resided in. There are restrictions to this in that the source view cannot have LOB columns, and the view must be relational with only scalar columns.

Here is an example of an export using this feature:

```
expdp scott/robert directory=mydir dumpfile=test.dmp views_as_
tables=emp_view:emp,dept_view:dept
Export: Release 12.1.0.1.0 - Production on Wed Aug 28 09:12:51 2013
Copyright (c) 1982, 2013, Oracle and/or its affiliates.  All rights
reserved.
Connected to: Oracle Database 12c Enterprise Edition Release 12.1.0.1.0
- 64bit Production
With the Partitioning, OLAP, Advanced Analytics and Real Application
Testing options
Starting "SCOTT"."SYS_EXPORT_TABLE_01":  scott/******** directory=mydir
dumpfile=test.dmp
views_as_tables=emp_view:emp,dept_view:dept
Estimate in progress using BLOCKS method...
Processing object type TABLE_EXPORT/VIEWS_AS_TABLES/TABLE_DATA
Total estimation using BLOCKS method: 128 KB
Processing object type TABLE_EXPORT/VIEWS_AS_TABLES/TABLE
. . exported "SCOTT"."DEPT_VIEW"                         6.007 KB
4 rows
. . exported "SCOTT"."EMP_VIEW"                          8.765 KB
14 rows
Master table "SCOTT"."SYS_EXPORT_TABLE_01" successfully loaded/unloaded
************************************************************************
********
Dump file set for SCOTT.SYS_EXPORT_TABLE_01 is:
  /home/oracle/dumpfile/test.dmp
Job "SCOTT"."SYS_EXPORT_TABLE_01" successfully completed at Wed Aug 28
09:13:10 2013 elapsed 0 00:00:17
```

Note that when you use the **views_as_tables** parameter, only a table mode export occurs. Thus, only the views you list will actually be exported. You can also use the **views_as_tables** parameter with the **tables** parameter to export other tables. Also, note that the data stored in the import file is the actual data, not the definition of a view that can later be imported. This is important to understand, since this has security implications. If the export is not encrypted, then the data in the dump file will not be encrypted.

Now, when this file is imported, as shown next, you will find that the old views called DEPT_VIEW and EMP_VIEW are now actually tables. A quick reference of the USER_TABLES view will show that DEPT_VIEW and EMP_VIEW now exist as tables:

```
impdp testing/robert directory=mydir dumpfile=test.dmp remap_schema=scott:testing
Import: Release 12.1.0.1.0 - Production on Wed Aug 28 09:14:56 2013
Copyright (c) 1982, 2013, Oracle and/or its affiliates.  All rights reserved.
Connected to: Oracle Database 12c Enterprise Edition Release 12.1.0.1.0 - 64bit
Production
With the Partitioning, OLAP, Advanced Analytics and Real Application Testing options
Master table "TESTING"."SYS_IMPORT_FULL_01" successfully loaded/unloaded
Starting "TESTING"."SYS_IMPORT_FULL_01":  testing/******** directory=mydir
dumpfile=test.dmp remap_schema=scott:testing
Processing object type TABLE_EXPORT/VIEWS_AS_TABLES/TABLE
Processing object type TABLE_EXPORT/VIEWS_AS_TABLES/TABLE_DATA
. . imported "TESTING"."DEPT_VIEW"                   6.007 KB      4 rows
. . imported "TESTING"."EMP_VIEW"                    8.765 KB     14 rows
Job "TESTING"."SYS_IMPORT_FULL_01" successfully completed at Wed Aug 28 09:15:03 2013
elapsed 0 00:00:06
```

There are a couple of things to note in this example. First, I am logged in as TESTING. Obviously, this schema would need the appropriate privileges to create the tables, such as the appropriate quota on the tablespace the tables will be created in (which would be the default tablespace for that user unless you use the **remap_tablespace** clause). Secondly, note that I'm using the **remap_schema** clause to move the objects from the SCOTT schema into the TESTING schema.

Oracle Data Pump Import and the views_as_tables Parameter

When you use the **views_as_tables** parameter as a part of a Data Pump Import operation, you are indicating that the listed views should be created as tables on the target of the import. This functionality does not require that the views first be exported using the **views_as_tables** parameter. Also, there are two different flavors of this functionality: one for a non-networked import, and the other for a network import.

Non-Networked Import   In our first example, I will look at the non-networked import. First let's create two views in the SCOTT schema:

```
select view_name from user_views;
VIEW_NAME
--------------------------------------------------------------------------
DEPT_VIEW
EMP_VIEW
```

As you might expect, these views are built off of the DEPT and EMP tables in the SCOTT schema. So, let's look at an example of this operation. In our example, I will first do an export of the SCOTT schema. Note that I'm not using the **views_as_tables** parameter in this export, as demonstrated in the previous section. Thus, the view definitions will be exported as you would expect:

```
expdp scott/robert directory=mydir dumpfile=test1.dmp reuse_
dumpfiles=TRUE
```

Now, let's import the views, but do so such that they are created as tables, not as views. I will import them into the TESTING schema (which I assume does not have the objects I am importing in it already). Here is the **impdp** command that I used:

```
impdp testing/robert views_as_tables=scott.dept_view, scott.emp_view
directory=mydir dumpfile=test.dmp remap_schema=scott:testing remap_
table=dept_view:dept, emp_view:emp
```

The **views_as_tables** parameter defines which views I want to convert into tables during the import. I also defined the directory and the dump file that will be used. Further in this example, I used the **remap_schema** parameter to move the tables to the TESTING schema. If I hadn't done this, the import would try to create the objects in the SCOTT schema instead of in the TESTING schema, even though I am logged into the TESTING schema. Finally, I used the **remap_table** parameter to rename the view names to names that are more appropriate for tables. In this example, I renamed the EMP_VIEW view to EMP and the DEPT_VIEW view to DEPT.

After the import is completed, the objects are created in the TESTING schema as tables:

```
select object_name, object_type from user_objects;

OBJECT_NAME        OBJECT_TYPE
------------------ ----------------------
EMP                TABLE
DEPT               TABLE
```

One thing to note when using the **views_as_tables** parameter is that it makes the import a table mode import. Thus, the remaining objects in the dump file are not imported. You can also use the **views_as_tables** parameter with the **tables** parameter to import additional table objects.

Network Import   If you are performing a network import, then the **views_as_tables** parameter takes a slightly different format. In this case, you would include the view name (and optionally the schema name) and then the name of the table that is the source of the metadata for the creation of the new table. For the next example, assume that you have a view in SCOTT called EMP_VIEW and that you want to create it as a table in the TESTING schema. In this case you could use a network import to do so.

First, I have created a database link between the database with the SCOTT schema and the database with the TESTING schema. Now, I am ready to execute the import, as shown here (note, I removed any previous copy of TESTING.EMP and TESTING.DEPT before I ran this import):

```
impdp testing/robert network_link=db_scott views_as_tables=scott
.dept_view:dept, scott.emp_view:emp directory=mydir remap_
schema=scott:testing remap_table=dept_view:dept, emp_view:emp
```

In this case I am logging into the TESTING schema to perform the import. I have already created the database link DB_SCOTT that is mentioned in the **network_link** parameter.

Looking further at the **impdp** command, I find the **views_as_tables** parameter. Here I am importing SCOTT.DEPT_VIEW and SCOTT.EMP_VIEW into the TESTING schema (as demonstrated in the setting of the **remap_schema** parameter) as tables. Note the mention of the DEPT and EMP tables in the **views_as_tables** clause. These are known as *template tables*. These template tables will be used to supply the metadata (such things as tablespace and various other **create table** parameters) that you want **impdp** to use when it creates the tables during the imports. The template tables are defined optionally, and **impdp** will use default template tables if you do not explicitly define a template table for an object.

If you do include template tables in the import job, each template table name must be unique for the view being imported, and the template table must be in the schema that is being imported from. So, for example, an error would have been generated if we had used the following **views_as_tables** clause:

```
views_as_tables=scott.dept_view:emp, scott.emp_view:emp
```

The temporary template tables (created if you do not define a template table) are prefixed with KU$VAT, followed by an underscore and a sequence number that makes the table unique. These are removed at the end of the import.

Finally, note that the **views_as_tables** import is a table-level import, as it was in the previous example. As a result, the remaining objects in the SCOTT schema will not be imported (unless you also use the **tables** parameter).

Moving Databases Across Platforms, Regardless of Byte Format, with Transportable Tablespaces

If you have ever had to move an Oracle database between platforms with different endian byte formats, you know what a chore this can be. For example, moving from Windows to Solaris (little endian byte format to big endian byte format) in previous incarnations of Oracle Database is difficult and time consuming. Typically, this involves using the network capabilities of Oracle Data Pump to move the data between the two different machines, taking advantage of the parallel features of the product to speed up the migration as much as possible. Still, moving several terabytes of data via such an operation can take a long time and is dependent on factors such as network speed, memory, CPU availability, and the speed of the database itself (of course, Oracle Database is blindingly fast!).

Moving between the same endian byte format is less of a chore. You can simply use transportable tablespaces and move the tablespaces from one platform to the other platform. You then just use Oracle Data Pump to move the tablespace metadata to the target machine and plug in the tablespaces. Voilà, a new database!

Oracle calls this new feature Data Pump Full Transportable Export and Import. This section discusses the following topics related to this new feature:

- Compatible platforms

- Restrictions and limitations

- Executing an Oracle Database move using Data Pump Full Transportable Export and Import

- Executing an Oracle Database move using Data Pump Full Transportable Export and Import over the network

NOTE
While this feature is supported with Oracle Database 10.1.0.3 and later, it is not a supported method to upgrade a given database to Oracle Database 12c at the time of writing. I suspect that this is true because not all platforms support this feature yet, but that's only a guess.

Compatible Platforms

To use Full Transportable Export and Import, the platform must support this new migration method. The V$TRANSPORTABLE_PLATFORM view provides a listing of all the platforms that are available for Full Transportable Export and Import. Here is an example of such a query (I have cut out some of the output to save space):

```
column platform_name format a50
column endian_format a20
select platform_id, platform_name, endian_format
from v$transportable_platform
order by platform_id;

PLATFORM_ID PLATFORM_NAME                                      ENDIAN_FORMAT
----------- -------------------------------------------------- --------------
          1 Solaris[tm] OE (32-bit)                            Big
          2 Solaris[tm] OE (64-bit)                            Big
          3 HP-UX (64-bit)                                     Big
          4 HP-UX IA (64-bit)                                  Big
          5 HP Tru64 UNIX                                      Little
          6 AIX-Based Systems (64-bit)                         Big
          7 Microsoft Windows IA (32-bit)                      Little
          8 Microsoft Windows IA (64-bit)                      Little
          9 IBM zSeries Based Linux                            Big
         10 Linux IA (32-bit)                                  Little
         11 Linux IA (64-bit)                                  Little
         12 Microsoft Windows x86 64-bit                       Little
         13 Linux x86 64-bit                                   Little
```

So, if the platform is on this list (again, this is partial output), then you can move it using Full Transportable Export and Import! Note in the preceding output that there are two endian formats, big and little. If you are transporting a database between platforms that are of a different endian byte format, you will need to perform a conversion on the datafiles of that database, as discussed later in this chapter.

Also of interest is that the ability to move datafiles across platforms with different endian byte formats also applies to transportable tablespaces. So now, if your data warehouse is on a different platform with a different byte format, you can move your tablespaces back and forth between the two platforms at will!

Restrictions and Limitations

As you may have anticipated, some other restrictions and limitations apply to Full Transportable Export and Import transportation of databases:

- General limitations and restrictions on transporting data

- Limitations and restrictions specific to Full Transportable Export and Import

General Limitations and Restrictions on Transporting Data   The following general limitations and restrictions apply to all methods that you might use to transport tablespaces across Oracle databases in Oracle Database 12c:

NOTE
The assumption in this section is that you are moving the entirety of user-defined tablespaces from the source database to the target database. As such, this section assumes certain constraints normally associated with transportable tablespaces, such as the requirement that the transport set be self-contained.

- The character sets on the source and target database must be compatible. I chose to use the word "compatible" because there are a lot of detailed restrictions if they are, in fact, different. If you are moving between two databases with different character sets, then please refer to the appropriate Oracle documentation for more information on compatibility between those character sets.

- The NLS character sets on the source and target databases must also be compatible. As with the previous point, check the Oracle documentation if you are using different NLS character sets, to ensure that they are compatible.

■ If the source database is a version earlier than Oracle Database version 10.1.0.3, then the tablespaces cannot contain columns with data types that are NCHAR, NVARCHAR2, or NCLOB.

■ Specifically for Data Pump Full Transportable Export and Import (not using the network version) :

   ■ The default tablespace of the user running the export must not be one of the tablespaces being transported.

   ■ The default tablespace of the user running the export must be writable.

■ If you are transporting into a non-CDB database, the tablespace(s) being transported from the source to the target database cannot be named the same as a tablespace that already exists on the target database.

■ If you are transporting into a CDB, the names of the tablespaces being transported into the given container (the PDB) must be unique. Thus, different container databases can have tablespaces with the same names.

■ If you are using a CDB, you cannot use the default Data Pump directory called DATA_PUMP_DIR if you are importing into a PDB (you can use DATA_PUMP_DIR if you're importing into the CDB itself).

■ If you are transporting objects with XMLTypes, you should reference the various restrictions for these column types in the Oracle documentation. This query can help you determine if you are, in fact, dealing with any XMLTypes in your database movement:

```
select distinct p.tablespace_name from dba_tablespaces p,
dba_xml_tables x, dba_users u, all_all_tables t where
t.table_name=x.table_name and t.tablespace_name=p.tablespace_name
and x.owner=u.username;
```

■ If you are transporting columns with a data type of TIMESTAMP WITH LOCAL TIME ZONE, first review the data movement considerations in the Oracle documentation. In short, tables with this data type will not be transported and a nonfatal error will be generated (thus the import continues). You will need to transport that data using a different method. Other objects in the tablespace will be moved across.

Specific Limitations and Restrictions on Full Transportable Export and Import
There are also specific limitations and restrictions that accompany the use of Full Transportable Export and Import:

■ You cannot move an encrypted tablespace across platforms that have different endian byte formats.

- Tables with LONG and LONG RAW columns that are in administrative tablespaces (for example, SYSTEM) are not supported when transported over the network.

- Objects that reside in both administrative and nonadministrative tablespaces at the same time (for example, table partitions) cannot be transported.

- Auditing cannot be enabled for tables stored in administrative tablespaces (for example, SYSTEM) when the audit trail is stored in a nonadministrative tablespace.

NOTE
*Don't forget that you can use the **remap_tablespace** parameter on Oracle Database Data Pump to map the objects being imported into a different tablespace.*

Executing an Oracle Database Move Using Data Pump Full Transportable Export and Import

Oracle Database 12c makes moving your database across platforms quite easy. In fact, using the Data Pump Full Transportable Export and Import method to move databases to different platforms might be as easy as using RMAN to do so. This section first provides the basic steps involved in moving a database using Data Pump Full Transportable Export and Import. Then it provides you with an example.

Basic Steps to Transport a Database Using Data Pump Full Transportable Export and Import   The basic steps for moving a database with Data Pump's new Full Transportable Export and Import feature are as follows:

1. Create the target database (the one to which you will be moving your datafiles) with the Oracle DBCA. Configure memory and other settings as appropriate.

2. Make all user-defined tablespaces on the source database read-only.

3. Export the database. Use the following parameters:

   - **Transportable = always**

   - **full =Y**

   - If the source database is Oracle Database Release 2 version 11.2.0.3 or higher, the **version** parameter must be set to **12**.

   - If you have encrypted tablespaces or columns that are encrypted, you must use the **encryption_pwd_prompt=YES** parameter or the **encryption_password** parameter.

NOTE
When you create the Data Pump Export in this manner, the resulting dump file will contain the metadata for all user-defined tablespaces, but not the actual data itself. The export dump file will also contain the data for user-defined objects within any administrative tablespaces such as SYSTEM or SYSAUX.

4. Copy the Export dump file to the target database.

5. Copy the database datafiles for all of the user-defined databases to a location that is accessible to the target database.

   For movement across platforms that are of the same endian byte format, you can simply move the datafiles across. There is no conversion needed.

   For movement across platforms that are of different endian byte formats, you will need to convert the datafiles into the byte format on the target platform. This is done by using one of two methods:

   ■ You can use the procedures **get_file** and **put_file** in the **dbms_file_transfer** PL/SQL-supplied package. These procedures will automatically convert the database datafiles for you.

   ■ You can use the RMAN **convert** command to convert the database datafiles.

   The benefit of either method is that you can convert the datafiles on either the source or target database platform.

6. Once the file moves are complete, you can make the datafiles on the source database read-write.

7. Import the dump file into the target database to complete the database move. Once the import is complete, the tablespaces will be read-write and the objects in them will be ready for use.

Oracle Data Pump Full Transportable Export and Import: Example   In our example we will use Oracle Data Pump Full Transportable Export and Import to move an Oracle Database 11g (11.2.0.3) database called ora11g to an Oracle Database 12c database called ora12c. First, I will create the 12c database, ora12c, with the DBCA. As an astute DBA, you already know how to do that, so I won't demonstrate that for you.

First, we should determine which directory we want to use when we generate the export file. In our example we will use the default directory **data_pump_dir**. Let's check to make sure that directory has been created in our database:

```
select * from dba_directories where directory_name='DATA_PUMP_DIR';

OWNER       DIRECTORY_  DIRECTORY_PATH
----------  ----------  --------------------------------------------------------
SYS         DATA_PUMP_  /u01/app/oracle/admin/ora11g/dpdump/
            DIR
```

After I have created the target database, I need to put the tablespaces of the source database in READ ONLY mode. First I will generate a list of those tablespaces:

```
select tablespace_name from dba_tablespaces;

TABLESPACE_NAME
------------------------------
SYSTEM
SYSAUX
UNDOTBS1
TEMP
USERS
```

In this case, the only tablespace we need to put in READ ONLY mode is USERS because it's the only tablespace that is not system managed. Here is the **alter tablespace** command to put the USERS tablespace in READ ONLY mode:

```
alter tablespace users read only;
```

Now that the tablespace is in READ ONLY mode, it's time to export the target database, ora11g. Here is our **export** command:

```
expdp "'sys/robert as sysdba'" full=y dumpfile=movedb.dmp
directory=data_pump_dir transportable=always logfile=export.log
version=12
```

This **expdp** command should seem pretty normal to you. I am logging in as the SYS user, using SYSDBA. This is required to get all the metadata that we need for the entire database. Also, I am using the **full=y** and **transportable=always** parameters, as these are required to move the database. Since I am exporting from an 11g database (version 11.2.0.3), we have to include the **version=12** parameter. If you were running this on Oracle Database 12c, you would not need to use the **version** parameter.

The output from the **expdp** command is a bit too lengthy to reproduce here. The end result is that we have created a dump file called movedb.dmp, as shown here:

```
[oracle@server12c ~]$ ls -al /u01/app/oracle/admin/ora11g/dpdump/
movedb.dmp
-rw-r----- 1 oracle oinstall 145883136 Jun 26 20:20 /u01/app/oracle/
admin/ora11g/dpdump/movedb.dmp
```

Now, we have our dump file. I will then copy it over to the target system using SFTP, SCP, or some similar file transfer protocol. We could also use the **dbms_file_transfer** package, which I will discuss shortly.

Having moved the export dump file, we need to find out which physical datafiles need to be copied. We know that the only datafiles that we need to "move" across are those associated with user-created tablespaces. In our case, the USERS tablespace is the only user-created tablespace in the source database, so it's the only one I will need to move. We can find out which physical datafile(s) are part of this tablespace with a quick query against the DBA_DATA_FILES view, as shown here:

```
select tablespace_name, file_name
from dba_data_files
where tablespace_name='USERS';
TABLESPACE_NAME FILE_NAME
--------------- --------------------------------------------------
USERS           /u01/app/oracle/oradata/ora11g/users01.dbf
```

From this query, we find that there is just one datafile that needs to be copied across to the target system: users01.dbf.

To facilitate this transfer I will use the **dbms_file_transfer.get_file** PL/SQL procedure. I will execute the procedure on the target machine, pulling the database datafile from the source database server over to the target database server. We could just have easily used **dbms_file_transfer.put_file** on the source machine to push the file to the target machine. Also, you can run these file transfers in multiple sessions, which will facilitate parallel datafile movement.

Before I show you an example, I should also note that in our example, I am moving from one Linux system to another. As a result, endian byte conversion is not a concern. However, the method I will use to move the datafile would serve to convert the datafile during the datafile move, should that be required.

There are a couple of considerations to be aware of when using **dbms_file_transfer**:

- The datafile to be copied must be less than 2 terabytes.

- The size of the file must be a multiple of 512 bytes.

If you cannot meet these requirements, then you could just scp or sftp to move the files across. If you needed to convert the file endian format, you could use the RMAN **convert** command on either the source or target system to convert the datafiles.

Here is the command that I used to move the single datafile that belongs to the USERS tablespace:

```
begin
    dbms_file_transfer.get_file('MY_DATAFILES','users01.dbf',
                                'ora11g', 'MY_DATAFILES','users01.dbf');
end;
/
```

Recall that I am executing this operation on the target database server. Thus I am pulling the datafile across. The first parameter of the **get_files** procedure shown here is the name of an Oracle database directory (MY_DATAFILES) that is defined by using the **create directory** DDL command. This directory is on the source system that I am pulling from. This directory is a database directory that is pointed to the location of the files to be moved. In our case we called the directory MY_DATAFILES and we pointed it to the operating system directory /u01/app/oracle/oradata/ora11g, which is where the datafile we want to copy resides.

Next we have the name of the datafile we want to copy, users01.dbf. Following that is the database TNS entry for that database. In this case we have a TNS entry called ora11g that points to the target database. We then have another directory, MY_DATAFILES, which is an Oracle database directory created on the target database with the Oracle **create directory** command. Finally, we have included the name of the datafile that should be created on the target system. Once this procedure is complete, I am ready to begin importing the Data Pump export we took earlier!

NOTE
*The ability to use **dbms_file_transfer** or RMAN to convert the datafiles and move them across endian platforms is the really "big" part of this new feature. Removing the need for a logical Data Pump load of all the data is a great improvement.*

Once the transfer is complete, we can make the tablespace on the source system read-write again. Here is the command to perform that action:

```
alter tablespace users read write;
```

From the target database server, we make sure that the Oracle environment is set correctly, and we import the metadata, as shown here:

```
impdp "'sys/robert as sysdba'" full=y dumpfile=movedb.dmp
directory=data_pump_dir transport_datafiles='/u01/app/oracle/
oradata/ORCL/datafile/users01.dbf' logfile=import.log remap_
tablespace=users:new_users
```

Note in this case that we have used the **remap_tablespace** parameter to rename the tablespace. This is required because there was already a USERS tablespace in the database that we were moving to.

At this point the import will begin, and the tablespace will be imported into the new database, along with all the relevant user-owned data in the system-owned tablespaces. The output from the import process is, again, quite lengthy, so it's not included here.

Once the import is complete, you will find that the tablespaces have been imported and made read-write, as shown here:

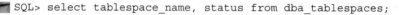

```
SQL> select tablespace_name, status from dba_tablespaces;

TABLESPACE_NAME                 STATUS
------------------------------- ---------
SYSTEM                          ONLINE
SYSAUX                          ONLINE
UNDOTBS1                        ONLINE
TEMP                            ONLINE
USERS                           ONLINE
EXAMPLE                         ONLINE
NEW_USERS                       ONLINE
```

Executing an Oracle Database Move Using Data Pump Full Transportable Export and Import: Network Mode

One of the downsides to using Oracle Data Pump Full Transportable Export and Import that we just discussed is the need to create dump files. This slows things down since you have to spend the extra time and IO to create the dump file on the source system. Then you have to copy it from the source system to the target system. Then the dump file has to be read to load the data into the database on the target system. That time adds up on large Data Pump export and import operations. Fortunately, you can save some time and hassle by using Data Pump's network mode to move your metadata between the source database and target database. In this section I will discuss that process and provide some details on how to use this Data Pump feature.

Oracle Data Pump Full Transportable Export and Import: Network Mode   If you have never used Oracle Data Pump's network mode import functionality, let me quickly describe how it works. Essentially, you create a database link on the target database that you want to import data into. You can then start an Oracle Data Pump import session and "suck" (that's a technical term) the data from the source machine to the target machine through the database link you created. This eliminates the need to create a dump file on the source system, move it to the target system, and then import that dump file. These imports can be parallelized and compressed, allowing you to make the most of the network bandwidth that you have available. Thus, given a sufficiently robust network infrastructure, Data Pump's network mode can speed up imports significantly. This provides a method of using Full Transportable Export and Import without having to create the Data Pump dump file. You still need to transport the database datafiles across, just as you did earlier, which will also entail putting the related tablespaces in read-only mode. Let's look at a quick example in the next section.

Oracle Data Pump Full Transportable Export and Import: Network Mode Example

The steps you perform in this example are quite similar to those in the previous example, so I will abbreviate the steps that are alike. Because each step requires less commentary, they are presented here in table format for easier reading:

Step	Description	Example (if required)
1	Create a database link on the target database to the source database using **create database link** command. The user on the target database must have the DATAPUMP_IMP_FULL_DATABASE role. The user on the source database must have the DATAPUMP_EXP_FULL_DATABASE role. Neither user needs SYSDBA privileges.	```create database link ora11g connect to scott identified by robert using 'ora11g';```
2	Make all user-defined tablespaces read-only on the source database.	```alter tablespace <name> read only;```
3	Transport all datafiles related to the user-defined tablespace from the source database to the target database. If you are converting between endian formats, you need to use either the **dbms_file_transfer** PL/SQL-supplied procedure or the RMAN **convert** command to convert the datafiles.	```begin dbms_file_transfer.get_file('MY_DATAFILES','users01.dbf', 'ora11g', 'MY_DATAFILES', 'users01.dbf'); end; /```
4	Import the database metadata using the **impdp** command. Make sure you set the following parameters as shown: **Transportable = always** **transport_datafiles** = {datafiles to be moved} **full = y** **network_link** = name of db link created in step 1 **version = 12** (if source database is Oracle Database 11g Release 2 version 11.2.0.3 or higher) If you are using encryption, then include the **encryption_pwd_prompt** or **encryption_password** parameter. Once the import is complete, the tablespaces on the target database will be available in read-write mode.	
5	If you wish, make the tablespaces on the source database read-write again.	```alter tablespace <name> read write;```

Transform Clause New Features

The transform clause on Data Pump Import has been enhanced with new features. These include capabilities to do the following:

- Disable some archive logging, which can improve performance

- Alter the LOB storage type when creating tables with LOB columns

- Change the **compression clause** of tables being created during the import

Let's look at each of these in a bit more detail next.

Disable Archive Logging

When using Data Pump **impdp**, you can use the **disable_archive_logging** option of the **transform** parameter to disable archive logging during imports. This parameter defaults to N, but when set to Y Oracle will set the **logging** parameter for tables and indexes such that logging is disabled during the import process. After the data is loaded, the logging parameters are restored to their normal values. Here is an example where I am importing data into a new schema and disabling archive logging:

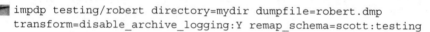

```
impdp testing/robert directory=mydir dumpfile=robert.dmp
transform=disable_archive_logging:Y remap_schema=scott:testing
```

Modifying LOB Storage

When you are importing LOBs, you might want to change how the LOB segment storage types are created. The **lob_storage** option of the Data Pump Import **transform** parameter provides the ability to make these changes while importing the LOB data. The following options are available:

- **SECUREFILE** Creates the LOB segment as a SECUREFILE LOB

- **BASICFILE** Creates the LOB segment as a BASICFILE LOB

- **DEFAULT** Creates the LOB segment with the default storage specification

- **NO_CHANGE** Uses the same storage as defined in the import file

Here is an example:

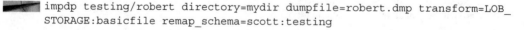

```
impdp testing/robert directory=mydir dumpfile=robert.dmp transform=LOB_
STORAGE:basicfile remap_schema=scott:testing
```

Changing the Table compression Clause

Suppose your organization has just bought Oracle Exadata, with compression included as a part of the purchase. Now you need to move your database over to Exadata and also change the **compression clause** of the tables while you are at it. You can use the **transform** parameter with the **table_compression_clause** option to have Data Pump Import create tables using a specific **compression clause**.

The default value is NONE, in which case the default value of the tablespace will be used. Otherwise, you can indicate the **compression clause** to be used (for example, COMPRESS BASIC, NOCOMPRESS, etc.) when the table is created:

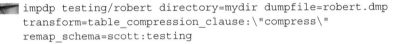

```
impdp testing/robert directory=mydir dumpfile=robert.dmp
transform=table_compression_clause:\"compress\"
remap_schema=scott:testing
```

Notice that we had to include the **compress** parameter in quotes.

Data Pump Fully Supports Oracle's New Multitenant Database Technologies

Oracle Data Pump Export and Import utilities can easily export and import data in a number of ways, including:

- From a non-CDB database to a PDB

- Between two PDBs

- From a PDB to a non-CDB database

In general, Data Pump works the same way with Multitenant databases as it does with databases that are not using Oracle Multitenant. If you try to connect to the root or seed database, Oracle Data Pump will generate an error that indicates that operations typically don't occur against these entities.

Tom Says
Hybrid columnar compression is a feature of Exadata and requires no additional license. Also, basic compression is a feature of Enterprise Edition as well, with no licensing required. Only OLTP compression for table compression requires the purchase of an additional licensed product.

To perform a Data Pump operation on a PDB, you connect to the PDB using its network service name, as shown in this example where I am connecting to a PDB called **target**:

```
impdp scott@target directory=scott_dump dumpfile=scott.dmp tables=emp, dept
```

You may be used to using the default Data Pump directory object DATA_PUMP_DIR, which is created by default in non-tenant Oracle databases, and is also created in the root of a Multitenant database. This default directory will not work within the different PDBs that are contained within the CDB of a Multitenant database. Thus, you need to create a directory in each PDB for Data Pump to use.

If you create a dump file in a PDB, and then import that dump file into another PDB that is associated with the same CDB, an error will occur when the import process tries to create the common user (C$$name). This is quite normal, since the user already exists. If you are moving the dump file to a PDB that resides on a different CDB, you will need to create that common user in the target CDB if that user owns objects in that PDB. An alternative to this would be to use the **remap_schema** parameter of Data Pump to move those objects into another user schema.

Enable Unified Auditing for Data Pump Jobs

If you have read Chapter 8, which covers the new security features, you are aware of Oracle Database 12c's new Unified Auditing feature. Oracle Data Pump activities fully support Unified Auditing. For example, if you want to audit all activities for Oracle Data Pump Export and Import, you simply create an audit policy and then enable it, as shown here:

```
-- Create the policy.
create audit policy audit_dp_policy
actions component=datapump all;

-- enable the policy
audit policy audit_dp_policy;
```

NOTE
If you have not enabled Unified Auditing, this command will have no real effect. You can check if Unified Auditing is enabled by issuing the following query:

```
select value from v$option where parameter='Unified Auditing';

VALUE
-----------------------------------------------------------------
TRUE
```

If the value that appears is FALSE, then Unified Auditing is not enabled. Enabling Unified Auditing requires relinking the Oracle kernel. Refer to Chapter 8 for more information on Unified Auditing and how to enable it.

Now, all Oracle Data Pump operations will be audited and can be displayed in the view UNIFIED_AUDIT_TRAIL, as shown here:

```
EXEC DBMS_AUDIT_MGMT.FLUSH_UNIFIED_AUDIT_TRAIL;
SELECT DP_TEXT_PARAMETERS1, DP_BOOLEAN_PARAMETERS1 FROM UNIFIED_
AUDIT_TRAIL
WHERE audit_type='Datapump';
DP_TEXT_PARAMETERS1
---------------------------------------------------------------
-------------
DP_BOOLEAN_PARAMETERS1
---------------------------------------------------------------
-------------
MASTER TABLE:  "TESTING"."SYS_IMPORT_TABLE_01" , JOB_TYPE: IMPORT,
METADATA_JOB_
MODE: TABLE_EXPORT, JOB VERSION: 12.1.0.1.0, ACCESS METHOD: NULL,
DATA OPTIONS:
0, DUMPER DIRECTORY: NULL  REMOTE LINK: db_scott, TABLE EXISTS:
SKIP, PARTITION
OPTIONS: NONE
MASTER_ONLY: FALSE, DATA_ONLY: FALSE, METADATA_ONLY: FALSE,
DUMPFILE_PRESENT: FA
LSE, JOB_RESTARTED: FALSE
```

Note that this only indicates that an Oracle Data Pump job executed. It does not provide detailed audit records of what happened during that Data Pump job. To get detailed audit records, you would need to audit specific actions, such as the creation of tables or the insertion of records into tables. See Chapter 8 for more information on how to enable auditing for these kinds of actions.

Miscellaneous Enhancements to Data Pump

About once a week my wife throws all the leftovers from the previous week into some magic pot and makes an awesome supper. Sort of like that pot, this section contains the leftover enhancements to Data Pump that didn't quite warrant their own section.

First up is the new **encryption_pwd_prompt** parameter, which indicates to Data Pump that you want to be prompted for the encryption password rather than just entering it on the command line.

The second miscellaneous enhancement is the fact that Data Pump supports the extended data string sizes of VARCHAR2, NVARCHAR2, and RAW data types if the database **max_string_size** parameter is set to EXTENDED.

Finally, a new parameter called **logtime** will cause Data Pump Export and Import to put a timestamp on messages that are output by the utilities. The **logtime** parameter comes with the following options:

- **NONE**   Default value. No timestamps appear in logfile messages.

- **STATUS**   Messages with status information will have timestamps.

- **LOGFILE**   Only messages in the log file will have timestamps.

- **ALL**   Timestamps will appear in both the logfile and status messages.

Oracle SQL*Loader Enhancements

Oracle SQL*Loader is used to load data within external physical files into the Oracle database. Oracle Database 12c has added some nice functionality to SQL*Loader that makes it easier to use, and even more powerful. This section discusses these enhancements:

- SQL*Loader express mode

- SQL*Loader support for identity columns

- SQL*Loader support for extended data types

- SQL*Loader support for Unified Auditing

- SQL*Loader dNFS-related features

- SQL*Loader control file enhancements

- SQL*Loader command-line enhancements

SQL*Loader Express Mode

SQL*Loader files can be a pain to create. Creating even the simplest of them probably requires you to pull out the documentation for a quick example, or perhaps you have a template that you use. Oracle Database 12c introduces

SQL*Loader express mode to address the more elementary data loading configurations. To use SQL*Loader express mode, you must

- Be loading into a table that contains columns that are only character, number, or date data types

- Be loading data from an input file that contains delimited character data

The beauty of express mode is that you do not have to create a control file at all in most cases. SQL*Loader will simply use the table column definitions to define the order of the input data in the source file, and also the data types of that data. SQL*Loader has defined default values for other settings, which you can override if needed.

Let's look at an example first, after which we can dive into some details. Let's say that we have a source table called HOLIDAYS. This table contains the holidays that our particular company recognizes. Here is the format of the table:

```
create table holidays (id number, hol_date date, hol_name varchar2(1000) );
desc holidays
Name                                       Null?    Type
------------------------------------------ -------- -----------------------
ID                                                  NUMBER
HOL_DATE                                           DATE
HOL_NAME                                           VARCHAR2(1000)
```

We need to load this table from an external file called holidays.dat. The data in the External Table is comma delimited, and each record is on an individual line, terminated by a CR+LF sequence. It looks like this:

```
01,01/01/2013,New Years Day
02,07/01/2013,Canada Day (My wife Carrie made me)
03,07/04/2013,Fourth of July
04,09/30/2013,Robert's Birthday
05,11/28/2013,Thanksgiving
06,12/25/2013,Christmas
```

Now, we want to load this data into **holidays**. With SQL*Loader express mode, this is quite easy. First, let's look at our table called HOLIDAYS:

```
show user
USER is "TESTING"
select * from holidays;
no rows selected
```

Now, I will host out and change to the directory where our holidays.dat file is located:

```
SQL>host
[oracle@localhost Downloads]$ cd /u01/Downloads/testload/
[oracle@localhost testload]$ ls -al
total 12
drwxr-xr-x. 2 oracle oinstall 4096 Jun 30 14:50 .
drwxr-xr-x. 4 oracle oinstall 4096 Jun 30 14:45 ..
-rw-r--r--. 1 oracle oinstall  202 Jun 30 14:49 holidays.dat
```

Now we need to make sure that the NLS_DATE_FORMAT matches the date format in the holidays.dat file. SQL*Loader will assume the database date format by default, so we need to override that. Here is the NLS_DATE_FORMAT setting:

```
[oracle@localhost testload]$ export NLS_DATE_FORMAT="mm/dd/yyyy"
```

Believe it or not, I am ready to load the data. Here is the SQL*Loader command line that we execute:

```
[oracle@localhost testload]$ sqlldr testing/robert table=holidays
SQL*Loader: Release 12.1.0.1.0 - Production on Sun Jun 30 14:53:48 2013
Copyright (c) 1982, 2013, Oracle and/or its affiliates.  All rights
reserved.
Express Mode Load, Table: HOLIDAYS
Path used:      External Table, DEGREE_OF_PARALLELISM=AUTO
Table HOLIDAYS:
  5 Rows successfully loaded.
Check the log files:
  holidays.log
  holidays_%p.log_xt
for more information about the load.
[oracle@localhost testload]$ exit
```

We have exited out and back into SQL*Plus. Now, let's see if the data got loaded:

```
SQL> select * from holidays;
        ID HOL_DATE  HOL_NAME
---------- --------- ----------------------------------------
         1 01-JAN-13 New Years Day
         2 01-JUL-13 Canada Day (My wife Carrie made me)
         3 04-JUL-13 Fourth of July
         4 30-SEP-13 Roberts Birthday
         5 28-NOV-13 Thanksgiving
```

Sure enough, our data has been loaded into the database. This is pretty simple, isn't it! Notice that a log file called holiday.log was created. That log file contains some interesting information:

- That express mode load was used.

- The formatting that SQL*Loader used to load the data into the HOLIDAYS table.

- The name of the input file, the bad file, and the discard file. These are automatically generated by SQL*Loader.

- Number of records loaded, number of errors, and other related load information, including the elapsed time of the load itself.

- A **create table** statement that can be used to create an External Table in the Oracle database. This provides a way for you to directly access the datafile from within the database, rather than having to execute SQL*Loader.

- The actual **create table** statement that was used to create the temporary External Table used to load the data.

- The **insert** statement that was used to load the table from the External Table.

The following are rules of the road and default assumptions for SQL*Loader express mode:

- Express mode expects

  - The name of the input table to be the same name as the table with a .dat extension.

  - Log files to be created using the table name with a .log extension.

  - A bad file to be created using the table name with a %p.bad extension.

  - An Oracle Database log file to be created using the table name followed by a %p.log_xt extension. This log file can be useful when debugging failures.

- External Tables are used as the load method. In some cases, direct path mode might be used.

- Fields are set up using the table column names, and they must match the table column order.

- Field data types are matched to the column data types.

- Newline is the record delimiter and commas are the field delimiters.

- The **degree_of_parallelisim** is set to **auto**.

- NLS settings are used for date and timestamp formats.

- The NLS client character set is used.

SQL*Loader express mode does allow you to override the default settings from the SQL*Loader command line. These are known as express options. The express options are documented in *Oracle Database Utilities 12c Release*. Additionally, you can configure a limited SQL*Loader express mode parameter file if you prefer. The parameters and configuration values for express mode are quite a bit more limited than those available for a full-blown SQL*Loader operation, as you might expect.

SQL*Loader Support for Identity Columns

Chapter 6 discussed identity columns in the context of SQL and PL/SQL new features. SQL*Loader provides support for direct-path loading of identity columns. The actions associated with a given identity column to be loaded are defined in the SQL*Loader control file. There are three different actions that SQL*Loader can perform with respect to identity columns:

- The column to be loaded is never loaded from the input file but is rather always loaded using the identity column sequence generator. This is done using the following column specification:

   ```
   colx NUMBER generated always as IDENTITY
   ```

- The column can be loaded explicitly. If it is not, then the identity column sequence generator will provide a value. NULL values will be rejected, as columns with a type of IDENTITY have a NOT NULL constraint. This is done using the following column specification:

   ```
   colx NUMBER generated by default as IDENTITY
   ```

- Same as the action described in the previous bullet except that NULL values are replaced by the sequence from the identity column sequence generator:

   ```
   colx NUMBER generated by default on NULL as IDENTITY
   ```

SQL*Loader Support for Extended Data Types

SQL*Loader now supports extended data types. VARCHAR2, NVARCHAR2, and RAW data types can now be 32MB in size. This feature requires that the database **compatible** parameter be set to 12 and that the database **max_string_size** parameter be set to EXTENDED.

SQL*Loader Support for Unified Auditing

As discussed earlier with respect to Oracle Data Pump, you can now audit SQL*Loader direct path mode using Unified Auditing. Just as with Oracle Data Pump, you need to create an audit policy and then enable it to audit SQL*Loader operations.

When creating the audit policy, you set the **component** clause of the **create audit policy** command to DIRECT_LOAD. This causes all direct path load operations to be audited, including those through Oracle Call Interface (OCI) programs. You can then reference the UNIFIED_AUDIT_TRAIL view column DIRECT_PATH_NUM_COLUMNS_LOADED for the related audit information. The following is an example of the creation of a policy:

```
create audit policy audit_sqlloader_policy
actions component=direct_load load;
```

The output from the unified audit trail might look something like this after the data load we did in the previous section on the HOLIDAYS table:

```
select userid, action, ojb_owner, obj_name, direct_path_num_columns_loaded
from unified_audit_trail
where audit_type = 'direct path api';

USERID  ACTION OJB_OWNER OBJ_NAME  DIRECT_PATH_NUM_COLUMNS_LOADED
------- ------ --------- --------- ------------------------------
TESTING INSERT TESTING   HOLIDAYS  5
```

SQL*Loader dNFS-Related Features

A new SQL*Loader parameter, **dNFS_enable** (with valid values TRUE or FALSE), has been introduced to provide the ability to enable or disable the use of Direct NFS (dNFS) during a SQL*Loader operation. An additional parameter, **dNFS_readbuffers** (default value 4), provides the ability to control the number of read buffers used by the direct NFS client.

NOTE
If you are using NFS but are not taking advantage of the benefits of dNFS, you might want to investigate Oracle's dNFS features. dNFS provides the ability for the Oracle database to connect directly to NFS servers using an internal NFS client. If you want more information about dNFS, reference the installation guide for your specific platform (for example: Oracle Database Installation Guide 12c Release 1 (12.1) for Linux).

SQL*Loader Control File New Clauses

The SQL*Loader control file has several additions and modifications to its parameters that improve functionality and ease of use. The following table highlights these changes:

Clause	Change
infile	Now accepts wildcard characters when specifying datafiles. Not allowed if using FIELDS CSV clause. Example: `INFILE 'dept*.dat'`

fields csv	Directs SQL*Loader to access data within the files as comma-separated values (CSVs). SQL*Loader expects the file to be a stream record format file, with normal carriage returns.
	
	Syntax diagram:
	
	`FIELDS CSV [WITH EMBEDDED|WITHOUT EMBEDDED]`
	`[FIELDS TERMINATED BY ','] [OPTIONALLY ENCLOSED BY '"']`
	
	You can indicate if record terminators are embedded in the individual data fields. If they are embedded, then the record terminators must be enclosed. TERMINATED BY (default ',') and OPTIONALLY ENCLOSED BY (default '"') are available and can be overridden.
	
	Only the following data types can be used as control file fields: CHAR, DATETIME, INTERVAL, and numeric EXTERNAL.
	
	Blank trimming is the default. The PRESERVE BLANKS clause, LTRIM or TRTIM functions are available as well.
	
	`load data`
	`infile "testdata.dat"`
	`truncate`
	`into table testing_data`
	`fields csv with embedded trailing nullcols`
	`( id char, test integer external, test2 char)`

date/ timestamp format masks	You can define DATE, TIMESTAMP, TIMESTAMP WITH TIME ZONE, and TIMESTAMP WITH LOCAL TIME ZONE date format masks at a table level. Only column-level masks will override the format masks.
	
	Here is a SQL*Loader that defines the date format for a DATE datatype:
	
	`load data`
	`infile "testdata.dat"`
	`truncate`
	`into table testing_data`
	`fields terminated by ","`
	`date format 'mm/dd/yyyy"`
	`( id char, test date, test2 char)`

nullif clause at the table level	You can now specify NULLIF at the table level. Syntax: `NULLIF {=|!=}{"char_string"|x'hex_string'|BLANKS}`

Clause	Change
field names	The **field names** clause provides the ability to control the field order. This overrides the default behavior of the fields being in the order of the columns in the database table. Instead, you can indicate that there is a header record in the input file that contains a list of field names that is associated with the column names in the associated tables.

Syntax:

```
FIELD NAMES {FIRST FILE|FIRST FILE IGNORE|ALL FILES|ALL FILES
IGNORE|NONE}
```

The options for the **field names** clause are

- **FIRST FILE**   Indicates that the first datafile contains a list of field names that map between the fields in the datafile and the columns in the target table. The list of columns uses the same delimiter as the data in the input file.

- **FIRST FILE IGNORE**   Indicates that there is a record in the first datafile with a list of field names, but that it should be skipped when processed.

- **ALL FILES**   Indicates that the first record of all datafiles contains a list of field names that maps between the fields in the datafile and the columns in the target table. The list of columns uses the same delimiter as the data in the input file. SQL*Loader will read this record in each file and use it to determine the mappings between the fields and columns of the tables. Note that this means that column mappings can be different in each file if required.

- **ALL FILES IGNORE**   Indicates that there is a header record in each datafile but that it should be ignored.

- **NONE**   Default setting that indicates there is no header record in the input files.

SQL*Loader Command-Line Enhancements

The SQL*Loader command line (sqlldr) has had new parameters added and others modified in Oracle Database 12c. These parameters are outlined in the following table.

Parameter	Change
trim	Overrides the **trip-ldrtrim** default setting when using the External Tables option.
degree_of_ parallelisim	Provides the ability to specify the degree of parallelism used when loading tables using the External Tables option.
bad	You can now specify only a directory name. A default filename will be used for the bad file.
discard	You can now specify only a directory name. A default filename will be used for the discard file.
log	You can now specify only a directory name. A default filename will be used for the log file.

Oracle External Tables Enhancements

Because the Oracle External Tables feature is closely related to SQL*Loader, many of the new and changed features in SQL*Loader are implemented in External Tables. All of the new parameters and features listed in the preceding "Oracle SQL*Loader Enhancements" section are available with External Tables (except, of course, the new **sqlldr** parameters!).

Additionally, you can specify a level of compression when writing to External Tables using the ORACLE_DATAPUMP access driver. The **compression** parameter defines the level of compression for the entire unload operation. The levels of compression are the same as you would find in Oracle Data Pump: DISABLED (the default), ENABLED, BASIC, LOW, MEDIUM, and HIGH. To use this feature, the database **compatible** parameter needs to be set to 12.0, and you must have a license for Oracle Advanced Compression to use anything other than basic compression.

Tom Says

External Tables are one of my all time favorite features. In fact, I've taken to calling SQLLDR the legacy data loading tool of the 20th century and External Tables the way we load data in the 21st century. As you saw earlier in the discussion of SQL*Loader express mode, even SQLLDR is using External Tables to load data these days!

Oracle Log Miner Enhancements

You may not use Oracle Log Miner directly, but several features of the Oracle database use Log Miner or various components of Log Miner. So, any enhancements to Log Miner can spider out to other features in the database. As such, let's quickly review the new features of Oracle Log Miner:

- Full support for SecureFiles LOBs, including de-duplication and SecureFiles Database File System (DBFS) operations

- Support for objects and collections

- Support for Multitenant databases

- Support for extended data types

ADR DDL and Debug Logs

The Oracle Automatic Diagnostic Repository (ADR) was introduced in Oracle Database 11*g* Release 1. It is a centralized location for all database-related files that can be used to diagnose and solve various database problems. It is where Oracle Database stores the alert log, trace files, and other diagnostically relevant files for problem analysis and resolution.

There have been a few changes to the ADR structure that you will want to be aware of. First, there are new logs that remove some messages from the database alert log, cleaning it for easier use. These first of the two new log file types are the DDL log file, which provides information on database DDL operations. The second is the new debug log files, which provide information on warnings and unusual database events.

The DDL log file can be found in the following directory: $ADR_BASE/<database_name>/<instance_name>/log/ddl. This feature needs to be enabled by setting the database parameter ENABLE_DDL_LOGGING to TRUE. The directory $ADR_BASE/<database_name>/<instance_name>/log contains a text version of this log file, called ddl_<sid>.log.

The new debug log files can be found in the following directory: $ADR_BASE/<database_name>/<instance_name>/debug. This directory contains an XML version of this log file. As with the DDL log file, there is also a plaintext copy of the debug log file in $ADR_BASE/<database_name>/<instance_name>/log, called debug_<sid>.log

Oracle SecureFiles Enhancements

A few quick notes on SecureFiles-related changes. First, SecureFiles LOBS now fully support parallel DML (PDML). Also, as mentioned earlier, Oracle Data Pump has a new parameter that indicates what kind of LOB that Data Pump should create when importing data from a dump file. Finally, when the **compatible** parameter is set to 12.1.0.0 or higher, SecureFiles will be the default for LOB storage.

Oracle R Enterprise, Hadoop, and MapReduce

Oracle Database 12*c* introduces Oracle R Enterprise and Hadoop natively in the Oracle database. Hadoop in the Oracle database facilitates Oracle In-Database MapReduce (IDMR), which provides the ability to analyze data stored in your Oracle database without having to move that data to an external Hadoop cluster. So let's look a bit closer at Oracle R Enterprise and Hadoop/MapReduce in the Oracle database.

Oracle R Enterprise

If you are using R now, you will want to know that Oracle R Enterprise is now a part of the Oracle database and it is licensed as a part of the Oracle Advanced Analytics Option. Oracle R Enterprise can be used with the Oracle database to make the open-source R statistical programming language and environment available for use in a secure and enterprise-ready environment.

Oracle has integrated the R language with the Oracle database so users can now run R commands and scripts for statistical and graphical analyses on data stored in the Oracle database. Oracle R Enterprise can average the parallelism and scalability of the Oracle database to automate data analysis. Oracle R Enterprise runs as an embedded component of the database, and can run any R package either by function pushdown or via embedded R. Finally, the database services the data served to the R engine, keeping that data in a safe and secure enterprise-ready environment.

Hadoop/MapReduce in the Oracle Database

Oracle database provides new functionality called In-Database MapReduce (IDMR). IDMR includes the following Oracle components:

- **SQL MapReduce**   Provides SQL analytic functions and table functions along with aggregate functions and SQL pattern matching

- **In-Database Hadoop**   Provides the ability to configure native Hadoop Reducers from within the Oracle database

With IDMR, you can deal with some of the more common issues related to "big data" processing, including:

- IDMR addresses the security issues that are present in many big data processing infrastructures.

- You can invoke Hadoop MapReduce through SQL interfaces, reducing the dependence on Hadoop-specific skills.

- You can reduce the technical sprawl and cost of another infrastructure.

- IDMR provides a seamless integration with the Oracle database server and your big data solution.

Discussing the basics of Hadoop or MapReduce is beyond the scope of this book, but I wanted you to be aware that this functionality is now available in Oracle Database 12c.

CloneDB

Although this is not a new feature in Oracle Database 12*c* (it's been around since 11*g* Release 2), it has not been fully documented except in Metalink (see Metalink note 1210656.1 for more information on using this feature in versions of Oracle Database previous to 12*c*). I wanted to mention it quickly to make sure you are aware that it's available.

Cloning Oracle databases has always been time consuming. Many enterprises have resorted to using expensive disk snapshot technologies to create these clones quickly. Oracle Database now offers the dNFS CloneDB feature, which provides the ability to stand up clone databases, almost instantly, based on an existing database copy.

The clone can be made based either on a restored RMAN backup, or a storage snapshot that is taken on the relevant database files. Oracle uses copy-on-write technologies to reduce the overall storage overhead associated with the clone databases.

CloneDB requires the use of Oracle dNFS. So, this is very powerful cloning technology if your storage machines are using technologies such as Oracle's ZFS file systems. In fact, ZFS file systems have some enhancements that may well make CloneDB perform even better on those environments.

Providing the basic steps to create clones would be somewhat lengthy and is beyond the scope of this book, but here are some quick highlights of how creating clones is accomplished:

1. Create a directory (on dNFS) for the source files for the clones.

2. Copy/restore from a backup the datafiles of the master database to the directory created in step 1. These datafiles can be from an online backup, a cold backup, or a restore from an RMAN backup.

3. Create a backup controlfile trace file. Modify it such that it contains the name of the first cloned database. The datafiles will point to the source clone, and the redo logs will point to a location specific to the clone database.

4. Modify the SPFILE for the clone database. In particular, the CLONE parameter needs to be set to TRUE.

5. On the clone database, run the **dbms-dNFS.clonedb_rename file** command for each datafile. The command takes two parameters: the existing datafile name (which was the source clone datafile as defined in step 3), and the datafile for the clone, which will be a new location defined for that clone.

6. Perform a **recover database** command if required.

7. Open the clone using the **alter database open resetlogs** command.

When the cloned database is open, you will be able to use it normally, issuing DDL and DML statements to it. The datafiles will consume no storage until changes are made to the database.

SQL Translation Framework

It may be that you are currently faced with client-side application code that is written for a database other than Oracle. It may also be that you desire to move to Oracle but the SQL issued by that client application is not compatible with Oracle databases as it uses a dialect that is unique to the database that it runs on.

Using Oracle's SQL Translation Framework, Oracle Database 12c can now take the text of a given SQL statement submitted from a client application and translate the code into Oracle-readable SQL code before it's submitted to the Oracle Optimizer. The client application must be using some open API, such as ODBC or JDBC, for the translator to be able to work. The SQL Translation Framework is installed when the database is created, but it requires the installation of at least one translator package in order to function properly. These translators may be supplied by Oracle or vendors of various products.

The translator code that is installed will be responsible for recognizing the non-Oracle SQL code and translating it into Oracle-compatible SQL code. Translation is supported by either simple lookup and replace, programmatic interface, or a mixture of both. The translation occurs inside the database and is registered with a specific SQL translation profile. The SQL Translation Framework also allows for results and errors to be translated and returned back to the application with values expected by that application. Additionally, the SQL Translation Framework maintains the ANSI SQLSTATE for the duration of the transaction.

End of Line

This chapter wraps up this book (except for some appendixes). If you have read the whole book from the beginning, you know that Oracle Database 12c is full of new features. It is, perhaps, the biggest major release for the Oracle Database product ever. In this chapter I've presented the odds and ends that are contained in the new release.

One thing I've noticed with my previous three books in the Oracle Database New Features series is that, after going to print, I inevitably discover additional new features and changed functionality. Also, with each new minor version change of the product, new features continue to pour in. That being said, I encourage you to keep an eye on my blog, which you can find at robertfreemanonoracle.blogspot.com. Here you will find lots of new information on Oracle Database 12c and other Oracle-related topics.

Finally, thanks for buying and reading this book. If you bought this book because you liked my previous books on Oracle new features, then I hope I've met your expectations. If this is the first book of mine that you've read, thanks for choosing it—I hope you have learned a lot! Feel free to write to me with any comments at the email link on my blog.

Enjoy Oracle Database 12*c*!

APPENDIX
A

Deprecated and Desupported Features in Oracle Database 12c

With every new release of Oracle Database, Oracle deprecates and desupports various features, parameters, and the like that were available in previous releases. Oracle Database 12*c* is no exception. This appendix briefly reviews some of the features, views, and parameters that are deprecated or desupported in Oracle Database 12*c*. The topics covered include the following:

- Defining deprecation and desupport

- Deprecated features in Oracle Database 12*c*

- Desupported features in Oracle Database 12*c*

- Deprecated views in Oracle Database 12*c*

- Deprecated parameters in Oracle Database 12*c*

Defining Deprecation and Desupport

You may have wondered what the difference is between deprecation of a feature and desupport of a feature. A *deprecated* feature in Oracle Database is one that Oracle has indicated it may stop supporting at some point in time, but that is still available in the product itself. A *desupported* feature is one that Oracle is no longer supporting, no longer making bug fixes to, and, in fact, will actually remove from the product in total. So, deprecation is like a shot across the bow—a warning. Desupport is like a direct hit and your taking on water—it's time to do something else.

Deprecated Features in Oracle Database 12*c*

Several database features have been deprecated in Oracle Database 12*c*. The following table lists many of the features being deprecated and provides some comment on those features. Though this list was complete when the book was written, it's possible the list will change. The *Oracle Database Upgrade Guide 12*c *Release* provides a complete list of all deprecated and desupported features in Oracle Database 12*c*.

Feature Deprecated	Comments
ignorecase argument of the **orapwd** tool	Deprecated in Oracle Database 12*c* in conjunction with the deprecation of the **sec_case_sensitive_logon** parameter. By default, all passwords are now case sensitive.
Oracle Restart	Deprecated in Oracle Database 12*c*.

Feature Deprecated	Comments
Svrctl utility single-character commands	Deprecated in Oracle Database 12*c*.
Catupgrd.sql script for upgrades	Deprecated in favor of the catctl.pl utility.
Oracle Streams	Deprecated in Oracle Database 12*c*. You should migrate from Oracle Streams to Oracle GoldenGate at some point because Oracle Streams may be desupported and unavailable in a later Oracle Database release.
Oracle Advanced Replication	Deprecated in Oracle Database 12*c*. You should migrate from Oracle Advanced Replication to Oracle GoldenGate at some point because Oracle Advanced Replication may be desupported and unavailable in a later Oracle Database release.
Stored outlines	Use plan baselines instead.
Various features of Oracle Label Security	See the *Oracle Label Security Administrator's Guide 12*c *Release* for more information on this feature.
Deprecation of Windows NTS Authentication using the NTLM protocol	Windows users can no longer authenticate using the NTS adaptor on Windows clients and servers that require the NT LAN Manager (NTLM) protocol. NTLM is deprecated as of Oracle Database 12*c*. Windows users can still use Kerberos. NTLM is still used for local user authentication, and in cases in which the database service runs as a local user.
Public Key Infrastructure for TDE	PKI is deprecated for TDE in Oracle Database 12*c*. To configure TDE in Oracle Database 12*c*, use the **administer key management** SQL statement.
XML_CLOBS option in Oracle Data Pump Export	Deprecated in Oracle Database 12*c*.
Database Vault Configuration Assistant and Database Vault Administrator	Deprecated in Oracle Database 12*c*. Use Oracle Enterprise Manager Cloud Control for Oracle Database Vault configuration and administration.
Certain Database Vault default rule sets	The Allow Oracle Data Pump Operation rule set and Allow Scheduler Job rule set are deprecated.

Feature Deprecated	Comments
Oracle Database Vault default realms	The Oracle Data Dictionary realm and the Oracle Enterprise Manager realm are deprecated in this release. The objects that were protected in the Oracle Data Dictionary realm have been migrated to new realms.
Oracle Database Vault deprecated API	The dvsys.dbms_macadm.sync_rules procedure is deprecated.
CSSCAN and CSALTER	Replaced by the Oracle Database Migration Assistant for Unicode (DMU).

Desupported Features in Oracle Database 12c

Several database features have been desupported in Oracle Database 12c. The following table lists many of these features and provides commentary on the desupport of that feature where applicable. Things change over time and the *Oracle Database Upgrade Guide 12c Release* provides a complete list of all deprecated and desupported features in Oracle Database 12c.

Feature Desupported	Comments
Oracle Enterprise Manager Database Control	Desupported in Oracle Database 12c. Replaced by Oracle EM Express. Oracle Database Control is no longer available in Oracle Database 12c.
Standalone deinstallation tool	This utility is replaced in Oracle Database 12c with a deinstall option in Oracle Universal Installer. Also, the **runInstaller** command includes **-deinstall** and **-home** options to allow for command-line-based Oracle Home removal and cleanup.
Oracle COM Automation on Windows	Desupported in Oracle Database 12c.
Oracle Objects for OLE	Desupported in Oracle Database 12c. Migrate your code to another supported application architecture (such as Java, .NET, etc.).
Oracle Counters for Windows Performance Monitor	Deprecated in Oracle Database 11g and now not available in Oracle Database 12c.
OCFS for Windows	Desupported in Oracle Database 12c. See the *Oracle Database Upgrade Guide 12c Release* for information on upgrading your database if you are using OCFS.

Feature Desupported	Comments
Support for raw devices	Desupported in Oracle Database 12*c*. This includes OCR and voting files for Oracle Clusterware.
Oracle Change Data Capture	Not included in Oracle Database 12*c*. Has been replaced with Oracle GoldenGate.
Specific cipher suites for SSL	The following cipher suites are desupported for Oracle Advanced Security:

- `SSL_DH_ANON_WITH_DES_CBC_SHA`

- `SSL_RSA_EXPORT_WITH_DES40_CBC_SHA`

- `SSL_RSA_EXPORT_WITH_RC4_40_MD5`

- `SSL_RSA_WITH_DES_CBC_SHA`

Feature Desupported	Comments
Oracle Net connection pooling	Desupported in Oracle Database 12*c*.
Oracle Names	Desupported in Oracle Database 12*c*. Migrate to directory naming.
Oracle Net listener password	Desupported in Oracle Database 12*c*. Security is enforced through local OS system authentication.

Deprecated Parameters in Oracle Database 12*c*

A few sqlnet.ora and database parameters have either been replaced or deprecated in Oracle Database 12*c*.

The sqlnet.ora parameter SQLNET.ALLOWED_LOGON_VERSION has been replaced by the parameters SQLNET.ALLOWED_LOGON_VERSION_SERVER and SQLNET.ALLOWED_LOGON_VERSION_CLIENT.

The following Oracle Database parameters have been deprecated in Oracle Database 12*c*:

- FILE_MAPPING

- SEC_CASE_SENSITIVE_LOGON

For a list of all deprecated parameters in the database, you can issue this query:

```
SELECT name from v$parameter WHERE isdeprecated = 'TRUE' ORDER BY name;
```

Deprecated Views in Oracle Database 12c

The following views have been deprecated in Oracle Database 12c:

- *_SCHEDULER_CREDENTIALS
- *_NETWORK_ACL_PRIVILEGES
- DBA_NETWORK_ACLS
- V$OBJECT_USAGE

APPENDIX B

New Parameters and Views in Oracle Database 12c

W ith every new release of Oracle Database, Oracle adds new parameters and views to the release. This appendix briefly reviews the new parameters and views in Oracle Database 12c.

New Parameters in Oracle Database 12c

Several new parameters are available in Oracle Database 12c. These are listed and described in the following table.

Parameter Name	Description
CONNECTION_BROKERS	Used to specify connection broker types, the number of connection brokers of each type, and the maximum number of connections per broker.
DNFS_BATCH_SIZE	Controls the number of asynchronous IOs that can be queued by an Oracle process when Direct NFS Client is enabled.
ENABLE_PLUGGABLE_DATABASE	A bootstrap initialization parameter to create a container database (CDB).
HEAT_MAP	When set to ON, causes the database to track read and write access of all segments, as well as modification of database blocks, due to DMLs and DDLs. Note that this feature does not work with Multitenant databases in the initial release of Oracle Database 12c.
MAX_STRING_SIZE	Controls the maximum size of VARCHAR2, NVARCHAR2, and RAW data types in SQL. Enable this parameter only when in upgrade mode, and run utl32k.sql script after enabling it.
OPTIMIZER_ADAPTIVE_FEATURES	Enables or disables all of the adaptive optimizer features.
OPTIMIZER_ADAPTIVE_REPORTING_ONLY	Controls reporting-only mode for adaptive optimizations. When set to TRUE, information required for an adaptive optimization is gathered, but no action is taken to change the plan.
PDB_FILE_NAME_CONVERT	Maps names of existing files to new filenames when processing a CREATE PLUGGABLE DATABASE statement, as well as when processing the ENABLE PLUGGABLE DATABASE clause of the CREATE DATABASE statement, if file_name_convert_clause is not specified and Oracle Managed Files is not enabled.

Parameter Name	Description
PGA_AGGREGATE_LIMIT	Specifies a limit on the aggregate PGA memory consumed by the instance.
PROCESSOR_GROUP_NAME	Instructs the database instance to run itself within the specified operating system processor group. All Oracle processes will be bound to the CPUs in this group and will only run on these CPUs.
NONCDB_COMPATIBLE	Provides behavior similar to a non-CDB when issuing SQL commands inside a pluggable database (PDB) in a CDB.
SPATIAL_VECTOR_ ACCELERATION	Enables or disables the spatial vector acceleration.
TEMP_UNDO_ENABLED	Determines whether transactions within a particular session can use a temporary undo log rather than a permanent one. The default choice for database transactions in prior versions of Oracle has been to have a single undo log per transaction. This parameter provides the ability for Oracle to split UNDO into two separate streams, one for permanent operations and one for temporary ones.
THREADED_EXECUTION	Specifies whether to enable the multithreaded Oracle model.
UNIFIED_AUDIT_SGA_ QUEUE_SIZE	Specifies the size of the SGA queue for unified auditing.
USE_DEDICATED_BROKER	Determines how dedicated servers are spawned.

New Views in Oracle Database 12c

There are a ton of new views included in Oracle Database 12c. The following table lists the various new ALL, DBA, and USER views contained in Oracle Database 12c.

ALL_ Views	DBA_ Views	USER_ Views
ALL_APPLY_ INSTANTIATED_GLOBAL	DBA_APPLY_INSTANTIATED_GLOBAL	
ALL_APPLY_ INSTANTIATED_ OBJECTS	DBA_APPLY_INSTANTIATED_ OBJECTS	
ALL_APPLY_ INSTANTIATED_ SCHEMAS	DBA_APPLY_INSTANTIATED_ SCHEMAS	

ALL_ Views	DBA_ Views	USER_ Views
ALL_ATTRIBUTE_ TRANSFORMATIONS	DBA_ATTRIBUTE_TRANSFORMATIONS	USER_ATTRIBUTE_ TRANSFORMATIONS
ALL_CODE_ROLE_PRIVS	DBA_CODE_ROLE_PRIVS	USER_CODE_ROLE_PRIVS
ALL_CREDENTIALS	DBA_CREDENTIALS	USER_CREDENTIALS
ALL_CUBE_NAMED_ BUILD_SPECS	DBA_CUBE_NAMED_BUILD_SPECS	USER_CUBE_NAMED_BUILD_ SPECS
ALL_CUBE_SUB_ PARTITION_LEVELS	DBA_CUBE_SUB_PARTITION_LEVELS	USER_CUBE_SUB_ PARTITION_LEVELS
ALL_ERROR_ TRANSLATIONS	DBA_ERROR_TRANSLATIONS	USER_ERROR_TRANSLATIONS
ALL_GG_INBOUND_ PROGRESS	DBA_GG_INBOUND_PROGRESS	
ALL_GOLDENGATE_ INBOUND	DBA_GOLDENGATE_INBOUND	
ALL_GOLDENGATE_ PRIVILEGES	DBA_GOLDENGATE_PRIVILEGES	USER_GOLDENGATE_ PRIVILEGES
ALL_GOLDENGATE_ RULES	DBA_GOLDENGATE_RULES	
ALL_HEAT_MAP_SEG_ HISTOGRAM	DBA_HEAT_MAP_SEG_HISTOGRAM	USER_HEAT_MAP_SEG_ HISTOGRAM
ALL_HEAT_MAP_ SEGMENT	DBA_HEAT_MAP_SEGMENT	USER_HEAT_MAP_SEGMENT
ALL_MEASURE_FOLDER_ SUBFOLDERS	DBA_MEASURE_FOLDER_SUBFOLDERS	USER_MEASURE_FOLDER_ SUBFOLDERS
ALL_METADATA_ PROPERTIES	DBA_METADATA_PROPERTIES	USER_METADATA_ PROPERTIES
ALL_PLSQL_COLL_ TYPES	DBA_PLSQL_COLL_TYPES	USER_PLSQL_COLL_TYPES
ALL_PLSQL_TYPE_ ATTRS	DBA_PLSQL_TYPE_ATTRS	USER_PLSQL_TYPE_ATTRS
ALL_PLSQL_TYPES	DBA_PLSQL_TYPES	USER_PLSQL_TYPES
ALL_POLICY_ ATTRIBUTES	DBA_POLICY_ATTRIBUTES	USER_POLICY_ATTRIBUTES
ALL_SQL_ TRANSLATION_ PROFILES	DBA_SQL_TRANSLATION_PROFILES	USER_SQL_TRANSLATION_ PROFILES
ALL_SQL_ TRANSLATIONS	DBA_SQL_TRANSLATIONS	USER_SQL_TRANSLATIONS
ALL_TAB_IDENTITY_ COLS	DBA_TAB_IDENTITY_COLS	USER_TAB_IDENTITY_COLS
ALL_TRANSFORMATIONS	DBA_TRANSFORMATIONS	USER_TRANSFORMATIONS
ALL_XML_NESTED_ TABLES	DBA_XML_NESTED_TABLES	USER_XML_NESTED_TABLES

ALL_ Views	DBA_ Views	USER_ Views
ALL_XML_OUT_OF_ LINE_TABLES	DBA_XML_OUT_OF_LINE_TABLES	USER_XML_OUT_OF_LINE_ TABLES
ALL_XML_SCHEMA_ ATTRIBUTES	DBA_XML_SCHEMA_ATTRIBUTES	USER_XML_SCHEMA_ ATTRIBUTES
ALL_XML_SCHEMA_ COMPLEX_TYPES	DBA_XML_SCHEMA_COMPLEX_TYPES	USER_XML_SCHEMA_ COMPLEX_TYPES
ALL_XML_SCHEMA_ ELEMENTS	DBA_XML_SCHEMA_ELEMENTS	USER_XML_SCHEMA_ ELEMENTS
ALL_XML_SCHEMA_ NAMESPACES	DBA_XML_SCHEMA_NAMESPACES	USER_XML_SCHEMA_ NAMESPACES
ALL_XML_SCHEMA_ SIMPLE_TYPES	DBA_XML_SCHEMA_SIMPLE_TYPES	USER_XML_SCHEMA_SIMPLE_ TYPES
ALL_XML_SCHEMA_ SUBSTGRP_HEAD	DBA_XML_SCHEMA_SUBSTGRP_HEAD	USER_XML_SCHEMA_ SUBSTGRP_HEAD
ALL_XML_SCHEMA_ SUBSTGRP_MBRS	DBA_XML_SCHEMA_SUBSTGRP_MBRS	USER_XML_SCHEMA_ SUBSTGRP_MBRS
ALL_XSTREAM_ ADMINISTRATOR	DBA_XSTREAM_ADMINISTRATOR	
ALL_XSTREAM_OUT_ SUPPORT_MODE	DBA_XSTREAM_OUT_SUPPORT_MODE	
ALL_XSTREAM_ TRANSFORMATIONS	DBA_XSTREAM_TRANSFORMATIONS	
AUDIT_UNIFIED_ CONTEXTS		
AUDIT_UNIFIED_ ENABLED_POLICIES		
AUDIT_UNIFIED_ POLICIES		
AUDIT_UNIFIED_ POLICY_COMMENTS		
AUDITABLE_SYSTEM_ ACTIONS		
DATABASE_EXPORT_ OBJECTS		
	DBA_ACL_NAME_MAP	
	DBA_ALERT_HISTORY_DETAIL	
	DBA_CDB_RSRC_PLAN_DIRECTIVES	
	DBA_CDB_RSRC_PLANS	
	DBA_CONTAINER_DATA	
	DBA_DIGEST_VERIFIERS	
	DBA_DISCOVERY_SOURCE	

ALL_ Views	DBA_ Views	USER_ Views
	DBA_EDITIONED_TYPES	USER_EDITIONED_TYPES
	DBA_GOLDENGATE_SUPPORT_MODE	
	DBA_HEATMAP_TOP_OBJECTS	
	DBA_HEATMAP_TOP_TABLESPACES	
	DBA_HIST_APPLY_SUMMARY	
	DBA_HIST_ASH_SNAPSHOT	
	DBA_HIST_CAPTURE	
	DBA_HIST_PDB_INSTANCE	
	DBA_HIST_REPLICATION_TBL_STATS	
	DBA_HIST_REPLICATION_TXN_STATS	
	DBA_HIST_REPORTS	
	DBA_HIST_REPORTS_CONTROL	
	DBA_HIST_REPORTS_DETAILS	
	DBA_HIST_REPORTS_TIMEBANDS	
	DBA_HIST_SESS_SGA_STATS	
	DBA_HIST_TABLESPACE	
	DBA_HOST_ACES	USER_HOST_ACES
	DBA_HOST_ACLS	
	DBA_ILMDATAMOVEMENTPOLICIES	USER_ILMDATAMOVEMENTPOLICIES
	DBA_ILMEVALUATIONDETAILS	USER_ILMEVALUATIONDETAILS
	DBA_ILMOBJECTS	USER_ILMOBJECTS
	DBA_ILMPARAMETERS	
	DBA_ILMPOLICIES	USER_ILMPOLICIES
	DBA_ILMRESULTS	USER_ILMRESULTS
	DBA_ILMTASKS	USER_ILMTASKS
	DBA_LOGSTDBY_EDS_SUPPORTED	
	DBA_LOGSTDBY_EDS_TABLES	
	DBA_LOGSTDBY_PLSQL_MAP	
	DBA_LOGSTDBY_PLSQL_SUPPORT	
	DBA_MINING_MODEL_TABLES	
	DBA_OBJECT_USAGE	USER_OBJECT_USAGE
	DBA_OPTSTAT_OPERATION_TASKS	

ALL_ Views	DBA_ Views	USER_ Views
	DBA_PDB_HISTORY	
	DBA_PDBS	
	DBA_PRIV_CAPTURES	
	DBA_ROLLING_DATABASES	
	DBA_ROLLING_EVENTS	
	DBA_ROLLING_PARAMETERS	
	DBA_ROLLING_PLAN	
	DBA_ROLLING_STATISTICS	
	DBA_ROLLING_STATUS	
	DBA_SENSITIVE_COLUMN_TYPES	
	DBA_SENSITIVE_COLUMNS	
	DBA_SQL_PLAN_DIR_OBJECTS	
	DBA_SQL_PLAN_DIRECTIVES	
	DBA_SR_GRP_STATUS	USER_SR_GRP_STATUS
	DBA_SR_GRP_STATUS_ALL	USER_SR_GRP_STATUS_ALL
	DBA_SR_OBJ	USER_SR_OBJ
	DBA_SR_OBJ_ALL	USER_SR_OBJ_ALL
	DBA_SR_OBJ_STATUS	USER_SR_OBJ_STATUS
	DBA_SR_OBJ_STATUS_ALL	USER_SR_OBJ_STATUS_ALL
	DBA_SR_PARTN_OPS	USER_SR_PARTN_OPS
	DBA_SR_STLOG_EXCEPTIONS	USER_SR_STLOG_ EXCEPTIONS
	DBA_SR_STLOG_STATS	USER_SR_STLOG_STATS
	DBA_SUPPLEMENTAL_LOGGING	
	DBA_TSDP_IMPORT_ERRORS	
	DBA_TSDP_POLICY_CONDITION	
	DBA_TSDP_POLICY_FEATURE	
	DBA_TSDP_POLICY_PARAMETER	
	DBA_TSDP_POLICY_PROTECTION	
	DBA_TSDP_POLICY_TYPE	
	DBA_UNUSED_OBJPRIVS	
	DBA_UNUSED_OBJPRIVS_PATH	
	DBA_UNUSED_PRIVS	
	DBA_UNUSED_SYSPRIVS	
	DBA_UNUSED_SYSPRIVS_PATH	

ALL_ Views	DBA_ Views	USER_ Views
	DBA_UNUSED_USERPRIVS	
	DBA_UNUSED_USERPRIVS_PATH	
	DBA_USED_OBJPRIVS	
	DBA_USED_OBJPRIVS_PATH	
	DBA_USED_PRIVS	
	DBA_USED_PUBPRIVS	
	DBA_USED_SYSPRIVS	
	DBA_USED_SYSPRIVS_PATH	
	DBA_USED_USERPRIVS	
	DBA_USED_USERPRIVS_PATH	
	DBA_WALLET_ACES	USER_WALLET_ACES
	DBA_WI_CAPTURE_FILES	
	DBA_WI_JOBS	
	DBA_WI_OBJECTS	
	DBA_WI_PATTERN_ITEMS	
	DBA_WI_PATTERNS	
	DBA_WI_STATEMENTS	
	DBA_WI_TEMPLATE_EXECUTIONS	
	DBA_WI_TEMPLATES	
	DBA_WORKLOAD_ACTIVE_USER_MAP	
	DBA_WORKLOAD_REPLAY_SCHEDULES	
	DBA_WORKLOAD_SCHEDULE_ CAPTURES	
	DBA_WORKLOAD_SCHEDULE_ ORDERING	
	DBA_WORKLOAD_USER_MAP	
	DBA_XS_AUDIT_POLICY_OPTIONS	
	DBA_XS_AUDIT_TRAIL	
	DBA_XS_ENB_AUDIT_POLICIES	
	DBA_XSTREAM_SPLIT_MERGE	
	DBA_XSTREAM_SPLIT_MERGE_HIST	
	DBA_XSTREAM_STMT_HANDLERS	
	DBA_XSTREAM_STMTS	
PDB_PLUG_IN_ VIOLATIONS		

ALL_ Views	DBA_ Views	USER_ Views
REDACTION_COLUMNS		
REDACTION_POLICIES		
REDACTION_VALUES_ FOR_TYPE_FULL		
SCHEMA_EXPORT_ OBJECTS		
TABLE_EXPORT_ OBJECTS		
UNIFIED_AUDIT_TRAIL		
		USER_PRIVILEGE_MAP

The following list provides additional GV$ and V$ views available in Oracle Database 12*c*:

GV$ Views	V$ Views
GV$AQ_BACKGROUND_COORDINATOR	V$AQ_BACKGROUND_COORDINATOR
GV$AQ_BMAP_NONDUR_SUBSCRIBERS	V$AQ_BMAP_NONDUR_SUBSCRIBERS
GV$AQ_CROSS_INSTANCE_JOBS	V$AQ_CROSS_INSTANCE_JOBS
GV$AQ_JOB_COORDINATOR	V$AQ_JOB_COORDINATOR
GV$AQ_NONDUR_REGISTRATIONS	V$AQ_NONDUR_REGISTRATIONS
GV$AQ_NONDUR_SUBSCRIBER	V$AQ_NONDUR_SUBSCRIBER
GV$AQ_NONDUR_SUBSCRIBER_LWM	V$AQ_NONDUR_SUBSCRIBER_LWM
GV$AQ_NOTIFICATION_CLIENTS	V$AQ_NOTIFICATION_CLIENTS
GV$AQ_SERVER_POOL	V$AQ_SERVER_POOL
GV$AQ_SUBSCRIBER_LOAD	V$AQ_SUBSCRIBER_LOAD
GV$ASM_ACFS_SEC_ADMIN	V$ASM_ACFS_SEC_ADMIN
GV$ASM_ACFS_SEC_CMDRULE	V$ASM_ACFS_SEC_CMDRULE
GV$ASM_ACFS_SEC_REALM	V$ASM_ACFS_SEC_REALM
GV$ASM_ACFS_SEC_REALM_FILTER	V$ASM_ACFS_SEC_REALM_FILTER
GV$ASM_ACFS_SEC_REALM_GROUP	V$ASM_ACFS_SEC_REALM_GROUP
GV$ASM_ACFS_SEC_REALM_USER	V$ASM_ACFS_SEC_REALM_USER
GV$ASM_ACFS_SEC_RULE	V$ASM_ACFS_SEC_RULE
GV$ASM_ACFS_SEC_RULESET	V$ASM_ACFS_SEC_RULESET
GV$ASM_ACFS_SEC_RULESET_RULE	V$ASM_ACFS_SEC_RULESET_RULE
GV$ASM_ACFSREPL	V$ASM_ACFSREPL
GV$ASM_ACFSREPLTAG	V$ASM_ACFSREPLTAG

GV$ Views	V$ Views
GV$ASM_ACFSTAG	V$ASM_ACFSTAG
GV$ASM_ESTIMATE	V$ASM_ESTIMATE
GV$BACKUP_NONLOGGED	V$BACKUP_NONLOGGED
GV$CLIENT_SECRETS	V$CLIENT_SECRETS
GV$CLONEDFILE	V$CLONEDFILE
GV$CON_SYS_TIME_MODEL	V$CON_SYS_TIME_MODEL
GV$CON_SYSSTAT	V$CON_SYSSTAT
GV$CON_SYSTEM_EVENT	V$CON_SYSTEM_EVENT
GV$CON_SYSTEM_WAIT_CLASS	V$CON_SYSTEM_WAIT_CLASS
GV$CONTAINERS	V$CONTAINERS
GV$COPY_NONLOGGED	V$COPY_NONLOGGED
GV$DEAD_CLEANUP	V$DEAD_CLEANUP
GV$DG_BROKER_CONFIG	V$DG_BROKER_CONFIG
GV$EDITIONABLE_TYPES	V$EDITIONABLE_TYPES
GV$ENCRYPTION_KEYS	V$ENCRYPTION_KEYS
GV$FLASHFILESTAT	V$FLASHFILESTAT
GV$GG_APPLY_COORDINATOR	V$GG_APPLY_COORDINATOR
GV$GG_APPLY_READER	V$GG_APPLY_READER
GV$GG_APPLY_SERVER	V$GG_APPLY_SERVER
GV$GOLDENGATE_CAPTURE	V$GOLDENGATE_CAPTURE
GV$GOLDENGATE_MESSAGE_TRACKING	V$GOLDENGATE_MESSAGE_TRACKING
GV$GOLDENGATE_TABLE_STATS	V$GOLDENGATE_TABLE_STATS
GV$GOLDENGATE_TRANSACTION	V$GOLDENGATE_TRANSACTION
GV$HEAT_MAP_SEGMENT	V$HEAT_MAP_SEGMENT
GV$INSTANCE_PING	V$INSTANCE_PING
GV$IO_OUTLIER	V$IO_OUTLIER
GV$LGWRIO_OUTLIER	V$LGWRIO_OUTLIER
GV$MAPPED_SQL	V$MAPPED_SQL
GV$NONLOGGED_BLOCK	V$NONLOGGED_BLOCK
GV$OPTIMIZER_PROCESSING_RATE	V$OPTIMIZER_PROCESSING_RATE
GV$PATCHES	V$PATCHES
GV$PDB_INCARNATION	V$PDB_INCARNATION
GV$PDBS	V$PDBS

GV$ Views

GV$SESSIONS_COUNT

GV$RO_USER_ACCOUNT

GV$SQL_MONITOR_SESSTAT

GV$SQL_MONITOR_STATNAME

GV$TEMPUNDOSTAT

GV$XSTREAM_APPLY_COORDINATOR

GV$XSTREAM_APPLY_READER

GV$XSTREAM_APPLY_SERVER

GV$XSTREAM_TABLE_STATS

V$ Views

V$SESSIONS_COUNT

V$RO_USER_ACCOUNT

V$SQL_MONITOR_SESSTAT

V$SQL_MONITOR_STATNAME

V$TEMPUNDOSTAT

V$XSTREAM_APPLY_COORDINATOR

V$XSTREAM_APPLY_READER

V$XSTREAM_APPLY_SERVER

V$XSTREAM_TABLE_STATS

Index

441

P

T

U

Oracle Technology Network. It's code for sharing expertise.

Come to the best place to collaborate with other IT professionals.

Oracle Technology Network is the world's largest community of developers, administrators, and architects using industry-standard technologies with Oracle products.

Sign up for a free membership and you'll have access to:

- Discussion forums and hands-on labs
- Free downloadable software and sample code
- Product documentation
- Member-contributed content

Take advantage of our global network of knowledge.

JOIN TODAY ▷ Go to: oracle.com/technetwork

Copyright © 2013, Oracle and/or its affiliates. All rights reserved. Oracle and Java are registered trademarks of Oracle and/or its affiliates. Other names may be trademarks of their respective owners. 157372

Are You Oracle Certified?

Showcase Your Oracle Expertise and Get Ahead

Top 5 Reasons to Get Oracle Certified

1. Demonstrate your mastery of Oracle's industry-leading technology
2. Raise your visibility so you stand out from the crowd
3. Gain a competitive edge and improve your earnings potential
4. Prove that you are dedicated to your professional growth
5. Increase personal performance

Over 1 million certified technologists testify to the importance of this top industry-recognized credential as one of the best ways to get ahead – and stay there.

Save with a Certification Discount Package and Get a Free Exam Retake

**Learn more at:
oracle.com/education/packages**

ORACLE
UNIVERSITY